CHANGING STRUCTURE
STRUCTURE
OF MEXICO

COLUMBIA UNIVERSITY SEMINAR SERIES

The University Seminars at Columbia University welcomes this study of *Changing Structure of Mexico: Political, Social, and Economic Prospects* edited by Laura Randall to the Columbia University Seminars Series. The study has benefited from Seminar discussions and reflects the advantages of scholarly exchange provided by the Seminar Movement.

Aaron W. Warner
Director, University Seminars
Columbia University

THE FUTURE OF AMERICAN BANKING
James R. Barth, R. Dan Brumbaugh, Jr., and Robert E. Litan

THE EVOLUTION OF U.S. FINANCE, VOLUME I
FEDERAL RESERVE MONETARY POLICY: 1915–1935
Jane W. D'Arista

THE EVOLUTION OF U.S. FINANCE, VOLUME II
RESTRUCTURING INSTITUTIONS AND MARKETS
Jane W. D'Arista

HOW CREDIT-MONEY SHAPES THE ECONOMY
THE UNITED STATES IN A GLOBAL SYSTEM
Robert Guttmann

THE ANTITRUST IMPULSE, VOLUMES I AND II
AN ECONOMIC, HISTORICAL, AND LEGAL ANALYSIS
Theodore P. Kovaleff, editor

FROM MALTHUS TO THE CLUB OF ROME AND BACK
PROBLEMS OF LIMITS TO GROWTH, POPULATION
CONTROL, AND MIGRATIONS
Paul Neurath

TOWARD SUSTAINABLE DEVELOPMENT?
STRUGGLING OVER INDIA'S NARMADA RIVER
William F. Fisher, editor

DEBT, CRISIS, AND RECOVERY
THE 1930s AND THE 1990s
Albert G. Hart and Perry Mehrling

CHANGING STRUCTURE OF MEXICO
POLITICAL, SOCIAL, AND ECONOMIC PROSPECTS
Laura Randall, editor

REFORMING MEXICO'S AGRARIAN REFORM
Laura Randall, editor

CHANGING STRUCTURE OF MEXICO

Political, Social, and Economic Prospects

Laura Randall
editor

M.E. Sharpe
Armonk, New York
London, England

Library of Congress Cataloging-in-Publication Data

Changing structure of Mexico: political, social, and economic prospects /
edited by Laura Randall.
p. cm.—(Columbia University seminars)
Includes bibliographical references and index.
ISBN 1-56324-641-4 (alk. paper).—ISBN 1-56324-642-2 (pbk.: alk. paper)
1. Mexico—Economic conditions—1982–
2. Mexico—Social conditions—1970–
3. Mexico—Politics and government—1988–
I. Randall, Laura. II. Series: Columbia University seminar series.
HC135.C44 1996
972.08´35—dc20
95-25404
CIP

Printed in the United States of America

The paper used in this publication meets the minimum requirements of
American National Standard for Information Sciences—
Permanence of Paper for Printed Library Materials,
ANSI Z 39.48-1984.

BM (c)	10	9	8	7	6	5	4	3	2	1
BM (p)	10	9	8	7	6	5	4	3	2	1

Contents

v

Part III: Quality of Life and Environment

List of Tables and Figures

Tables

Figures

List of Contributors

Miguel Alberto Bartolomé, Instituto Nacional de Antropologia e Historia, Oaxaca

Mariano Bauer E., Universidad Nacional Autonoma de México

Javier Beristain is Secretary of Finance for Mexico City

Mercedes Blanco, Centro de Investigaciones y Estudios Superiores en Antropologia Social

David Barton Bray, Inter-American Foundation

Nathan Buras, University of Arizona

Douglas A. Chalmers, Institute of Latin American and Iberian Studies, School of International and Public Affairs, Columbia University

Carlos Elizondo Mayer-Serra, Centro de Investigacion y Docencia Economicas

Anna. M. Fernandez Poncela, Departmento de Politica y Cultura, UAM-Xochimilco

Juan Guillermo Figueroa Perea, El Colegio de México

Haynes C. Goddard, University of Cincinnati and Instituto Tecnologico Autonomo de México

David M. Gould, Federal Reserve Bank of Dallas

Boris Graizbord, El Colegio de México

William Gruben, Federal Reserve Bank of Dallas

José Angel Gurria Treviño is the Secretary of Foreign Affairs of Mexico

Neil Harvey, New Mexico State University

Joseph L. Klesner, Kenyon College

Ana Langer, M.D., Population Council, Regional Office—Latin America and the Caribbean

Soledad Loaeza, El Colegio de México

xiv LIST OF CONTRIBUTORS

David E. Lorey, University of California at Los Angeles Program on Mexico

Rafael Lozano, M.D., Population Council, Regional Office—Latin America and the Caribbean

Nora Lustig, Foreign Policy Studies Program of the Brookings Institution

Catherine Mansell-Carstens, Department of Economics, Instituto Tecnologico Autonomo de México

Philip Martin, University of California at Davis

Jordy Micheli, Universidad Autonoma Metropolitcana—Azcapotzalco

Dra. Alicia Elena Pérez Duarte y N., Magistrate of the Tribunal Superior de Justicia del Distrito Federal

Kerianne Piester, Institute of Latin American and Iberian Studies, School of International and Public Affairs, Columbia University

María Angeles Pozas, Johns Hopkins University

Ma. Alicia Puente Lutteroth, Universidad Nacional Autonoma de México

Juan Quintanilla M., Universidad Nacional Autonoma de México

Laura Randall, Hunter College, City University of New York

Ramon Rodríguez M., Universidad Autonoma de Campeche

Crescencio Ruiz, El Colegio de México

William Siembieda, University of New Mexico

Elizabeth Umlas, Yale University

Francisco Valdés-Ugalde, Institute for Social Research at the Universidad Nacional Autonoma de México

Sidney Weintraub, Center for Strategic and International Studies, Washington, D.C., and University of Texas at Austin

John H. Welch, Lehman Brothers

Matthew B. Wexler, Department of Anthropology, Boston University

Francisco Zapata, El Colegio de México

Editor's Note

Some of the chapters in this volume were originally commissioned for publication in *Challenge* magazine. In conformity with the magazine's style requirements, those chapters do not contain footnotes or bibliography. A number of the commissioned articles did not appear in *Challenge*, however, because the publication of the magazine was suspended in June 1995. The authors of the chapters written for this volume included footnotes and bibliography, but in order to include as many essays as possible, only works cited in the chapters have been included in the bibliography.

The articles were written between December 1994 and June 1995. This note is written in June 1995. I have not updated the articles based on small changes that occurred after they were written. However, one change should be mentioned: The National Solidarity Program, known by its Spanish abbreviation PRONASOL, on June 14, 1995 was reorganized and renamed the Alianza Nacional para el Bienestar. In its new form, it is to be decentralized from federal government control, so that the states have more power.

Part I
Introduction and Overview

LAURA RANDALL

Introduction

Changing Structure of Mexico brings together the views of politicians, civil servants, and scholars from the United States and Mexico. It honors the tradition established by Professor Frank Tannenbaum, who was a noted scholar of Mexico, the founder of the University Seminars at Columbia University, and host to a wide variety of Latin Americans in his seminar, which established friendships between them and the graduate students and faculty privileged to attend. This book and the forthcoming *Reforming Mexico's Agrarian Reform* (Armonk, NY: M.E. Sharpe, 1996) are companion pieces, decades later, to two of his well-known books, *Ten Keys to Latin America* and *The Mexican Agrarian Revolution*.

There have been striking changes since Professor Tannenbaum wrote *Ten Keys* in 1962, summarizing a lifetime of observation and belief. He strongly admired rural villages. He shared with Gandhi a view that dignity, trust, and appropriate personal relations were found far more often in villages than in cities; independence and dignity would be crushed by too strong a government. The government, however, was to protect the most innocent and the weakest villagers, so that they could maintain the best parts of their traditional life.

This view developed from Professor Tannenbaum's early anarchism, which evolved into an appreciation that a society needed to have a balance of power among its institutions—the church, the economy, the family, and the state. No formal percentage distribution of the role of each is given. Instead, the concept of checks and balances is extended in its application beyond the various branches of government.

It is implicit that there are channels of access, means of communication, so that the needs of the most humble can be addressed—even if slowly. For this reason, Professor Tannenbaum profoundly admired President Lázaro Cárdenas and his trips to the countryside, on which Professor Tannenbaum sometimes accompanied him, to listen to his compatriots.

In *Ten Keys*, Professor Tannenbaum argued that Latin America—and particularly Mexico—would be understood by analyzing its human geography, race, religion, regionalism, the hacienda, education, leadership, politics, the United States and Latin America, and Castro and social change. These topics continue to define much of Mexico, but the list of key items has grown and the analysis has been transformed by the uneven modernization of Mexico.

When Professor Tannenbaum fell in love with Mexico, it was mainly rural. Now it is largely urban. Then, the symbols of nationalism—agrarian reform, a nationalized oil industry, restrictions on the Catholic church, and protection of workers' rights—were seen as defining a national style that would break an old, unjust order and make clear Mexico's separate identity from the United States.

Today, Mexico's changing structure reflects policies designed to increase efficiency by modifying agrarian reform, opening parts of the oil industry to private investment, obtaining increased political support for the government by recognizing the Catholic church, and making firms more competitive in the world economy by removing corrupt union leaders and reducing union control over work.

Professor Tannenbaum stressed the corporate basis of the governing party, PRI—that is, the representation of labor and agricultural interests as formal sectors of the ruling party and the representation of business through policy consulting at different levels. The increased complexity of Mexican society makes this too limited a means of communication and control. Thus, there is a proliferation of interest groups and nongovernmental organizations, some with international links, that supplement political parties as vehicles for influencing government policy. And the balance between the government and the rest of society is changed by the gradually increasing decentralization of government and the concomitant increase in municipal and state government power.

At the same time, increasing attention is being paid to issues reflecting both fashions in worldwide concerns and the transformation of Mexican society, such as the conditions of women and the environment.

In this book, distinguished Mexican and U.S. scholars have been asked to share their knowledge of the changing structure of Mexico. Both broadly defined issues and specific policy areas are discussed. Each of the essays in the book is organized according to the questions: What were the conditions at the beginning of the 1980s? What policies were adopted, especially by the Salinas administration, to address them? What changes have taken place? Are they the result of policies or other factors? What is the current outlook?

The essays indicate that although the specifics of policies recently adopted differ from those admired by Professor Tannenbaum, concerns for the balance of institutions in society, access to government of diverse groups of citizens, and the dignity of individuals underlie many of the recent policy changes and pay tribute to his understanding and respect for the Mexican nation.

SOLEDAD LOAEZA

Contexts of Mexican Policy

The questions about Mexico raised in the introduction are easier to answer after examining the context in which Mexican policy making took place. Soledad Loaeza writes that Mexico for many years differed from other Latin American nations. It combined authoritarian stability with economic growth and social change. The close ties between the governing party—Partido Revolucionario Internacional (PRI)—and the government were reinforced by large government participation in the economy. This is no longer the case. The economic crisis of December 1994 to the present not only reduced the government's participation in the economy, it also weakened the PRI, thereby making room for the expansion of other political parties and nongovernmental organizations. These developments were influenced by changes in the international environment and the transformation of Mexican society.

Mexico relied on its revolutionary heritage to legitimize its nationalist policies of self-determination in foreign affairs. But it faced increasing pressure by investors who feared the instability that might be engendered by an imperfectly democratic system. They urged the increased participation of the political opposition. Moreover, the severe allegations of fraud that surrounded the election of President Salinas made it necessary for him to proceed with political reform and to increase human rights. At stake was the legitimacy of the Mexican political system. Nonetheless, economic, rather than political, reform was the main priority of the Salinas administration. The increased participation of the middle class and the improved education of the whole population, along with its increased awareness of the outside world (made possible by radio and television and now the information superhighway), provided international standards for Mexican events. In the 1980s recession, social mobility and real wages fell, while the very rich got richer. Discontent was shared by those who were left behind by the modernization process. They could rebel because of the dismantling of political controls and the absence of coherently planned modernization—a modernization that is a top priority both for its own sake and for the restoration of a stable climate for economic growth. Loaeza adds that the Zedillo administration recognized the urgency of profound reform the first day in office, when it proposed the independence of electoral authorities from the government, the end of the privileged relationship between the government and the PRI, and a strict observance of the law. On January 17, 1995, the Partido Acción Nacional (PAN), the Partido de la Revolución Democrática (PRD), and the PRI agreed to negotiate these issues, and a truce was declared in Chiapas, where the Ejército Zapatista de Liberación Nacional (EZLN) had led an uprising on January 1, 1994. The truce ended, however, on February 9, when troops were sent to arrest the leaders of the EZLN—an action the government viewed as necessary to maintain order at home, and one that many analysts thought was necessary to restore confidence abroad.

For decades, Mexico has stood in strong contrast to other Latin American countries. It had succeeded in maintaining an impressive record of authoritarian stability, which it had used as a central pillar of economic growth and social change. Political continuity has been an essential characteristic of the Mexican experience for most of the second half of this century. It has been made possible by a relatively high level of political institutionalization, which is epitomized by a coherent and strong state, the sustained preeminence of a party closely linked to the State—Partido Revolucionario Institucional (PRI)—and the regular organization of elections. Electoral processes were not only a make-believe exercise intended to create a democratic facade, they also contributed to stability because they offered an institutional mechanism for the renewal of the elite. This arrangement provided an appropriate context for economic development because it guaranteed an important degree of predictability in the political processes and prevented dramatic swings between authoritarianism and democracy such as those experienced by other countries in the region.

But in the 1980s, the Mexican political system was beset by a severe financial crisis and economic recession. These difficulties forced a profound reform of the Mexican state's participation in the economy. Inevitably, the reduction of the state's interventionism weakened political institutions and brought about a loosening of political controls. The counterpart of this process was an unprecedented politicization of Mexican society. There was a substantial increase of autonomous political activities that induced an upsurge of nongovernmental organizations and the expansion of independent electoral participation. Since the mid- eighties, the latter phenomenon has led to the strengthened presence of opposition parties— namely Partido Acción Nacional (PAN), the long-standing conservative opposition, and Partido de la Revolución Democrática (PRD), an organization created in 1989 that rallied leftist groups of different shades, from former *guerrilleros* and communists to *priistas* opposed to the de la Madrid and Salinas reforms.

Thus, although the central pieces of the traditional political system are still in place, their persistence has not impeded the addition of new elements in the last ten years. Two important examples of this are an active and increasingly influential public opinion and the growth of autonomous political organizations, whose presence has induced substantial changes in the system. Many specialists and observers see a process of democratization in this evolution. But this view has proved to be overly optimistic. We witness the sustained power of the PRI and the conservative tendencies of large social groups, as expressed in recent elections. For instance, in 1994, the votes for the PRI and the PAN amounted to 77 percent of the vote. This suggests that Mexico has undergone limited political liberalization. This path of change may lead to a democratic regime. But liberalization is an open-ended process that can also follow an erratic course.

These economic and political transformations have had a profound impact on some of the assumptions of the almost legendary predictability of Mexican politics. Some of these affected assumptions were sustained economic growth, price and foreign exchange rate stability, political apathy, and conformity to the power of the presidency. Predictability and a general, if superficial, political uniformity had been the central characteristics of Mexican politics since World War II. But since 1982, uncertainty and political heterogeneity have developed as the dominant traits of that system. It can therefore be said that economic discontinuity created conditions for political discontinuity.

But the crisis of the economic model of import-substitution that prevailed from 1940 to 1982 does not suffice to explain the changing context in which Mexican policy has unfolded in the last decade. A complete picture of the environment in which economic restructuring and political liberalization have taken place requires the addition of two more components: (1) the dramatic transformation of world order, as an effect of the fall of socialism and by the enthronement of pluralist democracy as the only acceptable form of political regime; and (2) the demands of a complex society—politically aware, mobilized, and determined to achieve a modernization that today seems still unattainable. Even though genuine modernization remains elusive, it has been (since the 1910 revolution) and continues to be a permanent goal of the Mexican state.

These two elements—the international context and the transformation of Mexican society in the last quarter of this century—have determined the changing context of Mexican policy since 1982. In the past, their importance was not self-evident. The Cold War, on the one hand, and the social mobility induced by economic development, on the other, provided stable terms of reference for continuity. However, as predictably happens with fundamentals, their importance for the maintenance of the general balance of the Mexican political system would be properly appreciated only after they had disappeared.

The Influence of the International Environment

One aspect of Mexican nationalism (as shaped by the revolutionary experience) had been a certain political or ideological self-sufficiency. It sustained proud attitudes with respect to the relative success of what was considered an original political arrangement. This was seen as an ingenious formula that had given the country the stability that was required by economic development. Of course, the formula was not democratic. But it could always be seen as transitional. Until the beginning of the 1980s, whenever a political crisis arose, Mexicans believed that their only recourse was to turn to the"revolutionary heritage." Moreover, the association of the Mexican political system (however authoritarian it may have been) with contemporary nationalism was a crucial element of the general consensus regarding political institutions that had prevailed in Mexico for more than forty years.

The belief that Mexico had found a political formula of its own (effective, even if peculiar) was translated into a "protectionist" policy, in the face of possible external influences or "foreign models." This attitude also inspired Mexico's foreign policy during the decades of economic growth. It partially explains the Mexican government's traditional insistence on self-determination and its reluctance to join other countries in multilateral diplomacy.

While it is true that the effectiveness of the Mexican political arrangement was, in itself, a support of that same arrangement, it is also true that the Cold War offered a solid international framework for the maintenance of "special formulas," "uncommon democracies," and even "third ways." This approach prevailed as long as it did not alter the balance of power between the United States and the Soviet Union. The tolerance by Western democracies of political regimes of the third world that were not so democratic was, in itself, a stabilizing factor for these regimes. However, the debt crisis of the 1980s pushed this tolerance to a point of exhaustion, because governments and investors in Europe and the United States and international financial institutions were then forced to recognize the economic costs of undemocratic regimes that were dominated by corrupt political elites who ruled unaccountably. At the same time, the rise of the cause of human rights in the 1980s was instrumental in the battle of the Reagan administration against communism and the Soviet Union. Inevitably, this battle had repercussions in other countries whose regimes had been allies of the West in spite of very poor records in human rights matters. In this context, authoritarianism had become a cumbersome attribute of the third world for Western governments. The disintegration of the Soviet bloc, the fall of communist regimes, the transformations undertaken by Mikhail Gorbachev preceding the demise of the Soviet Union completed the shake-up of the post–World War II international order. The importance of the international environment for Mexican policy since the 1981–82 financial crisis has been widely stated and analyzed. But, while the economic consequences of this factor have been emphasized, the political effects are rarely mentioned, even though they were decisive.

During the de la Madrid years, at the height of the debt crisis, the Mexican political system came under close scrutiny by international investors, the media, the U.S. Congress, and Washington authorities. Their concern was not so much the expression of a deeply felt democratic conviction, as it was the manifestation of a sudden awareness of the dangers a chaotic situation in Mexico augured for the United States. Most of the expressions of concern were accompanied by suggestions of a political change that would preempt general unrest by opening up the system to the participation of the opposition. This pressure was translated into increasing criticism of the PRI's virtual hegemony and of electoral fraud and by support for the PAN. The need of the de la Madrid government for international credit and good will was so great that it probably considered a more liberal attitude toward party opposition and competitiveness a small price to pay for economic recovery. This explains, in part, the governmental permissiveness with respect to the progress of the PAN at the municipal and state levels in those years.

The influence of the international context on the liberalizing reforms undertaken by the Salinas government was recognized by President Salinas himself in his last State of the Union address, of November 1, 1994. In this speech (in which he generally reviewed his six years in power), the outgoing president emphasized the weight of the international factor in many of the decisions he took: "Mexico has changed intensely. . . . The goals of these changes were the establishment of a new relationship between the state and society, and to place Mexico in an advantageous position in the new international reality. . . ."

The international reality was an obvious frame of reference for the consolidation of a new export-oriented economic model: the North American Free Trade Agreement (NAFTA) was the kernel of that model. The democratizing wave that overtook Latin America and Eastern Europe after 1989 was a continuous touchstone of political reform—for the opposition as much as for the *salinista* government. For Salinas, the international context was a source of pressure for political reform, as it had been for de la Madrid. But the context was somewhat different. During his first year in office, Salinas succeeded in reducing the urgency of debt payments. Moreover, the appearance of a forceful populist opposition—led by Cuauhtémoc Cárdenas—in the presidential race of 1988 has cooled the enthusiasm of many politicians and opinion makers in the United States for immediate political reform in Mexico. However, the conflictual election and the severe allegations of fraud created an image problem that tarnished Salinas's claims of legitimacy. A president identified with and committed to the modernization of the Mexican economy could not afford to be perceived as the champion of time-worn authoritarian political institutions.

The international dimension of this "image problem" had two aspects: (1) the new relationship of Mexico with the outside world; and (2) the new international standards of "political acceptability." This dimension set important constraints on the direction of the Mexican government's policies with respect to the PRI—the opposition—as well as with respect to party competitiveness and human rights. It is also possible that some of the constitutional amendments Salinas introduced (for instance, regarding land property or relations with the Catholic church) were made with an eye toward events in Eastern Europe. Mexico could not remain far behind what was going on there. In spite of this, Salinas did not see political reform as a priority. While he recognized its importance, he also believed it could be subordinated to economic change. He therefore concentrated his efforts in this area, where his goals seemed much clearer and more well defined, rather than in the political domain, where his leadership tended to be reactive and dominated by a short-term perspective.

The Pressures of a Modernizing Society

In addition to a difficult and changing international context, which weighed heavily on the policy decisions of the Mexican government, President Salinas had to deal with the definition of new sets of relationships between the state and society. This need was imposed by the profound modernization that was experienced by Mexican society. Since the beginning of the 1970s, it was a foreseeable stage in a process that had transformed a relatively unstable and fluid society (in which social expectations were maintained by the promise of social mobility) into a dramatically unequal social structure in which class lines are more rigid than in the past.

This phenomenon of social stabilization was also the result of an accelerated modernizing process that, in spite of profound disparities, has penetrated Mexican society as a whole. By the end of the 1980s, the traditional political system that had been created to accommodate the political expressions of a predominantly rural society—parochial and inward-oriented—seemed to lag far behind what was needed to serve the urbanized society of the end of the twentieth century. It is a society that is aware of and in contact with the outside world and is eager to participate in the advantages of technological change and diversity. It has overcome the apathy and conformity that, for decades, stood behind the nonparticipatory attitudes that also supported authoritarianism.

In order to understand the recent evolution of Mexican society, it is necessary to remember that the years between 1970 and 1982 saw high rates of economic growth. This was the result, first, of international credit and, then, of the oil boom. But this period of prosperity was followed by twelve years of inflation (reaching 160 percent in 1987), recession, and adjustment policies. The rise of anti-authoritarianism among a number of social groups since 1983 has to be understood in the light of the increased participation of the middle classes in the benefits of the economic development of the 1970s and of the improvement of their relative position in the class structure. Other groups did not benefit as much from prosperity. Some examples of these groups were the urban, low-income groups, not to mention the rural population that still represented over 34 percent, in 1980, of the total population. Even they, however, were touched by some of its effects—namely, the expansion of education, the intense development of the media, and the access to information from the outside world due to the internationalization of Mexico. This means that events in other Latin American countries (elections in Nicaragua, for instance, or even the fall of the Berlin Wall) were frames of reference not only for the government but also for large social groups for whom the radio or television became a crucial agent of socialization. The electronic media became much more important than more traditional agents such as the school, the church, or the family.

The Indian peasant uprising in the southern state of Chiapas on January 1, 1994, has been interpreted as a rejection of modernity by groups who want to retain their traditional identity, and who feel threatened by NAFTA, land property reform, and the integration of Mexico in the international economic and political currents. However, this movement can also be understood as the extreme reaction of those who were being left behind in the modernization process, and who felt marginalized from the prosperity and well-being ideally associated with social change. In this perspective, their rebellion does not appear to be inspired by change itself, but rather by change from which they felt excluded. Thus, this movement shares a common ground with the demands for effective political participation by the modernized middle class and the urban low-income groups. These groups were activated by different phenomena in the 1980s—the 1981–82 crisis, the 1985 earthquakes, the development of the media, the recession, the upsurge of *cardenismo* in 1988, the dismantling of mechanisms of political control, the increased competitiveness of elections, or a simple and pure desire for change and new faces in the government.

The effects of social change on the Mexican political system have not been minor. Among them, the most noteworthy has been the appearance and increased importance of public opinion as a central element of political balance—a phenomenon that is derived from the new characteristics of Mexican society. It has also had a strong impact on the traditional institutional arrangement, which was built on the assumption that the only limits of government authority were self-imposed. But this impact has not yet found a solid institutional response.

The process of political change in Mexico has been plagued by contradictions and equivocal signals. The reaction of the government elite to demands of political change has been subordinated to the completion of economic modernization. It has had very high social costs. Paradoxically, many of these contradictions derive not so much from resistance to change, but from the difficulties in responding to the diverse demands of a society that has more political complexities than can be absorbed by the authorities in power or the existing institutions.

Since the de la Madrid government, policy makers and politicians have been more responsive to a heterogeneous public opinion. This phenomenon has found expression in the politicization of the media, an impressive upsurge of nongovernmental organizations, independent electoral participation, and, generally speaking, increased autonomous political participation. However, government responsiveness has not effected a predictable pattern of change, because it is not subject to a clear political design. Rather, it has been dominated by short-term reactions calculated on the basis of the priority of economic reform. The uncertainty that has apparently become a permanent feature of political dynamics in Mexico is related not only to the intensification of party competitiveness, but also to an institutional weakness that has to be resolved within the context of political modernization. That modernization has now become Mexico's top priority.

Zedillo's Response

From its first day in office, the Zedillo administration recognized the urgency of profound political reform. Immediately after taking oath as president of the republic, Zedillo launched a political offensive that was aimed at negotiation and establishment of new patterns of relationships with the opposition—namely with the PRD, the party that maintained an obstinate strategy of non-negotiation or dealings of any kind with government authorities or the PRI during the Salinas administration.

Zedillo's political offer consisted of three elements: (1) what he called "a definite electoral reform"—by which he meant the complete independence of electoral authorities from the government; (2) the disappearance of the privileged relationship between the government and the PRI; and (3) a strict observance of the law—a commitment that implied a reversal of the line of policy of the Salinas administration, which resorted to pragmatic agreements with the opposition to solve post-electoral conflicts.

The strategic importance of an accord with the PRD lay not so much in the electoral strength this party had mustered (well below its own predictions) as in its relations with the Ejército Zapatista de Liberación Nacional (EZLN) in Chiapas. The establishment of a working relationship with the PRD was seen as a necessary first step toward the deactivation of the potential of violence from the EZLN and the stabilization of a fragile political situation.

The sense of political urgency was intensified by the Mexican financial crisis that flared up in mid-December 1994. It precipitated a dramatic fall of the Mexican stock market and of the peso, and cast serious doubts on the success and viability of the economic restructuring that was undertaken by Salinas—the continuity of which was one of Zedillo's strongest commitments. Thus, after only two weeks in power, the new government had to face serious challenges simultaneously on the political and the economic fronts.

Contradicting all predictions that had been made on the basis of his technocratic background, President Zedillo seemed more prepared to tackle the political situation than the financial problems that seemed to threaten what Mexico had achieved in twelve years of economic adjustment and austerity. Thus, while the economic program of the government remained in many respects still undefined, on January 17, 1995, the media announced that the three main political forces—the PAN, the PRI, and the PRD—had signed a pact that was less an accord than a commitment to negotiate what amounted to an open political agenda. At the same time, the EZLN agreed with the federal government to an indefinite truce in Chiapas.

The announcement was well received, in general. But the PRI was less than enthusiastic and very suspicious of the accord, because it feared that the higher costs of the negotiations with the PRD would be paid by the priistas. The priistas would be forced to accept the demands of the *perredistas* to revise electoral results in Chiapas and Tabasco, where they have refused to accept the triumph of the PRI. Their fears were confirmed in less than a week because, after the signing of the accord, rumors began to abound that the minister of the interior had succeeded in bringing the PRD to the negotiating table, in exchange for the heads of the priista governors of Chiapas and Tabasco. The PRI then turned into the main opposition to Zedillo's political initiative, and the priistas of Tabasco organized what could be interpreted as a rebellion against the federal government in defense of their vote and of their governor. This reaction has only made the situation increasingly fluid.

At the beginning of February, President Zedillo and Attorney General Lozano (the latter, incidentally, being a member of the PAN) announced the government's decision to arrest the leaders of the EZLN. The decision was taken on well-founded information indicating that the EZLN was using the truce to expand its activities to other parts of the country. The effects of this decision are difficult to foresee. But, as the EZLN becomes more widely perceived as a real obstacle to political stabilization, it is expected that the arrests will contribute to a stable environment. Besides, it is probable that President Zedillo's image of political leadership will be enhanced by the decision.

3

DAVID M. GOULD

Mexico's Crisis: Looking Back to Assess the Future

In "Mexico's Crisis: Looking Back to Assess the Future," David Gould traces the events leading to Mexico's December 1994 economic crisis. He stresses that unlike the 1982 debt crisis, in 1994 markets were opening, inflation was low, and the public-sector budget was nearly balanced. The government intended to continue these policies, which were quite different from the protective measures designed to aid production for the domestic market that had been in force during much of the postwar period. They had led to annual per capita economic growth of more than 3 percent from 1954 to 1976. However, this growth often involved subsidies and inefficient allocation of resources that could otherwise have been devoted to education or more productive investments. Needed structural economic adjustments were postponed. The revenues from the oil boom financed the government's purchase of firms. In 1983, state-owned firms accounted for 18.5 percent of GDP. The 1981 fall in oil prices severely reduced the oil-exporting Mexican government's income, which in turn contributed to the exchange rate crisis, the 1982 moratorium on debt payments, and the nationalization of the banking system.

Despite the moratorium, almost 6 percent of Mexican GDP was transferred abroad from 1982 to 1985. The government created money to replace these sums. The resulting falling income and high inflation could be halted only by a radical shift in policy. This, in turn, could succeed only if the new policy was agreed to and supported by major sectors of the economy. Accordingly, in December 1987, the first of a series of pacts between the government and representatives of labor, farming, and business was signed. The first pacts included price

Catherine Mansell-Carstens, Ken Emery, Moises Schwartz, Sidney Weintraub, and Carlos Zarazaga offered many helpful comments for this article. All remaining errors are solely my responsibility. The views expressed in this article do not necessarily reflect those of the Federal Reserve Bank of Dallas or the Federal Reserve System.

*and wage controls, fiscal and macroeconomic adjustments, and debt renegotia-
tion. Later pacts emphasized deregulation, privatization, and liberalization of
trade and finance. In 1991–92, the government privatized the banks. In 1995, it
took additional steps to increase foreign participation in banking, other economic infrastructure, and activities servicing the oil industry. It is believed that
the anticipated increase in domestic and foreign private investment and technology transfer will increase efficiency, free government funds for essential economic, education, and health expenditures, and thus contribute to the belief that
the government will maintain its current economic policies.*

In early December 1994, the Organization for Economic Cooperation and
Development (OECD) and many private economists were predicting that
Mexico's real gross domestic product (GDP) would grow by at least 3.8 percent
in 1995.[1] Mexico appeared to be on the fast track to economic growth and
stability. For the first time in many years, its annual inflation rate was down to
less than 10 percent, the public-sector budget was nearly balanced, and exports
were growing at an annual rate in excess of 22 percent. Moreover, Mexico's
entry into the North American Free Trade Agreement (NAFTA) and its recent
uneventful presidential elections suggested a continuity in the country's economic reform policies.

A few weeks later, however, on December 20, 1994, international financial
markets were rocked by the devaluation of the Mexican peso. Then, what first
appeared to be a minor correction in Mexico's nominal exchange rate quickly
developed into a broader financial crunch felt in and out of Mexico. By March
1995, the peso had fallen more than 50 percent against the dollar, and monthly
inflation was growing at an annual rate in excess of 60 percent. Despite a $50
billion financial assistance package arranged by the international community to
help shore up liquidity problems in Mexican dollar-denominated debt, interest
rates on this debt remained twice as high as they were before the devaluation. In
May 1995, the Mexican government expected that the country's real GDP would
fall by 2 percent in 1995.

It may take several years for Mexico to fully recover the investor confidence
lost during this recent economic crisis. However, the speed with which Mexico
recovers will be fundamentally determined by the economic policies it chooses to
follow. The more Mexico relies on open markets and stable macroeconomic
policies, and the less it withdraws within itself, the faster the country will recover.

The purpose of this chapter is to put Mexico's current economic crisis into
broad historical context in order to assess the future trend in Mexico's economic
policies. Like many developing countries during the 1980s, Mexico's economic
paradigm shifted from a closed-market, inward-looking development strategy to
an open-market, outward-oriented development strategy. Unlike the period leading up to the 1982 debt crisis, the period before the latest crisis was one in which
markets were becoming more open, inflation was low, and the public-sector

budget was nearly balanced. Although there are forces in Mexico pulling away from market reforms as well as toward them, the trend in Mexico's policies has been toward greater openness. These economic reform policies have made future openness a more credible policy.

The first section of this chapter examines the history leading up to Mexico's recent economic policies; it then discusses Mexico's economic reform policies and how they have changed since the current economic crisis began, examines the factors that influence the credibility of Mexico's open-market policies, and briefly summarizes the likely trend in Mexico's policies.

The Historical Context of Mexico's New Policies

The Years of Inward Orientation

The economic reform policies that Mexico undertook in the mid-1980s were a shift away from policies that began shortly after World War II. Like many developing countries in the early 1950s, Mexico pursued an *import-substitution industrialization policy*.[2] The government kept Mexican markets relatively closed to foreign competition, restricted foreign direct investment, and tightly regulated domestic financial markets.

The original impetus for closed-market policies was the *dependency theory*, the idea that if poor countries want to grow, they have to break away from developed countries. Poor countries would have to start producing manufactured goods for themselves rather than continue to import these goods from developed countries in exchange for exports of primary goods. The fear was that poor countries would never catch up to the rich countries without major government intervention to manage international competition and support domestic industry.[3]

Despite the inherent problems of a closed, highly regulated economy, Mexico's real GDP per capita grew at an average annual rate of about 3.7 percent from 1954 to 1972 (Figure 3.1). Mexico did not grow as quickly as some other developing countries that followed more outward-oriented policies, such as Korea and Taiwan, but growth was stable and living standards were rising.[4] This period of Mexico's development has been referred to as *stabilizing development*.

During the early 1970s, Mexico's inward-looking policies generated economic inefficiencies, but increased government spending during the period may have made these costs less apparent.[5] While per capita real GDP grew 3.7 percent from 1954 to 1972, it grew only slightly less, 3.1 percent, from 1973 to 1976. The microeconomic costs of price controls, a growing government sector, and inward-based industrialization policies were beginning to increase (Bazdresch and Levy 1991). Moreover, resources that might have otherwise been devoted to education and other productive investment projects were spent on subsidizing a growing number of the state-owned enterprises.[6] The world recession and the spike in oil prices that hit in 1973 only made matters worse for

Figure 3.1 **Annual Growth Rate of Mexican Real Gross Domestic Product Per Capita, 1954–94**

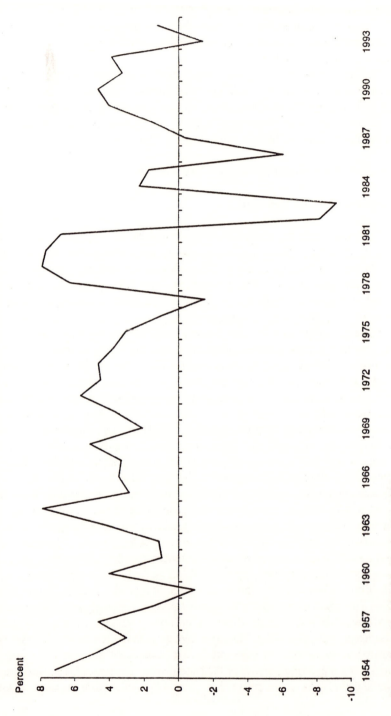

Source: Penn World Table, Version 5.6, 1995.

Table 3.1

Mexican Economic Indicators: 1954–72 and 1973–76

	1954–72 (percent)	1973–76 (percent)
Real GDP per capita growth	3.7	3.1
Inflation	3.5	20.1
Public deficit/GDP	1.8	4.3
Current account deficit/GDP	−1.5	−2.9

Mexico, which at the time was a net importer of oil (Lustig 1992).

In attempting to offset a slowdown in growth, Mexico pursed expansionary fiscal and monetary policies. However, as Table 3.1 and Figure 3.2 show, expansionary policies without real fundamental economic change simply generated inflation and large fiscal and current account deficits. In 1976, a balance of payments crisis erupted and led to a 60 percent devaluation in the peso, which had been fixed at 12.50 old pesos per dollar since 1954 (Table 3.2).

If macroeconomic policies had been as stable as they were in the 1950s and 1960s, Mexico might have been able to avoid the balance of payments crisis in 1976, even without structural change. But Mexico's increasing economic inefficiencies would have necessitated, at some point, fundamental change.

Mexico was ready for structural change in 1976, but huge oil discoveries appeared to lift fiscal and foreign exchange constraints, at least for the foreseeable future. Rather than implement the needed but difficult structural reforms, the new administration of President José López Portillo, expecting uninterrupted oil revenues, set out on a massive fiscal expansion. Without tight budgetary constraints, the state devoted more and more resources to purchasing private-sector firms that were no longer economically viable, with the hope of maintaining employment (Bazdresch and Levy 1991, 249). From 1950 to 1970, the number of para-statal firms in Mexico remained below 300; twelve years later, state-owned firms numbered 1,155. In 1983, state-owned firms accounted for 18.5 percent of GDP and employed more than 10 percent of the population (Aspe 1993, 181). Firms owned by the government included businesses such as the national oil company (PEMEX), the airlines (Aeromexico and Mexicana), the national telephone company (TELMEX), sugar refineries, and hotels.

Mexico's economic boom turned to bust when oil prices began to fall and U.S. real interest rates began to rise in mid-1981. The fixed exchange rate became extremely overvalued as the economic fundamentals changed. Investors' fear of another balance of payments crisis and devaluation led to capital flight. The government tried to maintain the exchange rate as long as it could, but foreign reserves were dwindling rapidly. In 1982, the government devalued the currency by more than 260 percent, declared a temporary moratorium on debt

Table 3.2

Overview of Mexican Finances, 1954–94

Year	Population[a]	Real GDP Per Capita[b]	Real GDP Per Capita Growth Rate (percent)	Inflation (percent)	Nominal Exchange Rate (new pesos)	International Reserves Minus Gold[c]
1954	31,419	2,397	7.15	4.85	0.0125	147.08
1955	32,348	2,514	4.88	15.99	0.0125	298.50
1956	33,483	2,590	3.02	4.85	0.0125	344.50
1957	34,617	2,711	4.67	5.10	0.0125	295.50
1958	35,757	2,751	1.48	8.17	0.0125	247.50
1959	36,891	2,726	-0.91	0.00	0.0125	316.00
1960	38,227	2,836	4.04	7.59	0.0125	306.00
1961	39,472	2,864	0.99	-2.03	0.0125	301.00
1962	40,754	2,897	1.15	2.15	0.0125	333.00
1963	42,074	3,019	4.21	-0.11	0.0125	409.00
1964	43,446	3,258	7.92	3.55	0.0125	418.00
1965	44,337	3,351	2.85	4.50	0.0125	379.50
1966	46,337	3,467	3.46	3.77	0.0125	454.99
1967	47,868	3,582	3.32	3.05	0.0125	420.00
1968	49,451	3,766	5.14	1.76	0.0125	491.92
1969	51,081	3,846	2.12	2.60	0.0125	493.39
1970	52,770	3,987	3.67	7.06	0.0125	568.10
1971	51,982	4,213	5.67	4.95	0.0125	752.09
1972	53,690	4,404	4.53	5.66	0.0125	975.88
1973	55,429	4,609	4.65	21.35	0.0125	1,160.21
1974	57,165	4,782	3.75	20.60	0.0125	1,237.63
1975	58,876	4,928	3.05	11.31	0.0125	1,383.46
1976	60,560	4,973	0.91	27.20	0.0200	1,188.00
1977	62,211	4,900	-1.47	20.67	0.0227	1,648.90
1978	63,836	5,208	6.29	16.17	0.0227	1,841.51

Year						
1979	65,445	5,621	7.93	20.04	0.0228	2,071.71
1980	67,046	6,054	7.70	29.78	0.0233	2,959.89
1981	68,637	6,467	6.82	28.68	0.0262	4,074.36
1982	70,225	5,942	-8.12	98.87	0.0965	833.89
1983	71,791	5,401	-9.10	80.77	0.1439	3,912.92
1984	73,309	5,524	2.28	59.17	0.1926	7,272.04
1985	74,766	5,621	1.76	63.74	0.3717	4,906.40
1986	76,178	5,283	-6.01	105.75	0.9235	5,669.82
1987	77,562	5,262	-0.40	159.16	2.2097	12,464.08
1988	78,933	5,349	1.65	51.66	2.2810	5,278.68
1989	80,312	5,566	4.06	19.70	2.6410	6,329.10
1990	81,724	5,827	4.69	29.93	2.9454	9,862.90
1991	83,306	6,018	3.28	18.80	3.0710	17,725.52
1992	84,967	6,253	3.90	11.94	3.1154	18,941.96
1993	86,557	6,167	-1.38	8.01	3.1059	25,109.61
1994[d]	88,054	6,244	1.25	7.00	5.0800	6,148.00

Sources: International Monetary Fund International Financial Statistics; *Penn World Table,* Version 5.6.; Banco de México.
[a]Thousands.
[b]U.S. dollars.
[c]Millions of U.S. dollars.
[d]Estimate.
Note: Data are for the end of the period. Real GDP is shown in terms of 1985 U.S. dollars and is adjusted for differences in purchasing power (using an equivalent basket of goods) between the United States and Mexico.

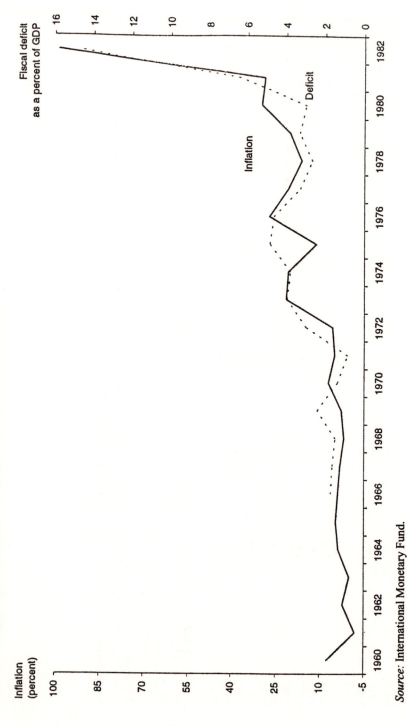

Figure 3.2 Mexico's Inflation and Fiscal Deficit as a Percent of GDP, 1960–82

Source: International Monetary Fund.

payments, and forced the conversion of dollar-denominated bank deposits into pesos at an unfavorable, below-market, exchange rate. As the crisis worsened, the government responded by tightening its grip on the economy. Toward late 1982, all trade became regulated, full exchange controls on capital were adopted, and the Mexican banking system was nationalized. But more government intervention spooked financial markets and only made matters worse. With the Mexican financial markets in disarray, a government fiscal crisis, and inflation pushing an annual rate of 100 percent, real per capita GDP declined 8.1 percent in 1982 and 9.1 percent in 1983.

Hindsight is always better than foresight. By 1982, it was obvious that Mexico should have pursued more market-based policies and limited foreign borrowing. However, with the price of oil increasing quite rapidly during the late 1970s and expectations of further price increases (expectations that other countries shared as well), the pressing need for change was not apparent (Lustig 1992, 21).

The Transition Years

In late 1982, Mexico's newly elected president, Miguel de la Madrid Hurtado, inherited perhaps the worst economic crisis in the country's history. During the early years of de la Madrid's administration, the first important stages of reform began, but it was only toward the end of his administration that structural reform policies genuinely moved in the direction of a more market-based economy.

From 1982 to 1985, Mexico's annual rate of inflation slowed from around 100 percent to about 65 percent in response to government spending cuts and tighter monetary policy. Real GDP per capita declined about 13 percent over these years as the economy adjusted to lower government spending and large foreign debt payments. Due to the high debt payments, Mexico's net transfers to the rest of the world totaled nearly 6 percent of GDP from 1982 to 1985 (Aspe 1993, 35).

Although the de la Madrid administration began reducing the public-sector deficit, it was not eliminating other fundamental causes of macroeconomic instability. Anti-inflation policies were not credible because the government still relied heavily on excessive money growth to earn inflation tax revenues. The inflation tax as a share of GDP was 8 percent in 1983 and 5.5 percent in 1985 (Figure 3.3).[7] The need for inflation tax revenues was due to debt payments, financial support of state-owned enterprises, and a weak tax system. Inflation began to accelerate in 1985, and by 1986, it was back up to more than 100 percent a year.

Although the economy was opening to trade, it was still relatively closed and the private sector was uncertain about the government's true commitment to open markets. Thirty-five percent of imports had to be licensed, and quotas covered 83 percent of the value of imports (Aspe 1993, 156). The export sector was being held back because resources were kept in import-competing sectors.

Figure 3.3 Mexican Inflation and the Inflation Tax, 1982–94

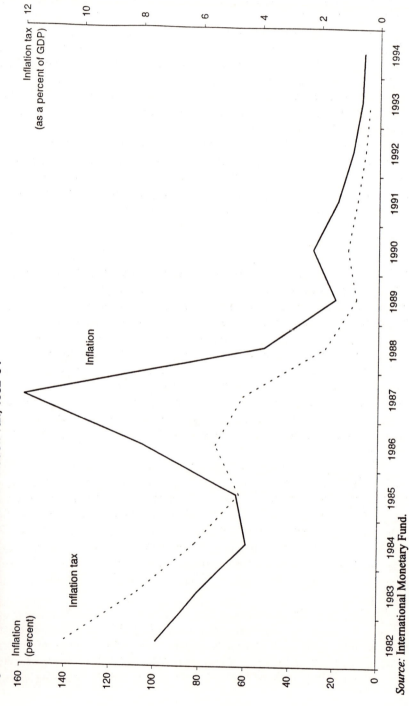

Source: International Monetary Fund.

Foreign investment was also weak because investors were suspicious of Mexico's commitment to open markets; laws still limited foreign ownership of business, and the government controlled the banking sector. The macroeconomic environment continued to worsen. After an earthquake in 1985, another oil shock in 1986, and a stock market crash in 1987, Mexico was ready for rapid and far-reaching reforms. The next package of reforms began to address some of its worst structural problems.

The Move to Open Market-Based Policies

During the early 1980s, Mexico's drop in real per capita income was almost as large as that which occurred during the Great Depression. As Figure 3.4 shows, in 1982 real per capita GDP fell 8.1 percent, while inflation rose to an annual rate of 98.9 percent. The experience convinced many people in and out of the government that Mexican policies were not working and they had to find an alternative (Aspe 1993, 14). Certainly there were those, mainly in the protected and state-owned sectors, who resisted changes in policy, but as the economy continued to contract, their political clout waned. The country embarked on a new policy direction.

In December 1987, President de la Madrid and representatives of the labor, farming, and business sectors signed the Pact for Economic Solidarity, which was followed by the Pact for Stability and Economic Growth under the newly elected administration of President Salinas de Gortari. These two measures, now jointly referred to as the *Pacto,* were designed to combine orthodox fiscal and monetary restraint with structural reforms and an incomes policy (controls on wages and prices).

The Pacto has gone through fifteen phases (or renegotiations, as they have been called) since its implementation in 1987.[8] The Pacto phases began as very short-term commitments, lasting about two months; they then grew to longer-term, one-year commitments.[9] During the first phases, a strong emphasis was placed on price and wage controls, fiscal and macroeconomic adjustment, and debt renegotiation; later stages focused on deregulation and privatization to promote economic efficiency and on trade and financial liberalization to enhance competition and reduce production costs (Schwartz 1994).

Incomes Policy

The incomes policy, or price and wage controls, has been and remains the most controversial part of the Pacto. Wage controls included programs that simply limited nominal increases as well as more complicated schemes of linking wage increases to productivity gains. Price controls were not uniform across the economy; the intention was to focus the controls on the leading sectors. Some have contended that the incomes policy was necessary to break the cycle of increasing

Figure 3.4 Real GDP Growth Per Capita and Mexican Inflation, 1980–94

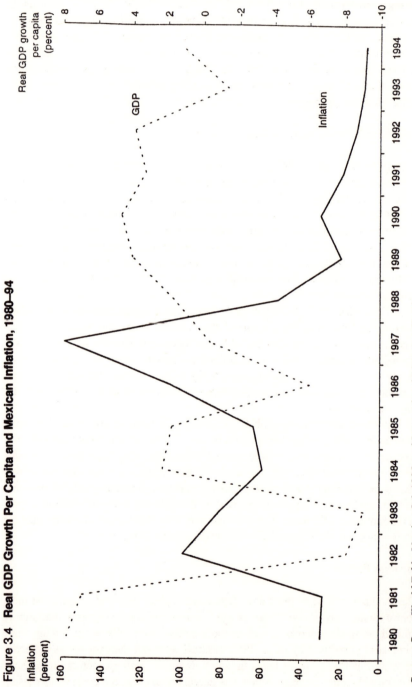

Source: Penn World Table, Version 5.6, 1995, and International Monetary Fund.

inflation resulting from the practice of indexing wages and prices to past inflation (Lustig 1992, 52). Others, however, have argued that the incomes policy
was unnecessary because, without fiscal and monetary austerity, the lifting of
price controls would simply result in a return to high inflation.

Fiscal and monetary austerity are sufficient to stop inflation, but some have
claimed that a benefit of the incomes policy was that it served to announce the
government's intentions to all concerned parties. An explicit statement of the
government's goals may have informed individuals what the inflation targets
were, which could have decreased the costs of adjustment. However, price and
wage controls, by themselves, can be costly because they tend to distort relative
prices in an economy. The exact cost or benefit of Mexico's incomes policy has
yet to be quantified.

The incomes policy was the most hotly debated during the first few months of
the Pacto, when prices and wages were adjusted on a monthly basis according to
changes in expected inflation. As inflation subsided, price and wage controls
became a less contentious policy. High inflation expectations were no longer
automatically built into wage contracts, and the strength of labor unions to negotiate large wage increases declined. Although the December 1994 exchange rate
devaluation was followed by higher inflation and attempts to impose more strin-
gent price and wage controls, the government subsequently abandoned further
attempts to impose controls.[10]

Public Finance

An important element of the Pacto has been public finance policy. In addition to
fiscal austerity, there has been a realignment of public-sector goods prices to
reflect costs, the divestiture of state-run enterprises, and changes in the tax structure. An often observed difficulty with plans to reduce fiscal deficits, not just in
Mexico but also in other countries undergoing economic reforms, is their structural inconsistency with other objectives. In other words, a government may state
that the fiscal budget will be balanced and inflation will be reduced, but without
a functioning tax system, inflation may be the only way to finance public expenditure. Although Mexico still has fiscal problems, changes in the public sector
have made fiscal prudence a more feasible policy than during the early 1980s.

Of the 1,155 enterprises held by the public sector in 1982, 940 were either
sold to the private sector, liquidated, or merged by 1994. State-owned enterprise
spending fell from around 18 percent of GDP in 1983 to 9.6 percent of GDP in
1994. The recent economic stabilization plan for Mexico calls for further
privatization of ports, public utilities, and some petrochemical plants. However,
some of these proposed privatizations are being contested, and PEMEX, the
national oil company and the largest state-run business, is not currently being
considered for privatization.

Since 1989, the tax system has been simplified, and tax rates are down to levels similar to those in the United States. The corporate tax rate was reduced from 42 percent to 35 percent, and the highest income tax rate paid by individuals fell from 50 percent to 35 percent. By simplifying the tax structure, lowering tax rates, and increasing enforcement, tax evasion has fallen and tax revenue has increased. In the early 1990s, tax revenues increased nearly 30 percent, mostly as a result of Mexico's expanding tax base (Aspe 1993, 108). The overall fiscal deficit as a percent of GDP fell from 16 percent in 1987 to 0.3 percent in 1994.[11] During the same period, total government spending fell from 43.7 percent of GDP to 26.3 percent of GDP, and inflation fell from 160 percent a year to 7 percent a year.

Mexico's stabilization plan of March 9, 1995, calls for increases in the prices of fuel, electricity, natural gas, and other goods and services provided by the public sector to reflect international prices and increase revenues. There are also plans to raise the value-added tax from 10 to 15 percent, reduce public-sector employment, and limit the growth of public-sector real wages.

Financial Liberalization

An important element of Mexico's new reform policies has been financial liberalization. Financial liberalization took a major step forward after 1988 with the elimination of compulsory bank reserve requirements and forced credit to public-sector enterprises. The elimination of these measures allowed greater financing for private-sector enterprises. Other changes have been the authorization of universal banking and other financial entities. In 1991–92, the government privatized all the banks and lifted capital controls imposed after the 1982 crisis.

Mexico is now increasing access to foreign banks and brokerage houses. In October 1994, it authorized virtually all the foreign banks, brokerages, and insurance companies that sought entry into the market. The finance ministry issued fifty-two licenses to eighteen commercial banks, sixteen securities firms, twelve insurance companies, five financial groups, and a leasing company.

Because of the recent economic crisis and stress on the banking system, the government has pledged to speed up implementation of provisions that would allow greater foreign ownership of existing financial institutions. Foreigners will be able to hold majority interests in all but the three largest banks. Before the recent economic crisis, foreign ownership of existing banks was severely limited, although the banking sector still faced increased competition in the market. In 1991, Mexico's three largest banks—BANAMEX, BANCOMER, and SERFIN—accounted for about 62 percent of total Mexican banking assets; in late 1994, they accounted for less than 50 percent.

Since the December 1994 devaluation, there has also been an easing of the rules keeping financial institutions from using the futures market to hedge uncertainty. Prior to the devaluation, the development of a futures market to hedge peso and equity volatility was suppressed. But although the government felt that these markets would add to unwanted speculation against the currency, the markets may have led to greater flows of trade and investment. The rules now allow for Mexican institutions to hedge movements in the peso and the stock market.

Trade Liberalization

On the trade side, Mexico started to gradually liberalize in mid-1985, but the process was solidified in 1988 when the number of goods covered by import licenses dramatically fell and the tariff structure was simplified. In 1983, the share of imports covered by import permits was close to 100 percent; by 1992, the share had fallen to less than 2 percent (Banco de México 1993). Mexico joined the General Agreement on Tariffs and Trade (GATT) in 1986 and cemented its open trade stance with the United States and Canada through NAFTA in 1993. NAFTA has generated a large increase in trade and joint business ventures between U.S. and Mexican firms. For example, total trade flows between the United States and Mexico (exports plus imports) grew by around 17 percent in 1994, compared with a 7 percent annual rate in 1993. These trade flows have averaged about 15 percent growth since 1988 (Figure 3.5). Mexico is now vying with Japan to be our second-largest trading partner behind Canada.

Monetary and Exchange Rate Policy

When Mexico began its economic reform, the key element of its monetary policy was the use of the exchange rate as a nominal anchor—that is, domestic prices were tethered to international prices by targeting the nominal exchange rate. During the initial stages of the Pacto, the exchange rate was fixed to the dollar; then it was held to a preannounced daily depreciation. In 1991, the exchange rate was allowed to float within a widening band. At first, the top of the band rose 20 centavos (0.0002 new pesos) per dollar a day; then it was increased to 40 centavos (0.0004 new pesos) per dollar a day (Figure 3.6). On December 20, 1994, however, under pressure from foreign exchange markets and dwindling foreign exchange reserves, Mexico abandoned its exchange rate band. The peso was devalued and then allowed to float freely against the dollar.

Some have argued that keeping the exchange rate closely tied to the dollar, especially during the early stages of Mexico's economic reforms, kept exchange rate volatility low and allowed investors a simple means of monitoring Mexico's monetary policy. For example, if expected inflation was higher in Mexico than in the United States, or prospects for growth in Mexico weakened relative to those in the United States, dollars would leave Mexico seeking better returns in the United States. This would lead to upward pressure on the exchange rate (increase the number of pesos per dollar) as people who held pesos bought U.S. dollars. If the exchange rate was to be kept within the band, Mexico would need to tighten

Figure 3.5 **Annual Growth Rate of Trade (Exports plus Imports) between the United States and Mexico, 1982–94**

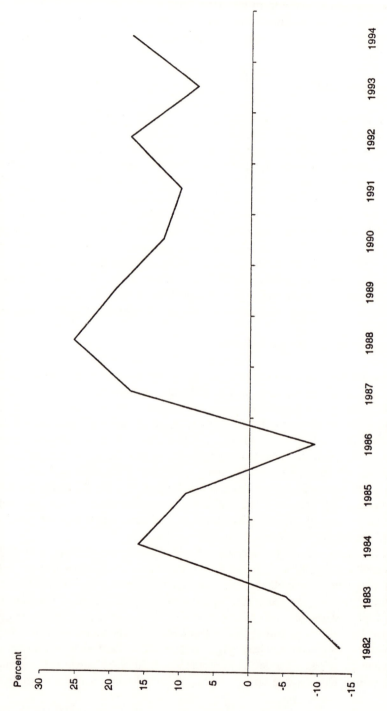

Source: International Monetary Fund; 1994 data annualized from first- and second- quarter data.

Figure 3.6 Mexican Pesos to U.S. Dollars Exchange Rate

Pesos per dollar

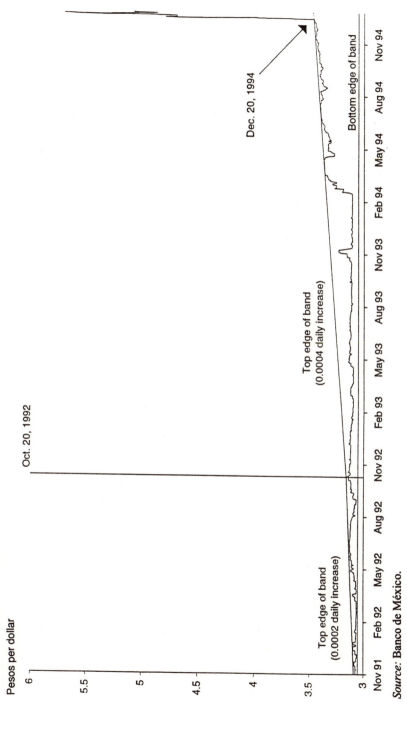

Source: Banco de México.

monetary policy and increase interest rates to attract dollars back into Mexico. As long as the exchange rate policy was maintained and was credible, it was argued, anyone who watched the movement of foreign reserves would know what would happen to monetary policy.

Of course, exchange rate policy does not make low inflation credible. Low inflation is made credible only through sustainable fiscal balance and low and stable monetary growth. Over the long run, it is these policies that keep exchange rate policy credible, not the other way around. If monetary policy is too loose and is inconsistent with maintaining the exchange rate, foreign reserves leave the country. Without any foreign reserves to defend the exchange rate, the exchange rate policy has to be abandoned.

From 1987 to the end of 1993, Mexico's monetary policy was consistent with low inflation and maintaining its exchange rate targets. Inflation fell from a high of nearly 160 percent in 1987 to around 7 percent in 1994. During 1994, however, political uncertainty in Mexico and rising interest rates in the United States began to drain Mexican foreign reserves. Investors were not being fully compensated for the greater perceived risks in the Mexican market, so they took their money elsewhere. Money left the country because interest rates did not rise sufficiently. A contributing factor could also have been that peso risks were difficult to hedge against. The central bank was suppressing the peso futures market because it feared the market would allow for inordinate speculation against the currency. Foreign reserves fell from around $25 billion at the end of 1993 to about $16 billion in July 1994 (Figure 3.7).

The election of Ernesto Zedillo in August 1994 brought new confidence to Mexico's policies and temporarily boosted foreign reserves and the peso. Following the elections, however, there were signs of investor uncertainty, and money began flowing out of Mexico again. Without dramatically higher interest rates, foreign reserves continued to leave the country. Eventually, foreign reserves dwindled to such a point that the exchange rate band had to be loosened and then completely abandoned after a continual pressure on the peso.

If interest rates had been kept higher after the 1994 presidential elections, perhaps the costs of abandoning the exchange rate, in terms of lost credibility and higher short-run inflation, could have been avoided. In hindsight, this may have been a better option than the one chosen, although dramatically higher interest rates could have also sparked an economic crisis. Perhaps a better option would have been to let the exchange rate float when foreign reserves were coming into the country, such as in late 1993. A floating exchange rate allows a country to weather domestic and international economic shocks without necessitating dramatic changes in domestic monetary policy and without calling into question the credibility of basic policies. Now that Mexico is floating its exchange rate, economic ups and downs will not generate speculation against a particular exchange rate policy. If monetary restraint continues, inflation—over the long run—will remain moderate.

Figure 3.7 **Mexico's Stock of Net International Reserves, 1994**

Billions of U.S. dollars, end of month

Assessing Mexico's Policy Credibility

What Determines Credibility

Perhaps economic liberalization never comes without a crisis. This has certainly been the case in Mexico. What becomes evident from looking across a broad spectrum of countries that have embarked on economic reform is that some have achieved great success, while others have failed miserably.[12] For example, Peru's trade liberalization attempt during the early 1980s was abandoned shortly after it was implemented. Will Mexico's economic reforms continue?

A common element of unsuccessful liberalizations seems to be the failure to create a credible economic policy. An example would be a government's pursuit of low inflation without addressing far-reaching structural problems, such as an inadequate tax system and a large budget deficit. In this case, pursuit of low inflation is inconsistent with the budget deficit and an inability to tax except through inflation. Another credibility problem occurs when a government's policies are time inconsistent. A time-inconsistent policy is one in which the government, at some later date, has an incentive to break its promise. For example, the government, for political reasons, may have an incentive to redistribute income from the rich to the poor.[13] Under this objective, a free trade policy may not be credible because the government has an incentive to provide more protection than expected to import-competing firms whenever the relative price of imports decreases. When the price of imports falls, the import-competing sector becomes relatively poor; consequently, the government has an incentive to renege on its free trade promise and redistribute income through protection to these sectors. Free trade, then, is not a credible policy because the private sector understands the government incentive structure.

Creating a credible policy that is time consistent can be problematic because it depends on the government's ability to precommit to a particular policy. In trade reform, for example, if a government cannot precommit to free trade, it may have to pursue a time-consistent but second-best policy of partial tariff protection. In other words, the government may never be able to create a credible policy committed to complete free trade; it may, however, be able to create a credible policy with less protection.

Consequently, to evaluate the credibility of any particular economic policy two questions have to be addressed: (1) Is the policy consistent with other objectives being pursued at the same time? and (2) Is the policy time consistent? In other words, does the government have an incentive to renege on the policy commitment? In the political economy context, the second question can be thought of as addressing whether the political forces that determine a particular policy are likely to change.

Almost universally, no policy—whether in a developed country like the United States or a developing country like Mexico—is completely credible. The lack of information about the government's incentives and uncertainty about future economic shocks make complete credibility impossible. However, the degree of policy credibility can be subjectively assessed by examining factors such as the government's behavior over time, the country's institutions, and the consistency of policies.

Assessing the Credibility of Mexico's Economic Liberalization

Since the December 1994 devaluation, Mexico's economic growth has stalled, and a growing number of people have become disenchanted with the current economic situation.[14] High interest rates have made it difficult for people to service their debts and have caused a decline in spending. While the current economic crisis can generate a political stimulus for greater economic liberalization and macroeconomic stability, it can also cause the abandonment of policies that enhance long-run growth in order to ease the short-run pains of adjustment. So far, the policies that have been adopted since the crisis began have favored greater economic liberalization and long-run macroeconomic stability, but their credibility over time will be determined by their consistency with other objectives and the strength of the constituency groups that favor such policies.

Because of Mexico's recent exchange rate devaluation, the credibility of another fixed exchange rate policy in Mexico is very low. Mexico's past monetary policy, although it generated a relatively low rate of inflation, was not consistent with its rigid exchange rate band. Its current floating exchange rate regime, however, is more credible because it does not require any specific commitment to tie Mexico's monetary policy to that of the United States. In addition, while a floating exchange rate may be more volatile on a day-to-day basis, it is unlikely to experience the kind of large discrete jump that is often seen in managed exchange rate regimes.

Compared with the period after the 1982 crisis and devaluation, however, Mexico may have a more credible low inflation policy. Although inflation has dramatically increased since the December 1994 devaluation, over the longer run Mexico may be in a better position to avoid high inflation. Unlike the situation during the 1982 economic crisis, the Mexican economy now has fewer government-owned enterprises that are taking funds from the public sector; many of these businesses have been privatized or liquidated. Moreover, the government budget is not in a large deficit, and because of a better tax system, the government does not have to rely solely on the inflation tax (printing money to pay for government expenses) to collect revenues (Figures 3.3 and 3.8).

Government incentives to maintain a more stable macroeconomic environment may also be higher today than in the past. Unlike the early 1980s, economic interdependence is much more important in Mexico today. Trade as a share of GDP increased from 8.7 percent in 1982 to 22.1 percent in 1993. The benefits of foreign investment and its sensitivity to bad policy choices have also

36

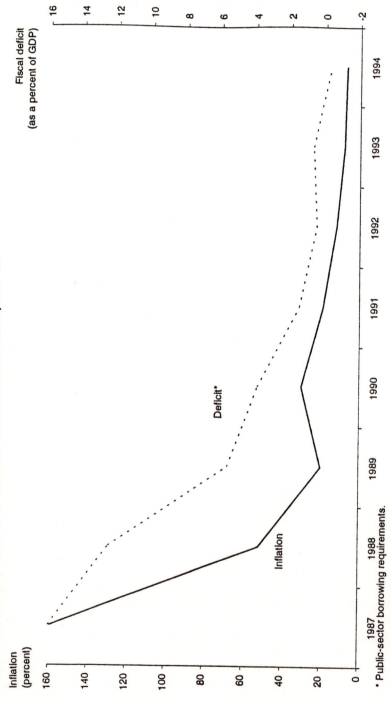

Figure 3.8 Mexico's Inflation and Fiscal Deficit as a Percent of GDP, 1987–94

* Public-sector borrowing requirements.

Source: Banco de México and International Monetary Fund.

become more obvious over the last decade. Countries that are more open and outward oriented—such as Chile, Hong Kong, Korea, Singapore, and Taiwan— have achieved much higher sustained economic growth than more closed, inward-oriented economies.[15]

The importance of market-based policies is apparent in Mexico's own experience. As discussed earlier, import-substitution industrialization policies were very costly for Mexico in terms of diminished economic efficiency and long-run growth. Moreover, while Mexico's 1982 crisis certainly hurt the country terribly, the poor policy response afterward, such as the nationalization of the banking industry, turned a bad situation worse by creating a massive capital flight, for which Mexico paid a tremendous price. Despite the recent exchange rate crisis, Mexico has yet to reverse its open-market stance.

Institutional arrangements can also increase the credibility of a policy. Although Mexico unilaterally reduced trade barriers in several areas before joining NAFTA and GATT, these multilateral agreements may be a much stronger commitment to future open markets, and not just because they are international agreements.

Free trade agreements create domestic coalitions against increases in domestic protection because of the threat of retaliatory response and possible collapse of the entire agreement. The greater the move to free trade, the more there is at stake and the greater the strength of these free trade coalitions. Usually, it does not pay for any one group to lobby against a single protective policy if the costs of such a policy to that group are relatively small. However, with NAFTA, a Mexican exporter has much more of an incentive to lobby actively against increases in Mexican protection because an increase in protection could induce a retaliatory response against its own products from the United States or Canada. The Mexican consumer also has a stake in seeing that the free trade agreement is kept because of the potentially large increase in the price of consumer goods if NAFTA is abandoned.[16]

Even though there may be coalitions in favor of sustaining open markets, in some sectors there is likely to be backsliding. Like the United States, Mexico is now using antidumping and countervailing duties against imports much more than in the past. Despite the fact that average tariff rates fell from around 34 percent in 1985 to 4 percent in 1992, the coverage of nontariff barriers went from 12.7 percent of imports in 1985–87 to 20 percent of imports in 1991–92 (Edwards 1993). The devaluation of the peso, however, may weaken the demand for nontariff barriers in Mexico. As the real value of the peso (adjusted for Mexican and U.S. inflation rates) has fallen against the dollar, the price pressure on import-competing firms in Mexico has decreased.

Conclusion

While continued economic reforms are not guaranteed in Mexico, they are more likely than often believed. During the 1980s, Mexico's economic paradigm shifted from a closed-market, inward-looking development strategy to an open-market, outward-oriented development strategy. Unlike the period prior to Mexico's 1982 debt crisis, the trend in Mexico's economic policies has been toward greater economic integration in the world economy and a reduced reliance on the government sector. This trend in Mexico's policies, although not immune to shocks, is more consistent with future low inflation and open markets than the country's previous inward-oriented policies.

Notes

1. In December 1994, the Blue Chip consensus forecast for 1995 Mexican real GDP growth was 3.8 percent. The OECD was predicting 4 percent growth for 1995 and 4.3 percent growth for 1996.
2. One of the main architects of this policy was Raúl Prebisch. For an insightful analysis of Prebisch's views, see Love (1980).
3. The underpinning of this theory was the idea that as world income rose, the demand for manufactured products would increase relative to primary products, and this change would lead to a lower relative price for primary products in international markets. As a result, if developing countries did nothing to change the structure of their output, their terms of trade would always move against them.
4. Over the same period, Taiwan and Korea both experienced around 4.6 percent real GDP growth per capita.
5. Although Prebisch was one of the main architects of the import-substitution industrialization policy, he realized the problems of protectionism as early as 1963. Hirschman (1968) quotes a very interesting passage from Prebisch (1963, 71): "As is well known, the proliferation of industries of every kind in a closed market has deprived the Latin American countries of the advantages of specialization and economies of scale, and owing to the protection afforded by excessive tariff duties and restrictions, a healthy form of internal competition has failed to develop, to the detriment of efficient production."
6. Gil Diaz (1984). As price controls were imposed to limit inflation, the profit margins of some private firms were squeezed.Those firms that could no longer produce profitability at the given prices were then purchased by the government. This was the case, for example, with sugar mills.
7. The real output that a government obtains by printing money and spending it is called the *inflation tax* or *seigniorage*. Money creation that leads to inflation erodes the real value of nominal money holdings. The formula used here to calculate the inflation tax as a share of GDP is: $INFTAX = (M/GDP) * \frac{\pi}{(\pi+1)}$, where M is monetary base, GDP is nominal gross domestic product, and π is the annual inflation rate.
8. If one includes the two stabilization plans announced on January 2, 1995, and March 9, 1995, as new Pacto phases, then there have been seventeen phases.
9. See Schwartz (1994) for the dates of Pacto announcements and durations.
10. The Mexican government's first stabilization plan, announced on January 2, 1995, allowed for a 7 percent increase in overall wages. On March 9, a revised plan included an additional 10 percent increase in the minimum wage, but those earning more than the minimum wage were free to negotiate their own wages.
11. The overall fiscal balance referred to here is the public-sector borrowing requirement, which measures the difference between total revenue and expenditure, which includes debt amortization in the interest component. The primary balance, which excludes all of the interest component in expenditures, has been in surplus since 1985.

12. See Michaely, Papageorgiou, and Choksi (1991) for an overview of the liberalization experience in several developing countries.

13. This is a case analyzed by Staiger and Tabellini (1987). In formal economic terms, the government's objective is to redistribute income from individuals with a low marginal utility of income to those with a high marginal utility of income.

14. Recent election results suggest such disenchantment. For the first time in its sixty-five-year history, the ruling Institutional Revolutionary Party (PRI) lost the governorship in the state of Jalisco, which includes Mexico's second-largest city, Guadalajara. The victory went to the National Action Party (PAN), which received 55 percent of the vote.

15. See Gould and Ruffin (1995).

16. See Gould (1992) for a more in-depth discussion of this topic.

Bibliography

Aspe, Pedro (1993), *Economic Transformation the Mexican Way* (Boston: MIT Press).
Banco de México (1993), *The Mexican Economy 1993* (Mexico City: Banco de México).
———. (1994), *Indicadores Economicos*, August. (Mexico City: Banco de México).
Bazdresch, Carlos, and Santiago Levy (1991), "Populism and Economic Policy in Mexico, 1970–1982" in *The Macroeconomics of Populism in Latin America,* ed. Rudiger Dornbusch and Sebastian Edwards (Chicago: University of Chicago Press), 223–62.
Edwards, Sebastian (1993), "Trade Policy, Exchange Rates and Growth," National Bureau of Economic Research, Working Paper No. 4511 (October).
Gould, David M. (1992), "Free Trade Agreements and the Credibility of Trade Reforms," Federal Reserve Bank of Dallas *Economic Review* (First Quarter): 17–27.
Gould, David M., and Roy Ruffin (1995), "Human Capital, Trade and Economic Growth," *Weltwirtschaftliches Archiv*, vol. 3.
Hirschman, A.O. (1968), "The Political Economy of Import-Substituting Industrialization in Latin America," *Quarterly Journal of Economics* 82 (February): 1–32.
Love, Joseph L. (1980), "Raúl Prebisch and the Origins of the Doctrines of Unequal Exchange," *Latin American Research Review* 15, no. 3.
Lustig, Nora (1992), *Mexico, The Remaking of an Economy* (Washington, D.C.: Brookings Institution).
———. (1995), "Income Distribution Problems in Mexico," *Challenge* (March): 45–50.
Michaely, Michael, Demetris Papageorgiou, and Armeane M. Choksi, eds. (1991), *Liberalizing Foreign Trade: Lessons of Experience in the Developing World*, vol. 7 (Cambridge, Mass.: Basil Blackwell).
Prebisch, Raúl (1963), *Towards a Dynamic Development Policy for Latin America* (New York: United Nations).
Schwartz, Moisés J. (1994), "Exchange Rate Bands and Monetary Policy: The Case of Mexico." Paper presented at XII Latin American Meetings of the Econometric Society, Caracas, Venezuela, August 2.
Staiger, Robert, and Guido Tabellini (1987), "Discretionary Trade Policy and Excessive Protection," *American Economic Review* 77 (December): 823–37.
Summers, Robert, and Alan Heston (1991), "The Penn World Table (Mark 5): An Expanded Set of International Comparisons, 1950–1988," *The Quarterly Journal of Economics* 106 (May): 327–68.

Part II

Economic Structures and Policies

4

SIDNEY WEINTRAUB

Mexico's Foreign Economic Policy: From Admiration to Disappointment

Sidney Weintraub highlights the shifts in Mexican economic policy that underlie the surprisingly rapid changes in popular understanding of Mexico's economic prospects. He states that Mexico's foreign economic policy as it exists in 1995 would have been unthinkable in the latter half of the 1970s. Protection of manufactures had helped promote steady economic growth but made Mexican manufactured exports uncompetitive. Oil reserves facilitated an inflow of foreign exchange that maintained the overvalued exchange rate and stifled non-oil exports.

The 1982 economic collapse forced a reevaluation of economic policy. Import substitution was replaced by a gradual opening to increased foreign trade and investment that culminated in NAFTA. New exports surged; inflation was reduced by eliminating the public sector deficit. A surplus was obtained in 1992 and 1993. The opening of Mexico to trade led to a current account deficit that in relation to GDP is four times that of the United States. However, NAFTA was expected to lead to sufficient investment to pay for imports. After all, the most important accords in NAFTA are those relating to investment, since trade barriers between Mexico and the United States had already been reduced. More than $50 billion was invested during the Salinas years, one-third in direct investment, the remainder in stocks and bonds—which would be fairly liquid if confidence in Mexico fell. Inflation was brought under control, but the annual economic growth rate was a modest 3.3 percent. On the other hand, the opening of trade led to the expected benefits of competition: greater choice and quality of products at lower prices. The composition of imports also is significant. Seventy-one percent of the imports were intermediate goods, which reflects the economic integration of Mexico and the United States. Some 40 percent of Mexican manufactured exports are sent to parent firms in the United States. Foreign exchange reserves increased through 1993. Although foreign investment had been attracted and dependence on oil exports reduced, political shocks led reserves to *decline to $17 billion at the beginning of December 1994. Mexico devalued the peso and adopted a floating exchange rate. By May 1995, the peso had fallen from 3.5 to 8.0 to the dollar. The high interest rate, to attract foreign capital, and an austerity program, to limit inflation, led to massive difficulties. The specter of the economic collapse of Mexico, with worldwide repercussions, led to the granting of $47.8 billion in credits from the United States, the IMF, and the Group of Ten.*

Both IMF conditions and the economic situation required President Zedillo to tighten the austerity program. This resulted in falling real wages and an increase in unemployment of 750,000 persons. Inflation was greater than expected but is coming under control. High interest rates led to demands for a debt moratorium for farmers and businessmen. And the fall in demand for imports ended Mexico's current account deficit. Despite its economic difficulties, in 1995 Mexico has a more developed economy and greater economic integration into the world economy than it did when it faced the debt crisis of 1982.

The views on Mexico's economic policy have been like a seesaw—given high grades for many decades until the 1960s, despised for two *sexenios* (six-year presidential terms) after that, lauded for a decade after the mid-1980s, and then reviled again in light of the devaluation in December 1994. We are reminded periodically that Mexico is a volatile, developing country. What follows examines mostly the last two episodes, the successful first five years of the administration of Carlos Salinas de Gortari, and then the collapse in the sixth year culminating in the drama that is still unfolding after the events of December 1994.

Mexico's foreign economic policy as it exists in 1995 would have been unthinkable fifteen years earlier. For all the talk of the inevitability of economic integration with the United States during the debate on the North American Free Trade Agreement (NAFTA), that outcome could not have been foreseen fifteen years ago. The turmoil that now exists in Mexico was equally unexpected, although it was building up during the first five years of the Salinas administration.[1]

Pre Salinas

The economic policy that dominated from roughly the 1930s to the 1980s was to look within Mexico for economic stimulus. The import-substituting industrialization (ISI) that prevailed was designed to provide more or less absolute protection against competing imports; the usual way to prevent competition from outside was to refuse to issue an import license. Imports that did enter Mexico legally consisted mostly of intermediate products not produced in the country and capital goods needed to equip Mexican industry. Most consumer imports were needed foodstuffs. Manufactured exports, consequently, generally were not competitive, burdened as they were by high tariffs and the requirement to use high-cost, low-quality national intermediate products.

The ISI model delivered steady growth of GDP of about 6 percent a year for about half a century, although this was accompanied by gross inequalities in income distribution.[2] However, the "easy" stage of import substitution has a finite beneficial life and must be buttressed sooner or later by more sophisticated production of intermediate and capital goods; and also by greater competitiveness and the ability to penetrate world markets. It had become clear to many economists, both inside and outside Mexico, that the ISI model had run its course by the early 1970s. What militated against change at that time—apart from vested interests who obtained rents from the status quo—was the discovery of large reserves of oil that came on stream roughly simultaneously with the presidency of José López Portillo at the end of 1976.

These were years of high oil prices. Oil as a percentage of the value of total Mexican exports climbed steadily after 1976, reaching a peak of 78 percent in 1982. In addition, based on the implicit guarantee of oil in the ground, Mexico went heavily into debt. The large inflow of foreign exchange permitted Mexico to keep the peso relatively unchanged for the six years before 1982 at between 22 to 23 to the dollar.[3] This overvaluation made non-oil exports almost impossible. Mexico had become an oil republic—better than other monocultures, perhaps, but still subject to the pressures of the marketplace.

The collapse came during the summer of 1982—after oil prices declined and international interest rates climbed due to the then U.S. policy of combating inflation. The Mexican authorities came hat in hand to Washington and announced that the country no longer could service its foreign debt. The Mexican treasury was bankrupt. Much of the 1980s were horrible years in Latin America, generally. However, to stick to Mexico, choices had to be made when Miguel de la Madrid Hurtado assumed the presidency at the end of 1982. The shift from ISI to what has been called *apertura*, or opening, began slowly and then gained steam under President Carlos Salinas de Gortari (1988–94). The culmination of this new policy was the coming into force of NAFTA on January 1, 1994.

What follows picks up the essentials of foreign economic policy under the Salinas administration and the issues that face President Zedillo in the first year of his sexenio.

The Salinas Years

Salinas and his *equipo* represented a new breed in Mexico—*técnicos* as opposed to *políticos* is the usual description. This shorthand is inadequate, however, because the technical expertise of the persons holding the key economic positions was of a high quality. The most prestigious U.S. universities rarely turned out as many first-rate Ph.D.s in economics for a single foreign country—save, perhaps, earlier in Chile under the Chicago boys. They were committed, by conviction and by what they felt was necessity, to a new structure for the economy.

The key elements of the new structure were elimination of the deficit in the

Figure 4.1 **Consumer Prices, the Salinas Years, 1988–94**
(percent change, December to December)

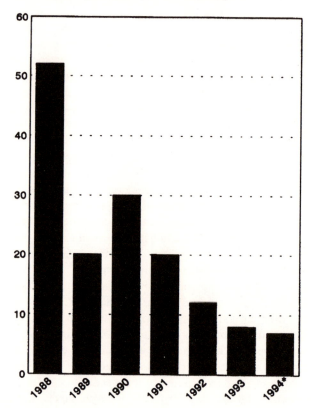

Source: Mexican Statistical Office.
*Estimated.

public-sector accounts, a steady reduction of inflation, a shift from a govern-ment-run apparatus to reliance on the private sector, an active search for foreign investment in lieu of the xenophobic suspicion that prevailed during the ISI years, the abrupt opening of the economy to import competition, and an objec-tive of export diversification away from excessive reliance on oil to manufac-tured goods. Figures 4.1 and 4.2 show how well two of these goals were accomplished. The rise in consumer prices in 1994 was about 7 percent com-pared with more than 50 percent in 1988 when Salinas took office; and the public-sector deficit that Salinas inherited was reversed and transformed into a balance, or even a surplus in 1992 and 1993—although some smoke and mirrors were required to achieve this, as is pointed out in note 7 below.

A high price had to be paid for the reduction of inflation. This was that overall economic growth—growth in gross domestic product—was not robust during the

Figure 4.2 **Public Sector Financial Deficit, the Salinas Years, 1988–94**
(as percent of GDP)

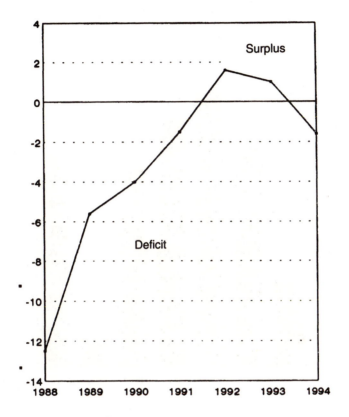

Source: Reforma, December 2, 1994.

Salinas years. This can be seen in Figure 4.3. For the six years as a whole, GDP growth averaged 3.3 percent a year—positive and more than population growth of about 2 percent a year, but hardly spectacular for a poor, developing country. For the economic technocrats who directed economic policy under Salinas, reduction of inflation took precedence over growth. Put differently, the argument made by the technocrats was that establishing the conditions for sustained growth in the future was more important than the gratification of growth now. There is a significant difference between career politicians, who in Latin America have had a tendency toward populism, and economists, who tend to take a longer-term view.

Yet higher growth in GDP is an imperative if the philosophical view of the Salinas reformers is to have durability. Bringing about this growth without sacri-

Figure 4.3 **GDP, the Salinas Years, 1988–94** (percent real annual growth)

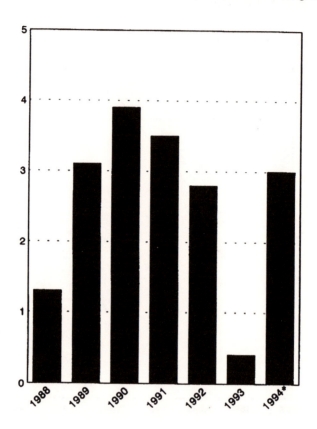

Source: Mexican treasury.
*Estimated.

ficing the achievements of the Salinas sexenio was perhaps the most economic and social challenge facing Zedillo when he took office, but that goal is more elusive now than ever. More on this later.

Opening the economy to imports and investment has had a profound impact on the daily life of Mexicans. Earlier, the only consumer goods generally available were from national production. Because of the import protection, oligopoly prices prevailed for these goods; and they were generally of second-rate quality. This, it was contended, was a necessary price of an ISI strategy. After apertura, all variety of products from the world at large could be bought in stores at prices that reflect competition under the prevailing exchange rate. Producers can purchase their intermediate products from the most competitive source for the quality desired.

Figure 4.4 **Current Account Deficit, the Salinas Years, 1988–94**
(billions of dollars)

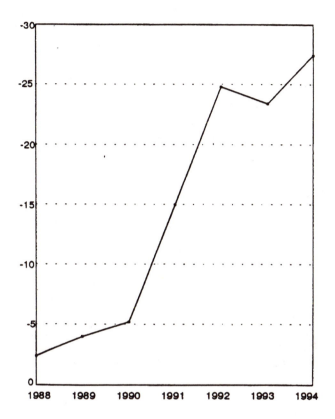

Source: Banco de México.

Under these circumstances, imports boomed. They were $19 billion in 1988 compared to $80 billion in 1994. Merchandise exports grew as well, but as Figure 4.4 shows, the deficit in the current account of the balance of payments (that is, the excess of imports over exports of goods and services) was almost $30 billion in 1994. This was 8 percent of GDP; as a point of comparison, despite its large trade imbalance, the U.S. current account deficit in relation to GDP is about one-fourth as large.

Despite the growth in consumer imports, the composition of total merchandise imports was still heavily weighted toward intermediate goods, that is, products needed for Mexico's own production. The merchandise import proportions in 1994 were 71 percent intermediate goods, 17 percent capital goods, and 12 percent consumer products.[4] The dominance of intermediate imports reflects the integration of production and marketing that exists between Mexico and the United States. U.S. multinational corporations produce parts of final products in each country (and throughout the world) for final assembly in either of them (or elsewhere). About 40 percent of manufactured exports from Mexico to the United States are intrafirm, that is, a subsidiary or affiliate shipping to the parent company.[5]

There had been continuing debate within Mexico as to whether a current account deficit of this magnitude was sustainable. The implicit answer of the responsible authorities was yes, as long as it was financed by voluntary movement of foreign capital into Mexico. This answer led to the current disaster. Over the Salinas period, foreign reserves increased at first from about $6 billion at the start of 1989 to $26 billion at the end of 1993. Put in layman's language, inflows of foreign capital more than compensated for the outflows required to finance the current account deficit. This was a different kind of capital movement from that which prevailed when Mexico resorted to debt financing before 1982; in the more recent period, holders of capital made their own decisions to move it to Mexico, whereas earlier it was the Mexican authorities who contracted the foreign debt.

But this kind of debate on the appropriate size of the balance-of-payments deficit has no end, only a decision regarding policy at a particular moment in time. Because of shocks to the Mexican economy during 1994—the continuing turmoil in Chiapas, the assassinations of presidential candidate Luis Donaldo Colosio and José Francisco Ruiz Massieu, the secretary general of the Institutional Revolutionary Party (PRI), and the raft of kidnappings taking place—there was a loss of reserves. They were about $17 billion at the start of December 1994, much less than they had been a year earlier.

Two other indicators of the performance of the economy under Salinas should be mentioned. These are that Mexico was attractive to foreign investors—despite the concerns over stability manifested during 1994. The inflow of foreign capital during the six years of the Salinas administration was unprecedented. Its cumulative total was more than $60 billion, about a fifth direct and the rest of a portfolio nature (buying Mexican stocks and bonds). The total was at least four times the capital inflow during the de la Madrid sexenio and ten times that which entered during the six-year term of López Portillo. The Salinas economic policy did attract foreign investment—precisely what was sought.

The other achievement was that reliance on oil exports was drastically diminished. Oil exports as a percent of the total declined sharply after 1982, but they were still about a third of the total in 1988. In 1994, manufactured goods accounted for more than 80 percent of total merchandise exports. This was not the result of a decline in oil exports, but of the increase in the exports of manufactures. Again, mission accomplished.

To end this discussion of the Salinas years, the crown in the jewel of Mexican foreign economic policy—the entry into force of NAFTA—deserves a prominent place. Salinas had no intention at first of entering into free trade with the United States or Canada. He was convinced that this was necessary when it became apparent that the foreign investment he sought would not be forthcoming from Europe or Japan, and that these markets would not absorb Mexican exports in the same manner as the United States. Once embarked on his policy of apertura, there was a logic to negotiating more secure access to the U.S. market, to which 60 to 70 percent of Mexican exports were sent; and looking only at manufactures, the U.S. market accounted for more than 80 percent of Mexican merchandise exports. One motive of NAFTA was to lock in the central economic policy changes wrought by the Salinas administration. This assurance was strengthened by the election of Ernesto Zedillo as president to succeed Salinas. But Zedillo was then confronted by a challenge that required reevaluation of all assumptions.

Zedillo's First Month

In a speech to a luncheon audience made up largely of foreign and Mexican business persons on December 2, 1994, the day after his inauguration, Zedillo emphasized that the word they should remember above all others about his administration was "stability." He made clear that he had in mind political and economic policy stability. This statement should be read in connection with what he said the day before in his inaugural address and be considered together with his choice of cabinet, which, on the economic side, was made up of people who played a large role in fashioning the Salinas economic policy.

Then, less than three weeks later, Mexico devalued the peso. The first effort was to change from a peso trading at about 3.50 to the dollar to one valued at 4.0 to the dollar, a depreciation of about 14 percent (from a peso worth 29¢ to one worth 25¢). The new value did not hold. The peso depreciated at one point to about 8.0 to the dollar, or a depreciation of more than 55 percent, and then recovered to about 6.0 to 1 by May 1995 and remained quite stable at that level. This amounts to a devaluation of about 40 percent.

What happened? Because of its high current account deficit—and the need this created for a steady inflow of foreign capital—Mexico was highly vulnerable to shocks, both internal and external. On top of all the other internal shocks during 1994, the one that seems to have been the straw that broke the camel's back was the reported renewal of the rebellion in Chiapas in December. This led to further losses of foreign reserves. Mexico also was subjected to the external shock of rising U.S. interest rates, which not only added to the cost of servicing the external debt, but required Mexico to further raise its already high internal interest rates (which in real terms, i.e., the nominal rate less inflation, are about double those in the United States) in order to attract the foreign capital required to finance the current account deficit. High interest rates, in turn, put a brake on overall economic growth.

Following the initial, modest devaluation, Mexico for a time sold more of its foreign reserves to buy pesos in a vain effort to hold its value at 4.0 to the dollar, but was forced to quit this intervention in the market when reserves dropped to $4 billion, a negligible amount in view of Mexico's needs. The peso then was allowed to float, and that is continuing.

The devaluation, in the face of continued assurances that it would not happen —the finance secretary, who has since resigned, gave such assurance only days before the devaluation—shattered confidence in the management of the Mexican economy. The technicians clearly were fallible—massively so. Many investors in Mexico took large losses from the decline in the value of the peso. Many foreign banks refused to roll over credits to Mexican banks out of fear of future losses, and this put the solvency of some Mexican banks at risk. Much of the foreign portfolio investment in Mexico was in government instruments, particularly those called *tesobonos*, which are peso instruments but which are indexed to the dollar to provide a guarantee against devaluation.[6] These are short-term instruments that must be amortized, but that found few buyers to roll them over at interest rates the Mexicans were able or willing to pay. Mexican firms with access to U.S. credit borrowed in dollars, at lower interest rates than prevailed at home, had to meet much higher servicing obligations.

In other words, Mexico had a horrible liquidity crisis, which, if not dealt with, could be transformed into a solvency crisis, bringing the peso—and the Mexican economy—crashing downward. This was the most immediate challenge, and the new Mexican treasury secretary, Guillermo Ortiz, found himself in continuous negotiation with foreign investment houses, banks, the International Monetary Fund, and wherever he could, to resolve this problem.

On January 3, 1995, two weeks after the turmoil began, President Zedillo introduced an austerity program calling for limits on wage and price increases, a drop in government expenditures, and privatizations in areas not previously considered, such as railroads, ports, telecommunications facilities, and electricity generation.[7] The president said that inflation in 1995 would be around 16 percent (the goal before the December events was 4 percent) and GDP growth about 1.5 percent (compared with an earlier goal of 4 percent). The current account deficit, he said, would be halved to about 4 percent of GDP. These were all optimistic estimates based on an exchange rate of 4.5 to the dollar and overcoming the liquidity problem. The initial program soon collapsed.

Zedillo's First Six Months

The collapse of the initial efforts of the Zedillo government made it evident that more comprehensive and drastic measures were needed. The U.S. government took direct action at this point. President Clinton proposed legislation to provide a credit of $40 billion to Mexico. This foundered because of congressional opposition, plus attempts to impose political conditions on the loan, such as requiring Mexico to rupture relations with Cuba or privatizing the state-owned oil company, Petroleos Mexicanos (PEMEX), which no Mexican government could accept. President Clinton, instead, provided a credit of $20 billion from the Exchange Stabilization Fund, which is controlled by the U.S. Treasury Department. This was augmented by an eighteen-month standby credit from the International Monetary Fund (IMF) of $17.8 billion, plus $10 billion in short-term support from central banks of the Group of ten Countries (the leading industrial countries) channeled through the Bank for International Settlements. The IMF credit was the largest ever approved for a member country.

The credits were designed to provide assurance to holders and potential buyers of Mexican government debt that there were funds available for repayment. Had Mexico not been able to meet its obligations, it would have been forced to resort either to import restrictions or exchange controls and a moratorium on payment of its dollar-denominated debt—or both. This could have led to what in technical jargon is called systemic repercussions, that is, declines in worldwide capital flows.

President Zedillo, in part to meet IMF conditions but also to take account of the real situation, instituted an economic program more severe than the one he had proposed initially. The Mexican authorities agreed to drastic fiscal tightening to achieve a public-sector surplus of up to 4 percent of GDP, and higher interest rates that for a time exceeded 100 percent in nominal terms on holders of credit cards. Wage increases have been limited to about 12 percent in face of an inflation the government said would be about 42 percent in 1995, but which is likely to be much higher. This is a precipitous decline in real take-home pay, and there undoubtedly will be later wage increases. The economy will decline, perhaps by as much as 4 percent of GDP, and unemployment already has increased by some 750,000 people. There will be little opportunity in 1995 for the one million new entrants into the labor force.

The situation by mid-1995 was that the financial medicine seemed to be working. The peso was holding steady at about 6.0 to the dollar, interest rates were declining to less than 50 percent for *cetes* (the government is no longer issuing tesobonos), the stock market was improving, and the high monthly inflation rates of the first few months were coming down. There was a dramatic turnaround in the trade account, and Mexico had a surplus in the first three months of 1995. There may be no current account deficit at all in 1995 because of the slack market in Mexico for imports and the export incentive provided by the undervalued exchange rate.

But the problems in the real economy—on individual incomes and employment —remain. The social situation in Mexico will continue to deteriorate for a time. The critical question is whether the decisive action taken will lead to a relatively rapid recovery, perhaps by early 1996, or the economic decline will last longer, as it did after the 1982 crisis. The government is betting on a quick recovery.

Looking Ahead

President Zedillo is off to a horrible start. Instead of the expected challenge to consolidate the economic changes of the Salinas administration, he is being forced to rescue them. Instead of being able to redress the issues of poverty and inequality, an objective he stressed in his inaugural address, he can promise only a year of austerity.

The technicians who ran economic policy under Salinas were the darlings of Wall Street and the foreign investment community. After massive losses resulting from the devaluation, there are now no financial darlings in Mexico, only a loss of confidence. The morbid betting taking place is on how long it will take Mexico to emerge from the present crisis. Zedillo is calculating about a year. That would be a good outcome, and the chances for meeting that timetable are probably better than even—but not more than that.

Yet, it is important to come back to the transformation that has occurred in Mexico from the depths of the depression that set in beginning in 1982. Mexico is now part of the production and marketing structure of North America. The country is also an exporter of a diversified range of products, and the devaluation of the peso will make Mexico's exports even more competitive. Mexico is facing the crisis of 1995 with strengths it did not have when it had to face the debt crisis that erupted in 1982.

Notes

1. One of Mexico's respected political analysts, Rafael Segovia, has characterized Salinas's six years as five plus one because unlikes cannot be added together.
2. See the Nora Lustig chapter in this volume.
3. López Portillo had promised to defend the peso like a dog, for which he was heavily mocked when the rate fell to 148 at the end of his term in office.
4. The figures are from the Banco de México for the first half of 1994. The proportions were almost identical in 1993.
5. U.S. Department of Commerce, Bureau of Economic Analysis, *U.S. Direct Investment Abroad: Operations of U.S. Parent Companies and Their Foreign Affiliates* (Washington, D.C.: U.S. Government Printing Office, 1993), tables II.H.5 and II.H.22. The figures are for 1991 and almost certainly understate the proportion of intrafirm trade that now exists.
6. The bank lines of credit up for renewal were about $20 billion. Outstanding tesobonos were about $28 billion, about $17 billion held by foreigners. In addition, there were about $9 billion outstanding cetes, peso instruments issued by the government, most of which are held by Mexicans.
7. One element of the austerity program was to reduce fiscal expenditures by 1.3 percent of GDP to achieve a surplus of 0.5 percent of GDP. What Zedillo did not mention was that the growth of lending by Mexico's development banks, which reached around 4.5 percent of GDP in 1994, would be cut in 1995 to about 2 percent of GDP. These loans were taken off budget a few years ago. In other words, the earlier figures on budget stringency were not fully candid.

5

Francisco Valdés-Ugalde

The Changing Relationship between the State and the Economy in Mexico

Francisco Valdés-Ugalde analyzes the internal and external reforms that determine the changing relationship between the state and the economy in Mexico. He argues that the Mexican state increasingly has faced a contradiction between market reform and the demands for economic development with social justice, as well as a democratic reform of the political system.

Traditionally, Mexico had combined a concentration of economic decision making and power in the presidency with, at first, social reforms, and, later, with an increased role of private enterprise. Conflicts over policy led to the bank nationalization of 1982. President Miguel de la Madrid took the first steps toward changing how economic policy was made in December 1982, when he submitted a constitutional amendment that restricted the state to intervention only in strategic areas and guidance in others, and gave Congress the power to issue and approve economic legislation.

Major changes from 1982 to 1994 were the sale of public enterprises, reduction of the federal budget, reduction of federal responsibility for municipal budgets, and transfer to the states of basic health services and education. In contrast to decentralization in the public sector, concentration of economic power in the private sector increased. An attempt to prevent a consequent immiseration of the masses was made during the Salinas presidency by establishing a National Solidarity Program, which directed aid to the poorest; reforming Article 27 of the constitution to allow communal landholders and small proprietors both to have definitive property rights and to sell their land; improving tax collection; and reducing transaction costs for domestic and foreign investment.

It will take time for these policies to take effect and the level and distribution of income to improve. If it does not, Valdés-Ugalde believes, "if the economy cannot meet social needs, and the state cannot make this possible, the only thing we can expect is the polarity of a minimally modern Mexico."

The application of market reforms to the Mexican economy has included the reorganization of state structures and economic functions. The reforms have strained all aspects of state economic intervention. This process has involved both external and internal adjustment. For example, insofar as the outside world is concerned, economic policies from 1982 until the present have focused on Mexico's external debt-crisis management and on its economic integration with the rest of the world through trade liberalization and expansion of foreign direct investment (FDI). The North American Free Trade Agreement (NAFTA) has been one of the most important steps in this effort. With regard to domestic adjustment, vast state reforms have been set in motion. As a result of both processes, the Mexican state increasingly has faced a contradiction between market reform, on the one hand, and demands for economic development with social justice (as well as a democratic reform of the political system), on the other. I shall address key aspects of these reforms and their impact on the relationship between the state and the economy.

Some History

Once the Mexican postrevolutionary state had built its basic structures, its relationship to economic development was distinguished by two outstanding features: (1) a concentration of economic decision making and power in the presidency; and (2) the adoption of social reforms, in order to achieve economic growth unaccompanied by increased inequity. This was the economic content of "revolutionary nationalism." It represented the economic statism of the contemporary Mexican state.

The Lázaro Cárdenas presidency (1934–40) carried out extensive land reform. The peasantry and labor organized big unions, which were affiliated with the Mexican Revolution Party—the progenitor of the PRI. And the government nationalized the oil companies. It also fostered economic growth with these reforms and gave birth to a significant number of modern enterprises and to a business class, which was aided by import substitution industrialization (ISI) strategy. But once the country had moved through this period of reform and had sustained economic growth, "revolutionary nationalism" became an increasingly contradictory process. This contradiction was, and continues to be, expressed as the one between the antiliberalism (in the classical sense of anti-economic freedom) of the postrevolutionary Mexican state and the market-oriented reforms that the government began to set in motion in the 1980s.

Previously—between 1954 and 1970—economic growth had reached the highest rates in Mexico's contemporary history. This growth was due to the success of recent policies and a favorable international business climate. Even though, in this period, state economic intervention grew, private enterprise also grew. Hence, market forces became more important. A new understanding between the public and private sectors gave birth to the idea that, in the long run, the economic importance of the government should be reduced and that of the private sector increased.

Some developing countries resisted the trend to market reform. They remained strongly in favor of policies that are protective of domestic industry and employment. Populism and socialism were extended widely throughout the third world. Being anti-imperialist, they continued to be hostile to market-oriented reforms. Nevertheless, the 1970s saw a growing consensus about the importance of market-oriented policies. But the increasing importance of liberalism was not as widely accepted as it would prove to be later. Mexico, among other countries, experienced this conflict during the Echeverría and López Portillo governments. From 1970 to 1982, under these administrations, state intervention was characterized by attempts to strengthen the weight of government in the economic process rather than to mitigate it. Echeverría's strategy of "shared development" and, later, López Portillo's "alliance for production" deviated from the implicit goal of market privatization. They assumed that it was inconsistent with Mexican history and with problems with which the governing alliance had to deal. One of these problems was the disagreement among the various economic actors and between them and the state about which economic and social policies were to be implemented. While business groups and organizations joined the chorus for neoconservatism and market reforms, trade unions demanded stronger state intervention in the attempt to improve income-distribution policies. They also insisted on a policy-making role. In turn, government demonstrated that it was torn by divisive attitudes between the nationalists in power and the technocrats who had been displaced from key policy positions.

Thus, from 1970 to 1982, the government sought a new equilibrium in economic policy among the state, the economy, and the society at large. But they failed to achieve that equilibrium. The essence of state economic intervention during that period lies in its refusal to give up ISI and, consequently, to redefine the division of labor between the state and the private sector. The overall result of these policies was, in the end, the opposite of their original purpose. The state came into increasing and intricate conflict with the private sector and failed to build a nationally centered economic model.

The end of this period was remarkable. President Luis Echeverría tried to modify these polarizing economic tendencies because they put state legitimacy in peril, but he was not only incapable of creating economic peace, he actually stirred up a unified opposition. His administration ended being unable to govern. Six years later, in spite of President José López Portillo's efforts to moderate the consequences of the 1970–76 sexenio, by the end of his term, economic crisis and social conflict had reappeared, as shown by the 1982 bank nationalization. The economic alliance between the private and the public sectors was broken. Economic problems became structural in nature. So too did the remedy.

A New Model

The central factors in this process of change that we should consider are: (1) the changing size, organization, and operation of the productive and administrative structure of the government; (2) budgetary, fiscal, and taxation measures; (3) privatization policies; and (4) changes in economic legislation and social policy. I offer here an overview of these aspects—considering first the de la Madrid administration, and second Salinas's.

From the first day of his term, President Miguel de la Madrid attempted to reorder state economic intervention. As early as his second day in office, he sent a bill to Congress to open a new "economic chapter" in the constitution—despite the opposition it raised among business representatives. But, only three months after the expropriation of private banks, this measure was seen as one following the same "state-centered economic path." Clearly, the purpose of this reform was to establish a difference between public and private responsibilities, in response to the demands of the business community. The state was to restrict economic intervention to "guidance" of the economic process and to intervene only in those "strategic areas" that were specified in the constitutional reform. In addition, new powers were granted to Congress. It could issue and approve economic legislation—powers previously granted solely to the executive office. This constitutional reform established the foundation for policies of adjustment and privatization. Reform was meant to reshape the structure of the relationships among the state, the economy, and the whole society.

Legal changes modified the structure of the federal government—from the ministries to state-owned enterprises. In the former, a huge redistribution of responsibilities took place. In the latter, the privatization process was set in motion. The reorganization of the state apparatus included the following changes: (1) from 1982 to 1994, 940 state-owned enterprises were sold off or eliminated; (2) the federal budget was significantly reduced by cutting government employment; (3) municipal reform relieved the central government of many of its budgetary obligations to local governments; and (4) decentralizing federal government transferred to state governments basic health services and education. The Salinas government later deepened this last change.

Privatization policies, on the other hand, have led to the restructuring of private business groups. They actually have increased concentration within an already concentrated economic system. In 1990, the top ten economic corporations represented 56 percent of total sales and 53 percent of employment generated by the 119 main economic groups. Three stock-exchange firms concentrated 40 percent of stock-exchange operations before the privatization of the banks in 1991–93. Besides, the same individuals who control the investment banks and banks control the main business umbrella organizations. These are a handful of individuals who comfortably preside over the relationship with the public sector. On the other hand, the five hundred biggest enterprises (including the banks, but also PEMEX—another state-owned enterprise) generated only 2.8 percent of total employment in 1990.

The building up of a new model has to be understood within the context of a lack of private confidence. It was critical throughout the de la Madrid administration and was not really solved until 1987–88, when a stabilization pact was signed between the government, the private sector, and organized labor. Two elements contributed to this: (1) the conviction that legal and economic changes could lead to an expanded, though reordered state presence; and (2) the natural uncertainty that is produced by changing policies at all levels. In sum, all economic actors shared the same institutional instability.

The 1987 Economic Solidarity Pact responded to the new economic crisis of October–December 1987. It addressed the need to find a stable framework for policy consulting, implementation, and control. It was meant to control macroeconomic variables in the short run through the control of wages and prices. Once the critical period had passed, it also proved useful in the satisfaction of private demands for an expanded privatization policy. In fact, President Carlos Salinas de Gortari undertook just that policy.

The "Pacto" established a format for policy negotiations that allowed the government to keep macroeconomic equilibria and to avoid unilateral actions on the part of single actors. It has worked to induce market reforms. But, for the same reasons, it has also worked to sustain the reform project within the old political structure.

The Politics of Modernization

In 1988 (and mainly from 1989 onward), the international climate for market-oriented reforms improved significantly. By the end of the 1980s, in contrast with 1982 (not to mention 1970 or 1976), the free-market mechanism was seen as the only way for domestic economies to become viable in the world economy. Consensus over "neoliberal" reforms, which support the engineering of the changes in the relationship between the state and society, was finally achieved.

State reform (along with economic reforms) was the key goal of Salinas's policies. It was meant to consolidate the modernization project that was initiated by his predecessor. It was presented by Salinas simultaneously as a break with the past of statism and as a continuity with the "original spirit" of the 1917 Mexican Constitution—the former being a distortion of the latter. According to Salinas's views, state economic centralism turned government into a "proprietor" whose goal of social justice was distorted by the activities that stemmed from the management of state enterprises. This situation, said the president, would come to an end with privatization measures. State structure would then be remodeled with the attainment of social justice with specific social programs in mind—mainly, "the national solidarity program." Obviously, this was an ideological operation that, in Salinas's own words, allowed for the deepening of privatization policies, justifying this before all of Mexico by claiming that the resources that would ensue from privatizations would be associated with social programs. In the same speech, Salinas asserted that this was the only way in which he could get congressional support to modify the constitution to privatize the banking sector.

In contrast with Salinas's words, it can be said that a strong role for the state in the economy comes from the very "original" writing (not just the spirit) of the 1917 Constitution. Its goal was to moderate social inequity and stimulate economic growth. That principle gave birth to a system of state enterprises. Salinas's state reform established a different principle for economic organization. But it still claimed its origin in the ideology of the Mexican revolution. Nevertheless, Salinas's reform reshaped state structure in order to reduce its economic intervention and to foster private investment as a substitute for the past role of public investment. Salinas's reform of the state basically concentrated on the economy and on social policy. It dissociated these from political democratization. Its basic operation consisted of deactivating the constitutional commitment to social justice in the economic process, and of transforming it into a separate branch of state policy.

One of the major turning points of Salinas's policies was the reform of the constitution's Article 27. Its objective was to set in motion certain structural changes in agricultural production: (1) officially finishing land distribution (excepting for that involved in previously filed demands); (2) giving definitive property rights to "*ejidos*" and small proprietors (ejidos are lands distributed after 1915 to groups of twenty or more land claimants or ejidatarios. Until 1992, these lands belonged to the state and were worked by members of ejidos. They could not be legally sold or rented. Roughly half of Mexico's rural land area is comprised of 28,000 ejidos on which 8 million members of ejidos and their families work); (3) allowing companies to buy land; (4) separating urban states from arable land and allowing communities to decide whether they would distribute the latter in individual parcels (or lots) among their members; and (5) allowing landowners of any kind to form productive associations or rent their land.

The ejido community assembly is meant to be the forum in which decisions on all matters concerning this law are made. The effects of this reform are still very uncertain. Potentially, this change is a turning point in agrarian social structure. But the question of whether it will succeed in increasing agricultural output has yet to be answered.

Fiscal policy has been another area of major reform. Fiscal adjustment (excluding extraordinary revenues due to privatizations) accounts for the 1991–94 surpluses. Besides, the new taxation policy (mainly precluding tax evasion) has shown remarkable results. It has increased tax revenues by 217 percent in the period from 1988 to 1993.

New economic rules and procedures have constituted another area of extensive changes. According to "neoliberal" economic theory, this area is fundamental to freer investment flows and simplified economic transactions. Among the most important is the new "automatic mechanism" for foreign investment. This mechanism has increased the number of operations (new investment as well as the constitution of new firms) that do not require previous government authorization. In 1994, direct foreign investment (DFI) reached a stock of more than $50 billion. This figure surpasses by more than 100 percent total foreign investment in 1988. However, a large amount of new DFI has been located in the stock market and in trade, rather than in industrial or agricultural production. A heated debate has developed over the proper role for foreign investment in a country like Mexico. The December 1994 devaluation, preceded by capital flight and its impact on internal debt and confidence crisis, has intensified this debate.

Other economic regulations have been changed. By mid-1993, around fifty major changes had been made in different areas to encourage microeconomic activity. These areas include transportation, trade and port operations, health, tourism, mining, electricity, and petrochemicals. Besides, "systemic actions" had been taken in key areas to reduce transaction costs and encourage competitiveness. Such areas include investment, money and stock markets, weights and measures, competitiveness, and consumer rights.

A key role of government in postrevolutionary Mexico had been as arbiter between labor and capital. In spite of the demands of the private sector to modify labor laws, the government has not attempted to change them. But everyday life in the working place has changed substantially. Economic adjustments have been made almost entirely on the backs of the laboring and middle classes. The proportion of wages in the GDP plummeted 12 percentage points between 1980 and 1990. Collectively bargained contracts have almost disappeared. Unemployment has remained at a very high level. Changes in the organization of labor have been possible without changing laws and with the acquiescence of trade unions. Nonetheless, sooner or later, a new federal labor law will be sent to Congress, though the timing could vary because of the political calendar. In any case, future regulations will basically give structure to that which is already happening in the labor market.

Privatization was one of the key policies of the Salinas administration. Among the businesses privatized were eighteen commercial banks, airlines, iron and steel works, sugar mills, and a substantial portion of CONASUPO—the staples distributor. Total privatization revenues yielded the equivalent of 6.5 percent of the GDP of 1991. Revenues for bank sales represented more than one-half of this percentage. At the outset of President Ernesto Zedillo's government, and even before the December 1994 financial blowup, the private sector had not managed to fuel the economy.

Social policy has been another area of major change. Traditionally, social welfare had been thought of as part of state action, combining strong government leadership, sectoral services (health, education, retirement, etc.), and subsidies (food, transport, etc.). The latter have been radically reduced, whereas specialized services have been rationalized. In addition, the National Solidarity Program (PRONASOL) was introduced by the Salinas government to deal with problems of poverty and social marginality. Pronasol has worked in the field as an organizer of social demand. It emanates from grassroots organizations, channeling funding to produce basic public goods—both in the countryside and in urban areas.

Limited Success

Economic adjustment has been achieved partly through the reform process. But the foundations for a new and balanced development have not yet been laid. This reveals a twofold problem: (1) a market economy cannot be created solely by reducing state economic intervention; and (2) state reform cannot be limited to economic matters; it has to address democratization of the political system.

Privatization measures and the reduction of state economic intervention do not automatically constitute either the adequate entrepreneurial function or the appropriate governmental regulation. Efficient resource allocation does not spring only from these policies. It needs proper economic, social, and political equilibria, which bring actors—both collective and individual—into a virtuous economic game. State and economic modernization in Mexico have not even come close to accomplishing their objectives. Mexico does not have a market economy in the modern sense of the term. Neither has it found an adequate way to focus on social justice. If the economy cannot meet social needs, and the state cannot make this possible, the only thing we can expect is the polarity of a minimally modern Mexico—one that is made up of a handful of giant enterprises and a few dozen technocrats on the one hand, and the vast impoverished majority of a backward Mexico on the other.

6

WILLIAM GRUBEN AND JOHN H. WELCH

Distortions and Resolutions in Mexico's Financial System

The Mexican financial system includes commercial banks, development banks, brokerage houses and securities markets, insurance firms, and other nonbank financial intermediaries, which include credit arrangements outside the formal banking system for the poor. William Gruben and John Welch provide an overview of the striking changes in commercial banking in the last decade, and a brief description of development banking.

Changes in government policy toward financial institutions are a major indicator of the changing relationship between the state and the economy. In 1982, the López Portillo administration nationalized the banks. It recapitalized and began to consolidate them. By 1990, only eighteen of the fifty-eight originally nationalized remained. The banks, however, had carried out diverse financial functions. In 1984, the de la Madrid administration began to sell brokerage houses, insurance firms, and other bank property. Nonbank financial institutions' assets increased from 9.1 to 32.1 percent of financial system assets. They bought public debt, freeing the government from financial dependence on borrowing from commercial banks. During the Salinas administration, the government eliminated many controls over banks, sold the nationalized banks, and moved toward universal banking.

The three largest banks had three-fifths of Mexican bank assets. Mexican banks' return on assets was almost 60 percent higher than that of U.S. banks. They were, however, roughly two-thirds as efficient as U.S. banks. Protection of Mexican banking explained this phenomenon. Competition would resolve the problem. In 1993, the number of Mexican banks almost doubled. In 1994, as a result of NAFTA, foreign banks were allowed to operate in Mexico, subject to size restrictions. Foreign banks as a whole were limited to up to 8 percent of

Opinions expressed in this document do not necessarily reflect the opinions of the Federal Reserve Bank of Dallas or of the Federal Reserve System.

total Mexican bank capital, an amount that would rise to 15 percent at the end of 1999. Some fifty-three financial institutions were licensed to operate in Mexico.

The Mexican banking system faced not only increased competition, but customers whose high interest costs and decreased profits led them to default on loans. Banks expanded consumer credit to customers about whom little was known. In 1995, to rescue Mexico's unsound banks, foreign banks were allowed to purchase any but the three largest Mexican banks. New rules allowed foreigners as a group to have up to 25 percent of bank capital.

A recapitalization program aided Mexican banks. The government purchased banks' nonperforming debt in exchange for bank purchase of special government bonds, allowing banks to restructure loan maturities and improve their balance sheets. William Gruben and John Welch believe that the favorable outlook for the Mexican economy brings with it an improvement of its financial sector, which, however, is not yet competitive and efficient by developed country standards.

Changes in Mexican policy toward financial institutions have moved them to a more open and riskier environment. But even without those alterations, Mexico's radical policy changes toward nonfinancial sectors would have meant a new atmosphere for financiers. To complicate this trajectory, United States' and other foreign nations' monetary and fiscal policies—together with policy changes and political shocks in Mexico—have pushed foreign financial capital in and out of the country. Together, these gyrations form a story of booms and busts, devaluation and bailout, but, behind it all, of a financial system headed toward greater efficiency and greater integration with world financial markets.

The Nationalization of Mexico's Commercial Banks

To elucidate the causes and effects of the Mexican financial system's volatile trajectory, we open with the close of the López Portillo administration in 1982, the first year of real economic decline since 1932. Faced with increasing pressure against the peso and attendant capital flight, the López Portillo administration forgot the real reasons capital flees a country and blamed the banks. As a punishment, the López Portillo administration nationalized them. To make sure they stayed nationalized, López Portillo incorporated the nationalization into the constitution.

The government's new prisoner was a sick one. The banks were suffering the effects of falling oil prices, of bursts of exchange rate instability and, ultimately, of regulatory laxity. Mexico recapitalized the banks and began to consolidate them. Of the fifty-eight originally nationalized, only eighteen remained by 1990 (Banco de México 1992).

Broadening and Deepening the Financial Markets

A financial crisis had preceded the bank nationalizations in 1982. The financial problems included an accumulation of government debt Mexico was hard put to pay. For years thereafter, government domestic borrowing crowded out private borrowers. The government absorbed domestic credit by decree, imposing heavy reserve requirements on the banking system and allowing them to be fulfilled only by the purchase of government debt. In 1986, for example, over 60 percent of net bank credit flowed to the government.

Crowding out was only part of the problem for the banking system, however. Until the late 1980s, Mexico was a classic case of financial repression.[1] Not only did the government force banks to lend to it, but it maintained interest rate ceilings on bank assets and liabilities and also dictated lending quotas to what it deemed high-priority economic sectors.

One of the most important events in Mexico's financial development of the 1980s was the rise of nonbank financial intermediation. When Miguel de la Madrid Hurtado replaced José López Portillo as president of Mexico in 1982, the new administration would not privatize the newly public banks. After all, nationalized banking was protected by the constitution. But perhaps everything those banks did was not really banking. In 1984, the de la Madrid administration began to sell off the brokerage houses and insurance companies and other bank property that did not involve taking deposits and making loans. Between 1982 and 1988, nonbank financial institutions' assets rose from 9.1 percent of total financial system assets to 32.1 percent.

One reason nonbank financial institutions grew was the rapid expansion of Mexico's securities market. This expansion in large part reflected the increased issuance of cetes, which are short-term government debt comparable to U.S. treasury bills. The point was to create a separate market for public debt so as to wean the government from the banks. Mexico had begun to issue these instruments in 1978, but it was not until the de la Madrid administration that these issues on the open market became major funding sources for the government.

By the late 1980s, the Mexican money market had become liquid and sophisticated. As a result, by the beginning of the 1990s, the Mexican government no longer relied at all on financing from the commercial banks. The biennium 1988–89 was among the most significant for financial liberalization in Mexico and for attendant broadening and deepening of financial markets there. Important events included not only the development of the money market, but freeing interest rates on bank assets and liabilities, eliminating the priority lending quotas, and ultimately phasing out both reserve requirements and liquidity coefficients. Moreover, banks were given greater opportunities to compete with the brokerage houses that had been taking market share from the banks at a rapid rate.

In 1990, even more choices became possible. Under Carlos Salinas de Gortari, who in 1988 succeeded Miguel de la Madrid Hurtado as president, the Mexican Congress amended the constitution to permit the sale of the nationalized banks, although only to Mexicans. Soon after, a new Financial Groups Law passed, heading the banks back toward the universal banking system to which they had been moving before the 1982 nationalization. Under universal banking —common in Europe but illegal in the United States—the same holding company may control an insurance company, a bank, a brokerage house, a leasing company, a factoring company, a bonding company, a mutual funds management company, a currency exchange broker, and a warehousing company.

Reprivatizing the Banks

The government sold its eighteen banks in fourteen months (June 1991 through July 1992) at the extraordinarily high average price-to-book-value ratio of 3.49. Mexico used the proceeds to reduce the public debt left over from the financial crisis of the 1980s. There is much anecdotal evidence to suggest that the buyers —mostly financial groups and brokerage houses—paid those high prices because they expected certain details of the Mexican banking system to remain in place.

The details included a banking market in which intense competition was not part of the landscape. With eighteen newly privatized banks, plus two others that for particular reasons had never been nationalized, there were only twenty commercial banks taking deposits and lending in Mexico.

Even among these twenty, market power was highly concentrated. At the time the last of the banks was privatized, the three largest accounted for about three-fifths of all Mexican bank assets. Profits were high. In 1992, when the government sold the last of its commercial banks, the net return on assets for Mexican banks was approximately 1.45 percent versus 0.91 for U.S. banks.

The new owners managed to mark loan rates up significantly above their costs of funds. Over the first five months of 1991, when the eighteen banks were still public, the spread between average cost of funds and average lending rates ranged from 5.31 percentage points to 6.29. During the last five months of 1992, when the eighteen banks were all private, spreads ranged from 8.09 percentage points to 10.69—even though inflation rates were lower in 1992 than in 1991. The spreads widened because banks paid lower interest rates to depositors in late 1992 than in early 1991, while the interest rates they charged borrowers were higher.

By the date of the privatizations, bank performance measures had already improved compared with the middle and late 1980s. But distractions from competitiveness still suggested themselves across the spectrum of bank financial ratios. Despite Mexican banks' high profits, low efficiency was chronic. At the end of 1991 a common measure of bank efficiency, the noninterest expense to total assets ratio, was 5.3 in Mexico compared with 3.6 percent in the United States.

Marketing seemed not to have received much attention, either. In 1991, Mexico had one bank branch for about every eighteen thousand people. In the United States, the number was about one branch per four thousand and, in Europe, about one for every two thousand.

These factors probably help to explain why financial penetration, a measure of the degree to which savings are channeled through the financial system to provide financing for investment, was also low in Mexico. As measured by M4/GDP (where M4 is currency, checking accounts and other short-term deposits, bankers' acceptances, long-term bank licensees' deposits, and government bonds held by the public), financial penetration grew markedly in the late 1980s and early 1990s. Nevertheless, by 1992, it was still only 46.1 percent, compared with 97 percent in Canada, 93 percent in the United States, and 71 percent in Italy.[2]

Increasing Financial Market Competitiveness

If the high price-to-book ratios they paid meant buyers of Mexico's commercial banks in 1991 and 1992 expected competitiveness to continue at these low levels, 1993 would be a surprise. After cutting the number of banks in the 1980s, Mexico began to open its banking markets to new domestic entrants in 1993. By 1994 a total of thirty-five Mexican-owned banks (including the eighteen that were privatized in 1991–92) had charters.

The wave of domestic bank charters that began to roll in 1993 was followed by another, of foreign applicants, in 1994. Before 1994, the only foreign bank chartered to operate as a deposit-taking and lending institution in Mexico in the 1990s was Citibank. But in 1994, new bank regulations attendant to the opening of NAFTA allowed foreign-owned banks to operate in Mexico.

Mexico had begun in the late 1980s to shed itself of trade protectionism by reducing tariffs and quotas and eliminating import licenses, but it opened trade in services more slowly. The craft of goods trade protectionism differs from that of services protectionism. Trade protectionism for goods usually means an attack on the product. The importer must pay a tariff on the product. Quotas limit the number of products one can import. Or products may enter the country only with a license.

Protectionism in services involves an attack on the producer. A government may let only domestic producers operate. Sometimes foreign producers may operate but only under different—read more restrictive—rules. Sometimes governments give some fortunate local producer a monopoly, freezing out even would-be domestic producers.

Before 1994, foreigners in Mexico could establish bank representative offices, but they could not set up actual banks that took deposits, built branches, and gave away toasters. Such familiarities were permitted only to Mexicans, and not to very many of them. Similarly, insurance companies, brokerage houses, and specialty finance companies (such as auto financing companies) could operate only if Mexicans had controlling interest.

The Introduction of NAFTA

The financial services sector of NAFTA, which changes all of this, is a principles-based agreement, and it is important to understand what that signifies. By contrast, the financial portion of the U.S.-Canada Free Trade Agreement laid out rules for banking, securities firms, and insurance companies but did not expressly base the rules on any underlying goals. Moreover, the U.S.-Canada agreement did not set up a framework for pushing toward goals that the original agreement did not achieve. One of NAFTA's themes is that the signatories have worked toward certain explicit general goals initially and will continue to work to realize them in the years ahead. That is the idea behind a principles-based agreement.

Two of the most important principles are national treatment and freedom of cross-border trade. National treatment means a country will treat foreign-owned firms within its borders as it treats domestically owned firms. This means that a Mexican subsidiary of a U.S.-based financial institution is supposed to face the same entry requirements and other regulations that a Mexican-owned financial institution faces in Mexico. Freedom of cross-border trade means a country does not interfere when its citizens try to use financial institutions in other countries. During the early 1980s, Mexico tried to keep its citizens from taking their money out of the country and putting it into U.S. banks. The cross-border trade principle is supposed to mean the Mexican government pledges not to do that again.

NAFTA opened Mexican financial markets enormously, and its initial rules moved toward full national treatment. Even so, they did not reach it. Canadian and U.S. firms that wished to purchase or start financial institutions faced size restrictions that Mexican financiers did not. These included maximum size restrictions per firm and by industry to make sure that foreigners did not finish by owning everything.

Consider first the implications of the by-industry rules. In 1994, foreign banks as a whole were permitted to purchase or start institutions with up to 8 percent of total Mexican bank capital, but no more than that. During a six-year transition period to end in 1999, the limit would rise steadily to 15 percent. Similarly, securities brokerage firms, factoring enterprises, and leasing operations could—as a group—start with as much as 10 percent of the Mexican market. By 1999, the limit would reach 20 percent. Most of the Mexican financial sector would open completely by the year 2000, and the entire Mexican market would open no later than 2006. Ultimately, this would signify a dramatic change.

Individual institutions also faced maxima. With the initiation of NAFTA, an individual foreign-owned bank—whether purchased or newly started—was allowed to own up to 1.5 percent of total Mexican bank capital until the year 2000, when a 4 percent maximum would apply. The same initial maximum of 1.5 percent of industry capital applied to foreign-owned insurance companies, while foreign-owned securities firms faced individual maxima of 4 percent. Thereafter, by the year 2000 an individual foreign-owned insurance or securities firm could account for up to 100 percent of the market. In any case, any of these institutions would be permitted to grow, once it had been purchased or started within these initial limits. Individual financial institutions would also face minimum capital requirements, but they would be the same as those the Mexican institutions faced.

Many foreign investors were undeterred by the capital restrictions. In October 1994, Mexico's Finance Ministry announced that it would issue licenses to foreigners to initiate eighteen commercial banks, sixteen securities firms, twelve insurance companies, and five financial groups. Although the opening of Mexico's financial markets was attendant to NAFTA, the opening for acquisitions and new charters was not restricted to Canadian and U.S.-based firms. Among the licensees were Banco Santander of Spain and the Bank of Tokyo.

Pressures on the System

The prospect of increasing competition, together with the consolidation of organizational changes, led to noticeable alterations in Mexico's commercial banking system. Between December 1991 and December 1994, the number of bank branches grew by one-eighth as total bank employment slipped and then fell hard. Measures of efficiency, including the ratio of noninterest expenses as a share of assets, edged downward. Although the improvement was slow, it was improvement.

But other pressures began to cause difficulties for the banking system. As part of Mexico's efforts in the late 1980s toward productive efficiency and low inflation, the country had not only lowered trade barriers but followed an exchange-rate–based stabilization policy. The government fixed the exchange rate during 1988. The next year, Mexico commenced a crawling-peg regime in which the rate of depreciation of the peso against the dollar was lower than the differential between the two countries' inflation rates.

The resulting increase in the real exchange rate, together with the trade apertures that had begun in the late 1980s, allowed international competition to discourage producers of tradable products from raising their prices. The nontradable products sectors, including real estate and construction-related industries together with various service producers, were less sensitive to such discipline. Recall that by definition, nontradable products are those that have little if any foreign competition. But nontradable products were typically among the inputs tradables producers used to make their products. When nontradables producers raised their prices, they imposed a squeeze between costs to and selling prices of tradable goods producers. The squeeze on these producers soon began to have implications for the banks that had lent them money.

Another important bank-related detail of Mexico's foreign economic policy was also related to the increasingly negative balance of trade. To maintain dollar reserves to defend the exchange rate, and to create capital inflows that would offset the outflows of funds to buy imports, Mexico held interest rates relatively high. Real interest rates rose during 1992 and 1993, making it more difficult for borrowers to repay their typically variable-rate loans.

Meanwhile, in the wake of the privatizations, banks began to expand consumer credit despite limited information on the creditworthiness of the borrowers. Well-organized credit reporting systems, so common in the United States, operated only on a very limited scale in Mexico.

These influences converged to make loan defaults more common and, then, even more common. The Indice de Morosidad, the ratio of nonperforming loans to total loans and discounts for commercial banks, rose from 5.5 in December 1992 to 8.3 in September 1994.[3] At the time, 8.3 seemed very high.

The Exchange Rate Crisis

During the presidency of Carlos Salinas de Gortari, which commenced in December 1988, the rationalizations of Mexico's fiscal, monetary, financial, investment, and trade policies—together with relatively high real interest rates in Mexico and low rates in the United States—precipitated large inflows of foreign capital. Mexico could use the resulting accumulations of foreign currency reserves to defend the peso. Capital inflows covered and to a certain extent caused the increasingly negative balance on current account.

By the first quarter of 1994, foreign currency reserves were converging toward $30 billion, after having fallen below $5 billion in March 1990. Investor optimism about Mexico's policies was so high that, when rebels occupied San Cristobal de las Casas in January, the markets shook off the shock and capital poured in.

Mexico's presidential election was to take place in August. However, when Institutional Revolutionary Party candidate Luis Donaldo Colosío was assassinated in March, the killing precipitated massive capital outflows. Foreign currency reserves fell from $29.3 billion in February to $16.5 billion in June.

Thereafter, the markets seemed to settle down. From June until mid-November, reserves fluctuated now and then, but not very much. In October, however, an assassin killed Institutional Revolutionary Party official José Francisco Ruiz Massieu. His brother Mario, an official in the attorney general's office, was appointed to investigate the case. In mid-November, Mario Ruiz Massieu resigned, complaining that his efforts were being obstructed. Reserves began to fall hard—from $17.667 billion at the end of October to $12.889 by the end of November. On December 20, Mexican Finance Secretary Jaime Serra Puche announced that the peso would devalue from 3.47 pesos per dollar to 3.99. This was not really a change in exchange rate regime, government officials explained; it was just an adjustment. The crawling-peg exchange rate regime would remain in place.

The crawling peg would remain in place? Investors knew that nearly $17 billion in dollar-indexed Mexican bonds were scheduled to mature in the first six months of 1995. Foreign currency reserves had not been that high for more than a month, and who knew how many bond holders would want to roll their bonds over? Market participants precipitated a run on the peso. After announcing on December 20 that the crawling-peg regime would remain in place, the government announced late on December 22 that the peso would float. The peso-dollar exchange rate quickly headed toward 5 to 1. Reserves fell from $12.889 billion at the end of November to $6.278 billion by the end of December and to $4.440 billion by the end of January.

The Financial Industry after the Devaluation

The devaluation triggered capital outflows and high inflation. As a result, interest rates rose so high that they put not only borrowers at risk, but, because major increases in interest rates push up loan default rates, also lenders.

To squeeze inflation out of the system, the central bank began to restrict central bank domestic credit to the commercial banking system and to slow growth in the monetary aggregates. After some gingerliness in its initial efforts, the Bank of Mexico began to impose highly restrictive credit and monetary policies in February and early March. Mortgage rates that had stood at 22 percent in November rose to 74 percent in early March. Also in March, the interbank loan rate rose briefly as high as 114 percent.

Under these conditions, even an inexperienced banker could correctly forecast a new wave of loan nonperformance. Some analysts claimed that problem loans had doubled between December and March.[4] Some banks were reported to have suspended all mortgage, auto, and consumer loans until further notice and to have canceled loans to farmers to purchase replacement parts and seeds for spring planting.[5]

As loan problems mounted, the government took steps not only to rescue the banks but to facilitate their purchase. NAFTA had decreed that, during the six-year transition period beginning January 1, 1994, a U.S. or Canadian financial institution could acquire an existing Mexican bank only if it did not account for more than 1.5 percent of total Mexican bank capital. This rule meant that, at the time of NAFTA's ratification, only two Mexican banks were eligible for direct acquisition.[6]

Beginning in February 1995, a new Mexican banking law permitted foreign banking organizations to purchase Mexican banks that accounted for up to 6 percent of total Mexican bank capital (*capital neto*), legalizing purchase of all but Mexico's three largest institutions. That this step was part of a bank rescue package may be seen by the 6 percent rule's application only to bank acquisitions. A foreign-owned start-up bank would still have to follow the old 1.5 percent rule.

Minimum capital limits were similarly segregated. Minimum capital for an existing bank to be acquired was set at 0.12 percent of total bank capital. As of this writing, that rule meant that the capitalization minimum would be about $63 million pesos. For a brand new bank, however, the minimum capital would be twice that.

Recall that NAFTA had also imposed limits on total bank capital that all foreign-controlled banks could hold. Under NAFTA rules, the limit in 1995 would have been 9 percent. The new Mexican banking law raised this limit to 25 percent.

To address mounting problems of undercapitalization of the increasing number of troubled banks, the government designed a special recapitalization program known as PROCAPTE. Under the PROCAPTE program, troubled banks could raise capital by creating and selling subordinated convertible debentures (bonds) to the nation's deposit insurance authority, FOBAPROA. The debentures would mature in five years. The government set forth criteria by which it could convert the debentures to equity if the bank turned out to be poorly managed or if insolvency was judged likely. Although this condition would make FOBAPROA (which is administered by Mexico's central bank) a commercial bank shareholder, the government has committed itself to sell such instruments as soon as they become shares.

In another effort to refinance the banks, Mexico introduced the Unidades de Inversiones (UDIs) program, which is a round-robin plan in which (1) banks repackage and restructure certain types of nonperforming private debt into bond-like instruments; (2) the government purchases this repackaged debt, issuing special bonds to raise the money for the purchases; and (3) the banks purchase the special government bonds that are used to fund the government's purchase of the banks' restructured debt. An important characteristic of the restructured debt is that it is denominated in so-called Unidades de Inversion, whose nominal value is indexed to the inflation rate, so as to preserve real value.

In a sense, the program is simply a trade of one type of bond for another. The program benefits the banks, in part, because bank balance sheets then look less problematic because the government holds the nonperforming loans. Differences between the returns from the banks' new holdings of the special government bonds and what the banks were receiving from the nonperforming loans makes the improvement for the banks more than just an accounting entry. A benefit to borrowers is that their payments, through the restructurings, are spread over a longer term.

More specifically, as of this writing, the plan permits problem banks to restructure (typically short-term) past-due loans that are adjudged likely to pay out ultimately. Under the restructuring program, loan maturities will be extended to a range of five to twelve years. The interest rate charged these past-due borrowers will be broken into a real component they must pay on schedule and a nominal component that is simply rolled into the existing principal. Borrowers, of course, will be able to pay out over a much longer period than under the conditions of the original loans.

These restructured loans will be placed in trusts and sold to the government, as noted above, as something very like bonds. The banks would reallocate the funds, that is, the deposits they had formerly used to support these repackaged loans. Specifically, the banks would use these newly freed funds to purchase special government bonds. When the government received this money for the sale of the bonds, it would use it to purchase the bondlike trusts from the bank.

Although the term "shell game" comes to mind, the intention is to allow borrowers and banks to win at the expense of the government. In the early years of the plan, at least, the government will be subsidizing the trusts. The nominal yields it will pay on government securities will exceed the income it receives from the restructured loans. If a loan in a trust defaults, it is the issuing bank's default. The bank, not the government, bears the default risk.

Additional Bank Finance: Development Banks

Although this discussion has focused on commercial institutions, Mexico has since the 1920s maintained a system of publicly owned development banks and trusts that focus on specialized categories of finance in which market failure has been perceived. Three of these institutions—Banco Nacional de Comercio Exterior (export finance), Banco Nacional de Obras y Servicios Publicas (public works finance), and Nacional Financiera (industrial finance)—currently account for more than three-fourths of Mexican development bank and trust-based financing.

From the 1970s through the mid-eighties, the development banks' primary role was financing the government, public-sector enterprises, and the large private-sector corporations, or *grupos*. The bulk of the lending involved direct financing or lending. Government officials themselves cite inefficiency and inadequate supervision of the system (Werner 1995), and corruption has also been noted (Mansell Carstens 1995a, 1995b).

Beginning in the late 1980s, the system was reorganized to focus more heavily on financing the private sector by rediscounting loans extended by other institutions, with special attention given small and micro enterprises, and on its chronic problems of high costs and low bad-debt recovery.

The development banks' importance in the financial sector ebbed through most of the 1980s as the publicly owned enterprises to which they lent were sold to the private sector. They regained their importance in the 1990s. Flows of finance to the private sector from the development banks as a share of total flows in the banking system rose from 10 percent in 1989 to 30 percent in 1993 and edged upward to 30.4 percent in 1994 (see Werner 1995). The form of development bank lending shifted from direct loans to rediscounting paper from banks. The role of development banks, therefore, is a crucial element in the discussion of a bailout of the Mexican banking system.

Conclusion

The Mexican financial market has changed markedly since the bank nationalization of 1982. First, the banking system has been privatized. Second, the banks have been allowed to move back to universal banking and away from the narrower version of banking that the government mandated during the early and middle 1980s. Third, after consolidating under nationalization, the number of banks has increased substantially in the few years since the privatization, and a few signs that suggest somewhat greater competitiveness have begun to surface. Fourth, during this period the government weaned itself away from the banks as a dominant form of funding and created a modern securities market.

Even so, 1994 saw a crisis just as 1982 did. Bad debts had become a serious problem in the two years before the December 1994 devaluation, and they worsened substantially thereafter. Although international markets initially reacted in 1994 and 1995 as they had in 1982, clear differences emerged. First, the government took steps to resuscitate the banks without nationalizing them. The Mexican government devised plans to bail out the banks through the rescheduling and securitization of their loan portfolios and also attempted to facilitate the purchase of existing banks.

Second, however, the structure of Mexico's nonfinancial private sector is different enough in 1995 to offer a prognosis for the financial market that is different from that of 1982. As they were for other Latin American countries, the 1980s were a "lost decade" for Mexico—a country whose exports were dominated by raw materials sales, and whose domestic production was state dominated, heavily regulated, and inefficient. Since then, Mexico's newly rationalized manufacturing sector has greatly increased its share of the nation's exports. While the devaluation has aggravated financial problems in Mexico, it also will have a more positive effect on Mexico's increasingly important manufacturing sector than it did on the oil industry during the 1980s. The exchange rate devaluations of the 1980s did not affect Mexico's ability to profit from oil sales then. In real-dollar terms, oil prices have not reached their levels of the middle and late seventies and very early 1980s. But the devaluation of the 1990s could ultimately increase the profitability of Mexico's increasingly important manufacturing industries. Devaluation allows manufacturers to raise their peso prices enough to beat the cost-price squeeze discussed above and yet remain competitive on world markets in dollar prices. Moreover, world demand for manufacturers is increasing more than world demand for energy. Mexico's economic restructuring over the last decade has made its nonfinancial sector more resilient to economic shocks over the long run and, accordingly, has made its financial sector more resilient.

Nevertheless, financial operating ratios, spreads between costs of funds and loan rates, and the other characteristics of Mexico's banking system suggest that Mexico's financial sector has some distance to go before it will be competitive and efficient by developed country standards.

Notes

1. For more comprehensive discussions of this issue, see Mansell-Carstens (1995b, 1993).

2. See Mansell-Carstens (1993) for fuller discussion on these issues.

3. Although the changes in the nonperforming loan ratio may be instructive, the ratios themselves are not easily comparable with U.S. nonperforming loan ratios. Mexican banks report as past due only the actual loan payment that is past due thirty days or more and not the entire remaining balance on the loan. In the United States, if a loan payment is past due ninety days or more, the entire loan balance is reported as past due.

4. See Crawford (1995), p. 4.

5. See *El Financiero: International Edition* (1995), p. 26.

6. For further discussion of these details, see Edmonds (1995) Gruben, Welch, and Gunther (1994).

Bibiliography

Banco de México (1992), *The Mexican Economy 1992* (Mexico City: Banco de México).

Crawford, Leslie (1995), "Lifeline Cast to Mexico's Troubled Banks," *The Financial Times*, March 30, p. 4.

Edmonds, Skip (1995), "Mexican Banks Open to Foreign Investors," Federal Reserve Bank of Dallas, *Financial Industry Issues* (First Quarter): 1–4.

El Financiero: International Edition (1995), "Outlook for Mexican Banks Tied to Peso," January 2–8, p. 26.

Gruben, William C., John H. Welch, and Jeffrey W. Gunther (1994), "U.S. Banks, Competition, and the Mexican Banking System: How Much Will NAFTA Matter?" Federal Reserve Bank of Dallas Research Department, Working Paper No. 94–10.

Mansell-Carstens, Catherine (1993), "The Social and Economic Impact of the Mexican Bank Reprivatizations," (Mexico City: Instituto Tecnologico Autonomo de Mexico).

———. (1995a), *Rediscovering a Forgotten Financial System: Popular Finance in Mexico* (Mexico City: Instituto Tecnologico Autonomo de Mexico).

———. (1995b), "Servicios Financieros, Desarrollo Economico y Reforma en Mexico," *Comercio Exterior* 45, no. 1 (January): 3–11.

Werner, Martin (1995), "La Banca de Desarrollo: 1988–1994, Balance y Perspectivas," *El Mercado de Valores* 55, no. 1 (January): 9–25.

7

Catherine Mansell-Carstens

Popular Financial Culture in Mexico: The Case of the Tanda

Financial intermediation in a developing country involves far more than private and government banks and nonbank intermediaries, whose activities dominate quantitative financial analysis. Within a developing nation, there are large numbers of people with small incomes and a clear need for credit. This need has been met traditionally by loans in cash or in goods and services from friends, families, pawnshops, and suppliers; recently, it has also been met by specialized banks that make very small loans.[1]

Catherine Mansell-Carstens points out that in Mexico, the poor do not have significant access to subsidized credit. Instead, they participate in a variety of ventures that mobilize their savings. An especially important technique for this is the tanda, *in which members contribute fixed—often weekly—payments in cash or in goods and services, for a given period of time, and one member collects the total amount paid in each week. In some cases, tanda funds finance a project jointly owned by its members. Tandas are likely to continue in importance, at least until bank accounts, cash machines, and other financial services are widely and affordably available.*

Why don't we see the poor opening bank accounts, using cash machines, obtaining bank loans or credit cards? The easiest answer is that they "lack financial culture." It's an answer a surprising number of people have. Some other easy answers include:

"Poor people are bad credit risks—they never pay anything back."

"If you give them a chance, they always indebt themselves beyond their ability to repay."

"They only borrow for frivolous purposes—you know, parties and funerals and booze."

"They're always exploited by moneylenders."

"Poor people can't save—they're too poor to save."

"The poor don't save—they lack the discipline to save."

If you believe these things, what is the solution? Logically, there isn't any because implicit in these clichés is the conviction that the poor will always be poor, and that people with money have fundamentally different character traits than those who do not. This is analogous to saying that people who cannot afford washing machines and the electricity, water, and detergent to run them every day "lack cleanliness culture." To insist that a sweetseller who manages to feed and clothe several children on her meager income nevertheless "lacks discipline" is obvious nonsense.

And yet, despite the logical inconsistencies, myriad government and charitable programs have attempted to help the poor with programs based on precisely these assumptions. They have therefore emphasized credits at below-market interest rates targeted for specific "productive" purposes (often dictated by the lender) and made no effort to capture savings. The results have been disastrous. Lending agencies have found themselves wading in red ink due to sweetheart deals (why lend to the poor at below-market rates when you can lend to yourself or your brother-in-law?) and inadequate collection policies, but above all, due to lending at below-market rates while facing the massive transaction costs involved in lending small amounts for targeted purposes. In consequence, subsidized credit has never been extended to any significant percentage of the Mexican poor. A sense of hopelessness has only been reinforced, and their needs for other financial services—particularly savings—have been neglected.

Of course the poor have fewer economic resources, less education, less information and experience in using formal-sector financial services, fewer powerful relatives, social connections, and so on. They may also, in some cases, suffer from lower self-esteem, lower expectations, and a tendency—quite natural under the circumstances—to plan with a shorter-term horizon. But a now substantial body of sociological, anthropological, and economic literature demonstrates that these common assumptions about how the poor use financial services are unfounded.

ROSCAs: Financial Intermediation

One of the most important areas of research in popular financial culture has been on rotating savings and credit associations, or ROSCAs. (A *rosca* is also a ring-shaped cake traditionally served on January 6, Three Kings Day. The acronym ROSCA, coined by economist J.D. Von Pischke, is unrelated to the ring-shaped cake, though serendipitously appropriate.) Known most commonly as tandas in Mexico, but also as *roles, rifas, vacas, vaquitas, mutualistas,* and *cundinas,* ROSCAs have been found flourishing throughout the developing world. For example, *tontines* are well known in Francophone Africa and the Caribbean; *hui, hye,* and *hwei* are found throughout Southeast Asia; Indonesia has its *arisans* and *paluwagons;* Egypt its *gamaiyah;* India, chit funds and *bishis;* Papua New Guinea, *wok meri;* and Bolivia, *pasanakus.*

While ROSCAs are organized at all socioeconomic levels—among secretaries, wealthy housewives, and even bank employees—for the poor, who rarely have access to formal-sector financial services, they play a crucial role in accumulating savings and obtaining credit. Accumulating cash in a bank account is usually out of the question—bank branches are too far away, lines too long, forms difficult to understand, minimum balances excessive, real returns often negative, and bank personnel intimidating. And keeping cash savings under the mattress can be problematic when living quarters—and the bed itself—must be shared with several others. Those with any savings are faced with multiple demands for loans from kin, neighbors, and friends. Having to make a payment to a ROSCA, however, is a legitimate reason to say no. In other words, participating in a ROSCA is a socially acceptable way to save.

How They Work

The basic ROSCA, or tanda, works like this: friends, neighbors, relatives, or coworkers get together and agree to contribute a fixed sum for a certain period of time, for example, ten pesos each week. Assuming there are ten participants, each week there will be a "pot" or "hand" of one hundred pesos. Each participant has a turn to take home the pot. At the end of ten weeks the tanda ends or begins a new cycle. Those who collect the pot at the beginning of the ten weeks are then using the tanda as a credit mechanism, and those who take the pot toward the end are using it to save. Usually there is an organizer who collects the contributions and distributes the pots. He or she may take a commission, take the first pot, or simply act out of goodwill.

What makes a tanda work is participants' trust in one another that all payments will be made until the last pot is taken home. Tanda membership is neither offered nor taken lightly. If one or more members fail to make payments, the others can suffer losses that may mean having to close a business, being unable to put on a new roof before the rainy season, or having to keep one's children home from school. Those who do not make all their payments on time can lose their reputation—and their friends. If she finds herself short of cash when she has to make a tanda payment, a participant will often sell an important asset (such as a sewing machine or livestock) or borrow from relatives or moneylenders. When all else fails, defaulting participants have been known to flee, or even commit suicide.

Variations on a Tanda

Tandas can easily be tailored to participants' needs. Groups in areas with little liquidity make their payments in foodstuffs such as rice, beans, and cooking oil rather than cash. Others, particularly during periods of high inflation, make payments in U.S. dollars. Some tandas assign the order of the pots by lottery, others by auction, by seniority, or according to need. Many will permit a member who has an emergency such as a hospital stay, a fire, or a robbery to take the pot out of order. Some tandas involve large amounts of money—enough to buy a house or a car—others involve the equivalent of a few pennies.

The most common variations on the basic tanda are:

• The "specific purchase" tanda: Members use their pot to make specific identical purchases such as a house, a blanket, a round of drinks, or books. (For smaller purchases, members often join more for social than financial motivations.)

• The "commercial" or "promotional" tanda: Similar to "specific purchase" tandas, these are organized by a merchant to promote sales of, for example, mattresses, furnishings, bedding, household appliances, or automobiles. The latter example is particularly well known in Mexico. Also called "commercialization systems" (*sistemas de comercialización*), Mexican auto-tandas were first introduced by Volkswagen de México's auto finance company AFASA through its dealers in 1977. Nissan, Ford, Chrysler, and other manufacturers and dealers have since developed similar plans.

The auto-tanda works as follows: Once a participant is approved (having provided proof of income, residence, and some guarantee, usually his house), he is admitted to a group of about 125 individuals. Each makes a down payment and agrees to make about forty more monthly payments to the dealer's or auto finance company's bank account. Each month the dealer assigns one or more cars (depending on the number of participants and total months before payment is completed), either by public lottery or by auction in which the customer who bids the greatest number of monthly payments receives his car first. This practice is so well known that in a popular movie, *Cómodas Mensualidades* (Convenient Monthly Payments), the overly indebted hero is prompted by his wife to bid an outrageous number of payments for his Volkswagen sedan.

• The "foodstuff or animal" tanda: These appear to be popular in cash-starved rural areas. Members make payments in dry foodstuffs or cooking oil, or purchase an animal and take turns feeding it, sharing the proceeds after its sale or slaughter.

• The Accumulating Savings and Credit Association, or ASCRA: An ASCRA is similar to the basic tanda in that it involves preestablished periodic payments and ends at some point. However, it is organized for an explicit profit for both the manager and participants, and the pot is not assigned on a rotating basis but is loaned out to both members and nonmembers for an explicit rate of interest, often similar to that charged by local moneylenders. At the end of a given period—usually fifty-one or fifty-two weeks—members' contributions are returned plus interest, net of a profit for the organizer. ASCRAs are usually termed *cajas* in Mexico (although it should be noted that there are a great variety of cajas in Mexico, many of which have little in common with ASCRAs, operating more as ongoing cooperative financial institutions) and appear to be popular in older, urban, working-class neighborhoods where members know each other well and have regular cash incomes.

Conclusion

Tandas should not be dismissed, as they often are, as a trivial bit of Mexican "folk culture." Make no mistake about it: tandas represent financial intermediation. Savers fund borrowers, borrowers repay savers, and in doing so they lengthen term structure, distribute risks more efficiently, and economize on transaction costs. The poor, in short, are doing for themselves on a private and voluntary basis what banks—both public and private—have proven unable or unwilling to do.

But there are numerous disadvantages to tandas, too. Based on trust, they are necessarily limited in scale; and once initiated, the amount and timing of payments are relatively inflexible. When bank accounts, cash machines, bank loans, credit cards, and so on become available to low-income Mexicans—or, when low-income Mexicans move into higher income brackets and are able to access those services—we should expect to see less enthusiasm for tandas.

Nevertheless, the widespread existence of tandas underscores the inadequacy and, in many cases, the inappropriateness of formal-sector financial services for the poor. Most important, it belies the shibboleths about low-income individuals' inability to save, poor creditworthiness, and general "lack of financial culture."

Note

1. Mansell-Carstens (1995).

Bibliography

Mansell-Carstens, Catherine (1995), *Las finanzas populares en Mexico: El redescubrimiento de un sistema fianciero olvidado.* (Mexico City: CEMLA, Editorial Milenio, ITAM).

8

CARLOS ELIZONDO MAYER-SERRA

Tax Reform under the Salinas Administration

Tax reform was a major part of the Salinas administration's economic strategy. If successfully enacted and implemented, it would increase government revenues, reduce inflation, and create a climate attractive to domestic and foreign investment.

Carlos Elizondo Mayer-Serra indicates that Mexico's unfair tax structure had been only partially modified before the Salinas administration, because of the need for the business community to invest its funds in the nation. Technical improvements were made in the mid-eighties to remove inflationary distortions. A rapprochement with business under President de la Madrid created a climate permitting tax reform during the Salinas administration. The three most important changes were reducing fiscal evasion by introducing a tax on assets, increasing the number of taxpayers by taking fiscal privileges away from 17 percent of productive Mexicans, and increasing penalties for tax evasion and improving the administration and enforcement of the law.

The pro-business stance of the Salinas government was an important reason for the acceptance and success of the tax reform. There was a significant increase in individual and business taxpayers and a consequent increase in tax revenue as a share of GDP. Yet the 1994 economic crisis called the entire Salinas economic project, and the recent increase in value-added tax rates, into question. Carlos Elizondo Mayer-Serra points out that this, and the increased competition with the states for tax resources, will affect the capacity of the federal government to raise and control revenue.

This chapter analyzes the tax reform implemented in Mexico under the administration of Carlos Salinas (1988–94). The main intention is to shed some light over the economic, ideological, political, and international conditions that either

I would like to thank Patricia Drijanski for collecting information. All shortcomings are my responsibility. Some parts of this article draw heavily from Elizondo (1994 and 1995).

existed or were created in order to achieve its success.[1] Some tax changes in the past help explain the capacity of the Salinas administration to reform, but this reform was more ambitious than previous ones. This chapter gives special attention to the relationship of the business community, especially of large businessmen,[2] with the Salinas administration in explaining its success.

The chapter is organized in four parts. The first part gives an overall picture of the fiscal issues that were important before 1988 and describes the major tax changes that took place from the late seventies up to 1988. The second part describes the tax reform of the Salinas government. The third part examines the conditions of its success. The fourth part examines the fiscal and political consequences of the tax reform. The conclusions summarize the main lessons suggested by this case study and provide an outlook for the near future.

Overall Picture

The modernization process of the Mexican fiscal system was initiated in the 1960s when the fiscal regime at that time was recognized to be unfair.[3] The government tried to introduce a profound reform in 1964 with the aim of increasing revenue by strengthening the fiscal base, but it was not able to impose it. The government's objective of industrialization through private investment implied, in its view, the need to give tax privileges.

Changes were implemented gradually after the failed Echeverría tax reform of 1972.[4] At the end of the seventies there was a gradual elimination of the fractionalized system of income tax. A value-added tax (VAT) was introduced in 1980, which replaced an inefficient federal sales tax and the specific taxation of many products, and in December of 1982, in the middle of the economic crisis, a reform was introduced to start the gradual elimination of the anonymity of bonds and shares not traded in the stock market.

The de la Madrid administration inherited a severe fiscal crisis from López Portillo, but the virtual rupture with businessmen that resulted from the incoherent economic policy of López Portillo and his decision to nationalize Mexican private banks a few months before his term ended made a profound tax reform extremely costly for businessmen. The de la Madrid administration was capable of increasing some tax rates and introduced some minor changes, but the impact in terms of revenue was minimal.

The most important reforms occurred in the last years of the de la Madrid administration. From 1986 to 1988 some steps were taken to remove inflationary distortions. Income tax, VAT, and excise tax on production and services were to be paid in advance monthly payments, as opposed to the previous quarterly payments. Interest payments and exchange rate gains and losses were settled so that only real interest would be of relevance for tax purposes. Capital contributions by stockholders and depreciation values were adjusted for inflation, deduction of the cost of sales was replaced with immediate expense of the purchase cost of inventories, and enterprises were permitted to index previous year's losses.

In terms of revenue the de la Madrid administration did not perform outstandingly, but it did achieve an improvement in the relationship with business. The expropriated bankers were compensated, some targeted subsidies were given to big businessmen, and the president's project of economic reform that included privatization and deregulation helped the administration to forge a new relationship with businessmen. This enabled the government in December 1987 to sign the Economic Solidarity Pact (PSE), which was a successful program to control inflation and help the economy to resume growth and a favorable framework for the introduction of tax reform in the Salinas sexenio.

Tax Reform under Salinas

There is a conceptual difference between changes in the tax law and a tax reform. The former does not attempt to change the basic structure of the system: it does not alter in a significant way who pays and how. It makes only marginal changes to increase revenue; that is, the same people pay, but most of them pay more. A tax reform, on the other hand, attempts to change this structure. It seeks to introduce new taxpayers or to oblige a specific segment of the population to pay more than before. The distinction between a reform and a change can be blurred when a significant number of changes are spread over the years, leading to a more general revision of the tax structure. The fiscal reform of the Salinas administration introduced a significant number of changes spread over the years of his regime. While the tax structure changed significantly, tax reform was not guided by redistributive objectives. The Salinas tax reform was part of a broader restructuring program of the Mexican economy.[5] The implemented measures were to contribute to the economic program by increasing government revenues and inducing economic growth.

We will focus analysis on the three most important changes introduced in the Salinas tax reform.[6] These were also the ones most loudly opposed by taxpayers. The three changes are:

1. Seeking to increase revenue instead of increasing after-revenue tax rates, the chosen strategy was to reduce fiscal evasion, which was widespread. A 2 percent asset tax on business was introduced in 1989, levied on the gross assets of enterprises. The tax was devised to avoid tax manipulations, which had previously enabled 70 percent of business to declare no profits.[7] Many had even declared losses, sometimes continuously for up to twenty years. This new tax is complementary to the corporate income tax. Thus, it does not affect those that pay income tax in an amount that is at least equal to 2 percent of their assets. It affects only those who had no profits or had devised ways to avoid the payment of income tax.[8]

2. In order to increase the number of taxpayers, in December 1989 special tax

provisions for so-called minor taxpayers (MTP) and the special tax basis (STB) were eliminated. These had covered around a million and a half firms (compared with 250,000 registered as normal taxpayers) that paid a specific quota depending on the activity and did not pay VAT. Through this legal change, the government took away fiscal privileges enjoyed by 17 percent of all productive Mexicans.[9] According to Pedro Aspe, secretary of the treasury, "These categories, which include agriculture, transportation, the publishing industry and an important number of small and medium size taxpayers produce 18 percent of GDP, but contributed with less than 1 percent of the Income Tax" (Aspe 1992, 415).

3. Increasing the penalties for tax evasion, changing the law to close loopholes, and improving enforcement of the law:

Prior to the Salinas administration, a tax evader was not prosecuted if he paid what he owed plus fines and charges. The law was changed to increase the grounds under which the government could imprison tax evaders. Under the new law, engagement in two or more related acts with the purpose of obtaining an unjustified fiscal benefit and not presenting the fiscal year tax return for more than six months are considered serious criminal acts, which makes it difficult to obtain bail. From 1921 to 1988 only two cases of tax evasion were taken to court;, between 1988 and 1993 the number of such cases conducted was 380.[10]

To improve control over taxpayers, several measures were established by 1992. More requirements must now be met for firms to deduct travel expenses, cars, etc. Other measures include higher frequency of audits. The responsibility to collect the VAT returned to the federal government, since the incentives for the states to raise taxes were negligible.

Tax reform was complemented with a restructuring of tax administration, with the aim of constructing a more efficient collecting system. The domestic tax administration was integrated with customs, which was also restructured. There was a reduction for regulations and barriers for custom brokers. Since 1992 the Mexican customs system has been entirely automated.

The organization of the tax administration has become more decentralized. The coordination offices are divided into four: audit, customs, legal, and revenue. Random annual rotation of personnel was established to minimize discretionality of the representatives of the coordination offices. Since 1993 a specialized administrative entity was created to deal with international tax issues.

Reasons For Success

Three main conditions seem to have made Salinas's tax reform possible.

First, the New Nature of the State Elite

During former administrations the different factions of the state elite were divided with respect to tax reform.[11] The more important actors of the government, in particular those in charge of raising taxes, have to be convinced of the need of tax reform; in the Salinas administration, most of the state elite accepted the need. Salinas inherited public finances in crisis and a distorted economy. This made his administration aware of the need to raise revenue without amplifying these distortions. The lack of foreign credit, the collapse of the oil crisis, and the cost of past deficits taught the Mexican political elite the need to generate a higher stream of tax revenue.

Second, the Relationship with Businessmen

The business community has a structurally privileged position with respect to policy making due to its control over resources. The government must reform without sacrificing future growth. If tax reform promotes capital flight or diminishes investment, it can backfire in terms of its aim of raising revenue. In Mexico the structural advantage of property holders (namely, the capacity to decide where to invest and save) is greater than in other countries, since capital has tended to be very mobile, for both geographic reasons (a long border with the United States) and cultural ones.

Moreover, the Mexican financial system has traditionally been particularly liquid and without currency controls. Property holders can move their assets very quickly. The menace of capital flight is a key constraint on government policies. It has been the preferred way to protect resources from any kind of threat against domestic assets, although not the only one, as tax evasion has also been used.[12]

The Salinas tax reform was careful in its making. It followed the World Bank's advice on fiscal policy, by expanding the tax base while increasing incentives to investment through lower marginal rates. This seems to have been even beneficial for the richest individuals and largest corporations due to the reduction in marginal rates. Since the tax reform is part of a broader reform of the state and redistribution is attempted by means of better targeted social programs, it does not menace property rights. Under Salinas there was no attack against businessmen nor against the principle of private property; his administration insisted that regardless of the short-term political costs, tax reform was consistent with his project of economic reform if long-term stability was to be achieved.

Salinas's overall project diminished the power of the government to act arbitrarily against business interests. The growth of the economy depended more than ever on voluntary saving and investment,[13] and the government had fewer tools to reward allies or punish enemies. This increased property holders' confidence in the government and enhanced the disposition of businessmen to accept more restrictions in the fiscal arena and to cooperate with the authorities.

The nature of Salinas's tax reform and of his economic program weakened the leverage of businessmen. They faced problems in articulating a coherent response. Some of the new policies, like trade liberalization and tax reform, could have been costly to their interests in the short term, but overall these measures did not go against the big business project. The differential impact on various categories of businessmen tended to divide them.[14]

Third, More Limited State Objectives

In the past, the state elite pursued many objectives besides raising revenue through the tax system, such as promoting industrialization. For this purpose, it gave subsidies to certain sectors, or devised tax privileges to promote investment or to avoid difficulties in tax collection, that afterward became loopholes in the fiscal system. This weakened the state capacity to raise revenue, since it propitiated the generation of corruption, which led to less state autonomy.[15] The economic reform included privatization of public enterprises and a newer interaction with the private sector in order to promote growth. By diminishing its size, the Mexican state could devote more attention to raising tax revenues.

Fiscal and Political Consequences of the Tax Reform

The first indicator of the success of the tax reform was revenue. It increased in spite of the decrease in the tax rates. This was possible due to an increase in the tax base and in the number of taxpayers. From 1988 to 1993 there was a 150 percent increase in the number of registered corporations and individuals with business activities.[16] Official data show that for enterprises the rise went from 1.8 million in 1988 to 5.6 million in 1993, and for employees the increase went from 11.1 million in 1988 to 14 million in 1993.[17] Corporate and individual income tax revenues increased from 5.1 percent of GDP in 1988 to 6.3 percent in 1993. VAT revenue increased from 3.5 percent of GDP in 1988 to 3.7 percent in 1991. There was a reduction to 3.2 percent in 1992 and 3.4 percent in 1993, because the general rate went from 15 percent to 10 percent. Import duties went from 0.5 percent of GDP in 1988 to 1.1 percent in 1993 as a result of the opening of the economy (see Tables 8.1, 8.2, and 8.3). Tax administration also improved; there is more fiscal presence and more efficiency in terms of cost. The number of audits increased. Between 1988 and 1992, 183,865 more audits were performed, 90 percent of which resulted in taxes payable to the government, while in 1988 only 13 percent led to more income.

Conclusions

Seven lessons can be drawn from the Salinas reform, indicating key conditions that made it possible:

First, unity of the state elite.

Second, a good relationship of the government with the business community. Salinas inherited this from the de la Madrid government, and it was not only

Table 8.1

Federal Budgetary Revenues (millions of new pesos)

	1988	1989	1990	1991	1992	1993	1994p
Total	69,037.2	92,434.8	120,625.1	177,288.0	214,947.3	203,417.2	213,467.1
Tax Revenues	48,098.5	64,367.0	83,219.4	104,934.6	132,031.3	152,808.4	160,128.1
Income tax	20,103.1	27,284.9	36,003.6	45,302.3	59,272.2	70,890.2	71,721.1
VAT	13,574.2	17,482.0	25,796.6	31,732.7	32,702.8	38,832.3	39,079.8
Excise tax on prod. & servs.	9,822.3	11,457.6	9,617.6	11,353.5	18,194.1	19,414.3	27,903.6
Import duties	1,856.5	4,153.0	6,461.3	9,911.4	12,884.2	12,683.5	12,736.2
Others	2,742.4	3,989.5	5,340.3	6,634.7	8,978.0	10,988.1	8,687.4
Nontax Revenues	20,938.7	28,067.8	37,405.7	72,353.4	82,916.0	50,608.8	53,339.0
Fees	15,711.4	20,328.7	28,468.1	35,148.8	38,684.5	39,413.3	36,592.4
Fuel	13,338.3	17,914.7	25,527.8	31,007.1	34,128.5	34,543.8	31,023.9
Others	2,373.1	2,414.0	2,940.3	4,141.7	4,556.0	4,869.5	5,568.5
Commercial governmental revenues	521.5	658.8	3,277.4	2,934.4	3,804.7	1,136.8	2,797.1
Administrative revenues[a]	4,705.6	7,079.9	5,656.9	34,268.9	40,426.7	10,058.7	13,949.5
Others	0.2	0.4	3.3	1.3	0.1	0.0	0.0

Source: 1988–93, Sixth Annual Government Report; 1994, SHCP (Preliminary).
[a]Includes extraordinary revenues from privatization of state enterprises, which were very important in 1991 and 1992.
p = preliminary.

Table 8.2

Federal Budgetary Revenues as a Percentage of GDP

	1988	1989	1990	1991	1992	1993	1994p
Total	17.7	18.2	17.6	20.5	21.1	18.0	17.0
Tax Revenues	12.3	12.7	12.1	12.1	13.0	13.6	12.7
Income tax	5.1	5.4	5.2	5.2	5.8	6.3	5.7
VAT	3.5	3.4	3.8	3.7	3.2	3.4	3.1
Excise tax on prod. & servs.	2.5	2.3	1.4	1.3	1.8	1.7	2.2
Import duties	0.5	0.8	0.9	1.1	1.3	1.1	1.0
Others	0.7	0.8	0.3	0.8	0.9	1.0	0.7
Nontax Revenues	5.4	5.5	5.4	8.4	8.1	4.5	4.2
Fees	4.0	4.0	4.1	4.1	3.8	3.5	2.9
Fuel	3.4	3.5	3.7	3.6	3.3	3.1	2.5
Others	0.6	0.5	0.4	0.5	0.4	0.4	0.4
Commercial governmental revenues	0.1	0.1	0.5	0.3	0.4	0.1	0.2
Administrative revenues[a]	1.2	1.4	0.8	4.0	4.0	0.9	1.1
Others	0.0	0.0	0.0	0.0	0.0	0.0	0.0

Source: 1988–93, Sixth Annual Government Report; 1994, SHCP (Preliminary).
[a]Includes extraordinary revenues from privatization of state enterprises, which were very important in 1991 and 1992.
p = preliminary.

Table 8.3

Federal Budgetary Revenues: Real Growth Rate

	1988	1989	1990	1991	1992	1993	1994p	Growth Rate 1988–94	Average
Total		6.44	0.79	20.84	5.81	−13.95	−2.74	14.79	2.33
Tax Revenues		6.39	−0.14	3.67	9.81	5.24	−2.88	23.60	3.59
Income tax		7.90	1.92	3.45	14.18	8.75	−6.24	32.45	4.80
VAT		2.38	13.97	1.13	−10.06	7.97	−6.73	6.88	1.12
Excise tax on prod. & servs.		−7.27	−35.17	−2.95	39.85	−2.98	33.20	5.47	0.89
Import duties		77.83	20.17	26.12	13.45	−10.49	−6.94	154.69	16.86
Others		15.65	3.39	2.14	18.09	11.28	−26.73	17.61	2.74
Nontax Revenues		6.56	2.93	59.03	0.01	−44.50	−2.32	−5.43	−0.93
Fees		2.86	8.16	1.51	−3.95	−7.36	−13.95	−13.53	−2.39
Fuel		6.77	10.06	−0.14	−3.94	−7.97	−16.77	−13.65	−2.42
Others		−19.13	−5.92	15.81	−4.00	−2.82	5.98	−12.88	−2.27
Commercial governmental revenues		0.43	284.24	−26.39	13.15	−72.83	128.04	99.13	12.16
Administrative revenues[a]		19.61	−38.29	398.05	2.95	−77.38	28.53	10.06	1.61
Others									

Source: 1988–93, Sixth Annual Government Report; 1994, SHCP (Preliminary).
[a]Includes extraordinary revenues from privatization of state enterprises, which were very important in 1991 and 1992.
p = preliminary.

maintained but even improved by the Salinas administration, in particular with the largest businessmen.

Third, the greater concern of businessmen with the harmful consequences of inflation than during other administrations. A new fiscal base was a reasonable price to pay for lower inflation, and the government committed itself to cooper-. ate in this aspect, imposing restraints on public expenditure.

Fourth, the making of decisions according to the particular reforms proposed. The other policies implemented in the overall economic project of Salinas did not threaten the interests of property holders, in particular those of big businessmen.

Fifth, the importance of a differentiated distributional cost among tax payers.

Sixth, the need for gradualism. Although profound, the Salinas reform was not introduced in a single year. It also benefited from changes conducted throughout more than a decade.

Seventh, good conditions of the international environment. The international attitude towards Mexico was highly positive. Foreign investment sustained the overall strategy of Salinas.

As a result of the Salinas tax reform, government finances improved without affecting private investment. The new tax system would in fact allow revenue to increase if the economy grew as expected.

The December 1994 crisis has, however, shown the limits of the overall economic strategy. To adjust to imprudent dollar-denominated internal debt and a high current account deficit and to penalize consumption, the government has raised VAT tax rates from 10 to 15 percent. This has not been enough to avoid lower tax revenues, as the adjustment program has pushed the economy into a recession, although public finances remain healthy, thanks to higher fuel revenue.

The VAT increase has fueled the debate regarding the legitimacy of the state to tax its citizens. In a more open political context and once the economic project of Salinas had shown its limits, the alliance with large businessmen with regard to taxation was severely damaged.

This crisis is just triggering a political reaction that could be expected under more normal circumstances. Once people start to pay taxes on a regular basis, demands for more accountability with respect to government expenditure, and for more efficient use of these resources, are likely to appear. Tensions with the states with regard to the distribution of tax resources will also tend to become a serious political issue, which will affect further capacity of the federal state to raise and control revenue.

Notes

1. "Success" is defined here in terms of (1) whether the reform is implemented, and (2) whether it achieves its explicit aims.

2. In this chapter businessmen, owners of capital, capitalists, property holders, and other similar terms are considered equivalent.

3. In the words of Nicholas Kaldor (1973, 36): "The exceptional favors that are conceded to different forms of income derived from property have no parallel in the legislation on income tax in other countries."

4. This reform is discussed more fully in Elizondo (1994).

5. A summary of the logic of the economic reform in less-developed countries can be found in *World Development Report: The Challenge of Development* (1991). For a collection of case studies, see Nelson (1990) and Stallings and Kaufman (1989).

6. For a detailed description of the tax policy from 1988 to 1992, see Aspe (1992).

7. The financial sector is excluded. New investments follow specific rules that allow for a period of exemption.

8. In the government's view, the majority of businessmen fall into the second group.

9. Figures given by Pedro Aspe, secretary of the treasury, *Excelsior*, January 6, 1990.

10. Numbers given by Aspe, *El Financiero*, February 10, 1993.

11. See for example the case of the Echeverría tax reform in Whitehead (1980).

12. Rojas-Suarez (1991, 83) states that there are two types of risk that may induce capital flight: "1) default risk associated with the expropriation of domestic assets; and 2) the risk of large losses in the real value of domestic assets as a result of economic policies that lead to a rapid inflation or to large exchange rate depreciations." Both have happened more than once in recent Mexican history. Salinas promised to avoid both attacks of property rights and followed policies that made this credible, although based as we now know on shaky premises.

13. Private investment grew 10.2 percent in 1988, 7.5 percent in 1989, 13.3 percent in 1990, 12.7 percent in 1991, and 20.4 percent in 1992. In 1993 it grew only 2.8 percent due primarily to the lack of growth of the economy (*Criterios generales de política económica*, 1989, 1990, 1992, and 1993). Direct private investment went from 2,880 millions of dollars in 1988 to 7,980 in 1994. Portfolio private investment went from 1,000 millions of dollars in 1988 to 8,186 in 1994 (Banco de México, INEGI, Sixth Annual Government Report).

14. Salinas's success confirms a suggestion by Richard Bird (1992), namely, the need to design a tax reform that divides property holders and ensures the cooperation of the more important businessmen.

15. State's autonomy is a necessary condition to promote development, not a sufficient one. To achieve development this autonomy has to be controlled by a state elite with a strategy to promote growth and the capacity to implement it. See Sorensen (1993).

16. Figures given by Aspe, *El Financiero*, July 9, 1993.

17. Data from the *Sixth Annual Government Report* (1988–93) and the *General Direction for Revenue Policy*, Ministry of Finance.

Bibliography

Aspe, P. (1992), "Tax Policy in Mexico," *Bulletin, International Bureau of Fiscal Documentation*, September 1992 (Amsterdam).

Bird, R.M. (1992), *Tax Policy and Economic Development* (Baltimore: Johns Hopkins University Press).

Elizondo, C., (1994), "In Search of Revenue: Tax Reform in Mexico under the Administrations of Echeverría and Salinas," *Journal of Latin American Studies* 26: 159–90.

———. (1995), "The Politics of Tax Reform in Latin America," CIDE, División de Estudios Políticos, Working Paper No. 32 (México).

Kaldor, N. (1973), "Las reformas al sistema fiscal en México," in L. Solis, ed., *La economía mexicana*, vol. 1, 29–39 (México).

Nelson, J.M., ed. (1990), *Economic Crisis and Policy Choice* (Princeton: Princeton University Press).

Rojas-Suarez, L. (1991), "Risk and Capital Flight in Developing Countries," *Determinants and Systemic Consequences of International Capital Flows*, IMF Occasional Paper No. 77, March 1991, 83–92.

Sorensen, G. (1993), "Democracy, Authoritarianism and State Strength," *European Journal of Development Research* 5, no. 1: 6–34.

Stallings, B., and R. Kaufman, eds. (1989), *Debt and Democracy in Latin America* (Boulder: Westview Press).

Whitehead, L. (1980), "La política económica del sexenio de Echeverría: ¿Qué salió mal y por qué?" *Foro Internacional* 20, no. 3: 484–513.

World Development Report: The Challenge of Development (1991), (New York: Oxford University Press).

9

José Angel Gurria Treviño

The Mexican Debt Strategy

The history and analysis of Mexican debt negotiations provided by foreign secre-
tary and former chief debt negotiator Angel Gurria traces the history of Mexican
debt strategy. In the short run, Mexico serviced the debt with about 6 percent of
its GDP each year from 1983 to 1988, severely limiting funds for domestic
investment and economic growth. The Mexican standard of living fell. Despite
various loans and rescheduling, commercial banks were reluctant to provide
new loans to Mexico and to other Latin American nations. Minister Gurria says
that the banking community was more interested in profiting from Mexico's
crisis than in solving it. Mexico, therefore, turned to multilateral financial insti-
tutions for loans with which to pay the debt service on commercial bank loans. In
1989, this was supplemented by debt swaps in which $3.6 billion of old debt was
exchanged for $2.5 billion in new bonds. The outlook for repayment improved.
The U.S. banks had been overexposed by their foreign-debt holdings. New loans
were needed to support future repayment of the debt. The banks would not
provide them. These loans had to come from the U.S. government if bank failure
was to be avoided. Then Secretary of the Treasury Nicholas Brady supported
Mexico's request for debt and debt-service reduction. The IMF, the World
Bank, the government of Japan, and the government of Mexico provided $7
billion of collateral. That made it possible to restructure $48.2 billion of Mexi-
can debt. As a consequence, investor confidence was restored; capital inflows
each year since 1989 averaged 4 percent of GDP. With a favorable outlook,
the foreign debt reached $160 billion in 1994. Foreigners provided 70 percent
of peso-denominated bonds (cetes) and about 80 percent of outstanding dollar-
denominated bonds (tesobonos). Devaluation made repayment of the debt more
difficult in the short run. Foreign loans and more attractive terms for rolling
over the debt were anticipated—in the short run, because of the $50 billion
rescue package and increased economic restructuring, and in the medium run,
because the intermediate and capital goods that had recently been imported
were expected to increase exports in the next two years and help to allay anti-

NAFTA fears that U.S. taxpayers (nominally aiding Mexico) would bail out U.S. holders of the Mexican debt.

The basic and often overlooked point is that both firms and developing nations routinely use debt. During its early development, the United States was in debt for 150 years. In the long run, the question was not how to eliminate debt but how to use it well. The question of how to regulate more speculative inflows of capital may soon be addressed.

On August 22, 1982, Mexico's official debt crisis began. On that day, the Mexican government requested a three-month extension for all Mexican public-sector debt that was scheduled to come due within the next ninety days.

In the main, the need for an extension was the result of the extraordinary rise in Mexico's cost of financing this debt and a deterioration in the terms of trade for Mexican exports. Specifically, in the early 1980s, oil prices (on which Mexico depended as a major source of income) dropped precipitously. At the same time, tightened U.S. and British monetary policies led to a sharp rise in international borrowing rates.

A miscalculation on the part of both Mexico and its foreign lenders that the spike in oil prices in the 1970s would be sustainable had led forecasters on both sides of the equation to project Mexico's balance of payments for 1981 and 1982 in excessively optimistic terms. Consequently, Mexico was able to overextend itself in both spending and foreign indebtedness. Moreover, a lack of early intervention in exchange-rate policy by Mexican officials resulted in a distortion of an array of other macroeconomic variables.

Rather than respond to these economic forces with changes in the Mexican macroeconomic infrastructure, the government of Mexico determined that its economic difficulties were temporary, and that the remedy was to obtain further commercial capital from overseas lenders. Because of the increased risks that resulted from Mexico's economic difficulties, foreign banks raised the borrowing rates for Mexico and shortened the maturities of the new loans that they made. In the process, commercial banks loaned Mexico another $2.5 billion.

But by mid-1982, it had become clear that Mexico's economic difficulties were not temporary. Commercial banks stopped lending. From that year until 1989, Mexico was forced to service its debt with internal capital. It didn't receive any new, voluntary funding from foreign banks. As a result, each year between 1983 and 1988, Mexico had to transfer about 6 percent of its GDP to other countries. This transfer made Mexico a new capital exporter and compounded its pre-existing problem of being "over-leveraged," thereby sharply limiting its capabilities for domestic investment and consumption.

The solution to this crisis was achieved only through four separate rounds of debt negotiations. In the first round, Mexico sought additional foreign capital, as well as a postponement of the maturity of the principal amounts of all existing foreign debt. However, Mexico promised to continue to make scheduled interest payments.

Early Negotiations

August 1982 marked the beginning of talks between the Mexican government and the U.S. Treasury to arrange a package of emergency loans for Mexico. While a solution was difficult to reach, Mexico ultimately received two separate loans. The first, effectively, was a $1 billion "advance" by the U.S. government on its future oil purchases from Mexico. For these funds, Treasury Secretary Don Regan proposed that Mexico pay an implicit rate of interest of 38 percent. The second loan (also for $1 billion) was granted to Mexico by the U.S. Commodity Credit Corporation. Separately, Mexico was able to obtain a third loan (for $1.85 billion) from the central banks of major industrialized countries through the Bank of International Settlements (BIS).

On August 20, 1982, Mexican officials met in New York with representatives of Mexico's most important commercial creditors. As a result of that meeting, the banks agreed to permit Mexico to defer repayment of $8.1 billion in principal. They also agreed to create an advisory committee to coordinate the debt rescheduling process. The establishment of this committee was indispensable for Mexico, because it permitted negotiations through a single entity, rather than through each of the more than 530 lenders worldwide that had extended credit to Mexico.

The final step in the first round of negotiations was to obtain the support of the International Monetary Fund (IMF). That support was crucial in gaining further assistance from the commercial banks. Through negotiations, the IMF agreed to give Mexico a $4.5 billion "extended fund facility" that would be disbursed over a three-year period. But, before it would approve the facility (and in an extremely novel move), the IMF insisted that Mexico's commercial lenders had to commit themselves to lending another $5 billion to Mexico. In addition to these new funds, Mexico was allowed by the banks to reschedule $23.1 billion in pre-existing debt payments.

Subsequent Rounds

In early 1984, when Mexico's "breathing room"—its postponement on principal repayments—began to run out, a second round of negotiations was initiated. Prior agreements with commercial lenders directed that major principal repayments would have to begin in 1985. But Mexico still had inadequate resources to fund these repayments. As a result, Mexican authorities began work on a comprehensive restructuring program to reschedule $48 billion in public-sector debt that would mature between 1985 and 1990.

Through the second round of debt restructuring, "multiyear rescheduling arrangements" (MYRAs) were introduced. The MYRAs extended the maturities of commercial loans, eliminated bank commissions, and reduced interest-rate spreads paid by Mexico from 2.25 percentage points to between 0.875 and 1.5

percentage points. While this new schedule ensured that foreign commercial lenders would not go bankrupt, it still did not address the problem that Mexico faced in its continuing transfer of wealth abroad. Though the debt schedule was more manageable for Mexico, the cost of repayment was still extremely high. To service its debt, Mexico had to generate large surpluses in its trade and current account balances.

The Baker Plan

In October 1985, a third approach began when U.S. Treasury Secretary James Baker announced that Mexico's debt crisis could be resolved by spurring Mexican economic growth with new financial resources from abroad. The so-called Baker Plan included the following three-part strategy:

• Mexico (and other Latin American debtor countries targeted by the plan) would adopt comprehensive new macroeconomic policies;

• the IMF would continue to play a central role in debt management, and multilateral institutions would support the adoption of new, market-oriented economic policies through increased and more structurally adjusted lending;

• commercial banks would further support these adjustment programs with additional lending.

Secretary Baker asked multilateral institutions and commercial banks to increase their lending significantly between 1985 and 1987. While some new funds were made available, economic conditions in Mexico and in the overseas commercial banking sector once again hindered efforts to restructure Mexico's foreign debt in a manner that was productive for Mexico and its creditors.

The Crisis of 1986

The year 1986 marked the climax of Mexico's worst economic crisis in the postwar period. Oil prices plummeted by more than 50 percent. That, in turn, cost Mexico 6 percent of its GDP and 20 percent of all public revenues. The government of Mexico responded to the crisis by tightening both fiscal and monetary policies. It devalued the peso and again sought new, more favorable debt-repayment terms with foreign lenders.

Once again, Mexico obtained more and more manageable debt. After considerable negotiation, Mexico reached an agreement with the IMF in September 1986. Commercial banks responded with new loans of $6 billion, and with even lower interest-rate spreads. This time they were just under 0.875 of a percentage point. But, even at such low borrowing costs, the assumption of new debt still did not help Mexico resolve the fact that a large portion of the wealth it created was needed to pay back its overseas creditors.

Furthermore, commercial banks ignored Secretary Baker's request. Gradually, they stopped participating in new financing packages to Mexico and other debtor countries. The banks had survived the debt crisis and avoided bankruptcy. They were eager to reduce their existing debt exposures by increasing the extent to which they had reserved capital relative to outstanding loans (so-called loan-loss reserves). To do this, the banks marked down the value of the loans on their books. Citibank, for example, marked down its loan portfolio for debtor countries by 25 percent. Several banks also sought to exchange the loans on their books for new assets in the emerging secondary and derivatives markets.

For several months after the IMF deal was negotiated, Mexico's only sources of new funds were multilateral institutions. Thus, Mexico was taking in institutional funding to pay the debt service on commercial bank loans. By 1987, the world economy was strong enough to permit Mexico to pursue market-based programs to reduce its debt. Moreover, with no improvement in Mexico's long-term ability to overcome its debt overhang, such a strategy was a necessity. Furthermore, there was a growing consensus among debtor and creditor countries alike that any solution to the problem of debt overhang must be permanent. And it must permit Mexico and other debtor nations to obtain resources sufficient to resume sustained economic growth.

A Permanent Solution?

The beginnings of Mexico's permanent solution emerged in early 1988 when, in an effort to lessen Mexico's overall debt burden, the Mexican government worked with the firm of J.P. Morgan to carry out a massive debt-for-debt swap. Through this offer, lenders could exchange the loans they had already given to Mexico for twenty-year bonds, the principal of which was guaranteed with U.S. Treasury zero-coupon bonds. As a result of the swap initiative, $3.6 billion of old debt was canceled and exchanged for $2.5 billion in new bonds. Mexico's debt balance was thereby reduced by a net $1.1 billion. The novel, market-based approach of this initiative was a watershed in the area of voluntary debt reduction. It influenced later multilateral efforts to further alleviate Mexico's debt crisis.

In the fall of 1988, Mexico elected President Carlos Salinas de Gortari. In his inaugural address that December, President Salinas outlined four objectives of Mexico's continued debt-restructuring program to reach a permanent solution to the country's economic turbulence. Salinas stated that these goals were:

• the conclusion of a multiyear debt arrangement that would eliminate uncertainty in long-term economic planning;

• a reduction in Mexico's net transfers of wealth to a level that permitted the resumption of national economic growth;

• a reduction in Mexico's total external debt balances;

• a reduction in the ratios between Mexico's total GDP and the costs of paying and servicing the national debt.

Toward these ends, the Salinas administration set out to reach agreements with Mexico's official, multilateral creditors, including the IMF, the World Bank, and the governments of major, industrialized countries. It was an attempt to ensure that these creditors would provide both political and economic support during anticipated negotiations between the Mexican government and its commercial lenders. In early 1989, in discussions between Mexico and its institutional lenders, it was agreed that Mexico must both eliminate its debt overhang and restore economic growth, in order to ensure against future debt crises.

The Brady Plan

Mexico presented an external debt reduction/management strategy to its institutional lenders. It requested continued international resources to help the country reduce its debt and its debt-service costs. Shortly after this strategy was presented, the U.S. treasury secretary, Nicholas Brady, developed a new plan for addressing the debt crisis in Mexico and similar crises in other developing countries. The Brady Plan supported Mexico's request for debt and debt-service reduction—specifically through the use of international resources that would "enhance" the collateral on new debt instruments issued by Mexico. The improved collateral would lower the risk associated with lending to Mexico, thereby reducing the interest costs to the Mexican government of taking on new debt. With this type of security, the collateral would also provide a guarantee to lenders that they would be repaid. In turn, they might be willing to reduce the amounts that were owed.

With the Brady Plan in hand, Mexico secured support from its most critical institutional creditors for a restructuring program on a scale that had never before occurred in the world credit market. The IMF and the World Bank agreed to set aside a portion of their programmed lending to support the reduction of Mexico's debt and debt-service costs. The IMF committed $1.7 billion to guarantee Mexico's principal and interest payments, and the World Bank put up slightly more than $2 billion. In addition, the government of Japan pledged nearly $2.1 billion to be committed through the international Export-Import Bank. Finally, the Mexican government set aside $1.3 billion of its own reserves, bringing the total collateral pool available to $7 billion.

With this new collateral secured, Mexico began discussions with commercial lenders in April 1989. After four months of intense negotiations, an agreement-in-principle (AIP) was announced. Through this agreement, a total of $48.2 billion in Mexican debt became available for restructuring. Each of the commercial lenders of these funds could choose one of the following options:

• *It could reduce the principal amount of Mexico's debt.* Banks could swap their eligible debt for thirty-year, floating-rate bonds whose principal value was 35 percent less than the value of the original debt. The bonds featured a bullet payment and bore an interest rate equal to 13/16 of a percentage point over international bank overnight lending rates.

• *It could reduce the interest rates on Mexico's debt.* Banks could swap their eligible debt for thirty-year bullet bonds whose principal value was "at par" with the value of the original debt. These bonds would bear a fixed interest rate of 6.25 percent.

• *It could provide new, secured funding to Mexico.* Banks could lend Mexico new money equal to 25 percent of existing eligible debt holdings over a period of three years.

For banks that selected either of the first two options, the principal amount of the new bonds they received was guaranteed by thirty-year zero-coupon bonds, with an additional guarantee equal to eighteen months' worth of interest payments of those bonds. Based on the choices they were given, 46.5 percent of the banks chose a debt-service reduction plan, 42.6 percent chose principal reduction, and 10.9 percent chose new funding. A massive restructuring had taken place. Since the negotiation of this deal, Mexico has put into effect additional voluntary debt-reduction initiatives through direct buybacks of its debt from commercial banks.

The success of the Brady Plan has been incontrovertible. Mexico's debt overhang has been diminished. It has fallen from an astounding 76.3 percent of GDP in 1986 to 33 percent of GDP last year. As a result, there now exists in Mexico an environment for investment, stability, and growth.

Not surprisingly, domestic interest rates declined considerably after the restructuring was completed. Both Mexican and foreign investment in Mexico have risen precipitously. Capital has been repatriated. And public finances have been consolidated. Once-legendary Mexican inflation has plummeted from triple-digit rates in the early 1980s to single-digit rates today. Consumer prices rise each year at a lower rate than they did on a monthly basis only five years ago. Mexico has switched from being a net exporter of its wealth to being a net importer, taking in capital flows each year since 1989 worth about 4 percent of its GDP.

On June 1, 1992, Mexico canceled nearly 9 percent of its total outstanding public-sector (external) debt. The country has also regained voluntary access to international capital markets and has taken in sizable capital inflows. It has accomplished this principally through direct and portfolio investment of the private sector, rather than through additional bank lending. Mexico's public-sector entities have achieved financing through the placement of many types of well-received bond issues in the European and U.S. markets. These bonds have provided these organizations needed capital access without creating further indebtedness to the world's commercial-banking sector.

After eleven years (and with considerable work), Mexico has achieved remarkable economic progress. In 1995, Mexico is the thirteenth-largest economy in the world, and has one of the world's most open economies. It has diversified its export structure considerably over the last decade, boosting non-oil exports by 400 percent and manufacturing exports by 500 percent.

Lessons Learned

The lessons that Mexico learned during the years marked by its debt crisis are numerous. It knows now that it cannot substitute external debt management for sound economic policy. It knows that packaging strategies for "debtor clubs" can result only in lowest-common-denominator solutions. It knows that negotiated financial packages must be as ample, simple, and flexible as possible. It knows that a timely agreement is better than an optimal, albeit extemporaneous, solution. It knows that progress must be measured using a number of different gauges. And it knows that, because each country has different circumstances and needs, what has worked for Mexico might not work elsewhere.

The Mexican experience over the past decade has proven that the best reforms utilize deep, structural programs, and that those reforms have an impact that will far outlast the terms and conditions obtained through the final round of restructuring negotiations. By freeing additional public resources that have become available through the restructuring and follow-up initiatives, Mexico can achieve continued reform and progress. It is well aware that, with negotiations behind it, its efforts must remain focused on the generation of a "virtuous circle" that will utilize continued economic reforms to fuel further improvements to the economy and that will build on the critical foundation of reform it has already established.

The Present Turmoil

In April 1995, Mexico again found itself in economic turmoil. A constant inflow of foreign resources from 1989 to 1993 caused gradual appreciation of the currency and a widening of the current-account gap to almost 8 percent of GDP. Exacerbated by political events, uncertainty turned into a loss of confidence and fueled a 50 percent devaluation in the last days of 1994. A financial package of $50 billion—put together by the U.S. government, the IMF, the BIS, and some commercial banks—was used to refinance short-term debt and stabilize markets. The fundamentals are still strong and sound. But two new lessons became clear: (1) Don't rely too much on foreign savings—especially if they are short-term; and (2) keep a close eye on your exchange rate.

10

NEIL HARVEY

The Reshaping of Agrarian Policy in Mexico

Two areas of the economy have long merited special attention. These are agrarian policy1 and oil and energy policy. The Constitution of 1917 made special provision for them; they became symbols of Mexican economic nationalism. Neil Harvey analyzes the reshaping of agrarian policy in Mexico. The decapitalization of agriculture and deteriorating conditions of agricultural workers and peasants in the 1980s resulted, in part, from the withdrawal of government support policies for agriculture. In 1993, the NAFTA agreement provided for the removal of barriers to trade in the staple crops of corn and beans. Imports of these crops would make subsistence farming even less profitable. This, and the reform of land tenure in 1992, contributed to the uprising in Chiapas on January 1, 1994.

Maximum tariffs on imports of food were set at 20 percent in 1986, as an anti-inflationary measure. It aided urban workers but harmed small producers who had higher production costs and lower subsidies than their U.S. and Canadian competitors. The United States produces four times as much corn and three times as much beans per hectare as Mexico. To enhance agricultural productivity, the Salinas administration reformed the legislation governing land tenure and passed a new agrarian law. It gave ejidatarios—*who previously had the right to work the land but not to sell it—the right to own land. Private companies could purchase it alone, or form joint ventures with ejidos. To provide security of private property, peasants no longer were allowed to petition for land.*

Opponents of the reform feared that land ownership would be concentrated, that small holders, especially women, would lose their land rights, and that unresolved land petitions would be rejected. Private owners who held more than the allowed maximum of land were granted one year in which to sell it, instead of having the excess holding expropriated. The agrarian reform is being implemented slowly. The government has established programs to expedite the granting of land titles and to provide direct payments per hectare to farmers who had produced corn, beans, and other specified crops. They were not required to continue to produce them.

Economic difficulties in agriculture were not confined to the subsistence sector. The economic austerity program imposed after the collapse of the peso led to interest rates estimated at 80 to 120 percent. In the spring of 1995, proposals for debt relief by agricultural producers were more prominent than those for changes in the only slightly implemented agrarian reform law. Acknowledging the difficulties of the agricultural sector, President Zedillo said that Mexico cannot afford to subsidize agriculture in the way that the United States and the European Union do.

Introduction

During the past decade the social and economic conditions of the majority of rural workers and peasants in Mexico continued to deteriorate. The long-term structural problem of decapitalization was not reversed by a set of new policies inspired by neoliberal economic theory. Out-migration from rural areas increased, as did the tendency for rural families to increase their nonagricultural sources of income. Rural families often had members who worked on ejidos, which are lands distributed by the postrevolutionary state to groups of twenty or more land claimants, or ejidatarios. Until 1992, these lands belonged to the state and were worked by ejidatarios. They could not be legally sold or rented. Roughly half of Mexico's rural land area is comprised of 28,000 ejidos, on which three million ejidatarios and their families work.

The majority of small holders, including those who work ejido land, suffered from the simultaneous withdrawal of price subsidies, the dismantling of state-owned marketing companies, the reduction of available bank credit, and the opening up of borders to free trade. The signing of the North American Free Trade Agreement (NAFTA) in November 1993 established a schedule for the gradual removal of all tariff and nontariff barriers for the sensitive crops of corn and beans. In 1992 a related set of reforms concerning land tenure were introduced by the Mexican government. These policies became politically contentious and culminated in the peasant and indigenous armed uprising in Chiapas on January 1, 1994.

This article focuses mainly on the administration of Carlos Salinas de Gortari (1988–94) and describes various policy initiatives and the political response they generated among rural social movements. Although earlier policies could not be sustained, I argue that the reform of Mexican agriculture lacked consultation with key actors, in particular new associations of producers, resulting in a lack of consensus about the general direction and specifics of rural policy. For example, the Permanent Agrarian Congress (CAP), a forum of the country's main peasant movements, developed proposals for a more gradual and negotiated process of trade liberalization, the introduction of new support programs for small producers, and legal protections against the concentration of private landholdings. However, in none of these areas was it able to significantly modify the policies favored by the president and his team of ministers. It appeared that the government was unwilling to contemplate any advice that differed from its own policy prescriptions.

Trade Liberalization

Until the mid-1980s Mexico maintained high import tariffs on most items of imported food. The decision to reduce or eliminate them was motivated by two problems: (1) the decline in productivity in the mainly rain-fed ejido sector and the related need to increase imports; and (2) the government's wage control policy, which could only succeed if the prices of basic foods were kept down in the major cities, particularly the capital. The first of these problems has been well documented, and it is generally agreed that the policy bias toward capital-intensive agroexports since 1940 accompanied the neglect of the ejido sector and a consequent decline in its capacity to meet domestic demand. The second problem arose from the policies adopted to confront the debt crisis that broke in 1982. Real wages fell by as much as 50 percent in the 1980s, leading to a contraction of the internal market and a reduction in food consumption. By importing cheaper food, principally from the United States, the government hoped to maintain control of prices for basic items in urban areas.

Following Mexico's decision to join GATT in 1986, the maximum import tariff was set at 20 percent, although the average fell to below 10 percent prior to the signing of NAFTA. The government was primarily concerned with controlling the prices of eggs, chicken, pork, beans, and tortillas. By keeping the cost of inputs low, consumer prices can be more effectively controlled. This anti-inflationary policy was a central component of the government's macroeconomic strategy of modernization.

The imports of cheaper foodstuffs had a negative impact on small producers, who continued to face higher production costs and lower subsidies than U.S. and Canadian producers. Even prior to NAFTA the effects of trade liberalization in some sectors were becoming apparent. Small producers of commercial crops such as rice, soybeans, and sorghum were left without markets in 1990–91 when import licenses were suddenly removed. In the case of sorghum, the system of guaranteed prices was replaced in 1990 by a system of negotiated prices (fixed between buyers, producers, and government). However, with the simultaneous withdrawal of import licenses, tariffs were effectively reduced to zero, and, by the time of the fall 1990 harvest, Mexican producers found that their projected market had already been saturated by cheaper sorghum imported from the United States. The new "negotiated" price did not hold, and thousands of small producers demonstrated by blocking highways and occupying government offices in central and northern states.

The fall in prices paid to producers was exacerbated by increasing production costs and the lack of agricultural credit. The consumer price index grew from 100 points in 1980 to 9,907 in 1988, while the cost of raw materials used in agriculture increased to 11,241, and guaranteed prices to only 6,746. After 1988 the agricultural credit supplied by BANRURAL was cut back in areas deemed to have a high risk of crop failure. By 1994 BANRURAL was financing less than 3 percent of ejido production in Mexico. With low crop prices and limited incomes from other sources, thousands of ejidatarios have seen their debts increase rapidly. The Salinas government's National Solidarity Program (PRONASOL) assumed many of the functions of BANRURAL in the poorer rain-fed areas, but credit provision did not meet more than half the production costs.

Rural indebtedness is particularly acute among the more productive middle peasants of northern and western Mexico. In response to the crisis of their operations, a new alliance of medium-sized private owners and small farmers was formed in 1993 under the name El Barzón. The *barzonistas* have staged several mass protests and rallies to demand that their debts be restructured on favorable terms and to call for new policies for financing agricultural production.

The dismantling of state-owned companies also had an immediate effect on small producers. The government's marketing board for basic grains (CONASUPO) underwent a process of rationalization that allowed private intermediaries to strengthen their operations in local and regional markets. The availability of cheaper food through imports may therefore benefit private traders rather than poor consumers.

Under NAFTA these problems may worsen, as protective tariffs on corn and beans are to be removed over a fifteen-year period. Since over two million rural families are involved in production of these goods, many feared that they would be forced to abandon cultivation completely and migrate to urban areas. It is clear that most Mexican producers are not able to compete with the United States and Canada. In the period 1985–89 average corn output per hectare was 1.7 metric tonnes in Mexico, compared to 7 tonnes in the United States and 6.2 tonnes in Canada. For beans, the output was 542 kg in Mexico, 1,661 kg in the United States, and 1,865 kg in Canada.

Reform of Land Tenure Legislation

On November 7, 1991, President Salinas sent an initiative to Congress proposing major reforms to Article 27 of the constitution, the legislation governing land tenure, and they were passed by Congress a month later. The new Article 27 was published in the government's *Diario Oficial* on January 6, 1992. After a debate in Congress, the implementing legislation, known as the Ley Agraria, entered into effect on February 26, 1992. This proved to be politically contentious and would be cited by the Zapatista Army of National Liberation (EZLN) as the catalyst for their decision to stage an armed insurrection in 1994.

The reforms to Article 27 of the constitution were followed in late February 1992 by the passage of a new Agrarian Law to establish the new regulatory framework for the social sector. For the government the modifications were seen as necessary steps to attract private investment in agriculture and increase productivity and welfare. Four of the main changes embodied in the new Agrarian Law were the following:

1. Ejidatarios were given the legal right to purchase, sell, rent, or use as collateral the individual plots and communal lands that make up the ejido.

2. Private companies were allowed to purchase land in accordance with the legal limits ascribed to different crops. At a maximum, a company with at least twenty-five individual shareholders could purchase holdings of up to twenty-five times the size of the individually permitted limit.

3. New associations were allowed between capitalists and ejidatarios, the latter providing land as "T" shares in joint ventures. (In joint stock associations for agricultural production, "T" shares are those shares that correspond to the value of the lands held by individual holders or ejidatarios and that make up part of the total value of the association.)

4. In line with the reform's intention of guaranteeing security for private property, the sections of Article 27 that allowed for campesinos to petition for land redistribution were deleted.

The debate surrounding the ejido reform raised several concerns. First, it was feared that the sale of ejido plots could lead to a reconcentration of land. Although the new law expressly forbids *latifundios* in Mexico, it also potentially allows for private companies of at least twenty-five individuals to own farms of up to 2,500 hectares of irrigated land, 5,000 hectares of rain-fed areas, 10,000 hectares of good quality pasture land, or 20,000 hectares of forested land. A company made up of twenty-five ranchers could also feasibly own an area equivalent to 12,500 hectares. In order for ejido land to be made available for private ownership, however, the assembly of ejido members must approve the measure by a two-thirds majority. Some commentators noted that the traditional control and manipulation of assemblies by ejido authorities could lead to forced votes in favor of privatization. In Chiapas the potential for land reconcentration is given by the politically powerful ranchers' associations, representing over 12,000 *ganaderos* organized in sixty local associations. Ranchers applauded the reforms to Article 27, arguing that greater security in land tenure would attract foreign investors wishing to create new meat processing plants in the region. The competition for land with indigenous campesinos should be understood in this context.

Second, the use of land as collateral or in associations with private investors involved the risk of farm foreclosures and loss of land rights. The effective exclusion of much of the social sector (which includes lands redistributed under the agrarian reform program: it is comprised of ejidos and indigenous people's communal lands as well as small private holdings not exceeding ten hectares, or twenty-five acres) from traditional sources of credit could influence the decisions of ejidatarios in putting land up as collateral. Women were placed at most risk since the male head of household could unilaterally decide how to dispose of what was family patrimony. The only special right that women received was the first option to buy the ejido land that their spouses decided to sell. In Chiapas it is possible that wealthier ejidatarios might concentrate land within communities as a result of foreclosures.

Finally, it was feared that most of the unresolved land petitions (*rezago agrario*) would simply be rejected. The government's claim that there was no more land to be distributed was contested by several organizations. Some (particularly in Chiapas) called for an investigation into private holdings that allegedly exceeded the legal limits, prior to decreeing the end to land redistribution. In fact, rather than providing for the immediate expropriation and redistribution of excess holdings, the new law gave private owners one year to sell off excess property. The end of land reform constituted a symbolic break with the past but one that offered no guarantees of improvement for the future.

These proposals did not meet with widespread protests. There was generally a lack of information about their content. However, there was an intense debate among the representatives of peasant movements, government officials and political parties. Salinas was able to co-opt some of his opponents in the peasant movement with a list of ten promises to increase rural welfare and mitigate the costs of trade liberalization. He was also able to win support through the PRO-NASOL antipoverty program and deflect opposition to the apparent break with the original spirit of Article 27. It would not be until the EZLN uprising that organized protest against these measures became visible.

As with the other reforms of the Salinas years, the EZLN felt that peasants and Indians had been abandoned by government policies and called for wide-ranging social, economic, and political reforms. The policy that most affected the landless Indians in Chiapas was the cancellation of land redistribution. Although this did not have the same impact elsewhere in the country, it did radicalize many peasants who had also felt the negative effects of the neoliberal restructuring noted above. Almost one-third of the backlog of unresolved land petitions were concentrated in Chiapas, and many feared that the reforms to Article 27 would simply institutionalize illegal practices of large private owners who exceeded the constitutional limits on small properties. Another potential effect of the ejido reform could be the reconcentration of land in few hands as poorer peasants are eventually forced to sell their land to wealthier neighbors.

By the third year of implementation of ejido reform, however, there was no evidence of a rapid reconcentration of land or a massive rush to sell, although good irrigated land in the northwestern states began to be sold to private owners. For the most part, the reform advanced very slowly. There was little information about the different steps needed to change ownership from ejido status to private holdings. In 1993 the government established an ambitious program to process individual certificates for all 2.5 million ejidatarios. The Program for the Certification of Ejido Land Rights (PROCEDE) has created a new level of bureaucracy that will take many years to document, resolve, and certify millions of individual land titles.

Alongside PROCEDE the Salinas government established a new rural subsidy scheme known as PROCAMPO. Under PROCAMPO, over 3.3 million producers of beans, corn, sorghum, soybeans, rice, wheat, and cotton were made eligible for direct payments in the form of individual checks, to be made on a per hectare basis. All those who had planted one of these crops during the period between December 1990 and December 1993 could request payment of approximately US$100 for each hectare cultivated during the winter crop cycle of 1993–94. PROCAMPO included 2.2 million peasants who produce for subsistence needs only and must purchase food in the market to complement their household production, and who had been isolated from official channels of credit. The other 1.1 million PROCAMPO members produce one of the above mentioned crops; many of this group also produce some of their own subsistence needs.

The PROCAMPO subsidy was designed to offset the reduction in the guaranteed price for corn and beans producers. As internal prices fell to the level of international prices, the PROCAMPO checks could be used to compensate for loss of income without obliging peasants to continue to grow the same crops. However, the costs of conversion to more lucrative cash crops are generally prohibitive, and many analysts saw PROCAMPO as a safety net for the poorest and a political measure to retain acquiescence in the countryside.

The failure of Salinas's rural reforms to attract significant amounts of private investment in Mexican agriculture also suggests limitations to crop diversification, while the limited access to credit, insurance, and technical assistance has already been noted. In 1993 less than 1 percent of foreign investment in Mexico went into agriculture. In addition, the decline in both public and private investment since 1982 is reflected in the deterioration of infrastructure, tractors, and machinery. Without a serious program to promote integral rural development, which would inevitably imply a much greater role for campesino and indigenous organizations in planning and policy making, initiatives such as PROCAMPO will be ineffective in reversing rural decline.

By the time Salinas handed over the presidency to Ernesto Zedillo in December 1994, the rural sector was experiencing continued recession with few signs of interest from the investor community. The structural problems that existed prior to the neoliberal reforms persisted: lack of investment, poor infrastructure, and low rural wages. Although the Salinas reforms contained a clear logic in favor of promoting new private investment, as long as there were more profitable attractions in the Mexican stock market and the industrial sector, investors remained reluctant to revitalize the rural economy. President Zedillo inherited a country in economic crisis but has preferred to continue with his predecessor's policies rather than reach out to producer organizations and peasant movements for their proposals and alternatives. The outlook for rural development continues to be bleak unless political reforms create the space from which more socially just and environmentally sustainable policies can emerge.

Note

1. See Laura Randall, ed., *Reforming Mexico's Agrarian Reform* (Armonk, N.Y.: M.E. Sharpe, 1996).

11

JUAN QUINTANILLA M. AND MARIANO BAUER E.

Mexican Oil and Energy

The Mexican oil industry, as well as the ejido (land owned by the state, use of which is granted to claimants), served as a symbol of economic nationalism. Although foreign oil companies had obtained concessions, the Constitution of 1917 restored the principle that oil deposits are the property of the Mexican nation. Disputes between these companies and the government led to the nationalization of the oil companies in 1938, with two major results: (1) greater attention was paid to production for domestic needs. The asphalt produced was used to create all-weather roads, considerably extending the effective size of the market. (2) The various oil workers' unions were given conditions previously enjoyed only by the best-off union. They obtained—and continued to enjoy—wages, fringe benefits, and extra-legal opportunities not available to the majority of Mexican workers. The Mexican oil industry fulfilled its mandate of supplying the nation, providing just over 80 percent of domestic energy supplies, but at a high cost.

Mariano Bauer and Juan Quintanilla indicate that hydrocarbon reserves have been falling steadily since 1984. Since higher priority for immediate development is given to other sectors, Mexico could obtain funds to develop new oil reserves and to provide a mix of products that are better for the environment by increasing hydrocarbon product prices to world levels and by redefining the oil industry in order to permit foreign investment. Mexican economic adjustment packages have led to world market prices for most oil products, and the oil and energy industry is being restructured. In 1992, Congress amended the law regulating the electric industry to indicate that the small-scale production and import of electric power no longer were considered a public service reserved to the government. The most important aspect is that it opens the door to large-scale independent power production for self-supply or for sale to the Comisión Federal de Electricidad (CFE); in addition, it allows imports for self-supply by private companies.

PEMEX was restructured. It became the holding company for subsidiaries for exploration, refining, natural gas, and petrochemicals and created a separate entity (PMI) for international trade. PEMEX's non-oil operations, such as hospitals for its workers, were transferred to other groups. Further, because profits came mainly from exploration and production, the government renewed its offer to sell selected petrochemical installations. In spring 1995, the regulatory law governing Article 27 of the constitution redefined the exclusive area retained by the state. By default, what is outside is subject to private participation, Mexican and foreign. As there are still some permits involved, one will have to wait and see how specific applications are resolved. As of mid-June 1995, it appears that PEMEX no longer will have a monopoly of the storage, distribution, and transport of natural gas. The gas industry was opened to private enterprise. At the same time, PEMEX formed a joint venture with Shell Oil Company in Texas to refine Mexico's heavy oil. This appears to take into account Bauer and Quintanilla's assessment that "exposing the Mexican oil sector immediately to a completely open market could be disastrous. It needs to be strengthened first."

The present financial crisis in Mexico once again brings its oil and energy policy to the fore. Stated bluntly, the United States would like the Mexican state monopoly of the energy sector to disappear. It would like to have a fully integrated North American energy free market.

Because it wishes to secure its energy supply and keep prices down, the United States is seeking assurances that Mexico's oil potential will be fully developed. It wants Mexico's capacity to export oil to be not only maintained but increased. If oil reserves in Canada, the United States, and Mexico were lumped together, the reserves/current-production-availability ratio would jump. For the United States, it would increase from nine years to twenty years. Naturally, for Mexico, it would drop from fifty-five years to twenty years.

The United States possesses the needed capital and technology. It would like to have full access to the upstream areas of the industry and be contractually bound in production-sharing agreements. Furthermore, because they have an excess of refining capacity, American oil companies wish to be allowed direct entry into the Mexican market of petroleum products. For instance, they would almost certainly wish to open gas stations in Mexico, which they would supply from the refineries in Texas. Finally, there is also American interest in Mexico's petrochemical industry. Its successful development would assure the feedstock supply of the United States.

There are many factors—economic, political, and even constitutional—that will need to be considered in this complex scenario. But before we move on to them, perhaps an overview of Mexico's energy supplies and policies would serve well.

The Mexican Energy System

Mexico is a country rich in energy resources. The oil discoveries of the 1970s rank it in eighth place, as measured by proven reserves. It is one of the world's leading oil producers and exporters. Its internal energy demand, supplied fully from indigenous resources, is predominantly and increasingly dependent on oil products and natural gas (mostly associated gas).

Oil (and the energy sector, in general) has become a cornerstone of the Mexican economic and political structure—both national and international. Because of the debt crisis of 1982, the need for growth after the difficult decade of the 1980s caused Mexican policy makers to move to an open economy. They signed free trade agreements—particularly the NAFTA with the United States and Canada—and obtained membership in the OECD. They have attempted to increase foreign investment through changes in legislation—including laws that govern the energy sector. Consequently, structural changes clearly have been taking place in Mexico's oil sector. Its percentage of the GDP, the government's fiscal income, and its share of export income have been falling (see Figure 11.1).

Mexico's proven hydrocarbon reserves reached a peak in 1984 of 72.5 billion barrels of crude oil equivalent (see Figure 11.2). Of that quantity, oil and gas liquids accounted for 78.8 percent, and gas accounted for 21.2 percent. At the beginning of 1994, proven reserves were down to 64.516 billion barrels of crude oil equivalent (78.7 percent of oil and 21.3 percent of gas). This includes the often-questioned Chicontepec basin—with 11.0 billion barrels of crude oil equivalent.

Production of crude oil has remained constant—more or less at the level of 2.6 million barrels per day (see Figure 11.3). According to PEMEX's classification, production is located in three areas. The main production area is the Marine Region. It is followed by the South Region, and last by the North Region. Proven reserves of gas also reached a peak in 1984 of 76,998 billion cubic feet. At the beginning of 1994, proven reserves of gas were 69,675 billion cubic feet (52.5 percent located in the North Region, 30.9 percent in the South Region, and the rest—16.7 percent—in the Marine Region).

Gas production is concentrated in two of the production areas—the South Region with 52.9 percent and the Marine Region with 34.8 percent of the production (see Figure 11.4). Even though the major amount of reserves is located in the North Region, its production was 12.3 percent—the smallest of the three. The reason for this is that gas production is strongly related to oil production, since 86.4 percent of gas production is associated gas and only 13.6 percent is nonassociated dry gas.

In 1993, the Marine Region contributed 73 percent of crude oil production and 35 percent of natural gas production. However, the Mesozoic area of Tabasco and Chiapas shows a high gas : crude oil ratio. For this reason, the South Region contributed 53 percent of natural gas production. We expect, in the very near future, a higher contribution from the Marine Region, due to the fact that the new fields of light crude oil show higher gas : crude oil ratios. Natural gas flaring has been systematically reduced during the last few years. In 1993, it was 124 million cubic feet per day, due mainly to the lack of storage infrastructure. It was expected that we would see an important reduction in natural gas flaring in 1994.

Figure 11.1 **PEMEX and the Economy** (percent contribution)

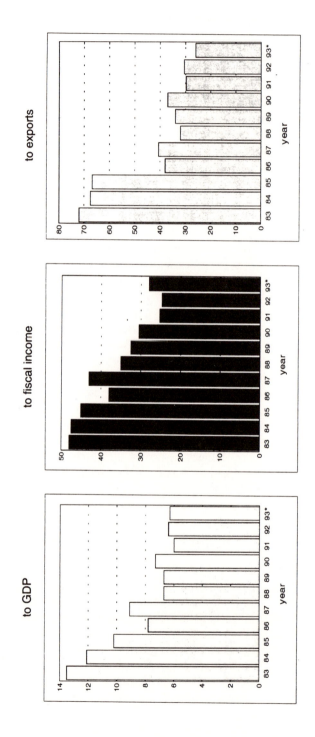

Source: PEMEX, *Memoria de Labores*, 1993.

Figure 11.2 **Hydrocarbon Reserves and Reserves to Production**

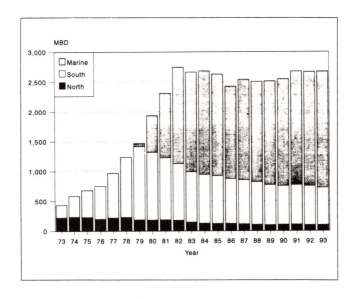

Source: PEMEX, *Anuario Estadistico,* 1994.

Figure 11.3 **Oil Production by Region**

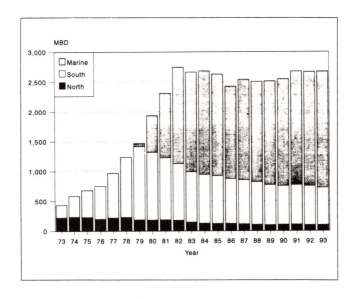

Source: PEMEX, *Anuario Estadistico,* 1994.

Figure 11.4 **Gas Production by Region**

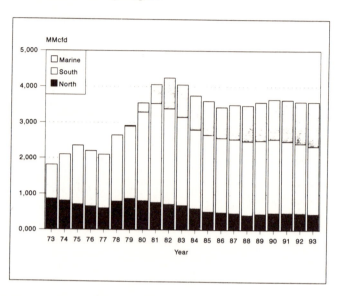

Source: PEMEX, *Anuario Estadistico,* 1994.

Supplies, Consumption, and Foreign Trade

Foreign trade data of oil and oil products for 1993 are shown in Figure 11.5. Exports of crude oil reached their peak in 1983 at 1.537 million barrels per day. Ten years later, in 1993, exports had fallen to 1.337 million barrels per day (13 percent less than in 1983)—about one-half of current production. Exports of natural gas began in 1980 and dropped to zero in 1985. After that, there were no exports until 1993—the year in which there was a marginal amount of exported gas (4.8 million cubic feet per day). And that was due to the contraction in the internal demand. However, for the country to change from being a net importer of natural gas to an exporter of significance, considerable investment is necessary.

For selected years during the period of 1980 to 1993, 89.4 percent (on the average) of the internal energy supply is represented by fossil fuels (see Table 11.1). The supply distribution of the different fuels is: oil (55.12 percent); gas (28.78 percent); and domestic coal (2.8 percent). Other primary sources are: biomass—bagasse and fuel wood—(7.46 percent); geothermal (0.64 percent); hydraulic (4.88 percent); and uranium (0.37 percent). Fuel wood still plays a significant but decreasing role during the indicated period. It is the sole source of energy for many small rural communities. On the negative side, it contributes to the country's deforestation problem.

In 1993, internal energy consumption showed that the energy sector itself—Petróleos Mexicanos (PEMEX) and Comisión Federal de Electricidad (CFE)—

Figure 11.5 **Foreign Trade of Oil and Oil Products, 1993**

Oil Exports

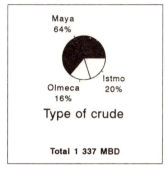

Exports and Imports of Oil Products

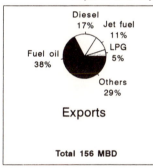

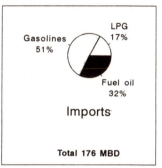

Source: PEMEX, *Anuario Estadistico,* 1993.

accounted for 28.4 percent, leaving 71.6 percent for end use. Of the latter, transport took 36.2 percent, industry took 30.5 percent, the residential, commercial, and public-services sector took 21.6 percent, and, finally, agriculture took 2.4 percent. Feedstocks (i.e., nonenergy uses) accounted for 9.3 percent.

The electricity sector in Mexico, as part of any energy system, plays an important role as a consumer of gas, oil products, and other fuels. Table 11.2 shows the power capacity by type of utility between 1980 and 1993. In 1993, hydroelectric power accounted for 28 percent of capacity, thermal energy based on hydrocarbons for 55.9 percent, coal for 6.5 percent, geothermal energy for 5.53 percent, and nuclear energy for 2.3 percent. Thus, in 1993, thermoelectric energy (fossil fuels, geothermal, and nuclear) constituted 72 percent of the total

Table 11.1

Internal Energy Supply Structure

	1980	1985	1990	1993
	(percent)			
Geothermal	0.24	0.36	0.99	1.08
Hydraulic	4.47	5.73	4.45	4.73
Biomass	8.39	7.64	6,78	6.85
Coal	2.26	2.64	2.68	2.92
Nuclear			0.56	0.93
Hydrocarbons	84.61	83.43	84.54	83.49
	Peta calories[a]			
Total domestic production	1,631.7	2,096.6	2,056.9	2,126.6
Total imports	18.9	28.7	62.2	101.9
Inventory changes	8.3	4.7	2.8	6.7
Exports	512.3	872.6	756.1	831.4
Other (pills, flaring, etc.)	50.5	31.9	34.3	41.8
Total internal supply	1,079.4	1,216.2	1,325.9	1,361.9

Source: Juan Quintanilla M., on the basis of SEMIP *Balance Nacional de Energia* (several years).
[a]1 peta calorie is approximately equal to $7 * 10^5$ barrels of oil equivalent.

capacity, while 62.4 percent of the total capacity was based on fossil fuels.

Table 11.3 shows the fuel consumption in the generation of electricity in the period from 1980 to 1993. The main fuel is fuel oil (67.4 percent), followed by gas (15.5 percent), coal (10.5 percent), uranium (5.4 percent), and diesel oil (1.2 percent). The generation by type of utility in the same period is shown in Table 11.4. Thermal generation accounts for 79.3 percent and hydroelectric generation for 20.7 percent.

The Role of PEMEX

Although the country has been self-sufficient with respect to its energy needs, some constraints and bottlenecks have appeared. In past years, internal demand continued to rise strongly even as reserves fell drastically. This was caused by a significant reduction in investment—20 percent lower in 1990 than in 1982. It was a direct result of the economic crisis. Environmental concerns, whether for political image or to solve actual problems, such as the air pollution of the metropolitan area of Mexico City and other large urban concentrations, and as a result of the pressure from NAFTA, highlighted the need for a large fraction of the available capital—domestic and foreign—for the oil sector. It also limited the needed expansion of production capacity and of exploration. In 1991, PEMEX created an "ecological package," the aim of which was to improve the quality of

Table 11.2

Installed Capacity by Type of Utility (megawatts)

	1980	1981	1982	1983	1984	1985	1986
Hydro	5,992	6,550	6,550	6,532	6,532	6,532	6,532
Hydrocarbons							
Steam	6,616	7,486	8,325	8,655	8,929	9,599	9,949
Combined cycle	540	1,223	1,223	1,223	1,227	1,450	1,450
Turbogas	1,190	1,539	1,686	1,698	1,760	1,789	1,789
Internation combustion	137	118	101	91	107	112	111
Dual							
Coal		300	300	600	600	900	900
Geothermal	150	180	205	205	205	426	535
Uranium							
Total	14,625	17,396	18,390	19,004	19,360	20,808	21,266

	1987	1988	1989	1990	1991	1992	1993
Hydro	7,546	7,749	7,761	7,804	7,931	7,931	8,171
Hydrocarbons							
Steam	10,299	10,450	11,301	11,367	12,553	12,788	12,574
Combined cycle	1,550	1,624	1,618	1,687	1,826	1,817	1,818
Turbogas	1,789	1,792	1,770	1,778	1,777	1,777	1,777
Internal combustion	111	89	89	82	115	149	149
Dual							1,400
Coal	1,200	1,200	1,200	1,200	1,200	1,200	1,900
Geothermal	650	650	700	705	720	730	740
Uranium				675	675	675	675
Total	23,145	23,554	24,439	25,298	26,797	27,067	29,204

Source: Juan Quintanilla M., on the basis of the *Informe de Operación,* CFE (several years).

fuels. It involved twenty projects, including the upgrading of refineries to produce unleaded gasoline. This fuel was needed to make possible compliance with the 1990 decree that all new cars sold in Mexico must be equipped with catalytic converters. Currently, 40 percent of domestically sold gasoline is unleaded. Both low-sulfur fuel oil and diesel oil are produced and directed to the most critical areas—like Mexico City. New plants will be needed to produce oxygenated compounds (MTBE and TAME). This will cost about $1.2 billion—with about 70 percent of these funds coming from the Overseas Economic Cooperation Fund (OECF) and EXIMBANK of Japan. PEMEX will supply the rest. Five projects have been completed and are now operating. Twelve projects are due to be completed in 1995. As of mid-1994, about $350 million had been spent. The largest single project—an HDS (hydro desulfuration, to reduce the sulfur

Table 11.3

Fuel Consumption for Electricity Generation (peta calories)

Year	Fuel Oil	Diesel Oil	Gas	Coal	Uranium (U_{308})	Total
1980	86.7	10.9	30.1			127.7
1981	90.7	10.5	25.6	0.04		126.8
1982	97.2	8.0	28.2	3.0		136.4
1983	110.7	3.0	23.3	6.0		143.0
1984	119.9	3.9	18.7	7.4		149.9
1985	123.2	2.6	19.6	8.9		154.3
1986	131.7	2.1	25.5	14.7		174.0
1987	144.4	3.2	27.5	16.8		191.9
1988	150.7	1.9	25.6	18.4		196.6
1989	159.6	2.9	27.0	18.6		208.1
1990	155.3	3.8	33.6	18.2	7.7	218.6
1991	159.0	4.1	40.4	18.8	10.9	233.2
1992	156.7	3.0	37.4	19.4	10.2	226.7
1993	159.0	2.8	36.6	24.7	12.7	235.8

Source: Juan Quintanilla M., on the basis of the *Informe de Operación,* CFE (several years); and SEMIP *Balance Nacional de Energia* (several years).

content) for the residuals installation at Tula—is now on hold. It will cost $650 million.

Continuation of these trends would severely restrict, and even suppress, Mexico's export capability in the near term. Had Mexico experienced an economic upturn (with a 4.5 percent annual growth rate of the GDP), the country would have ceased to export oil by the year 2000, unless production was increased. At the time, this projection (made by the University Energy Program in 1989 but not really disputed by oil experts) was based on the 2.55 million barrels per day rate of production. Finally, the needs of the petrochemical industry and (for environmental reasons) the planned use of natural gas in the power and transport sectors, coupled with lagging exploration and development, will have to be supplied with imports eventually. In 1992, natural gas was imported at the rate of 250 million cubic feet per day. Although demand (mainly from the fertilizer industry) fell in 1994, and resulted in a net export balance, this is a transient situation.

In addition, with respect to refined petroleum products—especially fuel oil, gasoline, and liquid petroleum gas (LPG), Mexico increasingly is becoming a net importer. This is the result, in part, of a strategy by which PEMEX buys products from abroad, if it is cheaper to do so (because of the transportation costs) than to supply them directly. That is the case in the northwestern states. But, more likely, the reason is a shortage of refining capacity due to the slowdown in capital investment and an unexpected surge in demand—especially in the trans-

Table 11.4

Electricity Generation by Type of Utility (GWh)

	1980	1981	1982	1983	1984	1985	1986
Hydro	16,740	24,446	22,729	20,583	23,448	26,087	19,876
Hydrocarbons							
Steam	37,012	35,527	40,025	44,822	46,342	48,322	53,247
Combined							
cycle	3,267	3,456	5,272	4,281	4,122	4,554	5,866
Turbogas	3,623	3,202	2,438	1,261	939	853	600
Internal							
combustion	311	251	187	107	100	43	63
Dual							
Coal		33	1,278	2,424	3,132	3,852	6,337
Geothermal	915	964	1,296	1,353	1,424	1,641	3,394
Uranium							
Total	61,868	67,879	73,225	74,831	79,507	85,352	89,383

	1987	1988	1989	1990	1991	1992	1993
Hydro	18,200	20,777	24,199	23,337	21,737	26,095	26,235
Hydrocarbons							
Steam	58,298	60,838	65,087	66,916	70,328	69,829	68,339
Combined							
cycle	7,440	7,047	7,150	7,487	7,748	7,214	7,982
Turbogas	602	474	629	669	659	281	277
Internal							
combustion	63	73	98	80	186	237	277
Dual							2,148
Coal	7,289	8,035	7,890	7,774	8,077	8,318	10,500
Geothermal	4,418	4,661	4,675	5,124	5,435	5,804	5,877
Uranium			372	2,937	4,242	3,919	4,931
Total	96,310	101,905	110,100	114,324	118,412	121,697	126,566

Source: Juan Quintanilla M., on the basis of the *Informe de Operación,* CFE (several years).

portation sector. Significant importation of gasoline began in 1989 with 28.2 million barrels per day. It reached 83.9 million barrels per day in 1993—equivalent to 17 percent of internal sales that year. The acquisition by PEMEX from Shell Oil of 50 percent of the Deer Park refinery in Texas will allow it to process over 100,000 barrels per day of Maya heavy crude and to obtain 45,000 barrels of unleaded gasoline per day.

The economic and confidence crises have also been felt in the petrochemical industry—both basic and secondary. The first is the responsibility of PEMEX. The second is under the private sector, but with limitations on foreign investment. A report (May 1991) to the House of Representatives by the U.S. General

Accounting Office attributes the following assessment to PEMEX officials and the Mexican Petrochemical Commission: The deficit in installed capacity led to a $5.5 billion import of basic petrochemicals between 1980 and 1988. And the trend continues. There is a need for $1.7 billion to construct twenty-one plants that were planned more than a decade ago. The industry requires between $5 billion and $10 billion by 1995 to avoid large trade deficits in basic petrochemicals —as much as $8.6 billion by the same date.

In spite of the economic crisis of 1982, the demand for electricity in Mexico has increased steadily at an annual rate of between 6 and 8 percent. Its continued growth is expected. The power and energy reserves of the electricity sector have been declining, due to insufficient investment since 1982.

There is a need to regain appropriate investment levels in all energy sectors. Accordingly, a basic element of energy policy has been to adjust energy prices to international levels and to phase out almost all subsidies. By the end of 1994, only LPG for domestic use and electricity for the agricultural and residential sectors remained subsidized. Financial analysts estimate that the development plans of CFE for the period between 1995 and 2000 will require $30 billion, while PEMEX will need $20 billion for the same period.

Under the present circumstances, it is too soon to know what changes are being contemplated by the Zedillo administration. But efforts to stimulate independent power production and to privatize the petrochemical sector will be intensified.

The Changing Legal Framework and Policies

In an attempt to open its economy, Mexico applied to enter the GATT in 1985. It has tried to recapture growth through market-oriented policies and free trade— for example, the NAFTA—as well as attempting to secure financial resources for the development of the energy sector. Some changes took place during the Salinas administration. However, care has been taken not to amend the constitution. NAFTA itself expressed full respect for the national constitutions of the United States, Canada, and Mexico. Consequently, Mexico is explicitly not bound to security-of-supply clauses such as those that appeared in the previously signed treaty between the United States and Canada.

The constitution of the United States of Mexico establishes: (1) the ownership by the nation of all natural resources, among which are "solid mineral fuels," "oil and all solid, liquid, and gaseous hydrocarbons," and the "nuclear fuels"; furthermore, ownership is unrenounceable (Article 27); and (2) the exclusive responsibility of the public sector for the "strategic" areas, and the necessary ownership and control by the federal government of the agencies and companies instituted accordingly (Article 25); the strategic areas include "oil and the other hydrocarbons; basic petrochemistry; radioactive minerals and generation of nuclear energy and electricity" (Article 28). Within this legal framework, two state companies were established—PEMEX (in charge of the oil sector) and CFE (in charge of the power sector). Later on, a Secretariat of Energy, Mines, and State Industry (SEMIP) was created.

The important fact is that the constitutional mandate has implied that, with respect to hydrocarbons, PEMEX has exclusive charge of all upstream and downstream activities. It has to be the sole supplier of oil, oil products, and those petrochemicals defined as basic within the country. It is also the sole importer and exporter. Similarly, CFE has been in charge of all electricity generation, distribution, and sales—as well as imports and exports. Its role is considered one of public service. The only exceptions have been instances of self-supply under special circumstances (PEMEX and some other large industries), and of small generators for emergencies.

With respect to the power sector, significant legislative changes have occurred. They have been aimed directly at bringing the private sector into the process of needed development. Indeed, the expansion plans contemplate the near doubling of installed capacity by the year 2001. This is in response to a sustained, strong increase in demand—even during a recession or in a slow economy. The law regulating the electric industry was amended by the Mexican Congress in December 1992. It widened the participation of the private sector—both national and foreign—in what had been considered "public service." It even allowed the participation of independent power producers. The essential legislative change arises in the modification of Article 3 of the Electric Energy Public Service Law, not of the constitution. It now states:

> The following are not considered public service: (1) The generation of electric power for self-supply, cogeneration, or small production; (2) the generation of electric power by independent producers to be sold to *Comisión Federal de Electricidad* (CFE); (3) the generation of electric power for exportation, derived from cogeneration, independent production, and small production, subject to a permit of the *Secretaria de Energía, Minas e Industria Paraestatal* (SEMIP); (4) the importation of electric power by physical or moral persons (i.e., companies) for their own use; and (5) the generation of electric power to be used during emergencies derived from interruptions of the power public service.

Congress has also passed the specific regulations and procedures that will apply in the above instances. A regulatory body has been created—the Comisión Reguladora de Energía. CFE expects 70 percent of the planned increase in capacity for the year 2000 to be privately financed.

In view of the growing environmental concerns and regulations, the lower required capital investment, and the shorter construction time, it is expected that private investors will favor natural gas combined-cycle power plants, thereby increasing considerably the demand for natural gas. The changes in the oil sector pertain more to a reorganization of PEMEX. They will bring about its modernization and make it more efficient and businesslike. The sheltered oil sector—upstream and downstream—which certainly has been supplying the country's needs, exhibited low standards when compared to the prevailing international yardsticks. In 1989, PEMEX's sales per worker were one-tenth that of Exxon or Royal Dutch. But we must qualify these comparisons. PEMEX was much more than just an oil company. For instance, it operated hospitals, schools, stores, etc., until recently. In the refining area, however, its productivity rate was 38 barrels per day per worker, as compared to 100 in the United States and Canada.

The new structure was sanctioned by the 1992 Ley Organica de Petróleos Mexicanos y Organismos Subsidiarios. It aims to establish independent operation and accounting along "business lines" within a corporate structure. PEMEX remains the parent company of four principal subsidiary companies that are in charge, respectively, of: exploration and exploitation of oil and gas; refining, production, and distribution of oil products; processing natural gas and natural gas liquids and manufacturing the basic petrochemicals; and the production of secondary and tertiary petrochemicals. In addition, there is PEMEX Internacional (PMI), in charge of international trade of crude and petroleum products.

The clarification of PEMEX's internal economic performance is already evident in the annual report for 1993 (from which Table 11.5 is extracted). Before the restructuring, a single balance sheet for the whole company was presented. It had been audited by external accountants, according to "standard practices." Thus, only the first column in Table 11.5 shows subsidiary net operating profit. Currently, there is a more detailed balance sheet and operation analysis for each of the subsidiary companies. It clarifies internal transfers from one company to the other, as well as the external transactions of each one. This was actually one (if not the main one) of the purposes of the change. PEMEX is evolving toward the presentation of financial statements that may comply with the requirements, for instance, of the Securities and Exchange Commission of the United States. Their purpose will be to secure access to capital via instruments other than outright loans, or by privatizing its secondary petrochemical operations.

More important, the oil workers' union's hold on the industry has been broken. It had led to increased inefficiency and an economic drain brought about by exclusive rights and corrupt practices. The new labor contracts have allowed the reduction of personnel from 210,000 in 1987 to about 106,000 in 1993. PEMEX has divested itself of activities it considered not to be proprietary or not pertaining to the mainstream of its business. For example, the production of lubricants, air transportation, the medical services, and others have been transferred to joint ventures in which PEMEX has a 49 percent participation. But the private partners manage the company.

PEMEX has clearly opened the exploration and development of several fields to international bids. There are direct contracts to foreign companies. Included among these are contracts with the Triton Engineering Corporation of Houston

Table 11.5

PEMEX 1993 (U.S. $ = 3.1 peso)

Subsidiary Net Operating Profit[a]	$ Million	Percent
Exploration and production	12,571.6	98.2
Refining	313.5	2.4
Gas and basic petrochemicals	150.3	1.2
Petrochemicals	(232.9)	(1.8)
Gross corporate profit	12,802.5	100.0
Corporate expenses	3,210.0	
Revenue before taxes and dues	9,592.5	100.0
Taxes and dues	8,545.5	89.0
Net revenue	1,047.2	11.0

Source: Prepared by the authors from *Memoria de Labores,* 1993.

[a]*Memoria de Labores* 1993 contains a separate balance sheet for each subsidiary, as well as for PMI and IMP. This had not been presented previously.

and the Sonat Corporation—the latter in partnership with the Mexican company, EPN Arval. PEMEX had done this, to a certain extent, in the past as well. Risk contracts are excluded, but "performance" clauses can be introduced in turnkey service contracts. Many other services are also contracted. The Mexican Petroleum Institute (created as the technological arm of the oil industry) now has to compete with national and foreign companies for the projects of the different PEMEX subsidiaries. On the other hand, it is now actively exploiting its expertise abroad. An important change in legislation was also made to finally reduce the number of the exclusive "basic" petrochemicals to only eight. It previously had been brought down from sixty-six to twenty. The petrochemicals that have been reclassified as secondary are open to private investment. PEMEX-owned plants of secondary petrochemicals may be sold, or opened to private investment through the stock market or joint ventures—depending on market conditions.

Although NAFTA does not touch the constitutional mandate, most observers recognize that it is desirable to strengthen the important role of the trade of energy goods and basic petrochemicals within the region, and to improve it through a gradual but sustained liberalization. A reference to GATT rules on trade in energy and basic petrochemicals has been incorporated. Also, the government procurement rules for the energy sector have been softened. NAFTA establishes that government procurements will be opened to suppliers in all three countries. In the case of state enterprises (like PEMEX and CFE), the rules will apply to procurements in excess of $250,000 for goods and services and $8 million for construction services. For Mexico, these provisions are being phased in. They begin with 50 percent of the contracts and increase to 100 percent by 2003.

Mexico's Present Dilemma

In the present crisis, given the constitutional restraints, what should Mexico do about conjoining its oil industry with that of the United States? From the U.S. point of view, what would be the advantages for Mexico? Sorely needed capital and technology would flow from north to south. Mexico's economic recovery would be accelerated. More jobs would be created. And the standard of living—so dramatically depressed during the past decade—would begin to rise again.

On the other hand, Mexico has again asserted strongly that the state will not relinquish its fundamental responsibility under the constitution. Certainly, to go beyond the changes already made would require constitutional amendments. Constitutional amendments are nothing new in Mexico; there have been quite a few in the past. President Salinas de Gortari carried out some very drastic ones, which he deemed necessary for his bold economic reform program. Indeed, he touched on areas (such as land ownership) that had been considered untouchable and politically risky—especially because of the large part they played for many years in the official credo, rhetoric, and policy. Now, the energy sector—oil especially, since the expropriation in 1938—is possibly the one that has been most systematically linked to the concept of the nation's sovereignty.

Besides the political risk, there are some very practical reasons to justify not letting go of the energy sector. For one, PEMEX has been, and still is, the main source of income for the federal government. The oil sector's share of tax revenue rose from 27 percent in 1981 (before the outbreak of the 1982 crisis) to a high of 45 percent in 1985. It is presently at 27 percent again. This, in addition to the drying out of foreign credits, explains the drastic drop in investments for development in the 1980s. Privatization would free the oil sector from the special fiscal regime, which is determined by the government.

There are also the questions of efficiency and productivity we mentioned earlier. Although there has been some improvement, there is a need to go further, before exposing the industry completely to foreign competition. For example, there is the question of installed refining capacity, which is 4 percent that of the United States. But it has been exploited to the limit. There are problems of upgrading—in both quantity and quality—because of lack of sufficient investment in the past few years. On the other hand, the United States and Canada have idle capacity. It can come on line on short notice.

Similar conditions prevail in the basic petrochemical area and in the electricity sector. Exposing the Mexican oil sector immediately to a completely open market could be disastrous. It needs to be strengthened first.

12

FRANCISCO ZAPATA

Mexican Labor in a Context of Political and Economic Crisis

Francisco Zapata points out that economic recession and changing ideology from 1982 to 1994 led to a 67 percent fall in minimum real salaries and a more than 50 percent fall in median salaries. More family members worked, increasingly in nonunionized service-sector jobs and in self-employment. Unions lost control of work processes and internal labor markets. Strikes were repressed. Payment systems increasingly reflected productivity. This was possible because of the pacts agreed to by labor, business, and the state. The pacts controlled inflation, limited salary increases, suppressed strike activity, and supported the PRI in elections, although with decreasing effectiveness.

At the same time, technological modernization led to massive layoffs in several industries. The unions lost control of hiring; closed shop; legal protection for labor leadership during its term of office; and other benefits were reduced. These measures were undertaken to increase productivity, which would make Mexican firms more attractive to investors. He points out that especially in some of the maquiladora industries (which benefited from U.S. tariff preferences) in northern Mexico, there are sweetheart contracts benefiting labor leaders and the firm but not its workers. He indicates that the changing economic and political relations in Mexico, and its increasing integration into world markets, make the relationship between the state and labor particularly hard to predict. After Dr. Zapata's article was written, Mexican unions refused to march in the traditional Labor Day parade, anticipating protests rather than celebrations.

Events that took place in Mexico from 1982 to 1994, such as devaluations, stock exchange debacles, inflation, adjustment policies, political assassinations, trade liberalization, guerrilla movements, privatization of state enterprises, and changes in foreign investment regulations, to mention only a few, had strong impacts on trade union action, collective bargaining negotiating capacity, and especially on the historic link between the labor movement and the political system. These were the result both of economic factors and of the changing ideology and role of the state.

Some of these impacts were the following: From 1982 to the present, Mexican GDP experienced negative growth rates in 1982, 1983, and 1986 and very low positive rates in the other years (see Table 12.1). Inflation levels reached their peak in 1987, to decrease after the signing of a pact committing business, labor, and the state (Pacto de Solidaridad Económica, December 15, 1987) to price and wage control and other economic matters. Minimum real salaries decreased during the entire period, cumulating in an overall decrease of 67 percent. By 1994, median salaries decreased to under half of their 1982 level. Open unemployment fluctuated from a minimum of 2.5 percent to a maximum of 6.1 percent of the population aged twelve years and more in a sample of thirty-seven cities in the 1982-94 period. This process resulted in an increase in the concentration of income and in a highly intensive use of human resources by poorer households through an increase in the number of household members in a position to receive monetary income.

These short-term data can be placed in the context of a drawn-out process of structural change that has been taking place in Mexico in the last decades as the evolution of the sectorial distribution of the economically active population shows (see Table 12.2). In addition to a massive increase in employment in the service sector of the EAP, changes in the structure of nonagricultural employment involve the growth of informal labor arrangements. As Table 12.3 shows, the proportion of self-employed people increased 8 percent from 1980 to 1992, while people employed in the formal sector decreased almost in the same proportion. Therefore, it is necessary to consider at the same time what happened both in the short term and in the medium term to understand that not all the impacts we will analyze here are mechanically related to the 1982 crisis. Events of the period 1982–94 are to be understood within a general process of social, economic, and political change, in which, obviously, one can neither dismiss what happened within the period nor forget the framework in which it was happening.

In addition to the business-cycle matters we have mentioned, collective contracts have also been changed and adapted to the new conditions, through the deletion of clauses that favored union control of work processes and of internal labor markets. The anti-union offensive that has been induced from the weakening of the bargaining position of unions—and especially through the implementation of the 1987 Pact—put into question the historic corporatist trade-off that resulted from the political arrangements consolidated during the Cárdenas presidency (1934–40). This process was reinforced by the policies of the ministry of labor that tended to impose salary increases systematically below increases in the cost of living and by the repression of strikes, especially those that took place in transnational companies such as Ford and Volkswagen. The ministry also instructed the federal and local conciliation boards to block union pressures in contract negotiations. At the same time, there were changes in the

Table 12.1

Output and Labor Force Indicators, 1980–94

Year	GDP	GDP–PC	OUE M	OUE W	OUE T	I	MS	MES	PRO	UCLF
									(1980 = 100)	
1980	8.3	4.9	3.8	5.9	4.7	29.8	-14.5	—	—	—
1981	7.9	5.5	3.5	5.6	4.2	28.7	-6.3	—	—	—
1982	-0.6	-3.0	3.9	4.9	4.2	98.8	-9.0	0.9	—	—
1983	-4.2	-6.5	5.3	7.6	6.1	101.6	-17.4	-21.0	—	—
1984	3.6	1.2	4.9	7.0	5.6	65.5	-5.6	-7.3	—	—
1985	2.6	0.2	3.6	5.8	4.4	57.7	-1.7	1.5	106.7	68.3
1986	-3.8	-5.9	3.7	5.3	4.3	86.2	-8.7	-5.8	104.3	66.1
1987	1.8	-0.5	3.4	4.8	3.9	131.8	-5.2	-0.3	107.1	64.7
1988	1.3	-0.7	3.0	4.5	3.5	114.2	-11.9	0.6	110.9	60.3
1989	3.3	1.4	2.6	3.6	2.9	20.0	-6.3	9.1	118.7	61.1
1990	4.5	2.5	2.6	3.0	2.7	26.7	-10.4	2.1	126.2	59.2
1991	3.6	1.7	2.5	2.9	2.7	22.7	-4.6	6.7	133.4	59.1
1992	2.8	0.9	2.7	3.0	2.8	15.5	-10.2	9.7	141.3	60.3
1993	0.6	-1.2	3.2	3.7	3.4	9.8	-6.4	7.9	134.1	58.2
1994	3.0	1.3	—	—	3.7	—	—	-0.8	—	—

Sources: GDP and GDP–PC: Inter–American Development Bank, *Social Progress in Latin America*, Washington, 1993; OUP (men, women and total): INEGI, *Cuadernos de Información Oportuna*, Mexico, 1985, 1989, 1993, 1994; MS and MES: Comisión Económica para América Latina, *Balance de la Economía Latinoamericana*, all years since 1980; PRO and UCLF: INEGI, *Indicadores de la competitividad de la economía mexicana*, no. 5, 1994.

Note: M = Men; W = Women; T = Total.

Table 12.2

Sectorial Distribution of the Economically Active Population, 1895–1980 and Yearly Variation (in percentages)

Year	Ag	% Var.	Industry	% Var.	Services	% Var.	Total
1895	62.50	—	14.55	—	23.0	—	4,761,914
1900	61.93	–0.1	15.66	7.6	22.4	–2.6	5,131,051
1910	67.15	8.4	15.05	–3.8	17.8	–20.5	5,337,889
1921	71.43	6.4	11.49	–23.7	17.0	–4.5	4,883,561
1930	70.20	–1.8	14.39	25.2	15.4	–9.4	5,165,803
1940	65.39	–7.0	12.73	–11.5	21.9	42.2	5,858,116
1950	58.32	–10.8	15.95	25.3	26.0	18.7	8,272,093
1960	54.21	–7.0	18.95	18.8	27.2	4.6	11,332,016
1970	39.39	–27.3	22.95	21.1	37.7	38.6	12,955,057
1980	25.98	–34.0	20.35	–11.3	53.7	42.4	21,941,693
1990	22.6	–13.0	27.9	37.1	46.1	–14.2	23,403,413

Sources: Instituto Nacional de Estadística, Geografía e Informática (INEGI), *Estadísticas históricas de México,* 1985, vol. I, p. 251. Data for 1990, INEGI, *XI Censo General de Población y Vivienda,* 1990.

Table 12.3

Structure of Nonagricultural Employment, 1980–92

Sector	1980	1985	1990	1992
Informal sector				
Total	49.1	51.3	55.5	56.0
Self-employed	18.0	23.5	30.4	30.5
Domestic employment	6.2	6.4	5.6	5.5
Small companies	24.9	21.4	19.5	20.0
Formal sector				
Total	50.9	48.7	44.6	44.0
Public sector	21.8	25.5	25.0	24.5
Large private companies	29.1	23.2	19.6	19.5

Source: Encuesta de hogares, in *PREALC Informa,* no. 32, September 1993.

institutional framework. For example, institutions such as the National Commission for Minimum Salaries became associated with rubber-stamp measures, rather than with their traditional function as places of bargaining about the terms of the commitment of social and political actors to the corporatist arrangement. Finally, the reduction in social expenses forced by the overall decrease in public spending affected the operation of health services, education and scientific research, social security, and other organs. They opted for survival strategies that limited their capacity to meet the demands of a growing population. (There was a 3.3 percent increase of urban population between 1981 and 1987.)

The transformation of labor markets, both external and internal, modified the way in which matters such as horizontal and vertical mobility, layoffs, subcontracting, and payment systems were managed in the enterprise. In all these matters, the common denominator was a higher degree of unilateral decision making at the shop-floor level geared toward achieving a greater ability to respond to changes in the national and international markets. For example, payment systems are much more a function of productivity than of hourly wages, and in recent Pact negotiations increases have been divided between these two elements, almost in a 50–50 proportion.

All of the above considerations and facts are indicators of changes within the institutional system of labor relations and of its interrelations with the political system. A series of processes, combined and linked to one another, has developed in parallel. On the one hand, the reduction of public spending and of social expenses has questioned the capacity of the state to continue to play its role in the political alliance with the labor movement, the peasantry, and the middle classes. It has become harder to find the financial resources with which to face the increasing demands of those social groups in terms of subsidies for food consumption, public transportation, education, and health and, in more general terms, to assure social mobility. On the other hand, tensions at the level of the corporatist structure, within the political leadership, have also resulted in divisions within the so-called revolutionary family between the renovators, or modernizers, and the traditional, patrimonialist leadership. It is within this context that one can analyze the role of unions in this phase of the implementation of the modernizing strategy undertaken in the 1982–94 period.

Continuity or Breakup of the Corporatist Structure

To correctly evaluate the relation between the modernizing project and trade union action, one can start with the hypothesis that unions, employers, and the state continue to interact within the corporatist structure that was established in the thirties during the Cárdenas presidency. The existence of the Pact does not substantially change the relations among these actors and with the state. Trade unions and business chambers recognize their subordination to the state and at the same time contribute to the implementation of its objectives.

From this point of view, the Pact did not change the structures of interaction among these actors as a result of the process of harmonization of policies that were put into place to face economic crisis. Maybe the institutions where those actors interact face to face, such as the National Commission for Minimum Salaries, the Mexican Institute for Social Security, and the Commission for the Administration of the Pact, reveal the nature of those static relations and the rhetorical character of much of what is said in those instances. A good example of this situation was the debate concerning the reform of the Federal Labor Law, in which, in spite of the fact that many good wishes were expressed to change it to make it compatible with the new economic model, nothing substantial happened, nor will happen given the political restrictions that those reforms imply.

On the other hand, in spite of the restrictions on public spending, the state confirmed its commitment to the institutions that administer the corporatist pact by using resources obtained in the privatization of state enterprises. More than $27 billion were collected in this process between 1989 and 1993. They were spent in a series of assistance programs in the countryside, and in urban areas in the so-called National Solidarity Program. Through this strategy, some of the negative impacts of the adjustment and restructuring processes were corrected and became instrumental in the recuperation of political support for the Institutional Revolutionary Party in the elections of 1991 and 1994. These measures point toward the construction of a new consensus where the historic trade-off of the period 1940-70 has to be reformulated. Some of the benefits that are not functional to the new economic model will be eliminated, while new ones, more associated with direct assistance, will be included in the package that assures cogency to the political alliance. This shows that the intervention of the Mexican state is being modified to be compatible with the new model of development.

One can conclude that both labor and business have agreed to renovate their traditional forms of interaction without proceeding to destabilize the system through the use of force and thus have been able to maintain the corporatist structure in operation.

All this means that the Pact played a fundamental role in the maintenance of the core elements in the corporatist structure while modifying its forms of operation. Labor, business, and the state interacted efficiently between 1987 and 1994 to control inflation, limit salary increases, suppress strike activity, and provide support for the PRI in municipal, state, and federal elections. The Pact, centered in the corporatist framework, bypassed the legislative power, and therefore political parties did not play a significant role in this process.

In general terms, one can say that this arrangement is operational when the central actors of the corporatist system can interact with one another on the basis of a nonideologically motivated consensus that results from a very long history in which these actors have played other roles in other "circumstances," more positive perhaps than the contemporary ones, and are able to confront the new challenges with these shared perspectives. It is possible to say that this method of structuring political support for the economic strategy followed in the last decade or so provided a basis that, seen retrospectively, was quite effective, while it lasted.

Corporatism and the Mexican Labor Movement in the Eighties

In addition to the rearticulation of the historic link between the Mexican labor movement and the state, framed within the corporatist alliance, the labor movement had to face technological modernization, massive layoffs, and revision of collective contracts, in sectors such as steel, telephones, and automobile production, where restructuring implied strong internal adjustments within companies. In these sectors, the labor leadership was willing to sacrifice jobs and accept drastic modifications of collective contracts. The leadership appeared more and more identified with the official neoliberal policy and with the managers of the companies. Surprisingly, this did not result in generalized discontent among rank and file workers at the level of the factories, but reflected itself in the partial loss of electoral positions on the part of the labor leadership, especially at the national level in the 1988 and 1991 elections. This involved a decrease in their leverage with respect to the government and to the managers. Thus, the present status of the labor leadership is very ambiguous: while it has not lost its credibility among workers, it is losing its capacity to deliver the votes to the PRI.

This situation has been particularly clear in the case of strikes. Between 1982 and 1994 a series of strikes took place where the margin of manoeuver that the labor movement had enjoyed up to that moment was seriously undercut. These strikes—by steel workers at the Siderúrgica Lázaro Cárdenas Las Truchas (SICARTSA) and Altos Hornos de México (AHMSA) plants in Michoacán and Coahuila, telephone workers in the Federal District, auto workers at Ford and Volkswagen, and beer-producing workers at the Cervecería Modelo plant in the Federal District—pointed toward the tensions that arose when the Mexican government searched for reform of prevailing labor conditions to strengthen economic restructuring. One characteristic of these strikes is that they started as a result of contract revisions that were judged detrimental by workers.

As has been shown by many analysts, the objective pursued by the government through the policies of the Ministry of Labor was to eliminate contractual clauses that maintained high levels of rigidity in the operation of factories or to make strikes very costly by systematically refusing to discuss demands that were not compatible with macroeconomic policy. Clauses such as union control of hiring, closed shop, and legal protection for labor leadership during its term in office were to be deleted from contracts. At the same time, the ministry opted for a discretionary application of the Federal Labor Law in matters such as layoffs, which became easier to implement through the use of arbitrary indemnifications that were not calculated according to years of service as the law provides, and repressed strikes, where both the local and federal conciliation boards tended to favor the business interests over the union interests.

Perhaps the workers that were affected first by this strategy were those at Fundidora de Hierro y Acero de Monterrey, where the government decided to declare the company bankrupt and thereby close it, and those at the national airline, AeroMéxico, where a similar strategy was used except that, instead of closing the company, workers were rehired after the collective contract had been purged of clauses that played against its competitiveness. Before 1987, these two cases are illustrative of the way the government used strikes to radically modify labor relations in both companies. Given the dramatic economic situation that Mexico was experiencing, workers could not face the radical "flexibilization of labor relations" that the government implemented and that were associated with various mechanisms located both inside and outside the factory.

After President Salinas took office in December 1988, this strategy was applied to other companies, such as the Cananea copper mine, the steel companies that were going to be privatized, such as SICARTSA and AHMSA, and especially Teléfonos de México (TELMEX). In different ways, the renegotiation of the terms of collective contracts was preceded or was followed by long strikes or conflicts that had to face either state or federal officials who intervened in the internal life of the respective unions by modifying union statutes, demoting uncooperative leaders, and repressing public meetings. The relatively high level of conflict derived from the profound changes that were being introduced into collective contracts. These changes included changes in clauses that had to do with the labor process, with internal labor markets, hours of work, overtime, and subsidies that companies gave to unions.

For example, in the automobile sector, modifications took place in the amount and rhythm of work, in the horizontal and vertical mobility of workers, in the degree of unilateral intervention by managers in the supervision of work, and in several other aspects that regulate work at the shop-floor level. In this process of flexibilization no new clauses related to the regulation of technological change were introduced. This reveals that the type of flexibilization going on in Mexico is not related to projects concerning productivity and the involvement of workers in the organization and production processes, as some government rhetoric has suggested.

Most changes have to do with the internal labor market, especially with the terms of hiring temporary personnel, promotion procedures, and horizontal mobility. They involve decisions about the proportion of union and nonunion personnel. In all cases it is possible to see an increase of managerial rights in the factory. This goes with increases in supervisory personnel and changes in the statute concerning union and nonunion personnel. For example, in Petróleos Mexicanos (PEMEX—the state oil company) in the seventies a significant part of the technical personnel of the company were placed in the category of unionized workers; at the end of the eighties they were returned to the category of nonunionized. This implies that PEMEX management recovered its authority over this critical mass of workers who, during the time they were a part of the national union, had been very militant in the defense of their demands.

In the case of SICARTSA, a company that was privatized in 1991, the negotiation of the 1989 collective contract culminated in a very long strike (August–September 1989). It was not successful in blocking changes in ten clauses that referred to types of work, payment of salaries, work during holidays, compulsory rest, vacant jobs, voluntary retirement, and the administration of the resources of the company. In all these themes, the common denominator is the search for greater unilateral decision-making capability of management, in order to make SICARTSA attractive for investors. Thus, the new contract stipulated "the absolute freedom of the company to manage the resources and install new equipment while it compels the union to provide the workers that the company requires." Last but not least, the failure of the strike was clear when the union was forced to accept the dismissal of 1,775 workers as well as the suppression of the same number of working posts in the company. Thus, SICARTSA found bidders when it was put on sale at the end of 1990.

Other changes that resulted from the flexibilization of collective contracts were the introduction of flexible hours of work, the decrease in the number of days of vacation, the flexibilization of shift work, the number of rest periods during working hours, the elimination of payments that the company had made to social security organs on behalf of workers, and the elimination of clauses that had to do with preferential retirement or voluntary retirement.

Finally, many privileges that had been enjoyed by unions and their leaders, such as donations (automobiles, for example) and long-term absences from work for the members of executive committees, were restricted. The same happened to members of health and hygiene committees and with the money that usually had been accorded sport activities.

This process indicates the deep modifications that were introduced in collective contracts to make working conditions less rigid so as to offer the best chance to companies in their struggle to be competitive in the international market.

Conclusion

On the basis of what has been said here, one can see a long period ahead in which the labor movement will decrease its historic leverage within the political system and local unions' rank and file workers will tend to lose their power at the shop-floor level. Perhaps this will result in increases of labor militancy, such as those that took place at the Volkswagen factory in July–August 1992 and at the Ford Cuautitlán factory in 1993–94. Given the resurgence of the economic crisis at the end of 1994, this scenario will tend to spread if the access to decision making is denied to labor organizations, and especially if the Pact tends to lose its centrality as a political mechanism to generate consensus.

Also, if layoffs increase, if subcontracting becomes a general practice, if conditions of employment are made even more flexible, if salary levels are tied to productivity, and if the trend of labor authorities to intervene in favor of business continues, then it is possible that the patience that both unions and workers have shown until now will tend to diminish.

This situation is exacerbated because there have been no initiatives directed toward collective bargaining where business and labor interact without the intervention of the state and within the enterprise. On the contrary, harmonization of policies in the Pact took place at the highest political level and was dependent on the participation of government officials who elaborated and wrote what labor and business representatives would have to sign. Although government rhetoric tended to speak about the need to establish levels of negotiation closer to the shop floor, that intention did not become a reality.

On the contrary, the distance has tended to increase, as the example of the maquiladora industry in the northern border indicates. Indeed, in those productive facilities, workers don't even know there is a union that represents them. Still worse, workers don't know that there is a collective contract, because unions are artificially created by spurious confederations and contracts written by personnel managers in collusion with those labor leaders. The total absence of workers from union life and the union practices mentioned lead toward an unprecedented situation: a labor movement without workers, something that seems to be the project of some managers and union leaders in the northern border of Mexico.

At the end of this brief reflection one can state that profound changes are taking place in the historic relationship between labor and the Mexican state. As a result of both the internationalization of the national productive and financial apparatus, and tensions within the political alliance that succeeded in representing diverse social interests in the country, one can see a tough period ahead in which neither the new economic model nor the modifications of the corporatist arrangement have a guaranteed future.

13

María Angeles Pozas

Flexible Production and Labor Policy: Paradoxes in the Restructuring of Mexican Industry

*An aim of the Salinas administration was to increase Mexican economic effi-
ciency. Mexican entrepreneurs wanted to reduce government regulation of labor
and to increase their control. Traditionally, the government, labor, and the private sector negotiate wage increases. In 1993, a new basis was established:
wage increases would be equal to anticipated inflation plus an amount linked to
productivity. Seven percent was frequently granted; no one knew how to measure
workers' productivity.*

*At the same time, the government reduced its contribution to social security
and increased that of workers and employers. Firms subsequently reduced fringe
benefits. Unions then pressured for measures needed to obtain greater produc-
tivity-based wage increases. Some improvements were the results of workers'
suggestions. In other cases, management took credit for enhanced productivity.*

*Unions have also lost control over working conditions. Unions could no
longer require that promotions be based on seniority. Training replaced it, while
workers no longer were restricted to only one task.*

*Mexico's inadequate and undemocratic unions, as well as the federal labor
law, need to be transformed for Mexican firms to become competitive. In the
short run, steps to achieve this will place labor at an increasing disadvantage.
And the opening of Mexico to international trade and investment threatens the
survival of Mexican industries. Professor Pozas urges a balance between modernization and social justice.*

This paper is a reflection led by the research I conducted between 1990 and 1994 in
more than twenty-five firms in different regions of Mexico (Pozas 1990, 1992, 1993,
1994a, 1994b). I would like to thank Patricia Landolt for her valuable help in editing this
paper.

Introduction

Following the first part of the last decade, the opening of the Mexican economy to international markets led to a process of technological conversion and reorganization in industrial firms. This process is characterized by the flexibilization of production within firms. It requires a new type of worker and contractual conditions that are much less rigid than is the norm under Mexico's current labor legislation. Therefore, the consequences of industrial modernization extend beyond the individual firm and cause a profound modification of Mexico's system of labor relations. This article focuses on the emergent trends of Mexico's labor policy from the perspective of the firm.

During the Salinas administration, labor policy was gradually adjusted to fit the needs of large industrial firms, with the overall objective of adapting the legislation to the requirements of a more flexible mode of production. Beginning in 1989, the entrepreneurial sector signaled the key elements in which it required changes in the Federal Labor Law. Entrepreneurs wanted to force a redefinition of workers' rights and labor conditions in accordance with the particular needs of each firm. The changes they asked for can be grouped into four types.[1] First, they wanted to eliminate the state as labor's interlocutor and to relocate negotiations between workers and managers to the realm of the firm. Second, legal restrictions on firing workers had to be eliminated to flexibilize the firm's use of the work force. Third, they sought to avoid efficiency and productivity problems by modifying the law's prescriptions with regard to wages, benefits, compensations, training, and seniority rights. Finally, entrepreneurs wanted to modify both workers' right to strike and the union's right to intervene in the hiring and firing of workers (COPARMEX 1989; CONCAMIN 1991). In short, the entrepreneurial sector pursued a labor legislation that granted their unconstrained access to a more deregulated labor force.

Given the potential political consequences of these changes, the Salinas administration did not alter Mexico's labor law. Instead, the new conditions for labor relations were gradually inserted through a series of tripartite pacts and agreements. Thus, the National Agreement to Improve Quality and Productivity (ANEPC),[2] signed in May of 1992, marked the take-off of a policy designed to eliminate obstacles to the flexible use of the labor force. Yet the implementation of the National Agreement gave rise to many problems.

The centrality of the wage relationship in a production regime has led certain authors to argue that the crisis of the Fordist and Taylorist mode of production is first and foremost a crisis of the wage relationship that determines the job structure and the process of wage formation (Leborgne and Lipietz 1988; Boyer 1990). In this light, this paper addresses two problems of the new agreement that are at the core of the redefinition of the labor system. The first set of problems relates to changes in the Mexican wage system. The second issue involves the role of unions and collective bargaining. The solutions to these problems will determine the new character of labor relations in Mexico.

Wages and Productivity

Unlike other countries, where wage agreements are reached within the firm, in Mexico the state has historically played the role of arbitrator and legislator of labor relations. This has given rise to a uniform wage system, enforced by law through "standard" sectorial contracts, a minimum wage, and a wage ceiling. Traditionally, the Congress of Work, an umbrella organization that represents the main Mexican unions, negotiates a wage adjustment with federal labor authorities and private-sector representatives. The resolutions reached in this agreement impact not just the unions represented by the workers' Congress but all Mexican workers, even those not unionized or affiliated with company or independent unions.

In 1993, however, in the annual tripartite pact, the government, the private sector, and the Congress of Work reached an agreement that signaled a change in the established wage system. The wage adjustment would now include a fixed wage increase of 5 percent, equivalent to expected inflation in 1994, and a discretionary increase linked to productivity. The value of this bonus would be decided in each firm according to its own measure of worker productivity. Under the agreement, firms were to establish a bilateral committee that would determine a measure of workers' productivity. Only for minimum wage workers, the increase was fixed at a 7 percent total. As well, for the first time in decades, no ceiling was set on contractual wages. Not surprisingly, most Mexican firms took the 7 percent increase as the norm on which they based their contractual revision in 1994 and did not address the issue of productivity bonuses. The problem, as will become evident, was that no one knew how to measure workers' productivity.

Concurrently with the liberalization of the wage system, the new labor policy included reforms of the Social Security Law.[3] The main aspect of this reform was the reduction of the state's contribution to the Mexican Institute of Social Security from 25 percent to only 5 percent of the institute's total budget (CEN-PROS 1993). This is a clear indicator that the Mexican state was abandoning its historic commitment to guarantee workers' social security. On the other hand, employers' and workers' contributions to the institute increased. In response to this increase, firms diminished other workers' benefits, such as their retirement funds, and the firm's contribution to workers' saving funds and family recreation facilities (Pozas 1994).

The tendency to diminish workers' benefits led unions to pressure the firms to expedite the constitution of the bilateral committees. Many firms postponed the creation of these committees. In particular, managers resisted providing the kind of information unions required to propose a productivity measure. In their view this information would give unions a dangerous degree of control over the production process.

At the same time, unions resolved to learn how to negotiate productivity agreements by looking at the experiences of unions in other countries. In general, they tried to identify the areas where workers could save the firms money by reducing overtime hours and diminishing the number of defective pieces and waste. In order to do this, unions required statistical information and an analysis of the advantages and disadvantages for workers of the introduction of each action that led to increases in productivity. These increases could involve developments in the area of technology, training, or reorganization of the production line.

Managers, however, did not accept the kinds of studies produced by the unions. As a manager of a large firm expressed it, "What percentage of increases to productivity can be imputed to the labor force? If we give a productivity bonus, will this be considered as part of the wages in the employers' contributions to the Social Security Institute? If productivity is negative, will we implement a negative bonus?"[4] Clearly, they had doubts about how to convert productivity into wage bonuses.

During 1994, unions and managers of large industrial firms experimented with different ways of measuring productivity. Nemak, for example, a firm that produces motor heads for large automotive companies, focused its efforts on decreasing its rejection rate. A union's committee studied and identified the source of defective pieces in different departments, and workers were able to reduce the rejection rate to just 2 percent (Pozas 1994). Consequently, a bonus proportional to the decline in the rejection rate was agreed upon. This was, however, a temporary solution. In that year, many firms introduced new technologies and other important changes in the organization of work. Computer aid systems, work teams, and other innovations on the shop floor contributed to major increases in productivity (Pozas 1993, 1994). Yet managers resisted attributing these increases to workers' performance.

Measuring productivity is also complicated by the fact that many workers are not directly involved in the production process. How do you measure the productivity of a storage worker or even a white-collar worker? In continuous-process industries, such as the chemical industry, it is difficult to identify productivity indicators even for workers on the production line. The large firms have been developing sophisticated systems to determine wages and salaries. Some have opted for setting salaries that have both a fixed and a variable component. To determine the employee's variable salary component three factors are considered: the performance of the firm as a whole, the performance of the worker's department, and the individual's performance.

Regardless of the solution that each firm is able to reach, Mexican industry is going through a process of change that is modifying the entire system of labor relations. The problems facing Mexican industry give rise to many questions.

What new mechanism can compensate for the gradual withdrawal of workers' protection? How can these mechanisms be flexible enough to address the disparities between large and small firms, or between more or less developed regions? How can a modern labor-capital relationship be developed when more than half of Mexico's industries have not been modernized and lack the resources to do it? If the labor legislation is modified to fit the needs of the modern industries, how will workers of traditional firms be protected? Any new labor policy will have to solve these contradictions.

Unions' Role and Flexibility

During the last year of the Salinas administration, the process of adapting labor relations to the requirements of the new flexible mode of production continued. In the international competition to attract industrial investment, control over the labor force became increasingly important internationally (Gertler 1988; Micheli 1991). In Mexico, unions were gradually losing power over working conditions.

The pattern of the unions' bargaining was based on a job structure and a system of benefits designed to fit the old forms of organizing the work process. In this system job security and promotions based on seniority played an important role. By making training and not seniority the driving force of vertical mobility, and by replacing the system of single-task jobs with the company's option of rotating workers from one task to another, the relationship established between employers and workers was modified de facto, undermining the union's credibility.

Moreover, the state made it easier for firms to introduce flexibility by resorting to the Ministry of Labor and the Conciliation and Arbitration Boards to suppress union resistance.[5] The Salinas administration undermined the bases of the corporatist system by weakening the groups that created it and modifying the social welfare institutions that sealed the old pact between government and society. In Mexico, the increase in management's power of decision making and the unions' loss of power over working conditions are now generalized trends (De la Garza 1992; Zapata 1992).

The weakening of corporatism places the issue of worker representation on the agenda. For the labor sector, it is essential to guarantee workers' representation in both the country's workplace and its political life. Labor's influence in Mexico's political arena used to be exerted within the framework of corporatism and the alliance with the state. While this meant a significant loss of autonomy, the labor sector gained a form of political representation that negotiated its most general interests and achieved essential conquests vis-à-vis the state and employers, largely reflected in the Federal Labor Law. Given the absence of a labor party or strong, autonomous trade unions, breaking the corporatist relationship at this time would leave workers at a severe disadvantage. On the other hand, the increasing union bureaucratism resulting from corporatism seriously affected workers' representation in the workplace. This is reflected not only in a failure to enforce labor laws, but also in the absence of mechanisms to address specific worker demands. The lack of union democracy divorced workers from their leaders, fostering corruption and the holding of union posts for life.

This contradiction is at the center of stymied efforts to improve labor relations in Mexico. The leaders of the most advanced sectors of trade unionism recognize the need to join the discussion on modernization and productivity (Trabajo 1, 1989; *El Norte*, May 1, 1993). However, such negotiations within the plant require a representative union organization that can speak for all the workers if the union's proposal is to carry any weight.

From the employers' point of view, the legal forms set in the Federal Labor Law and the traditional forms of collective contracts hinder implementation of the new forms for organizing production that their firms need if they are to become competitive. Therefore, they have spearheaded radical proposals to change labor law, demanding totally flexible labor relations. "Flexible" as applied to labor relations refers specifically to job descriptions, length of workday, worker mobility between tasks, and forms of hiring and firing. Control of all these elements would enable managers to adapt to changing demand and to handle workers so as to increase production efficiency and cut costs. Since the entire system of worker protection rests on the aspects that employers want to transform, an agreement is obviously not easy to achieve.

Conclusion

Finally, it is necessary to say some words about Mexico's current crisis. In December of 1994 the Mexican peso underwent a catastrophic devaluation that produced a panic reaction in the stock market and the flight of international financial capital. Foreign investors in Mexico left the country overnight, precipitating the crisis and seriously jeopardizing modernization of Mexican industry. In June of 1995 the direction of this crisis is not yet clear, but some signs of the paralysis and reversal of Mexico's industrial economy are evident. Practically all of the firms that were financing their reorganization with credits contracted in U.S. dollars have gone bankrupt. Others have interrupted their expansion process, and many alliances with foreign firms were broken. While the entrepreneurial sector continues to demand modifications of the labor law, old practices of the wage relationship have been revived. The annual wage revisions are once again subject to a wage ceiling increase of 8 percent. Simultaneously, the representative organizations of Mexico's industrialists (CONCAMIN, CONCANACO, CPNL, CANAINTRA) asked the new president, Ernesto Zedillo, to include the issue of modernizing labor relations in the traditional National Plan for the Country's Development (Plan Nacional de Desarrollo) that each new president presents to the nation during his first year in office.

It is too soon to predict the duration of the current crisis or the depth of the damage to the Mexican economy and its possibilities of recovering. A set of government mistakes and difficult international conditions combined to produce this crisis. Internally, the Mexican experience shows that it is not possible to create an economic model with national scope that is designed to fit the needs of only a small sector of society (large industrial, commercial, and financial sectors) while the rest of the population suffers the withdrawal of social welfare policies. Political instability and the loss of confidence of foreign investors were the price paid for this imbalance.

On the other hand, the policy of opening trade toward the north occurred at a disadvantageous time for Mexico because of the dependence of the Mexican economy on the U.S. economy. Although only 6 percent of the United States' foreign trade was with Mexico in 1990 when the NAFTA negotiations started, 60 percent of Mexico's exports and 65 percent of its imports were already with the United States (Destler 1992). Alongside this asymmetry, Mexico reoriented its economy toward the world market at one of the most competitive moments in the history of the global economy.

The disadvantages of this strategy for Mexican companies proved to be greater than the advantages. The complete liberalization of imports and the establishment of U.S.-owned firms in Mexico posed a real threat to the stability and survival of Mexican industries. The current crisis means a major setback to the modernization that is already underway within the firms. Perhaps the crisis demonstrates that the success of these changes demands that Mexican society establish a balance between modernization and social justice.

Notes

1. These demands were signaled in public documents of the main entrepreneurial sector organizations: COPARMEX (Confederación Patronal de la República Mexicana), CONCAMIN (Confederación de Cámaras Industriales), CAINTRA (Cámara de la Industria de la Transformación), CPNL (Centro Patronal de Nuevo León).
2. Acuerdo Nacional para la Elevación de la Productividad y la Calidad (ANEPC).
3. In Mexico, the social security system includes health care services offered through the Mexican Institute of Social Security (Instituto Mexicano del Seguro Social) and financed by a trilateral contribution of employers, workers, and federal government.
4. Corporate director of labor department in Alfa, quoted in *El Norte*, October 12, 1993.
5. Ministry of Labor intervened in the conflicts of large firms such as Volkswagen, Puebla, and Ford, Cuatitlán, when their workers resisted changes in work organization.

Bibliography

Boyer, R. (1990), "la informatización de la producción y la polivalencia" in Esthela Gutiérrez, ed., *La ocupación del futuro* (México City: Fundación Friedrich Ebert-México / Nueva Sociedad).

CONCAMIN (1991), "Una nueva concertación. Hacia un acuerdo para el desarrollo y la competitividad." Centro de Estudios Industriales, internal document (Monterrey).

COPARMEX (1991), *Informe Asamblea Anual*. Internal document (Monterrey).

————. (1989), "Propuestas preliminares que la Confederación Patronal de la República Mexicana presenta para la discusión del anteproyecto de una nueva Ley Federal del Trabajo." Internal document (Monterrey).

De la Garza, Enrique (1992), "El Tratado de Libre Comercio de América del Norte y las Relaciones Laborales en México" in *Ajuste estructural, mercados laborales y el TLC* (México City: El Colegio de México, Fundación Friedrich Ebert and El Colegio de la Frontera Norte).

Destler, I.M. (1992), *American Trade Politics*, 2nd. ed. (Washington, D.C.: Institute for International Economics; New York: Twentieth Century Fund).

Gertler, Mark (1988), "The Limits to Flexibility: Comments on the Post-Fordist Vision of Production and Its Geography," *Transactions of the Institute of British Geographers* 13.

Leborgne, Dominique, and Alain Lipietz (1988), "New Technologies, New Modes of Regulation: Some Spatial Implications," *Environment and Planning* D: Society and Space.

Micheli, Jordi (1991), "Nueva manufactura, globalización y producción de automóviles en México." Typescript.

Pozas, M.A. (1991), "Modernización de las Relaciones Laborales en las Empresas Regiomontanas" in *Ajuste estructural, mercados laborales y TLC* (México City: El Colegio de México, Fundación Friedrich Ebert and El Colegio de la Frontera Norte).

————. (1992), *Reestructuración Industrial en Monterrey*, Documentos de Trabajo No. 40 (Mexico: Fundación Friedrich Ebert).

————. (1993), *Industrial Restructuring in Mexico: Corporate Adaptation, Technological Innovation, and Changing Patterns of Industrial Relations in Monterrey*, Monograph Series 38 (San Diego: Center for U.S.-Mexican Studies, UCSD in association with El Colegio de la Frontera Norte).

————. (1994a), "Tecnología y Organización del Trabajo: Cambios recientes en dos empresas regiomontanas," *Estudios Sociológicos* 12, no. 35.

————. (1994b), *Modernización de la Industria y Relaciones de Trabajo* (México City: Fundación Friedrich Ebert and El Colegio de la Frontera Norte). Trabajo (1989), no. 1.

Zapata, Francisco (1992), "La crisis del sector sindical sobre la dinámica del mercado de trabajo en México" in *Ajuste estructural de mercados laborales y el TLC* (México City: El Colegio de México, Fundación Friedrich Ebert and El Colegio de la Frontera Norte).

14

PHILIP MARTIN

Mexican-U.S. Migration: Policies and Economic Impacts

Labor relations involve both conditions in Mexico and those available in its neighbors. Central Americans migrate to Mexico; Mexicans migrate to the United States. Attempts by Mexico's strongest unions, such as the oil workers', to obtain conditions enjoyed by their counterparts in the United States failed, predictably, because they are much better than those of other Mexican workers. The solution compatible with long-run full employment involves increased investment both in Mexican education and in its economy, and migration of Mexicans to the United States.

Philip Martin indicates that as much as 10 percent of Mexican workers earn most of their income in the United States. During the last twelve years, three million migrants have come to the United States from Mexico—a number equal to 20 percent of Mexican net population growth and to 35 percent of legal U.S. immigration. This comes to 150,000–200,000 legal and illegal immigrants each year—a number that may increase to 430,000 in 1995—and one to three million seasonal workers, as a result of the devaluation. Migration thus provides more jobs for Mexicans than the estimated 60,000 annually attributed to NAFTA, or than those likely to be created as an immediate consequence of the December 1994 devaluation of the peso. Moreover, changes in Mexican rural structure are expected to increase migration to the United States—perhaps by over a half million workers in the next five to ten years.

The structure of migration includes U.S. migration to Mexico. One hundred and fifty thousand U.S. citizens are permanent residents of Mexico. At the same time, Mexico is a magnet for unskilled Central American workers and for skilled foreign professionals. Although questions have been raised about Mexican treatment of foreign workers, far more attention has focused on U.S. treatment of Mexican workers—especially after California passed Proposition 187. If upheld and implemented, this legislation would prevent unauthorized aliens from attending public schools or receiving most health and other services. President

Ernesto Zedillo, therefore, promised to increase efforts to protect Mexicans who live in the United States. Philip Martin believes that a bilateral migration accord may be negotiated in 1995 or 1996. Under that accord, part of migrants' wages will be withheld in order to encourage their return. The Mexican ambassador to the United States, Jesus Silva-Herzog, said that progress has been made toward a bilateral treatment of the immigration problem and that the issue is regarded as so important that Mexico City has designated a Minister of Migration at its Washington embassy. In spring 1995, Mexico was considering legislation that would help to regularize the continuing migration.

On the other hand, Philip Martin notes that the amount of migration depends, not only on absolute differences in wages between Mexico and the United States, but also on the distribution of income within Mexico. Migration would be reduced by improved income distribution, by a reduction in the rate of development in border areas, and by binational cooperation on immigration control. The benefits of migration are underlined by Ambassador Silva-Herzog, who, following flood-induced increases in agricultural prices in the United States, pointed out that the price of vegetables from the Southwest would rise 20–25 percent if Mexican labor were not available.

The United States receives more immigrants than any other country in the world. More Mexicans emigrate from their native land than do any other people. For most of the twentieth century, the major linkage between the two most populous countries in North America has been the migration of people from Mexico to the United States. In the most rural parts of Mexico, for decades, the slogan has been "Go north" for economic opportunity. Today, some two to three million of Mexico's thirty million workers rely on the U.S. labor market for most of their annual earnings. The U.S. labor force of 130 million includes three to five million Mexican-born workers who have been in the United States for less than ten years.

Both countries fostered this extensive migration. The Mexican civil war between 1913 and 1920 destroyed the agricultural system in the central Mexican highlands. In 1917, U.S. farmers and railroad trusts, eager for immigrant workers, persuaded the U.S. Congress to exempt Mexicans fleeing north from the literacy tests and head taxes that were being imposed on other immigrants. Between 1942 and 1964, Mexican workers were recruited to work under a series of *bracero* agreements on U.S. farms. Indeed, Mexico permitted the rural economies in several of its states to become dependent on seasonal U.S. farm earnings. Finally, in the late 1960s, the United States granted permanent residence status to thousands of Mexicans because of letters from U.S. farmers and other employers who offered jobs to the Mexicans. It permitted U.S. government employers to knowingly hire illegal aliens, so that, in the 1970s and 1980s, these "green card commuters" were perfectly positioned to provide the information and contacts for other Mexicans who came illegally to seek U.S. jobs.

Several questions ensue from this state of affairs: What are the current dimen-

Figure 14.1 **Mexican Immigrants, Other Immigrants, and Apprehensions, 1981–93**

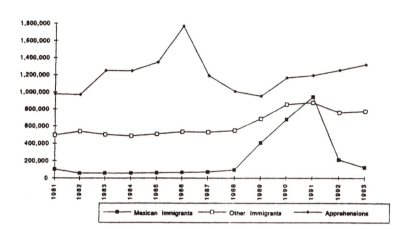

Source: Immigration and Naturalization Service, *Statistical Yearbook*, various years.

sions of Mexico-to-U.S. migration? What are the likely impacts of NAFTA on this? Most important, what are the prospects for U.S.-Mexican cooperation on migration issues?

Mexico-to-U.S. Migration

The volume of Mexico-to-U.S. migration is significant. Mexico has sent three million immigrants to the United States during the past twelve years. That number is equivalent to 20 percent of Mexico's net population growth and 35 percent of all legal U.S. immigration (see Figure 14.1). Most of these Mexicans were "illegal aliens" before they became legal immigrants. When many of them were acknowledged as legal immigrants in 1991, immigration from Mexico was greater than from all other countries combined.

Under U.S. immigration law, legal immigrants do not have to reside or be employed continuously in the United States. The result is that many legal Mexican immigrants live at least some of the year in Mexico, and many Mexicans who are not legal U.S. immigrants or visitors live some of the year in the United States. Between 1965 and 1992, some 21 million Mexicans were apprehended in the United States. During the same period, 3.7 million Mexicans became legal immigrants, including 2.2 million who became legal immigrants between 1989 and 1992.

The best estimates of the number of additional Mexicans—legal and illegal— who find U.S. jobs and settle each year (150,000 to 200,000) and of the number who work at least seasonally in the United States (one to three million) dwarf even the most optimistic estimates of job gains in Mexico due to NAFTA—such as the 60,000 additional Mexican jobs per year that Gary Hufbauer and Jeffrey Schott of the Institute for International Economics projected in 1992.

There is also a significant migration from the United States to Mexico, most involving Mexican citizens who are returning after seasonal employment in the United States. In addition, it is believed that many legal Mexican immigrants return to settle in Mexico. Return migration may be equivalent to 20 to 30 percent of annual Mexican immigration. Finally, some U.S. citizens (many of Mexican origin) return to Mexico each year, especially after they retire from their U.S. jobs. There are 150,000 U.S. citizens registered with Mexico's National Migration Institute as permanent residents of Mexico.

There are also several hundred thousand foreign workers in Mexico. According to press accounts, Mexico issues about 125,000 work permits to foreign workers each year. In addition, there are thousands more unauthorized foreign workers in Mexico. Most are unskilled Central Americans who are employed at the bottom of the Mexican labor market. They pick coffee beans, do unskilled construction work, and are employed in Mexican households as maids and gardeners. Violations of Mexico's minimum wage law and basic human rights standards are reportedly widespread where illegal Central Americans are employed.

There are also thousands of professional foreign workers in Mexico, including both legal and illegal "dryback" Americans. Unlike most other Western Hemisphere visitors, who get thirty-day tourist visas, two million Americans were issued six-month tourist visas to Mexico in 1993. Americans who live in Mexico can then simply cross into the United States every six months and get a new tourist visa on their return to Mexico.

NAFTA's Effects

Trying to determine the effect of NAFTA on labor migration is, at best, a very inexact science. There are several types of Mexico-to-U.S. migrants—legal immigrants, nonimmigrants, and unauthorized migrants. History shows that people can be shuffled among these U.S. categories by policy changes. For example, in 1954, "Operation Wetback" converted illegal aliens into legal nonimmigrants (braceros). Ten years later, in 1964, the end of the bracero program was followed by a U.S. policy that allowed U.S. employers to issue offers of employment to Mexicans, which enabled them to become permanent immigrants. In other words, it makes more sense to estimate the effects of an agreement such as NAFTA on the total flow of Mexicans to the United States, rather than on various subcategories of Mexican immigrants, because frequent changes of U.S. policies direct the flow into different subcategories (see Box 14.1).

Between 1982 and 1992, about three million Mexicans were recognized as being legally present in the United States. That made the flow of Mexicans to the

Box 14.1
Types of Mexico-to-U.S. Migration

Mexico was sending about 10 percent of the 600,000 immigrants to the United States in the mid-1980s. Mexico's share, as well as total immigration, jumped sharply in the early 1990s as a consequence of mid-1980s programs that permitted some illegal aliens to become immigrants and revisions to the immigration system in 1990.

The few migration provisions in NAFTA are similar to those of the U.S.-Canadian Free Trade Agreement of 1988. They permit four categories of "business persons" to enter the United States, Canada, and Mexico on a reciprocal basis, but they limit the number of Mexican professionals allowed to work temporarily in the United States to 5,500 annually.

Mexican professionals, unlike Canadians, receive NAFTA-TN visas only after their U.S. employer (1) files a Labor Condition Attestation (LCA) with the U.S. Department of Labor, which certifies that the employer tried and failed to attract American workers at prevailing wages for the vacant job; (2) files a petition with the INS that demonstrates that the Mexican alien has professional qualifications, generally a BS degree or more; and (3) the alien then applies at a U.S. consulate in Mexico for a TN temporary employment visa to work in the United States. U.S. employers do not have to file LCAs for Canadian professionals. Canadians do not require visas to enter the United States, and there is no numerical limit on how many may enter.

Illegal immigration has generally exceeded legal immigration from Mexico, but NAFTA does not include provisions that deal with the unauthorized entry of 1.5 to 2 million Mexicans annually, including 150,000 to 200,000 who are believed to settle every year in the United States.

United States the largest migration relationship in the world. Most of these Mexican immigrants were in the United States illegally and only subsequently had their status regularized. Approximately two-thirds of these Mexican immigrants are believed to be in the U.S. labor force.

How will NAFTA affect the net annual addition of at least 200,000 Mexican workers to the U.S. work force? There are a variety of models and methodologies, and all agree that there will be substantial Mexico-to-U.S. migration in the 1990s. Indeed, most of the migration models that consider NAFTA expect the agreement to increase the flow of Mexicans to the United States. The "smoking gun" in this migration-hump scenario anticipates that the free trade in agricultural products envisioned by NAFTA will displace Mexican farmers, who have a tradition of migrating to the United States.

The most widely cited projection of NAFTA's effects on Mexico-to-U.S. migration depends on Computable General Equilibrium (CGE) models of the U.S. and Mexican economies and labor markets. These models estimate that NAFTA would displace about 1.4 million rural Mexicans, largely due to changes in Mexican farm policies and freer trade in agricultural products. Most of the farm families displaced are expected to migrate internally and externally. The Raul Hinojosa–Sherman Robinson study projects that 800,000 will stay in Mexico and that 600,000 will migrate (illegally) to the United States over five to ten years.

Most econometric studies emphasize the likely effects of NAFTA on trade in maize (corn) and on production and employment in Mexico's countryside. The facts are straightforward. Between 30 and 50 percent of all days worked in rural Mexico are devoted to production of corn and beans. The United States can produce both crops more cheaply. Early in 1994, the U.S. corn price of $95 per ton was less than one-half of the Mexican price of $205 per ton. Liberalizing trade in corn (as NAFTA does over fifteen years) is expected to shift North America's corn production northward. Moreover, U.S. prices will prevail across the continent. After all, Iowa alone produces twice as much corn as Mexico. The argument goes that some Mexican corn farmers, discouraged by the prospect of lower corn prices, will have to leave their usually remote villages and wend their way along well-trodden roads to the United States.

CGE models suggest that trade liberalization in corn should be slowed in order to prevent a migration hump. What would be good for Iowa farmers, this argument goes, would be bad for unskilled workers in Los Angeles. While there is some truth in the general point, the Mexican government was concerned that the total cost of corn subsidies was large, and that these subsidies often did not reach the neediest corn farmers. In order to obtain the government-guaranteed corn price, the crop had to be delivered to a government agency—CONASUPO—and many corn growers were too far from a CONASUPO outlet, or produced corn only for their own subsistence. They, therefore, did not benefit from what was proving to be an expensive subsidy.

Recent Government Steps

Free trade in corn will be phased in over fifteen years. But the Salinas government took several steps that will probably transform rural Mexico in the 1990s— well before trade in corn is liberalized. First, in 1992, the Mexican Constitution was amended to permit those ejidos who communally control about 70 percent of Mexico's crop land and one-half of its irrigated land to sell or rent their parcels. Furthermore, in 1993, Mexico began to switch from supporting farmers by buying their corn at high prices to providing them with direct income payments instead. Finally, since 1987, Mexico has been reducing subsidies for the electricity, water, fertilizer, and credit that are used by farmers.

These policy changes amount to a revolution in Mexican government policies toward the one-third of the population in rural areas. Their net effect will undoubtedly be to promote emigration from rural Mexico. Although no one knows how many people will leave rural Mexico during its expected Great Migration of the 1990s, many echo Luis Tellez, the former undersecretary for planning in Mexico's Ministry of Agriculture and Hydraulic Resources. He suggested, on several occasions, that Mexico's rural population might shrink by one million annually, that up to fifteen million rural Mexicans might migrate "within a decade or two." This great migration should improve the allocation of Mexican resources. Tellez frequently reminds audiences that 27 percent of the Mexican population depends on agriculture for a living, but that this sector generates only 9 percent of GDP. For this reason, it includes two-thirds of Mexico's poor people.

In his final State of the Nation address in November 1994, Mexican President Carlos Salinas de Gortari condemned the approval of Proposition 187 in California —a state law approved by 59 percent of voters on November 8, 1994, that, if implemented, would establish a state-run eligibility screen to prevent unauthorized aliens from attending public schools or receiving most health and other services. According to Salinas, the movement of Mexican workers to the United States "is inevitable, and it is better to order and regulate it than to confront it with administrative measures that are not going to stop it, because the force of the economies is greater."

Deputy Foreign Minister Andrés Rozenthal predicted that, as North America integrates economically under NAFTA, "immigration is going to be the number one issue between the United States and Mexico for the next several years." However, it is not clear whether the immigration issue is going to be dealt with by negotiating a bilateral foreign-worker program, by attempting to slow displacing changes in Mexico, and/or by toughening enforcement efforts in the United States. Mexican President Zedillo has promised to step up efforts to protect Mexican citizens living in the United States. Each of Mexico's fifty-three consulates in the United States has a person who receives and investigates complaints that the rights of Mexican nationals in the United States have been violated. It is not yet clear whether Mexico will push for a bilateral foreign-worker program.

The scenario for Mexico requesting and for the United States negotiating a guest-worker program in 1995 or 1996 runs something like this: Labor shortages develop—perhaps in the May 1995 Oregon strawberry harvest. Meanwhile, the Immigration and Naturalization Service (INS) concludes that Operation Gatekeeper has succeeded in reducing the influx of illegal aliens and discusses ways to make legal border crossings easier. U.S. employers argue that the current H–2 programs under which foreign workers may be imported to the United States in the event of labor shortages are too inflexible. Mexico asks for a bilateral program that recognizes its proximity and the tradition of U.S. employers hiring

Figure 14.2 **The Migration Hump**

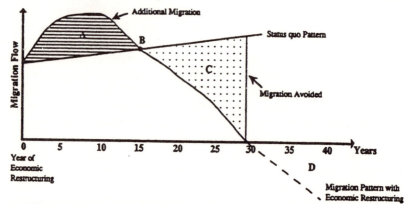

Source: Philip Martin, *Trade and Migration: NAFTA and Agriculture* (Washington, D.C.: Institute for International Economics, 1993).

Mexican workers. Given the passage of Proposition 187, it is already clear that guest workers would have little access to U.S. public services while in the United States and that a significant portion of their wages would probably be withheld to encourage their return.

The Migration Hump

The most likely migration trajectory is analogous to the demographic transition. Just as a country's population temporarily grows faster as death rates fall before birth rates do, and only later lower birth rates slow population growth, so too does the displacement and disruption associated with opening and privatizing the economy encourage more people to emigrate, and only later does job and wage growth slow emigration (see Figure 14.2).

The migration transition compares two scenarios. In the status quo scenario of a closed economy that, primarily, has migration linkages to the outside world, the level of migration depends on the gap between work force and job growth. If too few jobs are created, and if the work force is growing, and if there are opportunities to emigrate, then there will be a rising level of emigration. If the work force is not growing, as in much of Eastern Europe, then the status quo trajectory is likely to be flat.

The alternative open-economy scenario produces the migration hump. In economies that have been creating too few jobs to absorb new labor-force entrants, and where there are established international migration networks, the combination of displacement, disruption, and (in some instances) more money in extremely poor areas can temporarily increase emigration. If viewed in a figure in which time is measured on the horizontal axis and the number of migrants on the vertical axis, this temporary increase in emigration appears as a migration "hump."

The case for a migration hump is based on the expected behavior of the network, demand-pull, and supply-push factors that govern migration. This is the way it works:

• first, the establishment of networks that can move people across borders regardless of immigration controls;

• then, some demand-pull in the form of available jobs;

• finally, in the case of NAFTA, an increase in supply-push factors, as free trade displaces workers faster than additional investments create jobs for them.

The number of additional migrants may be small, especially relative to the amount of migration "saved" as a result of economic integration. Figure 14.2 illustrates this point for Mexico-to-U.S. migration. As drawn, there is additional migration as a result of NAFTA for about fifteen years. But this additional migration is a relatively small increment to an already significant flow—on the order of an additional 10 to 20 percent of an average 300,000 immigrants annually rather than 50 or 60 percent more migrants. Second, the figure is drawn to show that, when viewed over thirty rather than fifteen years, there is actually less migration with NAFTA, since C is larger than A.

The migration hump figure illustrates the likely effects of NAFTA on Mexico-to-U.S. migration. It is a reminder that the same policies that make immigration controls less necessary in the long run may make them more necessary in the short run. It should also be possible to make at least rough estimates of the A-B-C-D parameters of the migration hump for particular cases of economic integration.

Devaluation and Migration

Mexican migration to the United States, which has averaged about 300,000 settlers per year and 800,000 to three million sojourners over the past decade, is expected to increase as a result of the 40 percent peso devaluation in December 1994 and anticipated hard times in Mexico in 1995. The U.S. Treasury predicted a 30 percent (or 430,000) increase in illegal entries in 1995. It assumed a normal flow of 1.4 million unauthorized Mexican entrants and argued that the additional migrants would arrive if the United States did not extend to Mexico $40 billion in loan guarantees. President Clinton, among others, argued that the Mexican bailout package would "help us to better protect our borders." Previously, the 1982 peso devaluation was followed by a 35 percent increase in apprehensions in 1983—from 1 million to 1.3 million.

INS Commissioner Doris Meissner and Professor Ed Taylor of the University of California at Davis (who has a village economic model) predict that migration pressure will increase because the peso devaluation widens the wage gap between the United States and Mexico from 600 or 700 percent to 1,000 or 1,200 percent. Taylor's model finds that a 30 percent devaluation increases exits from Mexican villages by 25 percent.

Not everyone agrees that the peso devaluation will increase unauthorized Mexico-to-U.S. migration. Mexican migration expert Jorge Bustamante noted that the cost of being smuggled into the United States is set in dollars, and that some potential migrants might not be able to accumulate 40 percent more to pay smugglers immediately. There is general agreement that the migration effects of the peso devaluation will not become apparent until March or April 1995. That is when seasonal migrants seek U.S. jobs. These migrants will have to elude a beefed-up Border Patrol in order to enter the United States illegally.

Emigration pressure and migration flows will also depend on economic prospects in Mexico and California—the destination of most illegal Mexican immigrants. On January 3, 1995, President Zedillo made a speech that laid out plans to deal with the economic crisis that caused the peso to lose over 40 percent of its value in the last two weeks of 1994. The theme of the speech was sacrifice and austerity: Wages and prices are to rise more slowly than inflation; the government will try to sell off more public enterprises; and government spending will be cut. On January 17, 1995, the Zedillo government and the opposition parties signed a political reform agreement designed to minimize political unrest by ensuring honest elections—this in an attempt to restore the confidence of foreign investors.

A sluggish Mexican economy in 1995 could increase both internal migration to the northern border areas and emigration pressure. The Mexican economy is expected to grow less than 1.0 percent in 1995. Inflation is projected to be 15–20 percent annually. In addition, some foreign investors may put a temporary stop on plans to build or expand factories and stores in Mexico. However, the lower wages and costs wrought by the peso devaluation should make Mexico more attractive to foreign investors. Indeed, there has already been U.S. interest in shifting unused plastics and other light assembly work to the maquiladora in the border areas to take advantage of Mexican wages and benefits that have fallen from $2 hourly to $1.50. (About one-half of these wage costs are payroll taxes and benefits.) Since labor markets in Mexican border cities are fairly tight, such an expansion of maquiladora activity should attract internal migrants to the border. If the California and other U.S. border economies improve as expected in 1995, there could be more attempted migration across the border.

There is no doubt that Mexico will, over the next two decades, emerge as the low-cost manufacturing center of North America. But no one knows exactly when and how this economic transformation will occur. At least two to three million of Mexico's five to six million farmers (plus their families) are likely to leave the land over the next two decades. But it is not clear if foreign investment will create jobs for them in central Mexico or border areas, or if many will migrate to the United States.

Unlike East Asian tigers, Mexico's 1990s boom was fueled largely by foreign savings. An overvalued peso made imports of both capital and consumer goods cheap and could be sustained as long as foreigners believed that Mexico truly was the next "tiger." Mexico has learned that foreign money has an easy-come, easy-go quality. Mexico achieved more than 4 percent growth—4.5 percent—only in 1990.

An "orderly" peso devaluation was advocated by Mexico's new finance minister during the summer of 1994. But President Salinas reportedly wanted to be one of the few recent Mexican presidents to leave office without a massive devaluation. When the government that took office on December 1, 1994, announced its economic plans, local and foreign investors saw that the $30 billion trade deficit would not be reduced in 1995. With the Mexican Central Bank running out of reserves to support the peso, they bet that Mexico would have to devalue its currency. It did.

During the 1980s, Mexico managed to keep its unemployment rate low despite depression and economic restructuring. The official urban unemployment rate (open unemployment) for Mexico fell after 1983. It reached a low of 2.6 percent in 1991. Mexico's unemployment rate is low because it measures only people who are separated from formal job relationships, and because "unemployed" people not eligible for unemployment insurance are pushed into marginal jobs and considered employed. The unemployed in Mexico are those who can afford to search for work full time. They are usually better educated and more affluent workers.

The Border Problem

U.S. and Mexican presidents embraced NAFTA as a means to accelerate economic growth in both countries by encouraging each nation to specialize in producing those goods in which it has a comparative advantage. NAFTA also resolved that those goods will be traded without border barriers. For most of the twentieth century, Mexico's comparative advantage in the North American economy has been to export unskilled workers. NAFTA, it is hoped, can enable Mexico to substitute exports of goods and services for labor exports, and eventually reduce Mexican migration to the United States. Economic growth and development, which is accelerated by freer trade and investment, is a proven strategy to stop unwanted migration.

Of course, NAFTA will not provide a pure test of the effects of freer trade on migration. Mexico has unilaterally adopted policies that opened its economy and made internal reforms that will promote long-run growth. But these policies and reforms tend to drain people from the countryside. Simultaneously, the United States, with its easy legalization programs and ineffective enforcement of immigration laws during the 1980s, made it easier, rather than harder, for Mexicans to work in the United States.

Is there a way to open an economy and accelerate economic and job growth with a small migration hump? The answer is a qualified yes. Mexico could reduce internal and external migration by strengthening the institutions that broadly redistribute the benefits of uneven development. Nations such as Korea and Taiwan achieved both fast growth and an equitable distribution of that growth by not allowing rural–urban earnings differences to grow too large. Mexico, by contrast, has a very unequal distribution of income.

Second, Mexico and the United States might want to cooperate to avoid too much border development. Trade in low-wage manufactured commodities tends to decline sharply with distance. As U.S. apparel and footwear firms move to northern Mexico, many Mexican immigrants in the border areas of the United States may lose their jobs. This would confront the United States with the dilemma of either upgrading the immigrants" skills or risking demands for protection from Mexican imports. The latter would defeat the purpose of NAFTA.

Third, the United States and Mexico could cooperate on immigration control. In no other place do citizens of one nation mass, openly awaiting their chance to enter another country illegally. Mexican law prohibits Mexican citizens from leaving the country except at authorized ports. Mexican citizens who attempt illegal entry into the United States are also breaking Mexican law. It should be possible, without violating human rights, to cooperate at the border to reduce illegal border crossings.

15

NORA LUSTIG

The 1982 Debt Crisis, Chiapas, NAFTA, and Mexico's Poor

Income distribution is a key factor in migration; even more, it is important for political stability and for long-term economic growth. Nora Lustig analyzes the impact of Mexican development strategy on income distribution. Living standards are higher and incomes are more evenly distributed now than they were in 1963. But the 1980s marked a severe fall in per capita income and an increase in the share going to the richest people in Mexico: the upper 10 percent received 38 percent of the income in 1992, compared to 33 percent in 1984. Renewed growth in the early 1990s did not alter Mexican income distribution. The rich protected themselves by sending an estimated $36 billion abroad. The poor could not send money abroad. Instead, they exported themselves to the United States. Middle-income receivers could neither export capital nor migrate. Consequently, they were hurt disproportionately during the recession.

Health and educational services did not drop. But the rate of increase of educational attainment fell. Many children went to work instead of to school. Programs targeted for the very poor were severely reduced. They were implemented only toward the end of the crisis. The government, therefore, launched PRONASOL—the National Solidarity Program—to provide investment in infrastructure for and transfers of income to the poor. PRONASOL projects are often designed by their beneficiaries. Their cost was 1.0 percent of GDP in 1993. Nora Lustig states that extreme poverty could be eliminated by annual direct cash transfers of 0.25 percent of GDP to the very poor. The underlying causes of poverty, however, still must be eliminated. General economic growth is unlikely to adequately raise the incomes of the very poor in the immediate future. President Zedillo proposed a National Poverty Abatement Plan, which would provide guaranteed access to basic services and more employment opportunities for the needy. He also planned to guarantee the permanence of the PROCAMPO program of direct payments to farmers for at least fifteen years and to increase the direct financial support to the rural worker by almost 30 percent.

Concern for the welfare of the poorest was incorporated in the Mexican government's January 1995 adjustment plans. Technical assistance and some preference in government purchases would be provided to small and medium enterprises. Funds given to farmers through PROCAMPO would be 400 to 450 pesos per hectare (in early January, $30 per acre). Some rural groups complained that such funds were insufficient. Plans to help the poorest Mexicans were suggested—both on their own merits and because of the January 1, 1994, uprising in Chiapas. This rebellion reflected Chiapas's poverty, agrarian structure, and political difficulties. The Chiapas dilemma is the subject of special measures. The problems of Mexico as a whole are addressed both by the strategies described above and by long-run adjustments. The most important of these is the increased extent and level of education.

On December 20, 1994, Mexico was caught in a financial crisis triggered by the devaluation of the peso. What many thought should have been a "corrective" devaluation to reduce Mexico's large and rising trade deficit prompted a rush from foreign investors who held peso-denominated financial instruments. Without any doubt, the financial crisis will have a negative impact on the Mexican people's living standards. However, the severity of this negative impact will depend on the depth and length of the crisis. The rescue package put together by the international community will reduce both. However, even in the best-case scenario, real wages (and income, in general) will fall. In the first round, the group likely to be hurt the most is Mexico's middle class. These are the families who were used to buying imported goods, traveling abroad, making extensive use of credit cards. And they had purchased durable goods (houses and cars, for example) on credit with floating interest rates.

The financial crisis will also hurt the poor. A "stylized fact" in economic research is that whenever economic growth falters, poverty—in both numbers and intensity—tends to rise. But the clearest view of the impact of financial crises on the poor of Mexico, as well as on its middle class, can be gained from a historical perspective. One should bear in mind, however, that in 1982 the international community did not act with the same support that we've seen recently.

The 1982 Debt Crisis

Inequality and poverty in Mexico are undoubtedly high by international standards. But Mexico is less unequal and poverty is less pervasive today than it was thirty years ago. In 1963, for example, the wealthiest 10 percent of the population received 42 percent of the income, and the bottom 40 percent received 10 percent of total income. In contrast, in 1992 the top 10 percent got 38 percent of the income, and the bottom 40 percent received 13 percent. But the salient feature of the 1980s is that, after several decades in which the country was moving toward a more even distribution of income, the trend was reversed. Between 1984 and 1989, for example, the share of income that accrued to the wealthiest 10 percent increased by 15 percent (from 33 to 38 percent).

Following a similar pattern, poverty (measured by the proportion of households below the poverty line) fell during the 1970s and increased during the 1980s. However, with renewed economic growth in the early 1990s, poverty fell. For example, according to official estimates, 11 percent of households were living in extreme poverty in 1984. Each person was earning less than $20 per month. The percentage of poor households rose to 14 percent between 1984 and 1989 and then fell to 12 percent in 1992. In contrast, renewed growth left the distribution of income practically unchanged.

In spite of the fact that the rise in inequality and poverty during the 1980s took place at the same time as the tough adjustment program, their increase was more the result of the debt crisis and its aftermath than of the program. As was the case in all the highly indebted countries, the very sharp fall in real wages—over 7 percent per year, on average, between 1983 and 1988—was the consequence of the new adverse external conditions that were faced by these countries. In the case of Mexico, those adverse conditions included falling oil prices (then the main source of export revenues), rising world interest rates, and the drying-up of external credit. In Mexico, the debt crisis that started in 1982 (and the subsequent decline in wages) was also the inevitable fallout of the large and rising fiscal deficit that accompanied the oil bonanza between 1978 and 1981.

With inflation approaching a triple-digit level several times during the 1980s, no new lending from foreign private sources, and the domestic investors' capital leaving the country in leaps and bounds, stabilization and adjustment policies were not really a choice. They were a necessity. In country after country where the government either postponed a solution to, or was unable to cut down, its fiscal deficit and restore investors' confidence with market-oriented reforms, the results have been spurts of hyperinflation (or nearly so), sharp falls in real wages, and an absence of growth. This happened in Argentina, Brazil, and Peru, for example. It is still taking place in Venezuela. It is true that following the policies recommended by the Bretton Woods institutions (or some variation of them) does not guarantee a golden age or an avoidance of crisis. Neither Bolivia nor Mexico, for example, has been growing as expected. But, without the stabilization and adjustment policies introduced in the 1980s, the situation is likely to have been far worse.

Clearly, the costs of the debt crisis were not borne equally by all social groups in Mexico. The poor, and, even more so, the middle class, bore a higher share of the costs. It was reasonable to expect that, with Mexico's fall in average income and wages during the 1980s, poverty rates would expand. But why was the adjustment period accompanied by a rise in inequality? Why were the poor and the middle class, on average, less able to protect their living standards during the economic downturn than were the wealthy?

There is one explanation that stands out. The wealthy could always protect, and even expand, their wealth by simply transferring their assets abroad. And so they did. Between 1977 and 1987, capital flight was estimated at $36 billion. Access to dollar-denominated assets (or another strong currency) permitted the wealthy to have large windfall gains in the face of a devaluation of the peso—a process that occurred several times in that period. Those without savings—the majority of the population—did not have a similar option. Whereas capital can always find a safe haven, labor cannot freely move to other nations. Unlike asset owners who, on average, could substantially avoid the cost of adjustment in the 1980s, one of the most common safety valves available for the poor was to escape poverty by becoming an undocumented worker in the United States. While the United States welcomes Mexican capital without hesitation, undocumented migration from Mexico is becoming (if it is not already so) the major irritant in the bilateral relationship.

The middle sectors were hurt disproportionately—even in comparison to the poor—because of their reliance on wage income. Real wages fell by 42 percent in the five-year period that followed the eruption of the crisis in 1982. In Mexico, as in many developing nations, the poorest of the poor make a significant portion of their living outside the market economy. They home-grow and produce close to one-third of what they consume. Although, in structural terms, a lack of full participation in the market economy is one reason why many of the poor in Mexico remain poor, this relative isolation partially protects the real incomes of the poor during periods of crisis.

During the 1980s, in its attempt to attain fiscal discipline, the Mexican government stripped down all spending, with the exception of debt service. These cuts included the reduction in social spending (primarily, education and health) and the elimination of general subsidies (including food subsidies). The reduction in social spending did not lead to a reduction in the availability of teachers, doctors, nurses, schools, or hospitals. It was primarily the wages and salaries of the workers in the social sectors that bore the brunt of the reductions.

Even if the supply of education and health services was not reduced, the rate of progress of health and education indicators fell. The average years of schooling increased by one year to 6.4 years during the decade—half the increase of the previous decade. This slowdown occurred because junior high school graduates and high school graduates did not move on to the next level, and because there was a drop in the proportion of children entering primary school in relation to the total in the corresponding age cohort. Both phenomena clearly could be explained by the need of the children to join the work force at an earlier age or the postponement of school entry because of the high cost of the complementary expenses such as transportation and school materials. The infant mortality rate continued its downward trend and reached thirty-nine per thousand live births by the end of the decade. However, the proportion of children whose deaths were caused by malnutrition began to rise in 1982 after almost a decade of steady decline. Again, falling incomes might explain this reversal.

Protecting the employment of public-sector workers while the economy was shrinking (feasible because of the wage cuts) was an effective safety net in a country without unemployment insurance. It occurred at a time when other employment opportunities were not available. In addition, keeping the work force in health care and education more or less intact meant that provision of these services did not have to be reduced. Indirectly, this afforded some protection to those who are the large consumers of primary education and public health—the poor and the middle class.

However, some of the programs that were geared to the very poor suffered greater budget cuts than the rest. They were also decentralized. Because of a lack of resources, administrative capacity, and know-how at the local level, this decentralization seriously diminished their impact. There was also an attempt to replace the general food price subsidies with subsidized food targeted to the poor. But the subsidized food did not really reach them for several years. The Mexican government engaged in a concerted effort to channel resources to the poor with the launching of the program SOLIDARIDAD (also known as PRO-NASOL—the Spanish acronym of the National Solidarity Program). But this program was launched in 1989—seven years after the crisis had started.

PRONASOL and Mexico's Poor

In Mexico there have been a number of initiatives to reduce poverty over the last twenty years. A few were part of rural and regional development programs that were launched in the 1970s. In addition, the Mexican government tried for several decades to improve the living standards of the rural and urban poor through price-support mechanisms for some agricultural crops. They also increased generalized and targeted food subsidies, cheap credit, and the provision of free health care and education. And they expanded the provision of sewerage, running water, and electricity. Although no comprehensive evaluation of all these efforts exists, there are indications that some of them were not really giving priority to the poor. For example, the price-support mechanism or cheap-credit schemes did not reach the poorest producers or the poor landless peasants. The same was the case with the general food subsidies. They were targeted to the urban sectors, which did not include the rural poor as their beneficiaries. This ran counter to the fundamental objective of PRONASOL—to target resources to the poor in rural and urban areas.

PRONASOL was conceived as an umbrella organization in charge of coordinating health, education, infrastructure, and productive projects designed to improve the living conditions of the poor. The bulk of these have been investment projects that were designed to expand, rehabilitate, or improve the infrastructure available for the provision of basic services. They included health clinics, hospitals, schools, water-supply systems, sewage systems, electrification, roads, and food-distribution stores. A small number of projects took the form of transfers, such as a scholarship program to primary school children, interest-free loans provided to some production projects, and, particularly, the nutrition and health programs.

Due to its complexities and to a lack of information, it is difficult to make a global assessment of PRONASOL's impact. The projects that seem to have had a significant effect on large numbers of people are those that were directed toward investment in infrastructure, such as water-supply systems, sewerage, and electrification. In terms of spending, additional facilities, and beneficiaries, the numbers indicate that living conditions are improving. The projects that have concentrated on improving health and nutrition are very effective. But as of 1994, they had not been implemented on a large scale.

One disquieting factor is that PRONASOL's spending was not in balance with the incidence of poverty in the individual states. Some of its critics say that political/electoral criteria intruded. However, there also may be less Machiavellian reasons for this spending pattern. For example, demand-driven projects may omit the poorest because they live in isolated areas or lack the capacity to organize themselves. Whatever the reason, if the government wants to allocate the bulk of its resources to overcome extreme poverty, these programs will have to adopt a more "intentional" approach, rather than relying primarily on demand-driven projects.

Also, although investment in water sanitation, sewerage, electrification, health posts, and schools is crucial and increases the welfare of the poor, it will not reduce that aspect of poverty that is caused by the lack of adequate income. What is the advantage of having a good health clinic, a good school building, or running water if family income is too low to bring food intake to the acceptable nutritional minimum? The increase in infrastructure needs to be complemented with more direct transfers of purchasing power. There is a need for targeted health and nutrition programs and food for education programs.

Total spending on PRONASOL was equal to 0.45 percent of Mexico's GDP in 1989 and went up to more than 1.0 percent in 1993. As a point of comparison, the entire budget allocated for social development was slightly above 6 percent in 1989 and around 9 percent in 1993. Extreme poverty could be eliminated if an amount equivalent to 0.25 percent of Mexico's GDP was fully redistributed to the poor every year. This is a very rough calculation, since it does not take into account administrative costs or leakages to the nonpoor. However, rough as they are, these numbers indicate that the amounts required to eliminate extreme poverty are fiscally and politically feasible.

To what extent could one rely on "trickle-down" processes to eradicate poverty in Mexico? A very straightforward exercise shows that growth alone may reduce extreme poverty too slowly. For example, if the per capita income of the extremely poor grew at about 1.0 percent per year (a rate above the average in the last four years), the bottom 10 percent of the population would have to wait nearly fifty years just to overcome extreme poverty. Rough as this calculation may be, it shows that antipoverty programs should be part of Mexico's government agenda for many years to come. In fact, Mexico's new president, Ernesto Zedillo, has already made a commitment to fight poverty through a plan that will have two tracks: (1) guaranteed access to basic services such as education, health, nutrition, and housing to the poorest sectors; and (2) more employment opportunities for the needy. The problem is that the recent financial crisis will leave the government with fewer resources to undertake the antipoverty programs on any grand scale—at least in the short run.

Rural Poverty

Poverty in rural areas is close to three times higher than in urban areas and is concentrated in regions with large indigenous populations. According to the population census, in 1990, while 32 percent of the population lived in the eight poorest states in Mexico (measured by average per capita GDP), these same states had 65 percent of the indigenous population. Sixty-nine percent of the households lived in extreme poverty and received only 17 percent of Mexico's GDP. Chiapas, as expected, is one of these states. The remaining seven are Oaxaca (which has the lowest per capita GDP—even lower than Chiapas), Guerrero, Hidalgo, Michoacán, Puebla, Veracruz, and Zacatecas. These states are poor by any measure. Whereas the 1990 illiteracy rate for the entire population was estimated at 12.5 percent by the National Population Council (CONAPO), the average for these eight states was 22 percent. The percentage of people without electricity and running water was 13 percent. It was 21 percent for the country as a whole. The average was 24 percent for the poorest eight states and 36 percent for the nation. The indigenous population for these eight states is 16 percent of the total population, with Oaxaca showing the highest proportion (39 percent), followed by Chiapas (26 percent).

Countrywide figures, however, indicate that substantial progress was achieved in the expansion of basic services during the 1980s. For example, between 1980 and 1990, the rate of illiteracy fell from about 17 percent to 12.5 percent, and the proportion of people without running water and electricity fell from over 50 and 30 percent respectively to 21 and 13 percent. This progress must have benefited not only the richest but also the poorest states. However, in the latter, much still remains to be done.

Also, during the last few years, the government introduced reforms to decentralize decision making to the state and municipal governments. As a result, local governments now have more influence over public investment and services in their states and municipalities. In addition, as of 1990, the federal revenue-sharing formula was modified. The change resulted in a 64 percent real increase in federal transfers to the four poorest states (Chiapas, Guerrero, Hidalgo, and Oaxaca). The new revenue-sharing formula meant that the ratio of the transfers going to the richest states to those going to the poorest ones has been reduced by about one-third. In contrast, the federally financed investments, which are nearly twice that of revenue-sharing funds, are not driven by any formula. They are highly concentrated in a few states (not the poorest ones) and the federal district. Clearly, this is one area in which progress to redirect resources to the very poor can be made.

Chiapas and NAFTA

When the Chiapas uprising occurred on January 1, 1994 (the first day of NAFTA), many began to wonder whether NAFTA had been the cause of the rebellion. It is true that the implementation of NAFTA implies that some sectors will get hurt, and one of them is peasant agriculture. As liberalization brings the domestic price of corn down to international levels, the income of peasants is bound to fall. However, the exposure of corn and other crops to external competition is to take place in a period of fifteen years. In the meantime, the Mexican government has launched a program known as PROCAMPO, which, if adequately implemented, should partially compensate growers for their losses for that period. PROCAMPO compensates the rich as well as the poor growers. But it is likely to be more progressive than the previous system of price supports that usually left out the poorest growers. Zedillo has promised to keep PROCAMPO in place and to complement it with other policies to give direct support to rural workers. As a result of the devaluation, the price differential between imported corn (now more expensive in pesos) and domestic corn will narrow. Because of this, the required compensation because of lower trade barriers will also be smaller.

The connection between the Chiapas uprising and NAFTA is perhaps more symbolic in nature. The Chiapas revolt is the desperate protest of a group that feels it has been neglected for decades. It is a protest of those who feel they have been left behind while the rest pushed ahead. Although poverty in Chiapas has existed for a long time, the situation became aggravated when the international price of coffee dropped sharply (as a result of the unraveling of the existing international agreement), and no adequate safety nets were in place to cushion the blow. In spite of the fact that Chiapas received increasingly more PRONASOL resources, the anger expressed by a population ready to take up arms is an indication that something went wrong in the use of these resources.

It is beyond any doubt that poverty, lack of political freedom, and discrimination by the local elite (in particular) is at the root of the Chiapas uprising. Chiapas has the highest incidence of poverty (36 percent of the households live in extreme poverty) of all the Mexican states. However, one of the paradoxes is that the uprising occurred when the federal government had increased resources. More needs to be known about the leadership of the Zapatista National Liberation Army, its historical roots, and its ideological convictions to explain why government efforts to improve living conditions of Chiapas's poor did not convince the Zapatistas that armed struggle was neither desirable nor necessary.

Is NAFTA going to hurt the poor? When answering this question, the important thing is to net-out the positive from the negative effects and see what remains. Some will get hurt. Hence the need for a program such as PROCAMPO to avoid major dislocations of labor that will cause a rise in poverty in the rural areas. However, in the face of the new situation that arose in Mexico as a result of the financial crisis that started at the end of 1994, NAFTA's most important contribution in the short term and medium term will be to ensure market access for Mexican goods and stimulate direct foreign investment into Mexico. Capital inflows from other private sources will probably decline sharply as a consequence of the recent developments in Mexico. Once the financial crisis is over, foreign direct investment will play a very important role in sustaining growth in output and wages in the future.

In the longer run, the specific benefits that NAFTA will bring are probably difficult to imagine. As the adoption of more advanced technology gradually permeates Mexico's economic sectors, productivity will increase at a faster pace. This will translate into higher growth rates of national income and wages. It is true that economic growth is not the full answer to overcoming poverty. But, without growth, we can't even start to talk about reducing poverty. Also, the transformation that will occur in Mexico's productive structure as a result of NAFTA is bound to be large. So too will be the shifts of employment from low productivity to higher productivity and better-paid jobs. NAFTA can become one powerful factor in the quest for eradicating poverty in Mexico.

Part III

Quality of Life and Environment

16

DAVID E. LOREY

Education and the Challenges of Mexican Development

If you do not know what your country has, and what to do with it, your nation cannot grow. Modern economists find that the most important source of growth is educated people, whom they call "human capital." It has been the most important source of human development. Often carried out at home, in private schools, and by religious organizations, education has become the responsibility of the government. David Lorey notes that Article 3 of the Mexican Constitution of 1917 established education in Mexico as free, lay, and universal. The government has provided increased educational opportunities for its growing population. But the educational system has suffered from insufficient resources. Moreover, primary education is hampered by a dropout rate of 50 percent. Children leave school to work. Consequently, only two-thirds of the population is functionally literate. This is particularly important because primary education contributes more to economic development than do secondary and post-secondary training. Mexican educational policy, therefore, was designed to improve the quality of primary education as well as of college and post-college levels.

Attempts to change the content of the nationwide educational system has been resisted by the National Teachers Union. On the other hand, Carlos Salinas de Gortari's research (published in 1980) indicated that "rural dwellers see sending children to school as more important than voting." He also found that collective action by citizens at various tasks decreased their support for the political system. Nonetheless, his administration established PRONASOL educational programs, in which residents provided one-half the funds and labor for school projects. The government provided supplies and grants to children. These expenditures permitted them to attend school. Under President Salinas de Gortari and his Secretary of Education Ernesto Zedillo, the government gave incentives to universities. They matched their needs to government priorities and provided salary supplements to faculty for publication and outstanding teaching. In 1992, the share of federal spending on education was 3.50 percent of GDP almost equal to the previous high of 3.77 percent in 1982. On December 1, 1994, President Ernesto Zedillo pledged that all Mexican children would complete high school by the end of his administration.

Mexican policy changes leading to educational improvements indicate an understanding that the wealth of a nation is its people.

Article 3 of the Mexican Constitution of 1917 establishes that education in Mexico is to be free, lay, and universal. It traditionally has been interpreted to mean that the government is responsible for providing education through the primary and secondary levels—the key areas of weakness in the Mexican educational system at the beginning of the century. But, over time, Mexicans have increasingly considered themselves entitled to free education at all levels, including the university level. The two flagship public institutions of higher education —the National Autonomous University of Mexico (UNAM) and the National Polytechnic Institute (IPN)—charge only nominal fees for their services. Even with this high level of state commitment to public education, however, privately funded and operated schools exist at all levels in Mexico—especially at the secondary and university levels.

Weaknesses of Early Education

Many factors have complicated the achievement of the educational policy goals which were enshrined in the 1917 constitution—particularly that basic education be universal. Some factors are related to Mexico's historical past. For example, at least one hundred indigenous languages (most unrelated to each other) are spoken in Mexico's rural areas. Fully 10 percent of Mexicans—almost nine million—do not speak Spanish. Bilingual schools reach only a small part of this population.

By far the most serious problem at the basic level of education is high and persistent drop-out rates. Only about 50 percent of entering students at any level complete their studies. In rural areas of the country, approximately 75 percent of school children do not finish the first six years of primary education. Family economic factors seem to play the most important single role in the high dropout rates. Parents need children to contribute to family income. Dropout rates are higher in rural areas where families who make their living in subsistence agriculture are more likely to need the labor of children. Even in urban areas, the poorest Mexican families frequently rely on children's economic contribution in order to make ends meet. Schools do little to encourage attendance by poor children. There are few free-lunch or free-milk programs to help defray family costs or provide an incentive for study.

In addition to high dropout rates, teaching conditions at the primary and secondary levels are generally poor. Most classrooms in the country have over forty children per teacher. A single teacher is frequently responsible for as many as six grades. Many schools do not extend over the full six or twelve years.

Teachers are often very young and poorly trained, and are sometimes not even available in many areas of the country.

The primary and secondary school curriculum also inhibits learning. Controlled by the Ministry of Public Education (SEP), the curriculum is uniform throughout the country. As a result, it is often irrelevant to regional conditions. It ignores local occupational structure—particularly in rural areas. Furthermore, the curriculum is linked to the obligatory use of Free Textbooks (*Libros de Texto Gratuitos*), which also often do not reflect regional realities. Each grade has a standard curriculum. If children do not master it, they are forced to repeat the exact same curriculum. This discipline contributes to frustration, boredom, and dropping out.

Overall, the emphasis of national basic-education programs has been on access rather than on relevance or quality. The National Teachers Union (SNTE) is among the strongest political forces in Mexico. Historically, the primary objective of the union has been higher pay for member teachers. Little effort has been made by the SNTE to upgrade skills or introduce innovations in teaching techniques.

As a result of such continuing challenges, educational coverage and attainment in Mexico have been disappointing. At the primary level, entering-class coverage is 75.6 percent (ages 6–14), but coverage falls at every higher level. It is 40.1 percent at the secondary level (ages 12–16), 21.3 percent at the preparatory level (ages 16–19), and 14.9 percent at the university level (ages 20–24). Low completion rates further reduce coverage. There was an estimated population of about fifteen million fifteen-year-olds and older in 1990. Thirteen percent had never attended primary school; 7 percent had only two years of schooling; and 15 percent had three to five years. Such data on the primary level indicate that functional literacy in Mexico (found only among those who have completed the fourth grade) remains the domain of only about two-thirds of the Mexican population. Fully 60.8 percent of those aged fifteen and older had not completed secondary school.

Reform Targets

Some attempts at broad educational reform to address the obvious shortcomings of the primary and secondary system were made in the 1980s. In general, they resulted in an impasse, because the SNTE was intransigent in its support of the status quo. It refused to establish programs to retrain teachers, modify their outlook, or improve their capacity. In response, the government attempted to decentralize education to the states. This move would have weakened the SNTE by requiring sections of the union to deal directly with state authorities. But this strategy had few noticeable results. Attacking from another front, the government tried to modify the free required textbooks. This action was seen as a way to change the way school children were taught without taking on the SNTE directly. This effort also met with resistance from both the union and intellectuals who were unhappy with the books' untraditional portrayal of Mexican history. As a result, the new textbooks are not widely in use.

President Carlos Salinas de Gortari's alternative social program, Solidarity (PRONASOL), provided a significant boost to primary education policy between 1988 and 1994. In part because Salinas saw schoolchildren sitting on wooden crates during a campaign stop in a poor area of Mexico City during 1988, Solidarity provided funds for the building and refurbishing of schools in areas that were hard-hit by the economic crisis of the 1980s. Generally, residents provided one-half the funds and the labor for PRONASOL school projects. The government supplied equipment, building supplies, and technical advice. Solidarity also established a program of grants. Schoolchildren voted on which classmates would receive funds to help their families while grantees attended school.

Primary and secondary education remain an extremely important issue in Mexico. Forty-five percent of the population is under fifteen years old—roughly primary- and secondary-school age. While the percentage of those under fifteen years old has remained around 45 percent since 1950, the absolute number of school-age children has grown dramatically—from about 11 million in 1950 to about 36 million in 1990. In 1950, 3 million children were in school (27 percent of the school-age population). In 1990, 24 million were in school (67 percent of school-age population).

The issue of basic education in Mexico is also important to the United States and to U.S.-Mexican economic and social relations. Clearly, a population of limited functional literacy and numeracy may restrict the extent to which Mexico can take advantage of NAFTA. There is also an impact in the United States because, until recently, it received a majority of its Mexican immigrants from rural areas, where the basic education infrastructure is weakest.

The Public University System

University training has attracted more attention than any other educational level over the last few decades. The controversies that have swirled around the university system stem from the two most important aims of Mexican universities: (1) to produce the skills needed for economic development; and (2) to produce social mobility by providing access to professional careers. The ability of the university system to carry out each of these missions has been much criticized in the period since the late 1950s. Notions of a "university crisis" have become widespread among policy makers and the general public.

At the time of postrevolutionary political consolidation in 1929, the nation's flagship public university—UNAM—claimed one-third of national enrollment at the professional level. IPN was founded in 1937 as the nation's flagship polytechnic school. UNAM and IPN quickly consolidated their grips on the university scene. By 1938, they claimed 72.7 percent of all higher-level enrollment.

Until the 1950s, UNAM and IPN dominated all aspects of professional training. In the 1950s, their share fell as enrollment at provincial public universities and private institutions grew. By the mid-1960s, UNAM and IPN claimed less than one-half of Mexico's university enrollment.

Competing public institutions reduced the dominance of UNAM and IPN. The growth of regional public universities served to relieve the pressure of increasing enrollments at UNAM and IPN by keeping a part of increased demand for higher educational opportunities confined to the states. In 1974, the public Autonomous University of Mexico City (UAM) was established to counterbalance the political importance of the two public university giants, as well as to solve growing problems of overcrowding.

The Private University System

In the 1940s, the foundation of private universities picked up pace. After the late 1950s, they gradually came to achieve real influence. In 1929, Mexico had only five universities—all public. By 1958, it had 125 universities—53 of them private. By 1982, it had 315 universities—148 of them private. And in 1987, it had 362—191 of them private. The private share of university enrollment grew from 10.3 percent of total university enrollment in 1959 to 14.9 by 1964. In 1976, private university graduates accounted for 14.4 percent of all graduates. By 1985, they reached 19.8 percent. And in 1992, graduates from private universities accounted for 22.6 percent of total graduates.

Private universities were founded for two essential reasons: (1) to provide instruction that was not infused with the socialist ideology so strong at public universities; and (2) to fulfill needs for highly qualified professionals—primarily in the private sector. The Monterrey Technological Institute (ITESM), for example, was founded in response to the development of the robust industrial economy of Monterrey, Nuevo León. Adopting the California Institute of Technology and MIT as models, ITESM filled the needs for professional skills which were needed by regional employers. The more recently founded Autonomous Technical Institute of Mexico (ITAM) was established in Mexico City to produce non-Marxist business managers and economists to supplant the radical economists graduating from UNAM. Generally, private schools established curricula in line with government economic development policy and with the government's own needs for expertise. Historically, there have been significant differences in quality between public and private universities. These differences reflect responses to the demands of different market sectors for professional and technical skills.

Economic Development

The ability of the Mexican economy to absorb university graduates at the professional level has not grown as fast as the number of university students entering professional courses of study. After the 1950s, enrollment at the university level grew dramatically. It surged from 28,000 in 1960, to 270,000 in 1970, to 810,000 in 1980, and to 1,196,000 in 1990.

In the thirty-year period from 1950 to 1980, 622,257 graduates left Mexican universities to fill 440,000 new jobs for professionals. Between 1980 and 1990, 1,305,294 graduates were produced for 311,452 new professional-level jobs. By the 1960s, the demand for professionals was met and exceeded. By the end of the 1980s, there were about a million graduates for whom no professional jobs were available. Over the same period, the demand for technicians grew at a much faster rate than for professionals. As a result, university graduates increasingly found work below the level of their qualifications and expectations. This mismatch placed significant social and political pressures on the system.

Weak demand for university graduates resulted from at least two characteristics of the Mexican economy. First, employment opportunities for professionals were restricted by high levels of protection. Protection allowed Mexican industry to produce goods with outmoded equipment, minimal investment for research and development, and little innovation. These practices limited the need for associated professional knowledge. Second, the importation of capital goods also reduced employment opportunities for professionals. The reliance on imported capital goods meant that professional education was most stimulated in the countries that produced advanced capital goods. Such features of the Mexican economy greatly restricted the potential employment for university graduates with training in such fields as engineering, science, and business administration.

Public and private universities in Mexico increasingly acted together as a system in responding to the needs of the economy. They allocated university students among different labor markets. In general, the provincial public universities produced more dropouts than graduates. Most of those dropouts found employment as technicians or other nonprofessional workers. Private universities in economically dynamic regions produced the highest-quality degree holders. Most of these graduates went on to work as professionals. The majority of them found employment in the private sector. The oldest and largest public universities—UNAM and IPN—performed both functions. They produced high-quality graduates as well as large numbers of persons who found work at subprofessional levels. This pattern of public and private differentiation proved useful because of the importance of the social role of the public universities enshrined in official rhetoric.

University Reform Debate

A major controversy over university reform emerged with the economic crisis of the 1980s. Critical analyses of the university system exposed a wide variety of apparent problems in the public higher education system. Among them were obsolete curricula and inadequate laboratories, libraries, computer facilities, and other research infrastructure. Another was the low level of training among faculty. Two-thirds of professors had only the licentiate degree; just 2 percent held doctorate degrees; only 6 percent were actively involved in research. The analyses also revealed weak graduate programs. Only 3 percent of graduate students were Ph.D. candidates. Finally, the predictable financial stresses that were related to the reliance on government subsidies, poor secondary-school preparation of entering university students, and overcrowded campuses and classrooms (as universities absorbed unemployed college-age youths) exacerbated the problems.

President Miguel de la Madrid's term of office (1982–88) coincided with the most difficult period of the economic crisis and with the most concentrated criticism of Mexican universities. Shortly after taking office, de la Madrid introduced a policy to modernize higher education that focused on the geographical decentralization of university operations, shifting costs and responsibilities to the states. Results were limited. States did not have the financial resources to fund a geographical substitution of higher educational opportunities.

As President Carlos Salinas de Gortari (1988–94) began to reshape industrial production to make Mexican products competitive in the world economy, he encouraged the reform of the university system. His goal was to match it with the new economy of privatization and freer trade. Inefficient public universities received strong criticism under Salinas. Salinas's minister of public education, Ernesto Zedillo (later elected president for the 1994–2000 term), publicly questioned the "viability and future" of the public universities. He commented that a crisis of "quality and pertinence" had led many Mexicans to favor private institutions. Ideas for dramatic changes at public universities that were never before openly discussed emerged in the policy arena. Some of these were the limitation of the size of the student body, the raising of fees, the separation of university high schools from universities, the elimination of the automatic pass from public high schools to universities, and the establishment of closer ties with the private sector. Salinas established an informal system of incentives and penalties for public universities. Universities that supported government initiatives by tailoring their programs to government needs and orientations were rewarded with budgetary allocations that kept up with inflation. Universities that encouraged advanced research in priority fields were granted special salary supports for active researchers.

A new emphasis on faculty productivity resulted in a major expansion of the National System of Researchers (SNI). Established in 1984 to boost incomes among university researchers, it rewarded published research efforts. The government used the SNI to reward the most productive public-university academicians with bonuses that, in many cases, equaled 50 percent of their salary. After 1992, SNI was paired with programs that awarded salary supplements to outstanding academicians who dedicated most of their time to teaching. The federal government also established a special fund—the Fondo para Modernizar la Educación Superior (FOMES)—to support innovative quality-enhancement programs.

Internal university policy increasingly focused on the evaluation of university programs, faculty, and students. In line with the SEP's 1989 Educational Modernization Program, several projects were established to evaluate Mexican universities. Among them was the influential National Evaluation Commission (CONAEVA). In 1990, for the first time ever, almost all Mexican universities submitted self-evaluation reports to the SEP. They anticipated that the reports would play a role in determining federal subsidies. In 1991, interinstitutional peer-review committees were established to assess the quality of academic programs within universities. Increasingly, evaluation programs across the country were standardized. In 1994, a National Evaluation Center was established to design and administer pilot entrance and achievement exams.

Many of the new initiatives resulted from close consultation and collaboration with foreign countries and foreign education experts. This was a practice that previously had been taboo in Mexico. NAFTA established norms for developing equivalent procedures and standards for the certification of academic quality with a view toward the free flow of students and professionals in North America. When Mexico joined the Organization for Economic Cooperation and Development (OECD) in 1994, it was required to undergo a thorough evaluation of its higher education system by that organization. Many public universities in the Mexican states instituted far-reaching changes in faculty qualifications, curricula, admissions and degree requirements, and financing in attempts to win accreditation by U.S. university associations. Some universities hired the U.S. College Entrance Examination Board to institute admissions testing.

Looking toward the Future

The overall picture emerging in primary and secondary education by the mid-1990s is one of continuing expansion of coverage and extension of the successful Solidarity strategy of using community initiative to reinforce government policy. President Ernesto Zedillo took office on December 1, 1994, with a pledge to see all Mexican children through secondary school by the end of his administration. On the higher-education level, the trend toward thorough and serious evaluation and rapidly increasing quality and diversity throughout the Mexican university system is well established. Instead of an outmoded system that is dominated by a few public university giants and a focus on expanding enrollment at any cost, the university system appears to be shifting to a focus on the development of high-quality programs at many different institutions—public and private—in many regions of the country.

17

JORDY MICHELI

Technology Policy for a Weak Market

Research and development are extensions of education. In "Technology Pol-icy for a Weak Market," Jordy Micheli points out that Mexico has a weak research and development sector. During the Salinas administration, assis-tance to research and development was directed to research needed for eco-nomic development, rather than to "pure" research, preventing development of high technology for capital-intensive industries. Large firms invested in new technology and training of personnel, working toward standardization and environmental technologies.

The government adopted a new technology policy in the nineties. It required matching private funds for government spending on technology. Moreover, in order to increase the transfer of technology through foreign investment, the government decreased its intervention in the economy and provided better pro-tection of industrial property rights. This has led to a greater emphasis on the commercial nature of innovation and an increase in applications for patents. Although a variety of problems of technology policy were addressed by the Salinas administration, Micheli believes that it did not take sufficient action to protect the environment or to spread generic technology. This is especially im-portant because investment, technology, and population determine economic growth.

The Background

The size of its economy has placed Mexico among the top twenty countries worldwide; besides, Mexico has, for the past twenty years, had a government agency responsible for defining and implementing policies in science and tech-nology (the National Council for Science and Technology, CONACYT). Never-theless, when its efforts in R&D are compared with those of other nations, Mexico presents a situation of notorious weakness. The 1991 figures show that its proportion of gross domestic expenditure on R&D as part of total GDP was

Table 17.1

CONACYT: Evolution of Expenses by Technological Program
(basis = 100 in the starting years, constant 1980 pesos)

Program	1989	1990	1991	1992	1993
Innovation					
-Technological projects	100	250	—	—	—
-Shared risk	100	94	—	—	—
-Technology for production	—	100	—	—	—
-Technology for industry	—	—	—	100	110
Infrastructure					
-Incubators	—	—	100	1,900	2,400
Human Resources					
-Human resources	—	—	100	320	800
-Academy-industry	—	—	100	425	330
Total	100	520	110	940	1,300

Source: Calculated from CONACYT's unpublished data.

0.33 percent, while the total R&D personnel per thousand in the labor force was 0.9 percent (OECD 1994, 56). Such figures present Mexico as the worst ranked among members of the OECD countries.

Actually, what Mexico intended to accomplish during the 1988–94 sexennium was a process of modernization in the field of technology to help raise Mexico to world levels in capabilities, human resources, and innovation. This process was based on the needs of the market instead of on assigned priorities. Thus, it was a sectorial complement to the general economic model, characterized by its liberal creed (see Table 17.1). From the point of view of a scientist, the focus on economic development kept Mexicans from concentrating on the technological problem as such. This was especially unfortunate because now—just as this chapter is being written—the financial failure of this model, which used to be considered successful, is becoming widely known. One of the consequences of the model is that, because Mexico does not have a comparative advantage either in high technology or capital-intensive industries, the development of a privately financed market for technology to serve Mexican industry is inhibited. Consequently, the historical weaknesses of the Mexican R&D system could hardly be overcome within this context, which limited the development of a market for technological innovation. As the OECD recognized, "The most striking fact about science and technology in Mexico is the exceptionally modest amount of R&D performed by the business enterprise sector, whether local or foreign-owned . . . ; private industry is spending only 0.06 to 0.08 of GDP on

R&D" (OECD 1994, 165). Another survey showed that in 1991, the spending on R&D was 0.6 percent of the Mexican-owned enterprises' income, and the same ratio was 0.5 percent for foreign-owned enterprises.[1]

The Industrial Basis Changes, the Problem Remains

The import substitution model that prevailed over decades is the starting point of our analysis. As "structuralist" economists point out, technical progress is a weak participant in economic growth in Latin American countries, because its industrial behavior imitates that of other nations and is not based on an examination of internal needs and capabilities. This simply adds to the overprotected, oligopolistic, and socially excluding nature of the import substitution model, which reached its limits during the seventies.

Throughout the eighties, Mexico's economy was characterized by the carrying out of a deep macroeconomic adjustment and a process of long-run economic reform. The manufacturing sector went from extensive growth supported by the accumulation of capital and slow job absorption so typical of the late phase of import substitution, to slowed-down growth of an intense use of production factors. This phase was known for its generalized decrease in net capital funds and intense reorganization of labor relations, characteristic of the export-oriented automotive, maquila, and petrochemical industries that led the economy.

That shift exacerbated the duality of the industrial structure: one part had a dynamic nucleus, technologically and organizationally well developed, incorporated to the global tendencies; and another part had a passive manufacturing sector composed of micro, small, and medium-sized factories with a short life. In 1991, 85.5 percent of manufacturing enterprises were classified as micro (1–15 employees); 10.4 percent as small (16–100 employees); 2.2 percent as medium (101–250 employees); and only 1.8 percent as big (more than 250 employees). The total number of enterprises was 120,701, of which 70.6 percent were from one to fifteen years old, but the micro-enterprises represented 73.7 percent of that youngest segment.[2]

In the first nucleus, the firms have been successful in assimilating and adapting generic technologies, such as CAD, CAM, and total quality. Such generic technologies are characteristic for being evolutionary in terms of innovations, entailing the upgrading of firms' technological services. This requires the development of human resources with specialized training, software, maintenance for high-tech equipment, R&D, and "inverse engineering." Taken together, the adoption of these technologies has made the firms more competitive. Another aspect of technological development is that there has been an increasing search for standardization and environmental technologies, as a result of international pressure. That industrial reality forces us to think about the requirements of a technology policy.

New Objectives and Instruments

In the early nineties, the government established a new technology policy. The two main regulatory instruments that defined it were the National Program for Science and Technological Modernization and the Law to Protect Industrial Property Rights. They reflect a coherent vision, based on two assumptions:

1. Innovations in Mexico do not depend as much on the ability of the government to provide them or induce others to do so as they do on institutions' ability to meet the needs of the market. Therefore, without denying the importance and responsibility of the role played by public investment in technology, the market will be the one to generate signals for effective allocation of such expense. Furthermore, a requirement for matching public and private funds for technological innovation is definitely established.

2. Modern technology transfer itself depends on a context that favors foreign investment. On the one hand, it is assumed that the investing enterprise is the one that provides technological inputs, while, on the other hand, it is assumed that better protection of industrial property and less government intervention will increase the transfer of modern technology. An outstanding fact is that the Law to Protect Industrial Property Rights offer levels of protection comparable to those of developed countries.

Such a new approach and its availability through the instruments of public policy promoted an incipient cultural change within the research centers, recognizing technology as a process with economic value rather than "applied science." This starting point of a conceptual divide is very important if we consider that over many decades, there was a dominating idea that science automatically drove us to technology, and technology drove us to economic development. Therefore, it was difficult to distinguish the evaluation of inputs, the capability, and the results of technological activity separately from the scientific one. The research centers have begun to pay more attention to the commercial nature of innovation and the search for private cooperation and funding. Much the same way, the new industrial property regulation implies a culture of patenting unknown until recently. As a result of the new legislation, the number of patent applications increased by 32 percent between 1991 and 1992.

CONACYT's Modernization Program

Henceforth, the activity of CONACYT will be considered representative of public intervention in the scope of technology. According to the OECD, "CONACYT is the primary agency responsible for defining and implementing science and technology policy. From 1989, CONACYT's budget has been increased substantially: between 1989 and 1994 it increased by 600 percent, more than 230 percent in real terms. A number of innovative funds have been established to improve S&T infrastructure and ties between industry and academia. . . . But it is important to point out that the CONACYT handles only 27 percent of all federal expenditure on S&T" (OECD 1994, 44–45, 59). On average, during the 1989–93 period, only 12.3 percent of CONACYT's total spending on scientific research and technology development was for technology.

The rest of federal expenditure on S&T is shared among other secretariats, institutes and, mainly, the National Autonomous University of Mexico (UNAM). It received 12 percent, the Mexican Petroleum Institute (IMP) 7 percent, and the Institute for Forestry and Agriculture (INIFAP) 6 percent of this federal spending.

By specific activities, during the 1990-93 period, between 57 percent and 67 percent of federal expenditure on S&T were channeled to research and development, between 17 percent and 27 percent went to scientific and technical education, and funds devoted to scientific and technological services fluctuated between 11 percent and 22 percent. During the same period, federal expenditure on S&T ranged from 0.20 percent to 0.22 percent of GDP.

The funds for technology have come about in three different fashions: for innovation (with credits at commercial rates); for the R&D infrastructure (with subsidized loans); and for human resources (with nonreimbursable financing).

As shown in Table 17.1, between 1989 and 1993 the structure of the modernization policy became more complex. In terms of the funds assigned to innovation, however, a hesitant attitude can be recognized on CONACYT's part. It had four different policy instruments throughout the period. In terms of percentage structure in 1993, human resources received 50 percent of funds, innovation 36.8 percent, and infrastructure 13.2 percent. Altogether, this allows us to make a synthesis of CONACYT's program of technological modernization. It presents a contradictory picture: (1) It was given a wider range of programs, searching to identify market segments for its funds, so that an advantage of such policy has been that of finer tuning than in the past. (2) The sum assigned to the execution of that policy has been dramatically increasing. However, within the context of the council's funding, financing technological modernization represented a significantly low portion, confirming that the lack of policy priorities can become, too, an obstacle for efficient resource allocation.

Conclusions

Ironically enough, the dramatic change in the economic model did not represent an important modification of the weaknesses that were once attributed to the import substitution model. There was a prevailing lack of scrutiny with regard to the policies needed in order to create national ability in technological innovation. Moreover, public funds were insufficient to offset the negative impact of stabilization policy on innovation.

Regardless of its macroeconomic significance, technology is basically a phenomenon of individual performers who have their own characteristics in terms of business capability, time of response, competitive environment, etc. For instance, basic performers such as medium-sized and small enterprises did not have support programs that could be considered well defined. Problems known to have national priority, such as the deterioration of the environment, were not properly supported with programs specific to the development of appropriate technology. In addition, technology policy did not take action on the transferring of technology and the spreading of generic technology, which are strategies well known for their impact on the system of innovation and the industry.

All in all, the fact is that there were no solid answers for healthy preoccupations regarding the technological concern. In the end, the economic recession that is presently coming about will clearly manifest the weak and hesitant approach of the Salinas administration toward technological issues.

Notes

1. Preliminary results of the National Census of Employment, Wages, Technology and Job Training in the Manufacturing Sector, Labor Secretary and International Labor Office.
2. Instituto Nacional de Estadistica, Geografica y Informatica and Secretaria del Trabajo y Prevision Social (INEGI and STPs) (1995).

Bibliography

Instituto Nacional de Estadistica, Geografia y Informatica and Secretaría del Trabajo y Prevision Social (INEGI and STPS) (1995), "Encuesta Nacional de Empleos, Salarios, Tecnologia y Capacitación en el Sector Manufacturero, 1992" (Mexico City: Instituto Nacional de Estadistica, Geografia y Informatica and Secretaria del Trabajo y Prevision Social).
OECD (1994), *Reviews of National Science and Policy. Mexico* (Paris: OECD).

18

El Centro Mexicano para la Filantropia

Understanding Mexican Philanthropy

Mexican philanthropy is an important area that is not well known outside of Mexico. El Centro Mexicano para la Filantropia defines the welfare system to include all groups and institutions whose goal is the transfer, without profit, of all types of resources and surpluses to eliminate social inequalities. The Mexican welfare system from the colonial period through the mid-nineteenth century was centered in church activities. The state took over these activities as a consequence of its expropriation of church assets in 1861. A century later, during the 1960s and 1970s, social welfare activities diversified. They were carried out by progressive elements of the church and university students, often drawn from the social sciences or political student organizations with a leftist ideology. In the 1980s, defense of the environment and of human rights were newly emphasized. The increasing social problems of that decade led to the founding of new institutions to solve problems of health and education.

In 1995, the Mexican welfare system, therefore, included many old institutions —often with a religious orientation—aiding low-income and handicapped groups. They are supplemented by nongovernmental organizations that promote development of the poorest communities, as well as special groups in the nation. There are few foundations in Mexico to fund the various welfare organizations, although in the last decade new organizations were created to promote philanthropy and to provide technical and professional support to existing organizations, which have been handicapped by the absence of Mexican legal provision for tax-deductible contributions and of a well-defined and administered tax and legal code for nonprofit organizations. Thus, the human environment needs a better institutional framework for its development.

A brief description of Mexican philanthropy at the present time calls for, first of all, an attempt to define our concept of philanthropy, since there is no consensus, at least in Mexico, on the meaning of the term, and there is disagreement on the name to be given to this social phenomenon. Second, a description (at least in broad terms) of the main historical characteristics of philanthropy is necessary in order to better understand, third, the present status and problems facing philanthropic institutions.

Philanthropy as a Social System

Just like the political, educational, and economic systems, philanthropy or welfare is a social system. Philanthropy is not a system that is lost among the myriad of institutions; it is rather integrated by a universal communications code that sets it apart from other systems and that determines the role of institutions. For example, the power code corresponds to the political system, knowledge is the code of the educational system. The elimination of deficits and the covering of needs is the code of the welfare system. From this perspective, welfare is a phenomenon dating back to the first human groups. Even in archaic societies, welfare institutions were important for the group's survival. The welfare system has evolved and become complex just like society has evolved and its needs become complex. The way a social system evolves is through differentiation, by creating new institutions that respond both to the system's own problems and to the demands imposed by the environment.

Such a simple system as the sharing of food with those who have lost their crops has evolved into the impressive U.S. private welfare system composed of over a million institutions with annual resources in excess of $400 billion. The individual welfare that forced individuals to reciprocate in order to ensure the group's survival in archaic societies has evolved into the institutional, programmed welfare characteristic of societies of the late twentieth century. And the relationship between welfare and ethics still exists, since, as of the Middle Ages, the church preached and disseminated the moral obligation of helping the needy and turned Christian charity into one of the main human virtues.

The forms adopted by philanthropy or welfare have become even more complex during the final years of the present century. It could be said that the welfare system integrates all those initiatives whose goal is the elimination of social deficits. Philanthropy has to do with the way civil society, through its organizations, groups, and individuals, is capable of recognizing the existence of needs and problems; of being interested in coping with them; and of developing and procuring the means (resources, thinking, organization, relationship and communication with others, procedures and agreements with other institutional forms, determination of responsibility and competence fields, action and relationship codes and rules) necessary to face them efficiently.

From this perspective, it includes all those groups and institutions—regardless of their motifs (ethical, social, ideological, or political) and of their work methods and concepts (welfare, development, self-management, etc.)—whose goal is to contribute to the transfer, without profit, of all types of resources and surpluses, material or nonmaterial (time, money, organization capacity, technical, or professional help) to groups in need or to cope with collective problems and needs.

This concept includes many organizations that were not considered similar previously. The problem remains one of giving a name to this universal phenomenon. In Mexico, the term "philanthropy" is rejected in some sectors; and "nongovernment organizations" is a negative and too general a term. In the United States, it is called the "third sector" or the "independent sector." But what is important is to understand the phenomenon referred to.

Historical Issues of Mexican Philanthropy

The history of the Mexican welfare system can be broadly divided into three main stages. The first stage goes from the early years of the Colonial era (1521) through the mid-nineteenth century—when liberalism reigned over the church and conservatism, and when the secularization of power and society began. The second stage went through the 1960s, when society became complex due to an accelerated industrialization and urbanization process, which resulted in a similar growth and diversification of nonprofit welfare institutions (*instituciones no lucrativas de ayuda social*, or INLAS) and the system's differentiation.

The first stage occurred between 1524, when the first welfare institution of New Spain was created—the Hospital de Jesus—and 1860, when the Reformation Laws and the military defeat of conservatives marked the beginning of the decline of the temporal power (and more slowly, the spiritual power) of the church; the welfare system was dominated by this powerful institution and its doctrine.

If one is to understand the philanthropic movement of those days, it is necessary to take into account the prevailing social structure, the reigning ideology, and the existing social problems. The main social actors were those the Spanish crown, represented by the viceroy's government and the Catholic church, which were not totally differentiated from one another. Together with a small group of Spaniards, they shared the power and the economic surpluses. The Catholic doctrine provided the elements to understand and to get to know the reality. The stratified social order was the natural one; the aim of history and of individual lives was salvation. The orthodoxy of the Catholic church (as this was the era of the Lutheran Reformation) stressed (as a means of salvation) the acceptance of this doctrine, compliance with a strict ethics code, and membership in the church (the reservoir of true faith on earth).

Besides possessing half of the Mexican territory, the church was in charge of creating the philanthropic institutions for its flock to freely access salvation. The goal was to create spaces where Catholics could exercise their Christian charity. This was the beginning of the powerful linkage between ethics and welfare. First and foremost was to reach salvation while social problems could take a back seat.

The chronicles written by the Spaniards of those days and other studies indicate that the main problems were, first of all, the conversion of the natives; second, the poor health conditions of the indigenous population that was reduced by the frequent epidemic outbreaks (over fifty of such outbreaks lasted twenty-eight years and were registered during the first eighty years of the colonization) which in turn generated a shortage of labor available for both the construction of cities and farm and mining production. The third main problem was poverty manifested by hunger and diseases.

After detailing the above scenario, it is not difficult to indicate which were the most important philanthropic institutions of that time and their functioning: hospitals and conversion schools created, organized, funded, and operated basically by the various individuals comprising the Catholic church of those days (the various dioceses and numerous religious orders). The crown and wealthy Spaniards also contributed to their funding. It is important to make it clear that the hospitals of those days were health care institutions as well as asylums, food delivery centers, and conversion centers. Those schools where the Spanish language and the gospel were taught to the natives were all parochial. These institutions were later differentiated during the seventeenth and eighteenth centuries, with the creation of asylums for the elderly, nurseries, and orphanages.

During the first decades after Mexico's independence (1821–57), the Catholic church increased its power and wealth to the point of openly competing for the control of the state. Mexican liberals were thus forced to pass the Reformation Laws, which provided for the separation of the church and the state, the expropriation of all church assets and the control of its participation in education. This was the beginning of the second stage, characterized by the secularization of cultural and political life, the strengthening of the Jacobinic political elite, the retreat of the church from political life, and the increasing participation and development of the state as the key institution of the twentieth-century Mexican society.

The second most important change was noticed not in the social structure but in the ideology. (In the late nineteenth century, Mexico remained a rural country plagued with inequalities and widespread poverty ruled by an elite, a country with some touches of modernity here and there, budding industries and exporting farm regions, which were the origin of new social groups—the bourgeoisie and the small bourgeoisie, some trade unions and guilds.) The introduction and dissemination of liberalism through the lodges gave rise to an important thought current, which became first a law (the 1857 Constitution turned liberal principles into political and social organization standards) and then a government (by defeating the Conservative army and executing Emperor Maximilian, the Liberals took power, only to lose it until the Revolution). There was then an alternative to the religious concept of the world in the field of ideas, the schools and the press. First of all, it was a scientific vision of society (positivism was the dogma of the new rulers and of the few public schools), which contrary to the religious conception, explained the functioning of society from itself and not from divine will. Social inequality, for example, was not any more a natural situation, wished by God, but a social one. Second (and characteristic of the secularization process), religious issues were removed from public spaces and were confined to the individual in private.

Those changes experienced during the last decades of the nineteenth century had important consequences for the welfare system. First, the expropriation of the church assets in 1861 resulted in a number of the philanthropic institutions being transferred to the state, which then created the Public Welfare Funds Directorate to administer them. Due to the rickety government finances, its fate was no different than that of their beneficiaries: permanent poverty. Some other institutions remained under the control of the church through strawmen or in the hands of Catholic organizations closely related to the clergy. Besides the division between public and private welfare, this was a period conducive to neither the creation of new organizations nor the consolidation of the welfare system, since at least until 1940 the state had insufficient resources to foster them. The church and individuals saw their scarce philanthropic efforts restrained due to the enactment of a law that excessively limited and controlled this type of institution and that remains almost unchanged to date for private welfare institutions.

The second consequence of this liberal reform, and probably the most important one, was the redefinition of the terms "charity" and "welfare." Whereas charity was important for Catholicism as a means of salvation for those who practice it, regardless of its result (the social order was difficult to change since it was a natural order), positivism stressed the result of the charity action. Positivism advocated a society of people free from the ties of religious and metaphysical thought, a society based on the principles of science and technology. This called for the formation of new and useful people and good workers through an education separated from religious principles. Christian charity was conducive only to the perpetuation of laziness, mendicancy, and delinquency. On the contrary, true welfare, or "intelligent charity," was aimed at eliminating those social conditions that led people to poverty and vices. This liberal-positive concept gave rise to a new type of philanthropic institution: the school of arts and crafts, which served as a laboratory where the positivistic thesis of the creation of new and free people was put to the test. Some of these schools were organized by a minority of individuals who thought that welfare should be their responsibility and not that of the church or the state. And this issue has been strongly debated during the past few years.

Following the Mexican Revolution early in the twentieth century (1910–20), the state was consolidated, among other things, through a widespread social policy aimed at meeting the needs of millions of poor people and implemented by huge government agencies. For that reason, the supply of education, health, housing, and many other services has been mostly controlled by the bureaucracy. Limited public welfare activities were carried out by the "national volunteers group," whose members were the wives of government officials. It used the same spirit and welfare methods as the private charity organizations in creating asylums, distributing food, funding orphanages, etc.

After a fruitful but brief period reassessing its social activity, initiated by the *Rerum Novarum* encyclical letter (which resulted in the creation of Catholic farm and urban workers' groups that fought for the elimination of alcoholism and unemployment and tried to improve the standard of living of Indians, etc.), the Catholic church limited its nonspiritual actions to the traditional welfare institutions. These included orphanages, asylums, clinics, and, above all, schools. The church created thousands of religious schools in spite of the constitutional mandate.

One of the consequences of the predominance of two omnipresent institutions in the life of the country—the church and the state—has been a weakness of civil society as manifested by the existence of just a few organizations independent from the state power and a deeply rooted paternalistic and state culture in which most individuals expect the government to do everything for them. The business sector was remarkably absent from the welfare system through the 1960s, which mark the beginning of the third historical stage of philanthropy. As religion was limited to privacy and charity was thus a personal issue rather than a social one, and as the populist and benefactor state attributed to itself the sole responsibility for the well-being of the population, it was easy for the business sector to detach itself from its social role. While in the United States, the big companies have been forced to take on the social problems (such as education, health, and poverty) and to create large private institutions for fear of an interventionist state and the implementation of socialism as a means of improving workers' social standards, such conditions did not exist in Mexico, as the state's objective was to avoid these dangers. Though some Mexican businessmen may contribute personally through donations to institutions, most believe that businesses have no responsibility in such issues.

This lethargy of civil society via-à-vis Mexico's growing social problems and the statization of the welfare system was changed as of the 1960s, with a diversification of the institutions based on new phenomena and new concepts of social reality.

During the sixties and seventies, the worsening of social inequalities, which became the main problem to be solved by society, was interpreted as a structural phenomenon. From the Marxist perspective (the capitalist production and relations structures, the theory of dependency), this called for structural changes rather than welfare solutions. Development was to be attained through the transformation of the economic and political structures. And the Catholic church also began to renew itself. The Second Vatican Council and the Medellin Conference in Latin America had already taken place, with the latter resulting in the preference for the poor. The Theology of Liberation just began to expand.

These two phenomena resulted in the emergence in Mexico of numerous

groups and institutions devoted not to welfare but to the promotion of neglected groups in the rural and urban areas. Behind those groups and institutions were the church progressive sectors, social sciences university students,
and some political student organizations with a leftist ideology. The goal was
to change the structures and to overcome poverty through popular education
(Paulo Freire's influence on those groups was definite), production and consumption cooperatives, technical and organizational assistance, health promotion with popular and traditional techniques, and political integration and
organization. Included in this integral development promotion spree was an
important business contribution: the Mexican Foundation for Rural Development (Fundacion Mexicana para el Desarrollo Rural). It was fostered and
funded by Christian businessmen who searched for nonpaternalistic strategies
that would "help peasants to help themselves" (which was their motto) without changing the economic and political structures.

In the 1980s, the philanthropic system experienced a deepening of its diversification process because of the increasing seriousness of social problems resulting from the Mexican economic crisis and the new ideological trends (the
questioning of the benefactor state, its decreasing intervention in some sectors,
and the crumbling of real socialism). The oldest welfare institutions adopted new
approaches; without abandoning their nature, they began to stress preventive and
community development activities. Other institutions were created to face new
health and education problems such as cancer, cerebral palsy, Down's syndrome,
drug addiction, and AIDS. Several institutions tried to improve the efficiency of
their work through staff training, improvement of funding systems, etc. The most
important private foundations were created during this period (besides the Foundation for Rural Development, such institutions as the Miguel Aleman Foundation, the Mexican Health Foundation, the Environment Education Foundation as
well as the Televisa, BANAMEX and BANCOMER foundations, and others),
and also the first organized and professional steps of the private sector in the
welfare system were taken.

The development promotion institutions began to revise their objectives, strategies, and ideology so as to be adapted to the new realities and to open new work
areas such as human rights and ecology. The number of new groups dedicated to
these activities has increased significantly during the past few years—this is not
an exclusive area of the left. Community groups, businessmen, housewives, professionals, and private university students, among others, have strongly embraced the case for the environment and the defense of human rights.

Mexican Philanthropy at Present

Briefly speaking, the welfare system at present is identified as follows:

1. A considerable number of old institutions—some with a hundred years'
experience—offer welfare services (hospitals, asylums for the elderly, orphan-

ages, special health care) to low-income and handicapped groups. Most of these philanthropic institutions preserve a strong religious content due to their origins or their relationship with the clergy. They exist because of the incapacity of the state, despite its widespread intervention in many of these fields of social life, to care for the neglected groups, and the immobility resulting from a huge bureaucracy.

2. A considerable number of groups promoting the social development of both urban and rural neglected groups (but not welfare) emerged as of the 1960s. These groups are known by the name of nongovernment organizations (NGOs). They have promoted the creation of popular organizations in low-income neighborhoods and in rural communities, some of which have a great potential in changing their reality.

3. During the past ten years, Mexican society has witnessed the emergence of a number of institutions that are taking care of new problems or of those barely solved by the government agencies: the environment, human rights in general or special groups such as women (feminist groups) and children, cultural promotion, the preservation of archeological and colonial heritage, etc.

4. Even though there is not yet a study on the number and nature of Mexican philanthropic institutions, it can be said that the sector is not highly diversified; that is, most of the above-mentioned institutions try to use their own and scarce resources to meet all of their needs for funding, operation, management, assessment, etc. They have not yet created organizations that can meet their common problems efficiently and effectively. For that reason, Mexico has essentially no foundations, and those that exist were created to finance their own works or projects. The handful of Mexican foundations resembling those of the United States are rather new (no more than twenty years old) and face serious problems in getting resources. There are neither institutions offering advice and technical assistance in legal, financial, fiscal, administrative, and information issues, nor enough capacity to gather and coordinate the efforts of various institutions having common objectives and problems.

It is worth mentioning the creation of various institutions promoting philanthropy and offering technical and professional support to the existing organizations. The Community Support Foundation (FAC or Fundacion de Apoyo a la Comunidad) was created in 1985 as an effort of Mexican bishops to set a professional channel for the funds granted by the Catholic church for social works and projects. The Mexican Center for Philanthropy (CEMEFI) was created in 1989 and soon became the main support and promotion center for the Mexican philanthropic system. The Junta de Asistencia Privada, a government organization integrated by private welfare institutions, has also tried to promote and support philanthropy, although many institutions do not trust it in view of its origin and ties with the government.

The above issues may be rounded up with some of the most important problems found in a study carried out by CEMEFI in 1991:

1. Just a handful of institutions have solved their financial problems. Their main sources of funding are individual contributions—just like in the United States—but in very small amounts. Foreign foundations operating in Mexico are an important source for the NGOs, but the resources allotted for them have been greatly reduced during the past few years as other Latin American countries are given priority. On the other hand, there is not a philanthropic culture, with some exceptions, within businesses and corporations even though many businessmen take part in charity efforts and make donations to many philanthropic institutions. Philanthropy is associated with a religious duty and does not pertain to businesses.

2. Tax problems are closely related to funding issues. The Mexican tax laws have no clear and permanent provisions exempting philanthropic institutions from the payment of various taxes or for allowing donors to make tax deductible contributions. This results in the law being frequently applied in an arbitrary and discretionary manner. Additionally, there is not a single and clear set of rules to register and control the nonprofit organizations. The one in force is obsolete, as it was drafted back in the 1800s for the purpose of controlling those institutions closely linked to the Catholic church. Despite all the amendments, the law remains inoperative.

3. Most of the philanthropic institutions still have a long way to go in becoming more effective in the attainment of their goals and more efficient in the management of their resources. They lack a trained and well-paid staff, as well as managers with relevant experience, and have difficulties in assessing and improving work methods on a permanent basis.

4. Finally, Mexico lacks a research infrastructure that allows us to better know its philanthropic sector: how many institutions there are, where they are, the size of their staff, the resources they have, the type of services they provide, who their beneficiaries are, etc. Solution of the existing problems and the promotion of an increasing number of philanthropic institutions will be easier as we make progress in understanding them.

19

JUAN GUILLERMO FIGUEROA PEREA

Three Comments on Population Policies in Mexico from a Reproductive Rights Approach

In general, an increasing population reduces individuals' ability to save and invest; requires more investment in schools, hospitals, and other infrastructure; and consequently lowers the rate of economic growth. Resources can be used either to provide education and adequate living standards for a stable or slightly growing population, or they can be used to support a larger population in less fortunate conditions. The Mexican government, therefore, introduced family planning in its health services. Despite the need for these services, questions have been raised about both the goals of population policy and the way in which it is implemented. Juan Guillermo Figueroa Perea notes that after several decades of policies favoring population growth, in 1973 the Mexican government amended the constitution, acknowledging each individual's right to family planning. Government-provided health services significantly reduced both birth and death rates.

Mexico's changing cultural attitudes and resulting demographic patterns reduced the birth rate from over 46.5 per 1,000 in 1902 to 32.9 in 1981 and 26.3 in 1994. The government succeeded in reducing its population growth rate to 2.5 percent in 1982 and wishes to reduce it to 1 percent by 2000. Fertility rates declined more slowly than the government had hoped. The Salinas administration urged increased efforts for family planning. Figueroa believes that a 1 percent population growth rate would leave too small a number of economically active people to support Mexico's increasingly long-lived population in the twenty-first century. He also believes that difficult conditions faced by women give them insufficient control over reproductive decisions. In particular, poor rural women did not know the medical implications of the form of birth control

Translated by Susan Beth Kapilian.

selected, and often had not been consulted regarding its choice—especially in the case of tubal ligations. He notes that women might choose to have fewer children if social expectations were different and they had better educational and employment opportunities.

Introduction

After several decades of promoting large families and prohibiting the use of contraceptive methods, in 1973 the Mexican government modified its position regarding the regulation of fertility. To this end, amendments made to Article 4 of the Mexican Constitution acknowledge the right of each individual to decide freely, responsibly, and with proper information, the number of children he or she will have, and the timing of such children, based on the logic that would help improve the population's social conditions. Similarly, the government promoted family planning activities in the different institutions that provide health services, and in this way the actions that private agencies had begun several years previously in this area were strengthened considerably. The magnitude of the task faced by the government can be appreciated if we take into account the fact that, at the beginning of the nineties, it was estimated that two-thirds of the individuals using contraceptive methods in the country (63 percent of women aged fifteen to forty-nine who were married legally or by common law) got such methods from government agencies. Recently, the health services provided by nongovernmental agencies have come to play a more important role than before, although statistically speaking, the segment of the population they serve is not significant yet. And this is despite the fact that they have managed to establish a critical process of dialogue and exchange of proposals with government institutions.

We can report that decreases in the birth and death rates (and, consequently, in the population's natural growth rate, which is the birth rate minus the death rate) have been promoted and facilitated by government policies and programs (see Table 19.1). By this we do not mean to indicate that the change in the reproductive process was merely a result of the actions taken by the state, but certain interactions are acknowledged, in particular, in response to demands made by the population, which governmental institutions have been able to meet.

The purpose of this paper is to reflect on three aspects of reproductive dynamics considered in population policies in Mexico. Since an analysis of demographic processes such as those linked to a population policy touches on a wide variety of factors conditioning them in different ways and degrees throughout time, in this article we shall describe (1) some elements of the legal framework and the context of programs in which actions linked to reproduction are carried out, (2) relevant aspects of recent reproductive dynamics, so as to go on, in a third section, to (3) a discussion of the role of health institutions vis-à-vis the previously mentioned legal framework and reproductive dynamics.

Table 19.1

Population Indicators

Year	Birth rate[a]	Death rate[a]	Natural growth rate[b]	Total fertility rate	Infant mortality rate[a]
1902	46.5	33.4	1.31		
1909					301.8
1912	43.2	46.6	−0.34		
1922	45.3	28.4	1.69		
1925					219.2
1929–31				6.3	
1930					145.6
1932	44.6	25.6	1.90		
1935					128.9
1938–40				6.4	
1940					123.8
1942	44.6	22.0	2.26		
1945					110.7
1950					100.5
1952	45.1	15.1	3.00		
1951–54				6.4	
1959–61				6.5	
1962	44.4	10.4	3.40		
1967	44.3	9.8	3.45		
1970				6.8	68.5
1971	43.9	9.3	3.46		
1975				5.8	
1976	40.0	8.0	3.20		
1977					61.4
1981	32.9	7.5	2.54	4.4	
1982–87				3.8	47.0
1988	28.6				
1987–91				3.5	
1991					
1990–94				3.3	
1994	26.3	5.1	2.12	3.0	33.1

Sources: Birth, death, and natural growth rates: 1902–71, Alba, F., *La población de México: evolución y dilemas,* El Colegio de México, 1971; 1976, CONAPO, *Política demográfica 1978–82;* 1981, CONAPO-SPP, *Encuesta Nacional Demográfica 1982;* 1994, CONAPO, *Informe de avances del Programa Nacional de Población 1989–94,* 1994 (mimeo). Total fertility rate: 1930–60, Alba, F., op. cit.; 1970–81, CONAPO, "Revisión de los niveles actuales de facundidad y mortalidad en México," 1983; 1987–91, Cervera, M., "La fecundidad en 1993," *Demos México,* 1994; 1990–94, Camposortega, S., "El monto de la población," *Demos México,* 1994. Infant mortality rate: 1909–50, CEED, *Dinámica de la población en México,* El Colegio de México, 1981; 1960–70, Mojarro, O., et al., *La revolución demográfica en México 1970–80,* IMSS 1982; 1977, Bronfman, M., and R. Tuirám, "La desigualdad socialante la muerte, 1983; 1982–87, Secretaría de Salud, *Encuesta Nacional sobre Fecundidad y Salud 1987,* México, 1989.

[a]Per thousand.
[b]Percent.

These programs are important not only because of their contribution to achieving balance between demographic, social, and economic growth rates, but also due to the way in which certain aspects of human rights are ensured, in accordance with criteria that have been defined internationally for such purposes. According to evaluation reports on government programs, the data most useful for conducting follow-up refer to the number of talks provided, the number of individuals who received information, and, particularly, new male and female users of contraceptive methods, as well as the number of individuals who at any specific time are regulating their fertility within the institution in question. In addition, emphasis is placed on individuals who have chosen to use "modern" contraceptive methods; the promotion of service providers working in health institutions has focused on such methods, especially on bilateral tubal ligation, IUDs, and injectable hormones, to the extent that in these reports, local methods (spermicides or condoms) are not recorded, much less the so-called traditional methods (rhythm and withdrawal), despite the fact that these may be the methods actually chosen by users.

This has led to a situation in which, based on data obtained in surveys conducted in Mexico between 1976 and 1992, a significant decrease can be observed in methods such as the pill and local methods, with a very important increase in the use of bilateral tubal ligation, injectables, and IUDs. According to a national survey conducted in Mexico in 1987, 36 percent of the women using some sort of contraceptive had chosen bilateral tubal ligation, whereas one out of every five users had chosen an IUD (see Table 19.2).

When a national survey analyzed the quality of services received before choosing bilateral tubal ligation and IUD, it was found that, in the case of tubal ligation, 10 percent of a national sampling of sterilized women stated that they had not participated directly in the decision to be operated on, a quarter of the total had not received information concerning other contraceptive options or about the irreversible nature of the procedure, and 40 percent did not sign a consent form. Moreover, these irregularities were more frequent among marginal women in rural zones with a low level of schooling. In the case of IUDs, it was found that 20 percent of women using this method as their first contraceptive choice "had not requested it" from the institution or person providing care during delivery; rather, it had been a unilateral decision in which they had not been consulted (Figueroa, Aguilar, and Hita 1994).

Despite the fact that this data was generated between 1987 and 1988, and that the actions taken by government institutions were being questioned, it has not been possible to carry out rigorous monitoring processes of the way in which free decisions on the part of individuals are ensured (Figueroa 1994). This becomes an even more pressing issue when we consider that, first, a national survey conducted in 1992 indicated that the level of use of bilateral tubal ligations was nearly 45 percent and, second, at different population and health conferences held in 1993 and 1994 in Mexico and Latin America participants

Table 19.2

Women Who Use Contraceptive Methods, 1976–92
(percentage distribution by method and source)

Population, method, and source	Year of reference				
	1976	1979	1982	1987	1992
Use among married women	30.2	37.8	47.7	52.7	63.1
Method					
Pills	35.9	33.0	29.7	18.2	15.3
IUD	18.7	16.1	13.8	19.4	17.7
Tubal ligation	8.9	23.5	28.1	36.2	43.3
Vasectomy	0.6	0.6	0.7	1.5	1.4
Injectables	5.6	6.7	10.6	5.3	5.1
Condoms and spermicides	7.0	5.0	4.1	4.7	5.0
Traditional methods[a]	23.3	15.1	13.0	14.7	12.2
Total	100.0	100.0	100.0	100.0	100.0
Source					
Government institutions		51.1	53.2	61.9	66.6
Private institutions		48.9	46.6	38.1	33.4
Total		100.0	100.0	100.0	100.0
Within government institutions					
Pills		29.8	23.1	11.1	10.0
IUD		29.5	24.2	28.9	25.5
Definitive methods[b]		38.2	44.7	56.1	60.5
Injectables, condoms, and spermicides		2.5	8.0	3.9	4.0
Total		100.0	100.0	100.0	100.0

Sources: 1976 Mexican Fertility Survey; 1979 National Survey on Contraceptive Prevalence; 1982 National Demographic Survey; 1987 National Survey on Fertility and Health; 1992 National Survey on Demographic Dynamics.

[a]Includes rhythm and withdrawal.
[b]Includes bilateral tubal ligation and vasectomy.

expressed surprise and concern on hearing of such a high percentage, particularly when there is no evidence to indicate that this responds to demands made by the population. On the contrary, it seems that the high percentage in question is a result of decisions made by people working in health institutions.

Thus, we are witnessing an "apparent contradiction" between the state (which validates the right to good health and to decision making about reproduction) and the government institutions involved in the area of health, which frequently violate those same rights. That is why we underscore the dimension of reproductive rights; more has been documented on the subject of demographic dimensions and the dimensions of health. However, little information has been system-atized on the component of human rights, which is just as relevant as the others to the study of reproduction.

In the current debate, the essence of reproductive rights includes free and responsible decisions about reproduction, as well as the exercise of sexuality (respecting the rights of each individual with regard to his or her sexual prefer-ences, be they heterosexual or homosexual), child-rearing, and the possibility of interrupting a pregnancy. Moreover, among the conditions acknowledged for the exercise of such rights are access to information and services related to sexuality, health, and reproduction, and respect for the active participation of women in the decision-making process concerning reproduction on the part of their partner and at institutional and social levels. This conceptualization of the conditions explic-itly includes access to education, employment, and other social rights such as housing, food, and health (Aparicio 1993; Azzolini 1993).

First Comment: The Legal Framework and the Context of Programs

Aside from the constitution itself and various general laws, Mexico has specific laws on population, health, education, and labor (see Pérez Duarte 1993), on the basis of which population and health programs have been worked out to define actions that will help improve the quality of life enjoyed by the country's inhabitants.

The General Population Law (CONAPO 1976) defines its objective as "to regulate the phenomena that affect the population in terms of its volume, struc-ture, dynamics, and distribution throughout the national territory, so as to see to it that the population receives the benefits of economic and social development justly and equally." To this end, the need is acknowledged for conducting family planning programs through educational and public health services, and for ensur-ing that this is done "with absolute respect for the fundamental rights of man and that they preserve the dignity of the family unit, in order to regulate rationally and to stabilize population growth." The General Law on Health (SSA 1992) seeks "to regulate the right to the protection of health" and, within that ambit, family planning is presented "as a health service that helps enhance the condi-tions necessary for the well-being of the population."

These laws have promoted the development of National Programs for Popula-tion, Health, and Family Planning, which specify the strategies to be followed on the basis of the demographic and health dynamics of the population. Some of these programs include targets to be reached and elements useful for monitoring and evaluating their progress. In the National Plan for Family Planning (CPNPF 1977) and in the Global Development Plan 1980-82, a figure of 1 percent is mentioned as the rate of population growth to be reached by the year 2000. This is repeated in the National Population Plan 1984-88. In some programs, these demographic targets are translated into goals involving contraceptive coverage among married women of child-bearing age, the intention being to reach the desired fertility this way. Criteria for assessing family planning programs have laid emphasis on the fulfillment of goals involving contraceptive services, despite the greater breadth of the objective of family planning policies (Cervantes 1993; Figueroa 1993).

This intense process of government planning was begun in the context of demographic changes observed, in particular, as of the latter half of the sixties. During that decade, in Mexico it was possible to observe one of the highest levels of fertility occurring in the twentieth century. This, added to significant decreases in the death rate, led to a high population growth rate of 3.5 percent. There is evidence that the population began to lower its fertility levels during the sixties, even before population policies encouraging large families and prohibiting the use of contraceptives were modified. Within this setting, political change led to recognition in 1973, in Article 4 of the Mexican Constitution, of reproductive rights, although they were not referred to as such. One might point out that this coincides with the needs of some groups of the population that were already initiating reproductive transformations before the state changed its population policies.

The legal and programmatic context outlined in these notes holds significant potential for the exercise of reproductive rights through relationships between the population and health institutions, since the laws and programs make explicit such concepts as dignity, respect, and the integrity of the individual.

Nevertheless, there is an element that suggests possible sources of conflict: the success of the particular type of demographic dynamics that was planned assumed, in part, the modification of behavior with regard to which the right of the population to decide had just been confirmed. It called for immediate action, since short-term goals had been outlined.

From the beginning, there was a possibility that the decisions made by the population would fail to coincide with the estimates included in programs, which would not produce a contradiction if the actions taken by government institutions respect procedures involving interaction with the people seeking services from them.

However, if no procedures exist for monitoring this interaction, especially when it evolves in a setting characterized by unequal relations of power between physician and patient, the risks of jeopardizing the population's right to decision making in the area of reproduction are increased.

Second Comment: Reproductive Dynamics and Family Planning

In the first seven decades of this century, Mexico had an overall fertility rate of more than six children; throughout this period—and especially as of the forties—the gross death rate dropped from over 35 to 10 per 1,000 inhabitants, and this produced an increase in the population growth rate, since the birth rate continued to be higher than 40 births per 1,000 inhabitants. In the early sixties, some population groups began to reduce their fertility. As of the seventies, such decreases became more evident due to the strengthening of family planning policies promoted by the government (see Urbina et al. 1984). This pattern continued, although at a more moderate pace, during the eighties; in the early nineties, the estimated overall fertility rate was almost half the rate observed in the sixties. This significant decrease should be interpreted as a notable demographic change, but it should also be viewed as a relevant cultural change (DGPF 1989, p. 35).

The National Plan for Family Planning (NPFP), presented in 1977, placed emphasis on the right of the population to regulate its fertility, yet at the same time, it set targets to be reached for decreasing said fertility. The NPFP included subprograms for health services, education, and social and biomedical research, for the purpose of establishing a favorable environment for the population's efforts to regulate fertility. However, the goals defined for conducting a follow-up of activities included in the NPFP were focused on demographic growth and on levels of use of contraceptive methods, and also stressed the role of health institutions in this regard. Worth pointing out is the fact that this is not directly responsible for generating a contradiction in terms of the respect for the freedom of individuals in the area of reproduction, since that depends to a great extent on the procedures used for such purposes. What we should like to underscore is that such a form of reductionism can produce processes that have a coercive effect on reproductive decision making by the population because they generate a constant —and at times obsessive—supply of contraceptive methods without acting systematically in areas such as education and job opportunities, which would allow us to ensure certain basic human rights. This, in turn, would give reproductive decision making a more comprehensive meaning and would also foster the free nature of such decisions.

In demographic policies, the government proposed "adjusting the behavior of natural population growth by states, in such a way as to be able to meet the national targets regarding total demographic growth of 2.5 percent in 1982 and 1 percent by the year 2000." The demographic assumptions used to estimate these targets could not take into account the timing and expectations of the population, since there were no previous experiences of significant decreases in fertility like the ones expected in the latter part of this century. The NPFP stressed "that the targets should be adjusted throughout the execution of the program and according to periodic assessments that are made of it" (CPNPF 1977, 7). This proposed adaptation of demographic targets to reproductive dynamics has not been put into practice, despite the fact that said targets constitute the basic criterion for defining the goals of users of contraceptives within the different institutions belonging to the health sector.

At the end of the first government administration with a new approach to state policies and planning in the area of family planning (that of President López

Portillo), the demographic data seemed to indicate that the population and the policies "were moving along the same path," if we limit this statement to a comparison between the demographic target that had been mapped out and the estimated fertility rate among the population in 1982. One could say that there was a certain degree of convergence between the reproductive intentions of Mexican women and the expectations set by the policies. Despite this, there began to be talk of a series of irregularities in the provision of health services, since the population was being pressured to modify its reproductive patterns, and in some cases this was even done without respecting the decision-making process to be conducted in this regard (see Figueroa 1991).

Some researchers have stated that this initial "success" of family planning programs was the result of a latent demand on the part of the population, which it was possible to meet thanks to the promotion of family planning services in a substantial part of the country. Government programs have helped put into practice one aspect of the reproductive rights of the Mexican population by promoting access to the means to implement their decisions about the number of children they will have.

In 1987, the Mexican National Fertility and Health Survey measured levels of fertility and contraceptive use. It disclosed a series of surprises from the government's viewpoint, since evidently the rate of decrease of fertility rates had declined considerably: from 25 percent under President López Portillo to 17 percent under President Salinas, so that the fertility rates were higher than those predicted by the government (see DGPF 1989). This suggested the advisability of reconsidering the process of demographic planning, in particular with regard to the fertility component and the programs attempting to influence it.

At the beginning of the Salinas administration (1988-94), the Mexican National Population Council (Consejo Nacional de Población, or CONAPO), which coordinates the country's population policies, proposed a modification of the targets for demographic growth in an attempt to take advantage of past experiences in analyzing the population's reproductive dynamics. This proposal suggested that the target of 1.8 percent originally set for 1988 be backed up to 1994, and, naturally, this was going to produce a change in the target originally set for the year 2000.

The reaction of President Salinas was to reject the proposal and to argue that "if the institutions belonging to the health sector had failed to do their job, that was no reason to forget the targets and to reduce expectations that are considered as the most feasible ones for the country." He also took advantage of the occasion to request that "efforts be stepped up" in the activities conducted within institutional programs, and stressed "full respect for human rights" (see REPNP 1990). A possible confusion arises in the use of the term "human rights" and its relationship to "political needs," in particular, in the performance of health service providers, in that they are responsible for implementing said policy.

There are likely to be heterogeneous, ambivalent, and easily manipulated interpretations regarding the right of the population—in particular, the rights of women—to make decisions freely and on the basis of proper information about the options they have in the areas of reproduction and contraception if health care providers want to "incorporate users" into family planning programs and act in ways reflecting paternalism, authoritarianism, and gender inequality, despite guidelines and ethics committees to regulate and monitor the provision of these services. In this way there is a danger that institutional programs might come to "expropiate reproduction" (Figueroa 1991).

According to some researchers, the target of reducing the rate of natural growth to 1 percent by the end of this century cannot be attained. Aguirre (1986) claims that were it to be reached, "dramatic changes would be produced in the age structure, both if fertility and mortality conditions continue and if the level of replacement—when each woman has on average one daughter to replace her—is recovered in the next century" (472).

In a study prepared by CONAPO (1989), it is proposed that "if a growth rate of 1 percent were to be attained by the year 2000, it is likely that as of the sixties of the twenty-first century, a zero growth rate would be reached and the population would no longer increase, but rather might even experience a slight decline. In order to achieve this, the population living at that time would have to go through an extremely traumatic period lasting nearly sixty years. The marked imbalance that this would occasion in the age structure and its economic repercussions could reverse the achievements made in the first stage and even aggravate the existing set of problems" (28). It is concluded that "the scenario proposed in the population program, which would result in a 1.5 percent demographic growth rate (which is equal to the birth rate minus the death rate, plus or minus the migration rate) by the year 2000—a modification not accepted by the president—is really the most appropriate one for the country, since it would enable us to lay the foundations for an undistorted transformation toward a more balanced population structure and dynamics for the coming century" (29).

Third Comment: The Role of Health Institutions

One of our hypotheses is that in institutional programs, little attention is paid to the fact that reproduction is the object of free decisions on the part of individuals, and not a mere object of treatment and intervention, and that this is supported by international declarations on human rights (Freedman and Isaacs 1993). Institutional actions having a bearing on reproductive rights are framed in a context of authoritarian relationships that are seldom questioned. In such a context, reproduction is "medicalized" and transformed into an ailment or a health risk "which should be combated by the respective authorities," such as physicians, as the prototype of health service providers (Illich 1987; Figueroa 1991; Bianco 1991; Menéndez 1992; Sherwin 1992; Cervantes 1993; Castro and Bronfman 1993; among others). Little recognition is given to the limits of such interactions, and this makes it difficult to ensure the free participation of individuals in their reproductive decisions. The situation becomes even more complex when the education and training of service providers fails to include the theme of human rights as a relevant one (Figueroa 1993). Moreover, it is difficult for health service providers to emphasize the human right of each person to make his or her own decisions in an atmosphere of unfair gender relations, in which women encounter significant obstacles to decision making about their reproduction, and where, in addition, they continue to be the main ones responsible for resolving "reproductive matters." How can they do so in a context in which individuals are not guaranteed access to certain basic human rights necessary for decision making in the area of reproduction?

Data obtained in several research efforts show a conflictive relationship between males and females as regards reproductive decision making and illustrate part of the complexity characterizing interaction between them in these matters.

An initial approximation to this issue has to do with the contexts of social reproduction in terms of level of schooling and occupation, as two indicators of the conditions allowing for autonomy; usually, women have a lower degree of access to both schooling and employment opportunities. There is a high percentage of women who claim that they do not have paid employment due to the opposition of their spouse or because they have to care for their children. In a considerable number of cases, this occurs because the husband believes that it is the wife who should care for the children and the family home. On the other hand, it is pointed out that women discontinue their education because they have to help out at home; furthermore, the educational expectations for women are lower than those set for men, and this is something stated by women themselves, in view of the differential employment expectations for both sexes.

In the sphere of biological reproduction, it is acknowledged that men are the ones who should decide to a greater extent when to have intercourse and how many children to have, whereas it is up to women to do something to regulate their fertility, despite the fact that a significant reason for not doing so is precisely the opposition of her spouse. Another important element in terms of the setting for conception has to do with the value that intercourse has for women, more as a way of pleasing her mate than as a personal choice. Some even admit that such efforts to please him are made "to ensure that the man doesn't leave her or get involved with another woman," and that they are not made as a "more transparent" means of satisfaction for her or, at least, a less conflicting and tension-producing one.

An additional element involves child-rearing, affective interactions with children, and the expectations placed in them. Women acknowledge that had they not had children or were they not to have them in some future time, they would feel lonely and incomplete. This is understandable when they are asked to compare the love they feel for their children with the love they feel for their mate.

Among those who chose one or the other (over half the women surveyed), the majority focused on love for their children and stated that this is a sincere, disinterested, and permanent type of affection, something they cannot be sure of when it comes to their husbands. The data reflect a significant level of loneliness in the viewpoints of these women, although it may not be interpreted as such. But it does exist in terms of a significant lack of cohesion in defining her responsibilities and joint responsibilities shared with her mate.

In order to understand the exercise of human rights, we propose at least four dimensions, which are not mutually exclusive: ethical, legal, political, and social. We believe that (1) if the ethical principles of justice, freedom, and welfare were ensured (Macklin 1990; Cook 1994; United Nations 1994); (2) if legal channels for demanding compliance with the individual guarantees recognized in the Mexican Constitution existed and were known to the population; (3) if the minimum levels of well-being acknowledged by institutional programs and governmental policies, and documented as conditions for exercising reproductive rights, were attained (Lamas 1994); and (4) if gender equality and that of social groups were ensured, then decisions on reproduction would not require rigid norms. The establishment of norms regarding reproduction would be minimal, and when it occurred it would merely be for the purpose of ensuring the social negotiation of individual liberties.

As these conditions have not been met, it would seem that government policies in Mexico have attempted to establish norms for reproduction through their family planning programs, since they have been unable to ensure the minimal conditions necessary for decision making in the area of reproduction.

Expectations and Pending Conflicts

We should point out that the social approaches proposed in the field of family planning and the concept of reproductive rights have not permeated the training for and assessment of institutional family planning programs in Mexico. Such a discussion has taken place mainly in the sphere of nongovernment organizations and in academic circles, probably due to the inertia of said programs and to the feeling that such proposals seriously question the history of those programs, despite the fact that this kind of research would enable us to document the health needs yet to be met in the context of the exercise of reproductive rights.

Regardless of the limitations of certain health institutions, we should acknowledge that, according to the latest information, approximately two-thirds of Mexican couples who are regulating their fertility obtain the contraceptive method they are using from some government institution. We should also acknowledge the important efforts made by health institutions in the search for strategies to ensure the reproduction of the population under better health conditions, even though reproductive rights are not referred to directly as such. The creation of laws, the formulation of policies, and the implementation of programs have all created a setting allowing for the provision of services that could potentially enable the population to have access to the means they need for decision making in the area of reproduction. Nevertheless, for various reasons this has not been achieved to the fullest.

Epilogue

We can conclude this series of reflections by drawing the reader's attention to data observed in 1994, which confirm the urgent need to promote discussions such as the ones suggested in different ways in this article. We are referring to the demographic growth rate, which corresponded to the target of 1.8 percent suggested at the beginning of the Salinas administration by the Secretary-General's Office of the Mexican National Population Council and rejected by the president, i.e., a target that was not reached despite the fact that the president exhorted health institutions to "step up their efforts." Such institutions may well have stepped up their efforts, and that is why it is pertinent to document the characteristics of the procedures they followed. We could state that strictly speaking, the Mexican government "failed to achieve" what it had intended—those were the words of President Salinas himself—i.e., to reach a growth rate that would assure a rate of 1 percent by the year 2000, although it was successful if we take into consideration the realistic goals set by the National Population Council in 1989, based on the conditions observed in our country's recent population dynamics.

Bibliography

Aguirre, A. (1986), "Tasa de crecimiento poblacional de 1 percent en el año 2000: una meta inalcanzable," *Mexico: Estudios Demográficos y Urbanos* 1, no. 3: 443-74.

Aparicio, R. (1993), "Políticas de población, políticas de planificación familiar y derechos reproductivos en México," *Fourth Latin American Conference on Population,* vol. 2 (Mexico City: INEGI-IISUNAM, 809-24.

Azzolini, A. (1993), "Legalidad y legitimidad en torno al derecho de la mujer a la reproducción." Presented at the forum entitled Public Policies, Women and Maternity: An Urgent Debate (Grupo de Educación Popular con Mujeres, A.C.), Mexico City, 29 pp.

Bianco, M. (1991), "La medicalización de la reproducción humana" in S. Azeredo and V. Stolcke, coords., *Direitos Reprodutivos* (Sao Paulo: Fundaçao Carlos Chagas/Prodir).

Castro, R., and M. Bronfman (1993), "Teoría feminista y sociología médica: bases para una discusión," *Cadernos de Saude Pública* 9 (3): 375-94.

Cervantes, A. (1989), "La preocupación por las coberturas" (Planificación Familiar) (Mexico City: *Demos, Carta Demográfica sobre México*), 8-9.

―――. (1993), "México: políticas de población, derechos humanos y democratización de los espacios sociales," *Fourth Latin American Conference on Population,* vol. 1 (Mexico City: INEGI-IISUNAM), 759-89.

CONAPO (Consejo Nacional de Población) (1976), *Ley General de Población y Reglamento de la Ley General de Población.* Mexico City.

————. (1989), "Análisis sobre la factibilidad y las consecuencias de alcanzar una tasa de crecimiento demográfico de 1 percent en el año 2000." Mexico City.

Cook, R. (1994), "Feminism and the Four Principles" in R. Gillon, ed., *Principles of Health Care Ethics* (New York: John Wiley), 193-206.

CPNPF (Coordinación del Programa Nacional de Planificación Familiar) (1977), *Plan Nacional de Planificación Familiar.* México City.

DGPF (Dirección General de Planificación Familiar) (1989), *Encuesta Nacional sobre Fecundidad y Salud. Informe Final.* Mexico-U.S.A. (Mexico City: Mexican Ministry of Health and the Institute for Resource Development).

Figueroa Perea, J.G. (1991), "Comportamiento reproductivo y salud: reflexiones a partir de la prestación de servicios," *Mexico: Salud Pública de México* 33, no. 6: 590-601.

————. (1993), "Derechos reproductivos y el espacio de las instituciones de salud: algunos apuntes sobre la experiencia mexicana" in *Proyecto de investigación y acción sobre derechos reproductivos* (Mexico City: El Colegio de México and Universidad Nacional Autonoma de México).

————. (1994), "La práctica de los derechos humanos en la relación entre reproducción y salud: apuntes para su análisis" in *Propuestas teórico-metodológicas para el estudio de la mortalidad y la salud* (Mexico City: National Autonomous University of Mexico).

Figueroa Perea, J.G., B.M. Aguilar, and G. Hita (1994), "Una aproximación al entorno de los derechos reproductivos por medio de un enfoque de conflictos," *Estudios Sociológicos* 12, no. 34: 129-54.

Freedman, L., and S. Isaacs (1993), "Human Rights and Reproductive Choice," *Studies in Family Planning* 24 (1): 18-30.

Illich, I. (1987), *Némesis médica* (La expropiación de la salud) (México: Ed. Joaquín Mortiz).

Lamas, M. (1994), "La responsabilidad política de los feminismos ante el debate poblacional: la construcción de la conciencia reproductiva," *Revista FEM,* 18, no. 131: pp. 13-16.

Macklin, R. (1990), "Ethics and Human Reproduction: International Perspectives," *Social Problems* 37 (1): 38-51.

Menéndez, E. (1992), "Modelo hegemónico, modelo alternativo subordinado, modelo de autoatención. Caracteres estructurales" in R. Campos, ed., *La antropología médica en México* (México: 97-114).

Pérez Duarte, A.E. (1993), "El marco jurídico de los derechos reproductivos." Mexico City.

REPNP (Reunión para la Evaluación Nacional de Población) (1990). Mexico City: Stenographic version and fragmentary accounts published in various newspapers distributed nationally.

Secretaría de Salud (SSA) (1992), *Ley General de Salud.* México.

Sherwin, S. (1992), *No Longer Patient (Feminist Ethics and Health Care)* (Philadelphia: Temple University Press).

United Nations (1994), *Declaration on Ethics Propositions. Report of the Round Table on Ethics, Population and Reproductive Health.* Preparations for the International Conference on Population and Development, New York.

Urbina M., Y. Palma, J.G. Figueroa Perea, and P. Castro (1984), "Fecundidad, anticoncepción y planificación familiar en México," *México: Revista de Comercio Exterior* 34, no. 7: 647-66.

20

HAYNES C. GODDARD

Air Pollution and Its Control in Mexico

In Mexico the environment is increasingly considered important. When it is damaged, its physical and economic value is starkly revealed. The most important element is air. Mexico City, surrounded by mountains, is no longer the "most transparent region" but a smog bowl. Haynes Goddard points out that poor nations have a smaller demand for environmental quality than rich ones, and that rapid population growth and urbanization strain physical resources. Goddard states that there are not enough specialists in the prevention and control of pollution. Further, pro-environmental legislation is expensive to enforce, and corruption further limits its enforcement.

Mexico City is damaged by emissions from its aging industrial plants and automotive vehicles. At high altitudes, the low level of oxygen leads to inefficient combustion and higher rates of emission of carbon and nitrogen oxides. Stronger pollution control policies began under President Miguel de la Madrid and expanded during the Salinas administration. The use of catalytic converters and unleaded gasoline was required, and compliance with laws was verified by fully automated equipment. Oxygenates (MBTE) were added to fuel to improve combustion, and diesel emissions of public buses were reduced. Goddard believes that the requirement that every car not be driven one day a week led to the purchase of more cars and greater pollution.

In 1994 air pollution was worse than a decade before but better than in 1991. Progress is hampered, however, by the authorities' reluctance to provide information and by the difficulty of obtaining an open political system that assists environmental interest groups to have greater influence.

Introduction

Environmental problems in Mexico are frequent topics of discussion in environmental circles: the dramatic loss of biological diversity, continued deforestation in protected areas, groundwater depletion, severely polluted watersheds and coastal areas, greatly deteriorated air quality in the country's large cities, and pollution of all of the environmental media along the U.S.-Mexico border, to mention just a few. Mexico's environmental problems are distressingly typical of those found in most of the developing countries of the world, although they are viewed as among the most serious.

The causes of this lamentable situation are several. Part of the problem stems simply from the fact that Mexico is still a poor country. Low per capita incomes will cause the demand for environmental quality to be lower than in higher-income nations, as environmental quality is what the economists call a "normal" good, that is, one whose demand increases as income increases. This means that in general the nation will feel that it can afford less environmental quality than the amount it would "purchase" were it less expensive, that is, have lower opportunity costs. Further, Mexico's past high rates of population growth and continued concentration of population in urban areas led to great pressures on environmental resources, such as the dispersive and absorptive capacity of urban air and watersheds. Of all of its problems, however, it is the continued high levels of air pollution in Mexico City that seems to have caught the world's attention most often.

Mexico's air pollution problems do not stem from an inadequate legal foundation for regulating emissions, as its standards for air quality as codified in legislation closely mirror evolving international standards (Legorreta and Flores 1992). For example, the primary standards are 0.11 ppm for one-hour ozone exposure, 0.13 ppm (parts per million) for twenty-four-hour sulfur dioxide (SO_2) exposure, 0.21 ppm for one-hour exposure of nitrogen dioxide (NO_2), 13 ppm for eight-hour exposure to carbon monoxide (CO), and a twenty-four-hour exposure to respirable particles (PM10–particulate matter of 10 microns or less in diameter) of 260 $\mu g/m^3$ (micrograms per cubic meter) (*Diario Oficial*, 1994). That this very modern legal foundation is not fully applied stems in large measure from the recognition that a quick achievement of ambient standards would be very expensive. Further, there are insufficient human and economic resources to deal with the many environmental problems that confront the country, as environmental protection must compete with other important social objectives such as feeding, housing, and educating an expanding and youthful population, as well as with making provision for the economic growth needed to create employment opportunities for this expanding population.

Virtually all of the oil revenue bonanza of the 1970s was to be focused on those developmental and social goals. The failure to administer those revenues properly led to the financial collapse of 1982 and the ensuing austerity of the 1980s, the period called the "lost decade" in Mexico, and caused all of these programs to be reined in. Environmental protection in particular was assigned a lower priority and treated essentially as a luxury that might be more affordable in the future when the economy improved. Nonetheless, throughout the 1980s environmental institutions in Mexico continued to be strengthened at least organizationally. For example, both federal and state environmental protection offices were opened in many states, although the limited resources available greatly constrained their accomplishments. Having said that, everyone who works in Mexico becomes aware that official inefficiency and corruption have always been a factor in sometimes greatly reducing the effectiveness of governmental programs, and environmental protection has not been immune to its debilitating effects, such as permitting continued development in legally protected areas.

Of the various resource insufficiencies impeding environmental protection, perhaps the most critical bottleneck is a shortage of appropriate human resources to diagnose and devise cost-effective pollution control programs. Mexico's economic priorities since World War II have been focused on economic growth and development, and therefore education and training have been focused primarily on producing graduates to help fulfill those objectives: teachers, engineers, medical professionals, economists, agricultural specialists, etc. It is still largely true that the available environmental expertise in Mexico is concentrated in the engineering community (also largely true in the United States), particularly in the sanitary engineering community, a branch of civil engineering. This means that the focus of these experts is naturally on control technologies for pollution abatement, since that is their training, as opposed to a wider view of the problem that would also contemplate nonstructural approaches to pollution control that are not focused wholly on "end of the pipe" controls. Nonetheless, undertaking large physical investments in pollution control has been and will continue to be difficult for Mexico economically. This is another reason that progress on environmental protection has been slower than what probably most Mexican citizens would like to see, as environmental consciousness is rising in Mexico.

Conventionally, air pollution sources are classified into *fixed* sources and *mobile* sources. The high levels of emissions from both of these sources in Mexico are directly derivative of past strategies for economic development. The country's fearsome air pollution problems derive in part from the old policy of *desarrollo estabilizador* or stabilizing development. This policy was basically one of import substitution with high tariff walls to protect relatively inefficient national producers from international competition in order to allow them to establish themselves. Critical to economic development and growth is increased manufacturing production, and as Mexico has not had the capacity to produce its own machine tools, the required technology had to be imported. Much of this capital equipment was older and less efficient; frequently it was economically obsolescent machinery that had been previously used in industrialized countries. All manufacturing facilities are classified as fixed-emissions sources, and in manufacture it is largely true that inefficiency in production leads to excessively high consumption of material and energy inputs, resulting in greater environmental impacts, especially from the energy (fossil fuel) inputs. All of this was viewed as an acceptable trade-off at the time, as it was expected that economic growth would produce the income to allow greater attention to environmental protection in the future.

A related policy allowed the market to concentrate capital investments spatially in order to achieve agglomeration and external economies, and accorded rural employment creation a lower priority. Most of the rural investment has been in large irrigation projects and not in creation of employment opportunities. The net result of these policies was to concentrate job creation in the cities, especially Mexico City, thereby creating a magnet for internal migration and at the same time pushing an expanding population out of the rural areas. The result is a megalopolis with unprecedented environmental impacts on the air, water, and land.

For mobile source control, during the late 1970s and early 1980s there was also a conscious decision made to put off adoption of the most advanced control technologies, such as catalytic converters, unleaded fuel, and fuel injection, as too costly for Mexico's economic circumstances. Mexico's import substitution policy was not changed fundamentally until the Salinas administration, and the catalytic converter was introduced only with the 1991 model year, more than a decade after the United States adopted the technology. These facts mean that there is a significant inertia and bias toward high emissions built into the structure of the Mexican economy that will take significant time to be changed. For example, while the introduction of catalytic converters is already having favorable impacts on Mexico City's very severe mobile emissions problem, the average age of vehicles in Mexico City is twelve years, thus making the fleet renewal effect on air quality slow to be realized. The high average age is partly the result of a taxation policy (*tenencia*) that creates a significant tax advantage for owning autos that are ten or more years in age. This "dead hand of the past" due to the durability of capital is an important reason why the scope of environmental protection policy must be expanded beyond traditional end of the pipe approaches. Forcing economic obsolescence on the productive plant of Mexico with command-and-control-approaches to pollution control (ambient standards to be met with technological fixes) makes this control more expensive than necessary.

The remainder of this chapter will present: (1) a brief overview of some of the quantitative dimensions of air pollution in Mexico City, (2) a brief history of control policies, (3) current problems of control, and (4) future policy directions. The following highlights the air quality problems in Mexico City only, since as of this writing adequate information is not available on the air quality situation in Mexico's other cities. It is known that both Guadalajara and Monterrey, the other major industrial complexes in Mexico, have important air quality problems, especially from fixed sources and from particulate emissions from diesel-powered mobile sources, virtually all public buses and private trucks. The ozone problem that is so severe in Mexico City is not yet a serious problem in Guadalajara and Monterrey at the present time, but as vehicle populations grow, the problems will also appear there.

The State of Air Quality in Mexico City

Although the high levels of pollution in Mexico City are notorious, air quality has in fact improved somewhat—moving from "very bad" to "bad"—in the last three years as the result of some belatedly implemented control measures. Nonetheless, information in Mexico on pollution and its impacts is not easily obtained, due in large part to a generalized cultural propensity not to share information, an impediment that is frustrating equally to Mexican researchers and to foreigners. This proclivity is especially pronounced at all levels of government, and, needless to say, it has rather important negative impacts on progress toward sustainable development of the country, and on pollution control in particular. This is because the free flow of information is critically central to the achievement of efficiency and effectiveness of resource use. Space limits us to only the briefest description of air quality in Mexico City, and the following data are drawn from several published and unpublished government sources, of which the publicly available sources used here are listed in a short bibliography.

Mexico City's problems derive in part from its location in a high mountain valley with a long dry season characterized by intense solar radiation, a prominent factor in the atmospheric chemistry of ozone formation. This ozone problem is unrelated to the other frequently mentioned problem of ozone depletion in the upper atmosphere—the "hole" in the stratospheric ozone layer. The valley location causes regional ventilation to be poor, as the mountains in the south of the valley block the winds, causing contaminants to pile up against them. The high altitude (2,280 meters, or about 7,500 feet) means that oxygen concentrations are about 25 percent lower than at sea level, a cause of inefficient combustion in internal combustion engines, leading to higher rates of emissions of CO and NO_x (nitrogen oxides). The high altitude also permits more solar radiation to reach the ground, causing high rates of ozone formation. The fact that about 25 percent of the nation's total population and total economic activity are concentrated in the metropolitan area causes the already limited dispersive capacity of the regional airshed to be exceeded easily.

Legorreta and Flores point out that between 1950 and 1990 the vehicle population in the metropolitan area grew by 2,400 percent, a reflection of growing incomes and the suburbanization of the population, whereas the population grew only 340 percent by comparison. For the period 1985–90, the rate of population growth in the federal district (DF) was 2.2 percent annually, while in the adjacent state of Mexico the growth was 7.8 percent. This indicates a trend toward suburbanization and decentralization in the Mexico City metropolitan area, with important implications for the continued growth of vehicle use and associated emissions, as housing density is lower and the suburban areas are less well served with public transport, the conditions of which are very deficient (crowding and untrained drivers).

Although Mexico City is still the most important manufacturing center in

Mexico, the structure of the local economy is gradually shifting to services, with the result that it is estimated that 76.6 percent of all primary atmospheric contaminants as a weighted average are from mobile sources. Vehicle emissions and those from the associated fueling cycle (bulk storage, fuel transport, and vehicle fueling) are responsible for 83 percent of hydrocarbon emissions, an ozone precursor. Recent measurements suggest that the widespread use of liquefied petroleum (LP) in domestic and commercial applications is another important and overlooked source of hydrocarbon emissions. In Mexico City, 55 percent of nitrogen oxides are estimated to derive from mobile combustion sources (45 percent from various fixed sources), along with 98 percent of the carbon monoxide and 100 percent of the lead emissions. The environmental impact of these emissions is exacerbated by the fact that annually approximately 180 days are characterized by thermal inversions, principally between November and April, the dry season. Although mobile sources are the most important emitters in the valley, 8.4 percent of emissions come from fixed sources, and 15 percent from natural sources, principally particulates from the deforested areas caused by irregular human settlements, estimated at some 300,000 tons of particulate matter (soil) per year from some 22,000 deforested hectares. There were in 1988 some 30,000 fixed manufacturing sources in the metropolitan area, 75 percent of which are classified as very small (*microempresas*). Of the fixed sources, in 1988 32 percent were food industries, 15 percent textile, 21 percent machinery, 11 percent paper, and 7 percent petrochemical (Comisión Metropolitana 1992). For fixed sources, the principal fuel is natural gas, followed by fuel oil with reduced levels of sulfur and fixed nitrogen (*gasóleo*). The largest fuel oil user in the valley is a cement manufacturer. For emissions of NO_x and CO, just 62 firms were responsible for 82 percent of all fixed-source emissions based on an emissions inventory, and just 101 firms emitted 82 percent of all pollutants from fixed sources (NO_x, CO, HC, SO_2, and TSP—total suspended particulates).

A Brief History of Mobile Source Control in Mexico City

The institutional framework for dealing with Mexico City's air quality problems has evolved over time. Despite the numerous changes to the institutional aspects of air pollution control as well the growing body of environmental legislation since the late 1950s, it is really only since 1985 that effective policies have begun to be implemented, the effects of which are clearly evident. During the administration of Miguel de la Madrid both Actions against Pollution in the Metropolitan Zone of Mexico City (1986) and One Hundred Necessary Actions (1987) were promulgated, and in 1991 under the Salinas administration the Integrated Program against Air Pollution (PICCA or Programa Integral Contra la Contaminación Atmosférica) was announced (Legorreta and Flores 1992). This latter program required the use of catalytic converters and unleaded gasoline, a policy that went into effect in 1991. Additionally, a new line on the subway, the

Metro, was opened in 1994. Also implemented under this program were mandatory emissions inspections, recently extended to twice a year, using fully automated equipment in order to reduce fraudulent certifications. Fraud continues to be a major problem, and the authorities are studying the possibility of creating governmentally operated inspection stations. In order to improve the combustion efficiency of gasoline at Mexico's high altitude, oxygenates (MBTE) were added to the fuel. At least one scientist has alleged that this has led to an increase in evaporative emissions, and that the rapid growth in the ozone exceedences can be traced to this (Bravo 1980).

As is true everywhere with respect to environmental protection, it is public pressure that has led to improvements in emissions control in Mexico City. One of the first improvements resulted from concerted action taken by the authorities to reduce diesel emissions of the public bus company Ruta 100. A denuncia popular (public complaint) was brought by the Mexican Environmental Movement (MEM), which goaded the authorities into action; this complaint mechanism was later formalized in the 1988 General Law on Ecological Equilibrium. Control of these particulate emissions was perhaps the first clear evidence of progress in mobile source control, and as a result visible emissions from both bus and truck sources have been significantly reduced, although PM10 (particulate matter under ten microns in diameter) remains a matter of serious health concern.

After a series of well-publicized inversion episodes in 1980s, for lack of a better idea, the authorities accepted a proposal put forward by the MEM to restrict vehicle use. In November of 1989, a No Driving Day program (Hoy No Circula) was initiated and is administered now by the Metropolitan Commission for Prevention and Control of Pollution in Mexico City, established in 1992. Under this program all vehicles are to be parked one day a week in the period from Monday through Friday. Conceived initially as a measure for the dry season only (November through March), its visible impact on congestion and air quality caused it to be made permanent after the first few months of operation. However, as is analyzed elsewhere (Goddard 1995), this inflexible program has simply caused the driving population to acquire additional vehicles to get around the restriction. The palpably visible results are that traffic congestion has risen, parking even in residential areas is difficult, and emissions are likely up over what they would have been without the program. The authorities have not yet released data and information to allow independent examination of these propositions.

The vehicle fleet in Mexico City has been growing at 10 percent per year, with the result that traffic has increased so much that peak-hour congestion is becoming generalized (reduced differences between peak and off-peak congestion), and now serious congestion and elevated pollutant concentrations occur even on Saturday and Sunday. The air pollution index in Mexico City is the IMECA (Indice Metropolitano de la Calidad del Aire) and during recent years it has reached very high levels. It has been common for it to rise above the 300 level (very unhealthful). In it 1992 reached 392 (dangerous) in the southwest of the city and nearly 500 (very dangerous) in Tlanepantla (a municipality in the metropolitan region). The impact on health of these high levels has been underestimated, as they are taken at thirty feet above ground level and not at "nose" level. These exceedences are nearly always for ozone concentrations or for carbon monoxide. Such levels have not been reached in the last two years, most likely due to a combination of favorable atmospheric conditions (continued ventilation) and the gradual introduction of catalytic converters. Since it takes as long as eight to ten years to observe trends in pollution concentrations, it is not yet possible to say whether the improvement is due to short-run favorable atmospheric conditions or improved control.

The air pollution standard is 100 on the air pollution index, and in 1994 it was exceeded 345 days (94 percent), more than 100 points higher than a decade earlier. There were 95 days (26 percent) over 200, although that is lower than the 178 days measured in 1991. These exceedences occur principally for ozone, PM10, and TSP.

Current Problems

It is generally true that starting from a base of no or little emissions control, implementation of available air pollution control technology alone will be the least-cost approach over a significant range of emissions reductions. Mexico City has started that process. However, current policy relies exclusively on technology, and due to the average age of the vehicle fleet in Mexico City, many years will pass before there are any important gains made in reducing the ozone problem. In fact, if the experience in southern California is any guide, the day may never arrive. The No Driving Day program must be judged a failure in its current form—worse, it is positively perverse—but there is both theoretical (Goddard 1995) and empirical (Eskeland 1992) evidence to indicate that optimal restrictions on private vehicle use will form part of a cost-effective set of controls for reducing mobile emissions. The basic idea is seen in Figure 20.1, in which ER is emissions reduction, MC is marginal cost, K is capital (technology), and OC is opportunity cost, in this case the loss of consumer welfare from not being able to drive on a given day. At some empirically determined level of control (ER_0), it becomes less expensive to employ some efficient and equitable mechanism to discourage vehicle use than to continue to rely on technology alone to control emissions. The application of tradable permits as a possible policy to achieve cost effectiveness in this context is the object of current research of the author and is described more fully in Goddard (1995). In general, more attention needs to be focused on developing cost-effective control policies that combine both technology and incentive mechanisms for discouraging polluting behavior.

Figure 20.1 **Cost Effectiveness in Mobile Emissions Control**

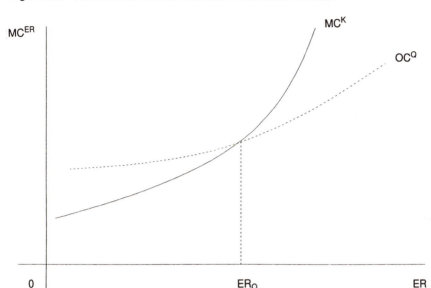

Sustainability and the Future of Mexico City

Mexico City is one of the world's largest cities, with a population of probably 22 million today. Despite the vicissitudes of the Mexican economy, it is a reasonable expectation that the population and economy of the area will continue to grow, placing ever greater pressure on its natural resources: the dispersive capacity of the airshed, the available water supplies, the land for receiving the population's solid wastes, and also on the built environment, such as the road system for moving the population. It is also a reasonable hypothesis that present trends are not sustainable. The No Driving Day program attempted to confront the unsustainability of private vehicle use, but because the policy was not well designed nor adequately analyzed prior to implementation, it is an easy conclusion that the restriction has made the situation worse, not better. This is a dramatic example of "intervention failure," unfortunately a rather common occurrence in Mexico. The root source of the problem is a failure of adequate diagnosis and appropriate policy prescription, in part due to a shortage of properly trained professionals, which makes it difficult for the government to identify effective and efficient solutions to its environmental problems. This situation is greatly exacerbated by the lack of dissemination of information, preventing independent analysts from critically evaluating proposed policies and analyses in order to increase the information base available to decision makers. The tendency is partly cultural, but perhaps it is mostly another social inefficiency generated by the lack of an open and truly competitive political system. The lack of openness in all authoritarian systems has very negative effects on environmental protection, as environmental constituencies are closed out of decision-making processes, and avenues for political redress and opposition are limited or completely closed. Nonetheless, it should be noted that even in open political systems environmental protection requires eternal vigilance, as economic interests have ready-made constituencies. In Mexico, government posts are still widely treated as opportunities for personal enrichment either by directly plundering the treasury and/or by selling favors, and since environmental protection does not generate a flow of economic rents to influence decision making, the advocates of increased environmental protection have a serious uphill battle to fight. Mexico's corporatist political organization has not made provision for environmental interests, and it is yet too soon to say whether this situation is changing.

It is gradually being recognized that unsustainable environmental practices have their root in the operation of the economies of the world, for after all, pollution is but the residual of consumption and production activities, economic activities quite clearly. Successful guidance of the world's economies along sustainable developmental paths will require the use of decentralized economic instruments that, on the one hand, cause polluters to be confronted with the social costs of their behavior, and, on the other, preserve a full measure of individual choice and freedom consistent with the ecological welfare of one's compatriots and, increasingly, of citizens of other nations. The identification and implementation of sustainable development paths require true and complete interdisciplinarity in the search and design of environmental policy, the recognition of which, although overdue, seems to be growing.

Bibliography

Bravo Alvarez, H., et al. (1980), "Efectos en la Calidad del Aire en C.U. por el Uso del Aditivo MTBE en las Gasolinas del Valle de México," *Memorias del VII Congreso Nacional de la Sociedad Mexicana de Ingeniería Sanitaria y Ambiental* (Oaxaca).

Comisión Metropolitana para la Prevención y Control de la Contaminación Ambiental en el Valle de México (1992), *Programa para el Control de Emisiones Contaminantes al Aire Provenientes de la Industria en la Zona Metropolitana de la Ciudad de México* (Mexico City, March).

Diario Oficial de la Federación del 3 de diciembre de 1994 (1994).

Eskeland, Gunnar (1992), "A Presumptive Pigouvian Tax on Gasoline: Analysis of an Air Pollution Control Program for Mexico City," Washington, D.C.: World Bank, August 13, unpublished manuscript.

Goddard, Haynes (1995), "Sustainability, Tradeable Permits and the World's Large Cities: A New Proposal for Controlling Vehicle Emissions, Congestion and Urban Decentralization with an Application to Mexico City," Instituto Tecnológico Autónomo de México and University of Cincinnati, unpublished manuscript (Mexico City and Cincinnati).

Legorreta, Jorge, and Ángeles Flores (1992), "La contaminación atmosférica en el valle de México" in Iván Restrepo, ed., *La contaminación atmosférica en México: Sus causas y efetos en la salud* (Mexico City: Comisión Nacional de Derechos Humanos).

21

DAVID BARTON BRAY AND MATTHEW B. WEXLER

Forest Policies in Mexico

Mexico holds tenth place in the world in forest cover. Its forests are home to some seventeen million people. Up to 80 percent of Mexican forest lands are held by ejidos or indigenous communities. Deforestation, however, is occurring rapidly as forests give way to agriculture and livestock production.

Private industries were allowed access to forests in 1943, and communities could sell only to them. On the other hand, in 1958, forestry was banned in 32 percent of the forest area. During the fifties and sixties, the government had an increasing role in the wood and paper products industries. By 1977, twenty-seven parastatal organizations controlled 56 percent of forest-sector production. They did not use optimal harvesting methods or fulfill their responsibilities for training peasants in management of timber production.

In the 1970s, the Forestry Subsecretariat began a program to empower forest communities to manage their own forests and forest industries. The 1986 Forestry Law ended private forestry concessions and began to dismantle forestry parastatals, emphasize environmental consequences of timber programs, and increase powers of local communities. Severe financial constraints and government reorganization limited the full implementation of this law.

The reform of Article 27 encouraged ejidos to enter joint ventures with private enterprise. The 1992 Forestry Law encouraged the development of forestry plantations, simplified administrative procedures, and privatized forestry services. The entry of Mexico into NAFTA, however, allows more efficiently produced United States and Canadian forest products to replace Mexican lumber in the north and center of Mexico. David Barton Bray and Matthew B. Wexler believe that Mexican community forestry, consequently, is likely to require special measures of support to survive.

David Bray would like to thank the U.S.-Mexico Fulbright Commission for support in collecting data for this article. Both authors would like to acknowledge support from the North-South Center at the University of Miami for a joint research project on community forestry in Mexico given to Gonzalo Chapela, Rodolfo López, Leticia Merino, Carol Zabin, and themselves. Helpful comments on earlier drafts of this article were received from Laura Randall, Eduardo Silva, and Laura Snook.

Introduction

There are many singular things about the forests of Mexico, not the least of which are the many policies applied to them. Mexican forest policy in the twentieth century has included virtually open doors to foreign investments, bans, industrial concessions, timber and pulp parastatals, a vigorous community forestry policy, and most recently, an effort to follow a plantation path of development. Although many of these policies were shaped by broad ideals such as forest conservation and efficient timber production, none of them have effectively delivered economic benefits to forest communities, reduced a persistent trade deficit in forest products, or conserved biodiversity. But perhaps the most singular thing about Mexican forests is the degree to which they are administered by local communities, giving Mexico what may be the largest community forestry sector anywhere in the developing world.

In marked contrast to most emerging economies, where forest lands are in state or private hands, the single most distinguishing fact of Mexican forest resources is that up to 80 percent of Mexican forest lands are held by ejidos or indigenous communities. The wealth of these forest resources represents perhaps the single greatest opportunity for many rural communities to participate in regional development. Mexico has some fifty million hectares of closed forest, 25 percent of the national territory, about half of which are highland pine and oak forests, accounting for most of the industrial production. While Mexico occupies tenth place in the world in forest cover, it is only twenty-sixth in forest production. The output from the wood products industries has consistently fallen short of its potential, contributing to Mexico's substantial trade deficit in this sector. Despite the low productivity, Mexico also has an accelerating rate of deforestation, estimated as high as 800,000 hectares per year and mostly tied to agricultural and livestock expansion, which threatens to eliminate Mexico's tropical forests in the early part of the twenty-first century (Téllez Kuenzler 1994, 260–72).

The deforestation rates threaten more than just timber production. Mexico is fourth in the world in biodiversity, much of it contained in its woodlands; its forests are also home to an estimated seventeen million people, many of them indigenous, including some of the nation's poorest and most marginalized peoples. For these people, the forests are not only an economic resource, but also a spiritual wellspring and a source of ethnic identity. Any comprehensive forestry policy grounded in the pursuit of "sustainability" must address not only the economic and environmental components of forest resource management, but also the cultural dimensions of Mexican forests. Mexican forests have many other extra-market or difficult-to-calculate values, as well, such as reduction of global warming and protection of watersheds.[1]

Bans and Concessions

Bans and concessions have been intertwined policies since the nineteenth century. In the late nineteenth century, the Mexican government granted timber concessions to attract foreign capital, opening the impenetrable southern jungles of Tabasco, Chiapas, Veracruz, and the Yucatan peninsula, with precious tropical hardwoods flowing out of coastal ports. After the Mexican Revolution, the government established the nation's first forestry law in 1926, to little regulatory effect. During the presidency of Lázaro Cárdenas in the 1930s, the wave of agrarian reform efforts included handing out four million hectares of woodlands, 21 percent of the land distributed, laying the land tenure basis for the contemporary achievements in community forestry. Some efforts were made at the time to promote forest community cooperatives, although most fell into corruption. Beginning in the 1940s, policies of banning commercial logging and industrial concessions held sway, sometimes, puzzlingly, even in the same region.[2]

Prompted by a shortage in pulp production during World War II, and signaling a turn toward a development model of import-substitution industrialization, a 1943 law created Forest Exploitation Industrial Units (UIEFs). The UIEFs allowed private industries access to large blocks of forests, limiting the communities' right to sell to anyone other than the UIEF, compensating communities with an extremely modest stumpage fee. Many of the UIEFs were enormous, vertically integrated enterprises, such as Industria Forestal del Poniente, which held rights to 178,000 hectares of forest lands in Guerrero and also owned a paper and cellulose processing plant. Twelve UIEFs would eventually be established between 1945 and 1972; some of them were given concessions for up to forty years, though twenty-five was more common.[3]

Concurrent with the industrial development policies, and born out of a concern for the damage to forests and watershed from deforestation (apparent even by the 1940s), the government pursued a vigorous policy of decreeing bans. By 1958, eleven states were under total bans, including such important forestry states as Michoacán and Veracruz, with partial bans in ten other states, covering an estimated 32 percent of the entire forest area. Most of these bans persisted into the 1970s. Their impact fell most heavily on the forest inhabitants, who desperately needed income. Patricia Gerez describes the situation in the Cofre de Perote area of Veracruz: "To avoid the forest guards they had to go down at night, whether it was foggy or rainy, by steep, muddy roads, to be able to return with food and money for family expenses. If the forest guards caught them, they had to give them a tip, or be left with nothing and go back to their communities empty-handed." It was also evident to most observers that deforestation continued apace under the bans.[4]

During the 1950s and 1960s, the government gradually assumed an increasingly larger role in the wood and paper products industry. In some instances, the government invested with private enterprise, as happened in 1956 in Oaxaca with Fábricas de Papel Tuxtepec (FAPATUX), a paper and pulp mill with initial timber rights of 251,825 hectares in the Sierra Juárez. By 1965 ownership of FAPATUX was completely transferred to the federal government. This movement culminated in the early 1970s when, under President Luis Echeverría's tremendous expansion of the federal government, new enormous timber parastatals, known as Decentralized Public Organisms, were formed in Guerrero, Chihuahua, Durango, the state of Mexico, Nayarit, Chiapas, and Quintana Roo, and provided a new state control over the forest sector. The parastatal enterprises in Guerrero and Chihuahua also clearly had rural pacification missions, in an effort to stem unrest that included a guerrilla uprising in Atoyac municipio of Guerrero, long known for pitiless timber exploitation by private interests. By 1977 there were twenty-seven parastatal organizations connected to forest activity that accounted for 56 percent of the total forest-sector production.[5]

The timber operations of the UIEFs and the parastatals generally based their forestry programs on the ultraconservative Mexican Method. The low harvesting volumes approved by this method leave a heavy shade cover and prevent sun-loving species, such as pine, from repopulating harvested areas. This approach resulted in sluggish and uneven regrowth in many regions, often accompanied by an unproductive shift in forest composition. In timber regions where loggers routinely exceeded the recommended extraction levels and based their volumes on the capacity of roads and machinery, selective cutting tended to remove healthy, marketable trees, leaving an ecologically damaged forest. Diseased and pest-ridden stands neighbored over-cut areas where severe soil erosion threatened water table levels and downstream agriculture. On the social side, the government charged the parastatals with educating and training peasants from ejidos and indigenous communities in the management of timber production, a responsibility that received little attention.

It was also during the 1970s and early 1980s that Mexico pursued its most aggressive tropical colonization policies, resulting in the devastation of hundreds of thousands of hectares of tropical forests. The tellingly named National Land Clearing Program (Programa Nacional de Desmontes) was a trust fund set up to transform forest lands "of little economic use" into agricultural or pasture lands. The program was responsible for destroying nearly twenty-eight million cubic meters of timber in five years during the 1970s, almost as much as the national timber production during the same period. However, some elements of the Forestry Subsecretary were able to enter the Uxpanapa colonization region in southern Veracruz (one of the major tropical colonization projects of the 1970s), where they were at least able to mount programs to market the fallen timber.[6]

The Rise of Community Forestry

As government programs mounted enormous industrial plants and slashed tropical forests, another division of the government was plotting a different strategy. In the mid-1970s an effort began, centered in a new division of the Forestry Subsecretariat, the General Directorate of Forestry Development, to empower forest communities to manage their own forests and forest industries. These efforts passed through various cycles and had many retreats and advances. Combined with intensive grassroots mobilizations against concessions, they would redraw the map of forest exploitation in Mexico and eventually create what is probably the most extensive sector of community-managed forests anywhere in the world.[7] As romantically expressed by a director of a community forestry promotion effort in northern Veracruz, foresters began to speak of "a country of silviculturalists, of forming social forestry enterprises, and of democratizing, in sum, the process of forest production." One of the first steps of the young reformers was to call for the lifting of the bans that still existed in many states, in order to create spaces for community forestry.[8]

This government effort was complex and inconsistent and emerged from the shifting alliances between cautious bureaucrats, production-oriented reformers, and more radical elements from the social left, with all tendencies springing from the Autonomous University of Chapingo.[9] It began with the idea of working only with small private property owners (*pequeña propiedad*), fighting the forest service's reputation for corruption, and only slowly began to work with ejidos and indigenous communities, where it would eventually find its greatest success. It would also begin in politically safe areas in Tlaxcala, Puebla, and Veracruz, where no large industrial concessions existed, and where bans had not allowed the growth of a legal forest industry. It would later expand, however, almost with guerrilla tactics, into the heart of some of the industrial concessions, particularly in Oaxaca. In silvicultural terms, it preached the abandonment of the so-called Mexican Method for Ordering Forests, a silvicultural technique that focused on the healthiest specimens, for the Silvicultural Development Method, which reduced "high-grading" (which leaves a genetically impoverished forest) and led to healthier, more even-aged stands of trees.[10] Philosophically, the young reformers promoted a concept called socioproduction, which attempted to introduce economic justice into production forestry, and encapsulated their efforts in the oft-repeated phrase that forest exploitation should be "controlled by the owners and possessors of the forest" (i.e., indigenous communities and ejidos, respectively). They also advanced the argument that increasing community productive control of forests would overcome Mexico's persistent trade deficit in wood products, and production gains were evident in the late 1970s, although they later stagnated.

In the early 1980s, frustrated with private concessions and state control of forest production, many forestry communities began to organize, often using aggressive pressure tactics that made some government reformers uneasy. In Oaxaca in particular, forest communities were galvanized into action when the federal government moved to grant a new twenty-five-year concession to FAPATUX, the parastatal pulp mill. The reaction from communities was intense and well coordinated. They blocked logging trucks from entering or leaving their forest lands, sought legal redress, and brought national attention to their demands to manage their own forests and receive the full value of their timber production. In Oaxaca and other states, political activists, who later became organized into nongovernment organizations (NGOs) that specialized in community forestry issues, also played an important role in providing organizational support, legal advice, and technical assistance to the forest communities.[11]

Grassroots mobilizations and support from reformers such as Cuauhtémoc Cárdenas (forestry subsecretary, 1978-80) and the leader of the reformers, Leon Jorge Castaños (forestry subsecretary, mid-1980s) helped community forestry reach a high point with the passing of the 1986 Forestry Law. This law reflected a significant policy change that (1) ended all private concessions and initiated the process of dismantling the parastatals; (2) required more detailed and environmentally sensitive studies for timber programs; and (3) began the transfer of technical services (which had been given in exclusive concessions to government administrative units) to local communities. The law marked the first time the welfare of forestry communities was the focus of legislative action. The passing of the law, however, would be the high-water mark for forestry reforms. Despite the momentum from local groups and government reformers, as the 1980s progressed, the forestry subsecretary experienced severe cutbacks in funding and staff as their actions began to directly affect economic interests. In addition, austerity measures resulted in a restructuring of Secretaría y Recursos Hidráulicos (SARII) in 1985 that eliminated the Forestry Subsecretariat and transformed it into the National Forestry Commission (CNF).[12]

Bureaucratic disorder has been a significant reason Mexico has not been able to achieve a well-articulated forest policy. As Mexican forest analyst Gonzalo Chapela noted during the Salinas period, three cabinet-level departments, four subsecretariats, and thirteen other government offices all have responsibility for different aspects of forest policy, with these agencies themselves frequently undergoing reshuffling. In 1986, President Carlos Salinas de Gortari reestablished the Forestry Subsecretariat within SARH, where it remained throughout his sexenio, although frequent changes at the top, culminating in the appointment of a medical doctor as forestry subsecretary, suggested little interest in forest policy as such. In the cabinet structure announced by recently elected President Ernesto Zedillo in December 1994, the forestry subsecretary has been taken out of Agriculture and incorporated into the new Secretariat of Environment, Natural Resources, and Fisheries. Although dropped from the subsecretary rank in the new agency, it will be part of a bureaucracy where, for the first time, all natural resources activities are gathered under one administrative roof.

The New Economic Environment

Beginning in 1991, the administration of Salinas de Gortari accelerated Mexico's program of deregulation and decentralization in the rural sector with three sweeping reforms that impacted the forest sector. They were the modification of constitutional Article 27, the 1992 Forestry Law, and the North American Free Trade Agreement (NAFTA), as well as a wave of privatization that affected all of the forestry parastatals. Taken together, they provide a policy and legal framework that encourages rapid market liberalization and privatization.

According to Article 27, forested lands are not subject to being subdivided and sold; they will remain communal property. However, the agrarian reform does encourage ejidos to enter joint ventures (Asociaciónes en Participación) between private investors and ejidos that the government hopes will stimulate the capitalization of timber production. To date, several forestry ejido unions have taken advantage of this opportunity to capitalize their timber operations. To attract these investments, however, forest communities have had to yield some control as they enter into partnerships. In the Costa Grande of Guerrero, several ejidos have recently joined with a private logging company from Washington State to form a joint venture that will export saw logs to the United States and Pacific Rim countries. The U.S.-based partner will provide millions of dollars in start-up costs and investments to upgrade machinery and road conditions, in exchange for financial control of the operations. Financial projections suggest that ejidos could more than double their income, although with more intensive cutting than has been done before.[13] The avowed intention of the law to prevent forest lands from being split up has also been called into question. One large forest ejido in Chihuahua has already been divided into a multitude of small production cooperatives, with the potential for a severe impact on the forest resource due to lack of centralized control.

The 1992 Forestry Law had four notable components: (1) a focus on developing plantations in Mexico (drawing heavily on the Chilean model and assisted by Chilean forestry specialists); (2) a dramatic simplification of the paperwork involved in cutting, transporting, and processing wood products; (3) the complete privatization of technical services; and (4) the use of some of the same language that had supported community forestry in the past, but with no provisions that recognize its special needs and accomplishments in the past decade.[14]

Until recently, Mexico had precisely one industrial plantation in the entire country, placing it far behind Latin American leaders like Chile, Argentina, and Brazil. The new legislation hopes to start remedying that situation. Plantations could recover degraded areas using adaptable, fast-growing species such as pine and eucalyptus to provide cheap timber and paper pulp. Plantations also provide environmental benefits through carbon sequestration and watershed protection, although if planted where natural forests once stood, they also occasion dramatic declines in biodiversity. Moreover, plantations provide fewer sources of income than does natural forest management, a significant consideration when so many of Mexico's poorest and indigenous peoples depend on forest resources for their livelihood. The difficulties of promoting plantations in Mexico, despite all the favorable legislation, was exemplified by the failed negotiations between a large U.S. timber company and the Náhuatl community of Pajapan in southern Veracruz. Local communities can still control their forest lands, and, in this case, analyses that demonstrated that they could earn more from corn, a notorious money-loser, than they could from a forest plantation on their land convinced the community that the timber company was not offering them a fair deal.[15]

A clear benefit of the new forestry law is the replacement of the elaborate harvest monitoring system that relied on lengthy paper trails (twenty separate documents by one count) with specially coded hammers that leave indented symbols on the logs, identifying the source of the trees and the responsible parties. This reduces labor costs for logging operations and would theoretically allow SARH officials to spend less time on paperwork and more energy on field inspections (although budget restrictions generally keep forestry officials at their desks). Unfortunately, this method also makes clandestine cutting much simpler, using a borrowed or forged hammer.

But the most important feature of the 1992 Forestry Law consisted of the complete privatization of the quasi-governmental regional agencies of professional forestry engineers (*servicios técnicos*). Among other duties, these engineers are responsible for the design and implementation of the timber harvesting and reforestation programs required by the government for all commercial logging operations. Privatization broke the monopolies held by agencies with government concessions and will lower costs for management plans, but there are also dangers involved. Forestry communities typically contract engineers for yearly tree-marking services and arrange separate agreements for the more costly design of timber programs. Because engineers will compete for low bids to gain contracts, the quality of services is likely to diminish, resulting in overharvesting and insufficient reforestation. Because most forestry engineers are paid per cubic meter harvested, the temptation to overcut is financially to their advantage, making sustainable harvests more uncertain. The new and distant stance of the SARH with respect to monitoring and sanctions makes this scenario all the more likely. In addition to providing this technical assistance, engineers serve as the organizational intermediaries between the forest communities and the government. As the government retreats from direct involvement in forestry production, the engineers will take on an increased importance in natural resource management as the bridge between the communities and government bureaucracies, frequently displacing ejido leadership.

NAFTA: Trade and Financing in the Forestry Sector

The Mexican timber industry is at an enormous disadvantage compared to the United States and Canada, two world leaders in forest production. During the 1980s, Mexican production was about 2 percent of that of the United States, with much higher production costs and with a persistent trade deficit in wood products. In Mexico, five big timber companies represent 17 percent of sales, while approximately 1,400 community forestry enterprises represent 66 percent of national timber extraction. In the United States less than 20 percent of timber companies generate over 80 percent of production.[16] In addition to being small, both the community and private timber industries suffer from antiquated equipment, low capitalization, and high production costs. Thus, for all the extra-market values it represents, and its genuine economic achievements, the community forestry sector is also a high-cost, inefficient producer of low-quality products, having emerged in a highly protected market. The competitive position of Mexican timber production is worst in the north, improving somewhat in the southern states due to higher transportation costs. Since Mexico signed the General Agreement on Tariffs and Trade (GATT) in 1986, cheap U.S. lumber has filled commercial centers such as Chihuahua, Monterrey, and Saltillo, and U.S. suppliers have also made deep inroads into Mexico City, the nation's largest consumer of wood and paper products. NAFTA will strengthen the position of U.S. producers in these areas, although the recent devaluation of the Mexican peso in January of 1995 raises the prices of imports and will buy a bit a breathing space for the Mexican industry.

Conclusions

The introduction of liberalized markets into Mexican forest production will undoubtedly bring some benefits in terms of increased investments and will force greater efficiencies in the industrial plant. But whether it will lead to improved forest management or economic opportunity for the millions of inhabitants of Mexican forests remains a question.

In the case of community forestry, as Laura Snook has argued, "free market competition seems likely to undermine the financial viability of both community forest industries and forest management. In order to prevent the degradation and conversion of Mexico's forests (not to mention the increased poverty) likely to result, it would seem to be in the interest of the Mexican nation and the international community to provide support to these communities in such a way that they can continue to maintain their forests for the benefit of all" (Snook 1995, 34).[17]

Some community forest industries may be able to survive by moving into "niche" markets for sustainably harvested timber, if they can improve their silvicultural methods. Recently, a coalition of NGOs called the Mexican Civil Council for Sustainable Silviculture has emerged to promote this opportunity. Mexico has rich human and natural resource capital in the forestry sector, and a more nuanced application of policy instruments, as well as support from the international community, could still maintain the enormous biodiversity of the highland pine and oak forests, and secure the remaining tropical forests for future generations of Mexicans.

Notes

1. For an excellent comparative review of native forest policy in Brazil, Mexico, and Peru, see Silva (1994).
2. See Salas Reyes (1989) and Vazquez Soto (1971).
3. See Baca Castillo (1984).
4. On the bans policy, see Hinojosa Ortiz (1958), 44. For Gerez quote (my translation), see Gerez Fernández (1993).
5. On state involvement in the forestry sector in the 1970s, see Francisco Xavier Ovando H. (1979).
6. See Castillo Fragoso (1978).
7. Former Forestry Subsecretary Leon Jorge Castaños (1992) offers figures showing that 40 percent of commercial timber production and 15 percent of sawnwood in Mexico is produced by the organized community forestry sector. For profiles of some of the most successful community forestry enterprises, see Bray, Carreón, Merino, and Santos (1993).
8. For overviews of community forestry, see Alatorre (1992). For silviculturalists quote, see Alfonso González Martínez (1992, 8); see also SARH (1973).
9. The forestry reform movement may have been one of the most long-lasting in recent Mexican history. Jonathan Fox (1992) provides a penetrating study of how reformers briefly moved to the top in food policy in the early 1980s and provides an analytic framework for approaching forest policy as well.
10. See Laura Snook and Patricia Negreros (1986).
11. For accounts of the community forestry movement in Oaxaca, see Abardía Moros (1992, 125); Bray (1991, 13–25); Chapela (1992); and Szekely and Madrid (1990).
12. The Comisión Nacional Forestal was created on February 6, 1986, and was composed of several cabinet secretaries whose agencies were involved in forest issues and the directors of the timber parastatals. See Alcocer Medina (1989).
13. See Wexler (1994).
14. See Téllez (1993, 80). It is worthy of note that Claudio X. Gonzaléz, who helped the government design the new law, is the son of the chairman of Kimberley-Clark, Mexico's largest pulp and paper manufacturer. See "Officials Pin Hopes on New Forestry Law," *El Financiero Internacional*, January 25, 1993.
15. For the official view of plantations, see Téllez Kuenzler (1994, 75–78); for the point of view of a national network of community forest organizations, see Red Nacional de Organizaciones Campesinas Forestales (1992); on the case of Pajapan, see Paré (1992).
16. Merino (1992). Very little is known about Mexico's industrial timber sector, an important area for future research.
17. A Spanish translation of Snook's work will be published in Mexico in a volume on sustainable grassroots development edited by Luisa Paré, David Barton Bray, and John Burstein.

Bibliography

Abardía Moros, F. (1992), "Oaxaca: Historia de Familia. O de como se transformó el uso de los bosques comunales (1950–1985)," *Ecologia, Municipio, y Sociedad Civil* (Mexico City: Fundación Friedrich Nauman).
Alatorre, Gerardo (1992), *La empresa social forestal* (Mexico City: Programa Pasos).
Alcocer Medina, Gabriel (1989), *La Planeación Nacional y su Vinculo con la Política, la Legislación, y la Administración Pública Forestal en el Periodo 1982–1988* (Chap-

ingo: Forest Sciences Division, Autonomous University of Chapingo), thesis in Forestry Engineering.

Baca Castillo, J.C. (1984), *Situación Forestal del Estado de Guerrero: Tendencias y Oportunidades de Desarrollo* (Chapingo: Universidad Autónoma de Chapingo), thesis.

Bray, David Barton (1991), "The Struggle for the Forest: Conservation and Development in the Sierra Juárez," *Grassroots Development* 15:3, 13–25.

Bray, David Barton, Marcelo Carreón, Leticia Merino, and Victoria Santos (1993), "On the Road to Sustainable Forestry . . . ," *Cultural Survival Quarterly* 17.

Castaños, Leon Jorge (1992),"Situación del sector forestal a nivel nacional," *Foro Nacional: El Sector Social Forestal a Nivel Nacional*, Pátzcuaro, Michoacán.

Castillo Fragoso, Rubén (1978), "El presupuesto de la Federación en el sector forestal," *Mexico y Sus Bosques* 18, no. 2 (April–June).

Chapela, Francisco J. (1992) "¿Complementariedad o conflicto? El manejo de bosque en Santiago Comaltepec, Oaxaca," *Ecologia, Municipio, y Sociedad Civil*. Edited by Dieter Paas, Diego Prieto, and Julio Moguel. Mexico City: Fundacion Friedrich Naumann, 93–112.

Chapela, Gonzalo (1990), "De bosques y campesinos: problemática forestal y desarrollo organizativo en torno a diez encuentros de comunidades forestales," *Los nuevos sujetos del desarrollo rural* (Mexico City: ADN Editores).

Fox, Jonathan (1992), *The Politics of Food in Mexico: State Power and Social Mobilization* (Ithaca, N.Y.: Cornell University Press).

Gerez Fernández, P. (1993), "Marginación Social, Deforestación y Desarrollo Rural: Un Estudio de Caso en el Cofre de Perote, Veracruz, México." Paper presented at conference, On Common Ground: Interdisciplinary Approaches to Biodiversity Conservation and Land Use Dynamics in the New World, December 1–4, 1993 (Belo Horizonte, Brazil).

González Martínez, Alfonso (1992), "Los bosques de las tierras Mexicanos: la gran tendencia . . . ," *El Cotidiano* 8, no. 48 (June): 5.

Hinojosa Ortiz, M. (1958), *Los Bosques de México: Relato de un Despilfarro y una Injustica* (Mexico City: Instituto Mexicano de Investigaciónes Económicas).

Merino, Leticia (1992), "Contrastes en el sector forestal: Canadá, Estados Unidos y México," *El Cotidiano*, no. 48 (June): 69.

Ovando H., Francisco Xavier (1979), "Los Diversos Sistemas de Organización en la Rama Forestal," *Mexico y Sus Bosques* 18, no. 2, Nueva Epoca.

Paré, Luisa (1992), "El eucalipto y la integración de México al mercado internacional," *El Cotidiano*, no. 48 (June).

Red Nacional de Organizaciones Campesinas Forestales (1992), *Documentos de Debate sobre la Iniciativa de Ley Forestal* (Mexico City).

Salas Reyes, G. (1989), *La Política Forestal Oficial de 1934 a 1952* (Mexico: Universidad Autónoma de Chapingo), thesis.

SARH (1993), *Levantamiento de Vedas Forestales, Febrero 1973* (Mexico City: SARH, Subsecretaría Forestal y de la Fauna).

Silva, Eduardo (1994), "Thinking Politically about Sustainable Development in the Tropical Forests of Latin America," *Development and Change* 25, no. 4: 697–721.

Snook, Laura (1995), "Community Forestry, Sustainability, and Forest Conservation in Mexico: Past Experiences and the Implications of Recent Policy Changes," unpublished manuscript.

Snook, Laura, and Patricia Negreros (1986), "Effects of Mexico's Selective Cutting System on Pine Regeneration and Growth in a Mixed Pine-Oak (*Pinus-Quercus*) Forest," *Current Topics in Forest Research: Emphasis on Contributions by Women Scientists*, USDA Forest Service, Southeastern Forest Experimental Station, General Technical

Report SE–46 for an Evaluation of the Mexican Method for Ordering Forests (Método Mexicano de Ordenación de Montes).

Szekely, M., and S. Madrid (1990), "La Apropriación Comunitaria de Recursos Naturales: Un caso de la Sierra de Juárez, Oaxaca," in E. Leff, ed., *Recursos Naturales, Técnica y Cultura: Estudios y Experiencias para un Desarrollo Alternativo* (Mexico City: UNAM).

Téllez, Luis (1993), *Nueva Legislacion de Tierras, Bosques y Aguas* (Mexico City: Fondo de Cultura Económica).

Téllez Kuenzler, Luis (1994), *La Modernización del Sector Agropecuario y Forestal* (Mexico City: Fondo de Cultura Económica).

Vazquez Soto, J. (1971), *La Política Forestal de México y el Aprovechamiento de Sus Bosques* (Mexico: Universidad Autónoma de Chapingo), thesis.

Wexler, Matthew B. (1994), "Community Forestry Challenged by Market Reforms: How the Privatization of Technical Services and Free Trade Are Restructuring Forestry in the Costa Grande of Guerrero." Report for the Ejido Reform Project, Center for U.S.-Mexican Studies, University of California, San Diego, October 17.

22

NATHAN BURAS

The Water Resources of Mexico: Their Utilization and Management

The availability of clean water is increasingly recognized as an essential ingredient of economic development. Mexico's renewable water resources, some 4,000 cubic meters per capita, are unevenly distributed across the nation, and only 15 percent are utilized. Most of the water is used for agriculture. Treatment of municipal-industrial wastewater could increase the supply of water by about 9 percent.

Nathan Buras writes that Mexico has a long history of planning its water development. Nonetheless, the scarcity of safe drinking water, insufficiency of wastewater treatment facilities, and competition for water among users led to a reexamination of water policy in the eighties. In 1989, the National Water Commission was created as the only federal authority dealing with water. The Salinas administration's water policy was designed to increase efficiency of water use and limit and control pollution. Public and private funds would be used to implement this policy, and, although water is a national resource, water services would be decentralized by fostering user associations and utilities: efficiency of water use increased when control of water was transferred to user associations. In 1992, a new national water law was enacted, which promoted these developments; it also incorporated economic incentives for compliance and introduced full-cost pricing for water services.

Although the 1995 economic crisis has lowered the priority given to water development, the drought in northern Mexico and consequent appeals for access to water from Texas make Mexican and U.S.-Mexican water issues an area of increasing domestic and international importance.

Introduction

Water has played a crucial role in Mexico's economic development. With the conclusion of the Mexican Revolution in 1926, a National Irrigation Commission was established for the purpose of building a hydraulic infrastructure that would supply water primarily for agricultural production. As the country settled down following the upheaval of the revolution, the Irrigation Commission was upgraded in 1946 to cabinet status, becoming Secretaría de Recursos Hidraulicos (Ministry of Water Resources). The new Secretaría pursued vigorous water resources development policies, mostly through River Basin Commissions and large-scale regional water plans. Thirty years later, in 1976, the Ministry of Water Resources was merged with the Ministry of Agriculture to become the Secretaría de Agricultura y Recursos Hidraulicos (Ministry of Agriculture and Water Resources), thus reflecting the priority given to solve water-related problems in the agricultural sector. This organizational structure persisted through the administration of President Carlos Salinas de Gortari.

Mexico is a country of approximately two million square kilometers, with a population in excess of ninety-three million (World Resources Institute 1994) and growing at a yearly rate of about 2 percent. The mean annual rainfall is 780 mm, which yields about 357.4 billion cubic meters of renewable water resources. On a per capita basis, the availability of water translates to slightly over 4,000 cubic meters annually—not an insignificant amount. The distribution of this resource over the territory of Mexico varies considerably, from the extreme humid tropics of the southeast to the deserts of the northwest. This diversity was one of the major reasons for constructing a complex and sophisticated hydraulic infrastructure.

Of the available renewable water resources, only about 15 percent are currently utilized, some 54.2 billion cubic meters, or 583 cubic meters per capita per year. This indicates that Mexico still has considerable amounts of undeveloped water resources in certain parts of the country. However, long distances and very difficult topographical barriers are enormous obstacles in the path of large-scale projects of inter-basin transfers of water. A reasonable conclusion could be that the management of water resources in Mexico should include a significant component of demand management on a regional basis, so as to minimize the need for the very large investments required by projects for interbasin water transfers.

About 86 percent of the water withdrawn from streams and aquifers in Mexico was supplied to the agricultural sector in 1987 (World Resources Institute 1994), 8 percent to industry, and 6 percent for domestic use. No comparable data are available for treating the wastewater generated by various human activities. One should consider, however, that about two-thirds of the water supplied to a municipal-industrial region is transformed into wastewater, or about 9 percent of the total water withdrawn annually in Mexico. The percentage may appear small, but it translates into about 4.9 billion cubic meters annually. The point is not that a few billion cubic meters of water can be added annually to Mexico's water availability; the point is that reclaiming wastewater can add a significant resource in regions of chronic water scarcity, in addition to contributing to the overall improvement of the public health situation. This was first recognized in the first National Water Plan in 1975.

The National Water Plan, 1975

The water policies of the Salinas administration are rooted in the National Water Plan of 1975. Without the groundwork laid by the plan, it is difficult to envision the transition that has occurred during the last two decades, from a policy that focused mostly on construction of dams and large-scale hydrosystems to a management orientation that placed increased emphasis on water demand and utilization.

Shortly after assuming office, the Echeverría administration (1970–76) realized the need for a National Water Plan (Buras 1976). The Mexican government began negotiations in 1971 with the United Nations Development Program and with the World Bank for technical and financial assistance. In February 1973, a formal agreement was signed between these parties, which defined the goals and objectives of the Mexico National Water Plan. At the national (as contrasted with regional) level, the *goals* of the plan were as follows:[1] (1) improve income distribution; (2) reduce dependence on foreign interests; and (3) achieve the highest possible rate of development compatible with economic and social stability.

Of course, a National Water Plan by itself, however sophisticated, could not possibly attain any of these goals without accompanying social and economic legislation. Nevertheless, it is quite remarkable that the Mexican government at that time recognized that these goals were essential for the proper functioning of the economy. Regrettably, the required accompanying social and economic legislation was not forthcoming.

The *objectives* of the National Water Plan were somewhat more specific. Two of the main objectives were the following: (1) formulation of alternative water development programs at the regional level for the short, medium, and long term, including preliminary identification of specific projects; and (2) adoption of key policy decisions concerning water development, with recommendations for the necessary institutional measures.

After a gestation period of almost twenty years, some of these policies were instituted under the Salinas administration. What is remarkable, however, is that more than two decades ago a comprehensive water plan was attempted in a country of the size and diversity of Mexico. That in itself was, at that time, a unique planning project on a world scale.

Some of the accomplishments of the 1975 National Water Plan, briefly stated, are as follows (World Bank 1976):

1. Identification of present and likely future water-use conflicts, and preparation of proposals for their solution, including transfer of available water from low-value to higher-value uses.

2. Proposals for new administrative structures to deal with the resolution of these conflicts.

3. Outlining different strategies for water development and management policies, depending on specific regional conditions.

4. Beginning of studies and evaluations for the identification and measurement of existing and potential water-use inefficiencies, particularly in irrigation, together with the analysis of potential alternatives to minimize these inefficiencies.

5. Development of mathematical models for major hydrologic basins, as tools for analyzing alternative regional hydraulic development projects.

6. Initiation of a systematic program of groundwater evaluation with proposed management structures to deal effectively with groundwater basin utilization.

7. Commencement of a systematic program of land-use evaluation, using, as a first approximation, ERTS satellite imagery.

8. A first systematic attempt to evaluate the implications of the proposed medium- and long-term development programs on the current and future budgets of the Secretaría de Recursos Hidraulicos.

9. An initial attempt to evaluate skilled personnel needs within and outside the Secretaría de Recursos Hidraulicos, including evaluation of the existing educational facilities (and the required changes) to overcome the existing deficiencies in the education, development, and training of personnel.

An immediate outcome of the Mexican National Water Plan of 1975 was the acceptance of some of its provisions by the ruling party, PRI, and their inclusion in the official platform for 1976–82. Article 78 of this platform stated, among other things, "It is advisable that in-depth analyses will be performed with the view of determining long-term irrigation needs, evaluating the implications of the competitive uses of water in agriculture, industry, and domestic supply, and deriving strategies adequate to the changing conditions of the national and international markets. It is advisable to change water prices with the object of providing incentives for the efficient use of this resource. . . ."[2]

The technical experience gained by the working team who produced the National Water Plan of 1975 was too valuable to be wasted. Consequently, toward the end of the Echeverría administration, the president of Mexico issued a directive transforming this ad hoc group into a National Commission for the National Water Plan. Subsequently, during the 1976 reorganization of the Mexican government, the two ministries of agriculture and water resources were combined into the Secretaría de Agricultura y Recursos Hidraulicos, all water-related activities were allocated to a Subsecretariat for Hydraulic Infrastructure in the new ministry, and the National Water Plan Commission became the Mexican Institute of Water Technology.

The National Water Commission

At the end of 1976, López Portillo, who was secretary of treasury in the Echeverría administration, assumed the presidency of Mexico. Regarding water resources, the new administration followed the guidelines established by the previous regime with some shifts in emphasis, continuing, however, the planning activities initiated under the Mexico National Water Plan of 1975. In fact, as behooves an effective planning agency, the 1975 plan was updated in 1981.

López Portillo's presidency was essentially a period of fairly rapid transition, from an era of active economic development to a crisis. The development projects initiated in the seventies were financed by the Mexican government with insufficient liquid funds, so that the national debt rose from 2.5 percent of gross domestic product in 1971 to 17.6 percent of GDP in 1982 (Secretaría de Agricultura y Recursos Hidraulicos 1988). This also contributed considerably to inflation and to social unrest.

Mexico started the last two decades of the twentieth century with a population almost five times as large as at the beginning of the century. The end of the decade of the seventies saw, among other things, an extraordinary growth in the petroleum production for export, which gave additional impetus to internal investments, without, however, adopting any policies for the improvement of the distribution of the national income. The atmosphere of crisis was upon Mexico.

Shortly after assuming the presidency in 1982, Miguel de la Madrid declared: "The country finds itself in a decisive moment in its national history."[3] Indeed, de la Madrid proposed a program of immediate action for reducing the inflation, protecting the industrial base and the employees, and picking up the economic growth again. Mexico had to embark on a road of great sacrifices in order to reestablish a development program based on sound foundations. However, at the beginning of 1986 a sudden drop in the world price of petroleum dealt the Mexican economy an additional blow.

The 1982 economic crisis had reverberations in the water resources sector. The scarcity of safe drinking water and of adequate wastewater treatment facilities in a large part of Mexico exacerbated the social frictions. The competition for water sharpened between the urban and rural areas, between cities, between states, and between regions. Inefficiencies were detected in all sectors of the economy. It was estimated that half the irrigation supply never reached the cultivated lands, and almost one-third of the water conveyed for domestic use was lost en route. It became necessary to establish a new water resources policy that would ensure the conservation of the resource, the adequate maintenance of the infrastructure and its efficient operation, the control of water pollution, and preserve the quality of available water.[4] The implementation of much of this policy occurred during the administration of President Salinas de Gortari.

In order to carry out these tasks effectively, a new organizational structure was needed. In February 1989, the Mexican government created the Comision Nacional del Agua (the National Water Commission). This new organization was an autonomous agency attached to the Secretaría de Agricultura y Recursos Hidraulicos (SARH) and was empowered to be the sole federal authority in Mexico to deal with water problems and issues (Comision Nacional del Agua

1990). By amending existing statutes, the National Water Commission (CNA) was given the authority to play a crucial role in the formulation of fiscal policies related to water rights and tariffs. The responsibilities of the commission included the following tasks: (1) definition of Mexico's water policies; (2) formulation, updating, and monitoring of the National Water Plan; (3) measurement of water quantity and quality and regulation of water uses; (4) preservation and enhancement of water quality in Mexico's rivers and other water bodies; (5) allocation of water to users and the granting of necessary permits; (6) planning, design, and construction of waterworks executed by the Mexican federal government; (7) regulation and control of stream flows and maintaining the safety of major hydraulic infrastructure; (8) provision of technical assistance to water users; and (9) definition and implementation of financial mechanisms necessary for the support of further development of Mexico's water resources and the provision of water-related services.

The implementation of this impressive list of objectives paved the way to a "new water culture."

A "New Water Culture"

Shortly after assuming the presidency, Salinas de Gortari formulated a new water policy, which had three main thrusts (Comision Nacional del Agua 1990): (1) add new components to the hydraulic infrastructure, so as to fill existing gaps and meet increasing water demands; (2) increase efficiency of water use; and (3) make a significant contribution to the abatement and control of water pollution.

The Salinas administration assumed three responsibilities in the implementation of this policy: (1) construction of large waterworks, in which public funds were to be augmented with private investments; (2) maintain authority and control over water, which, according to the Mexican Constitution, is a national resource; and (3) decentralize water services by fostering stronger user associations and utilities so as to provide better water services.

Shortly after being appointed, the director-general of the newly constituted National Water Commission enumerated some of the challenges facing CNA in its effort to establish a "new water culture":

1. *The political challenge.* Creating a new water culture demands, first of all, the rational resolution of internal conflicts in relation to allocation, use, and management of water resources. These conflicts have to be brought in the open and the political and socioeconomic issues debated and resolved through negotiation and compromise.

2. *The challenge of change.* It was obvious that the previous mode of managing Mexico's water resources had to give way to a new mode. In order to effectuate this shift, a vision of the future had to be outlined, which would determine the direction of change.

3. *The challenge of effectiveness.* The performance of the new National Water Commission can be effective only if it is linked with responsibility and accountability to the various groups of water users and other constituents in the Mexican society.

4. *The challenge of excellence.* CNA must attract the best-qualified people for any specific position and allow them to express their creativity. At the same time, the "deadwood" had to be removed as soon as it was discovered.

5. *The challenge of the future.* Always the next step, the next season, the next budgetary cycle, had to be considered.[5]

It was realized that the success of the new water policy depended to a large extent on a well-tuned balance between government actions and market forces (Gonzalez Villareal 1995). The result of this policy was a new water culture, which expressed itself in a number of different dimensions.

A Stronger Water Authority

The National Water Commission became the only Mexican federal authority charged with the management of the nation's water resources. Its organizational structure became decentralized to a considerably greater extent than previously, and it included six regional and thirty-one state water agencies. However, in order to strengthen both CNA and its regional and state branches, the support of the public was considered essential. Consequently, River Basin Councils were established by law, as a mechanism through which federal, state, and local governments, as well as water users and other interested groups, could share the responsibility for planning and managing the nation's water resources.

A New Water Law

In December 1992, the Mexican Congress passed a new National Water Law; its main provisions are:

1. Water is both a commodity and a public good. Its use requires licensing by the proper authority, as well as a payment for water rights and for the discharge of wastewater into the environment.

2. The river basin (and not an administrative subdivision) is the basic unit for water planning and management.

3. The management of water quantity and quality, as well as that of surface streams and groundwaters, needs to be integrated.

4. Market mechanisms have to be incorporated in the management of water resources.

5. Greater user participation in planning and management activities needs to be promoted.

6. Efficient water use and water pollution control have to be strongly emphasized.

Transfer to Users of the Management of Irrigation Districts

The National Water Commission started a program for the transfer of management to the users in seventy-eight large irrigation districts, covering 3.2 million hectares and accounting for 50 percent of the total irrigated area of Mexico. This program is probably unique in the world and involves a complex process of negotiations with over half a million farmers. Paradoxically, perhaps, was the fact that considerable resistance to this transfer was encountered internally in many districts: apparently, it was easier to accept management decisions made in Mexico City than to assume responsibility for one's own choices. In any event, by 1993, 1.5 million hectares were transferred to user associations, and water-use efficiencies in those districts increased from 59 percent to 64 percent (Gonzalez Villareal 1995).

Water Utilities for Municipalities

A national program was launched to decentralize water utilities from state and local agencies, in order to reach a more efficient operation, both technically and financially. The investment part of the program included a mix of federal and state subsidies, loans from Mexican national institutions as well as international sources (such as the World Bank), investments by the utilities themselves, and private investments. From 1989 to 1992, 13.5 million people were provided with drinking water and 11.5 million people with access to sewer systems. For the first time in many years, the coverage of these basic services grew faster than the population increase. The private sector invested in these projects in excess of $350 million. The revenue collected from these water services increased during these three years by more than 250 percent in real terms, due to more rational tariffs and an increased billing coverage (Gonzalez Villareal, 1995).

Water Quality

Water users must comply with specific conditions for the discharge of their wastewater as determined by the National Water Commission. In addition, users must pay a fee for the right of discharging wastewaters into national water bodies and must inform CNA periodically about the quality of their discharges. This system was set up so that it would be less costly for a user to treat its own wastewater than to pay discharge fees. The legislation provided for a two-year grace period of not paying fees related to water quality for industries and municipalities that demonstrate that they are in the process of building appropriate wastewater treatment facilities (Gonzalez Villareal 1995).

Financial Aspects

Two main objectives were formulated regarding water-related finances: first, the recovery of the full costs of providing water services through realistic tariffs;

second, the investment by the private sector of two dollars for every federal dollar invested in the construction and operation of water resources systems.

Management

In addition to issuing licenses and collecting fees, the National Water Commission also updated the water rights register. The transfer of water rights was now permitted with due consideration of third-party effects and other externalities, as well as social and economic objectives. This would allow some market mechanism to intervene in the management of regional and local water resources, for better water allocations and increased efficiency of water use (Gonzalez Villareal 1995). A "new water culture" was being created.

Summary

The policies of the Salinas administration in the broad and diverse field of water resources can be evaluated and appreciated only with reference to events that occurred in the preceding twenty years. These policies were in stark contrast with the attitudes that prevailed at the time when the first Mexican National Water Plan was produced in 1975. At that time, one could not even mention decentralization of management of water resources; and irrigation projects (dams, canals, pumping stations, etc.) took center stage, to the exclusion of other kinds of water-related projects, in the planning process, which was concentrated solely in Mexico City.

The National Water Commission pursued vigorously the implementation of the new policies instituted by the Salinas administration, in the face of considerable difficulties. It is significant, perhaps, that the first two irrigation districts that accepted the transfer of responsibilities from the federal government to manage their own water resources were an irrigation district in Hermosillo (Sonora) and a district in central Mexico;[6] they are both major suppliers of produce, the first to the Los Angeles market, the other to Mexico City. The free market economy seemed to be effective.

Another set of difficulties persisted in the tropical-humid Gulf Coast in southeastern Mexico, arising out of the prevailing land-holding pattern. The land is held in large cattle ranches, and their owners are enabled by law to utilize the land at a low carrying capacity per head of livestock. The ranch owners, who exert considerable political weight, are opposed to water-related projects, whether irrigation or drainage, that may restrict their extensive use of the land (Kirpich 1994).

The administration of Salinas saw the signing and ratification of the North American Free Trade Agreement (NAFTA). This agreement spilled over also into the area of water resources in the form of periodic symposia on the management of water resources systems in North America. The first two symposia (1990 and 1991) were one day long each and took place in Mexico. The third conference took place in Tucson, Arizona, in 1993 and assembled more than forty scientists and professionals from Canada, the United States, and Mexico (Buras 1995). This conference provided a forum for the Mexican engineers, scientists and professionals to present different aspects of the "new water culture."

The last year of the presidency of Salinas de Gortari was marked by considerable turbulence. A sudden acute financial crisis developed, which engendered a sharp drop in the public's confidence in the effectiveness of the government and resulted in a great deal of uncertainty regarding the future. The new administration of President Ernesto Zedillo was faced with almost insoluble social and economic problems, so that water-related issues acquired a lower priority. The National Water Commission was removed from the Ministry of Agriculture and Water Resources and placed in another ministry dealing mostly with the environment: its importance was deemphasized.

Hopefully, Mexico will emerge from this ordeal with a stronger sociopolitical structure. It is anticipated that as the turbulence subsides, opportunities will return for continuing the implementation of the positive water-related policies initiated under the Salinas administration.

Notes

1. Document no. MEX–71/534/C/101/42, dated August 1972 and signed by the UNDP, the government of Mexico, and the World Bank.
2. PRI, "Los Cien Puntos del Plan Basico de Gobierno 1976–1982," as published in *Novedades,* November 23, 1975, 23–25.
3. Poder Ejecutivo Federal, *Plan Nacional de Desarollo, 1983–1988*, Secretaría de Programación y Presupuesto, México, May 1983.
4. Ibid.
5. F.J. Gonzalez Villareal, director general, National Water Commission, 1989–94, personal communication, 1990.
6. E. Palacias Velez, director of irrigation districts, National Water Commission, 1989–91, personal communication, 1990.

Bibliography

Buras N. (1976), *The Mexico National Water Plan 1975: Evaluation.* Report submitted to the World Bank (Washington, D.C.).
Buras, N., ed. (1995), "Foreword," *Management of Water Resources in North America* (New York: American Society of Civil Engineers) iii-iv.
Comision Nacional del Agua (1990), *Water Policies and Strategies* (Mexico City: National Water Commission).
Gonzalez Villareal, F.J. (1990), personal communication.
———. (1995), "New Departures in Water Management in Mexico," *Management of Water Resources in North America III* (New York: American Society of Civil Engineers), (1995), 43–54.

Kirpich, P.Z. (1994), "Priority Regions in Latin America for Water Management," *Proceedings of the Interamerican Dialogue on Water Management*, Miami, Florida, October 27–30, 1993, 247–56.

Secretaría de Agricultura y Recursos Hidraulicos (1988), *Agua y Sociedad: Una Historia de las Obras Hidraulicas en Mexico* (Mexico City: Secretaría de Agricultura y Recursos Hidraulicos).

World Bank (1976), *Mexico: National Water Plan, UNDP Project MEX 71/534, Agency Evaluation and Recommendations*, report no. 1406-ME (Washington, D.C.: World Bank).

World Resources Institute (1994), *World Resources 1994–95* (New York: Oxford University Press).

Part IV

Politics and Social Structures

23

ELIZABETH UMLAS

Environmental Nongovernmental Organizations and Environmental Policy

The increasing national and international awareness of Mexico's growing environmental problems, combined with a more open political system, led to the effective action of Mexican environmental nongovernmental organizations, from the mid-1980s onward. The 1985 earthquake in Mexico City led to the formation of citizens' groups to aid quake victims, and a variety of nongovernmental organizations became active.

Environmental nongovernmental organizations have had to try to influence policy when the government's administrative structure dealing with the environment was changing and information was scarce. They were nonetheless able to pressure international agencies to deny funding for a dam that would have flooded Indian communities, and to successfully urge the re-routing of a highway in Chiapas. Further action by environmental nongovernmental organizations may depend on how environmental issues are linked to agrarian reform issues and to the relationship of the environment to other nongovernmental organizations working for the democratization of politics and the increasing mobilization of civil society.

Elizabeth Umlas discusses Mexican environmental non-governmental organizations (NGOs) and environmental policy from the mid-1980s to 1994, with emphasis on Mexico City–based groups. Many Mexican environmental NGOs are middle-class, urban, and fairly young, and they range from tiny volunteer organizations to well-financed conservationist groups with boards of trustees and members.1 Environmental NGOs are not associated with a particular corporate "pillar"—

The research for this essay was conducted from September 1993 to July 1994, with a grant from the Yale Center for International and Area Studies. All interviews cited in notes were conducted in Mexico City.

that is, labor, peasants, or popular classes—and present a relatively new challenge to the government.

While environmental NGOs were strongest in the mid to late 1980s, and instrumental in raising environmental awareness in government and in the Mexican population, the government has since reasserted control over the environmental agenda. However, Mexican environmental NGOs have been able to influence policy when they have coalesced around specific issues, when the issue has received substantial national or international press coverage, and when political conditions have further pressured the government to act on the issue. Federal environmental policy and the government's treatment of environmental NGOs under President Salinas combined reaction and preemption (Mumme 1992), traditional corporatist methods (the incorporation of environmentalist leaders into government positions, for example), and newer, technocratic solutions.[2]

Emergence of Environmental NGOs

There have long been conservationist organizations and environmental activists in Mexico, but it was in the mid-1980s that urban environmental (and other) mobilization surged. It was catalyzed in part by the earthquakes of 1985 in the capital, when Mexico City residents faced the stark reality of the government's lack of preparedness to deal with the catastrophe, and had to organize themselves to aid quake victims.

Although Quadri (1990) places the "birth of *ecologismo*" in Mexico between 1982 and 1983, with few exceptions there was little widespread environmental mobilization earlier.[3] Environmental groups gained a national presence with the Primer Encuentro Nacional de Ecologistas in 1985, just after the earthquakes. It was also in this period that some of Mexico's best-known environmental NGOs and networks formed. In 1985, the Group of 100, originally one hundred intellectuals, artists, and writers committed to the promotion of environmental causes, came together to protest environmental policy (or the lack thereof). In the mid-1980s the Alianza Ecologista was created, which would eventually form the Mexican Green Party in 1988,[4] and in 1986 the Pacto de Grupos Ecologistas, a horizontal, somewhat diffuse network of environmental NGOs, formed after the Primer Encuentro.

In the mid-1980s, President de la Madrid had instituted *foros de consulta popular*, public fora intended to provoke discussion of various issues, including environmental problems. According to Mumme, Bath, and Assetto (1988), the fora encouraged "the formation and proliferation of environmental interest groups," probably to a degree unintended by the government. In 1988 the legislature passed the Ley General de Equilibrio Ecológico y Protección al Ambiente, which calls for "encouragement of the participation of non-governmental actors in the environmental policy process" (Nuccio and Ornelas 1990, 44).

De la Madrid's actions helped boost environmental mobilization, and to the government's concern, "environmental activists began to link general environmentalism to a critique of the political system itself" (Mumme and Sánchez 1989, 4, 6). Mumme (1992, 129) makes the important observation that this mobilization in the late 1980s coincided with economic and political crises for the PRI. In the second half of de la Madrid's term, a national grassroots movement formed against the Laguna Verde nuclear power plant in Veracruz. The movement included Mexico City groups, social organizations and environmental NGOs from Veracruz, housewives, and students, among others, and was able to delay the plant's start-up. Laguna Verde went online in 1990, however, despite severe criticism about its safety.[5]

Government Reaction and Policy

With the beginning of Salinas's term, the government attacked on several fronts to regain legitimacy after the 1988 elections, the results of which were seriously marred by fraud. In the first half of his term, Salinas's environmental policy was "strikingly reactive to the challenge of environmental mobilization" (Mumme 1992, 131) and set the tone for his sexenio: environmental groups were put back on the defensive.

The start of the new sexenio also coincided with the decline of the Pacto de Grupos Ecologistas, which had attracted many of Mexico's most active environmental NGOs, as well as a good deal of government attention. By 1988 the Pacto was wracked by internal schisms based on personal and political differences, which emerged sharply in the 1988 elections.[6] In addition, environmental NGOs, like other nongovernmental groups, were affected by the economic difficulties of the 1980s and early 1990s.

In 1991, Salinas signed the Convention on International Trade in Endangered Species (CITES) and ordered the closure of the highly polluting March 18 oil refinery in Azcapotzalco, in northern Mexico City. While there had been some mobilization by environmental groups in favor of these measures, the timing of the decrees was probably heavily influenced by the fact that the North American Free Trade Agreement (NAFTA) negotiations were gaining importance, and Salinas was intent on portraying his government as environment friendly. In the case of the refinery, many observers feel the closure was one of several showy maneuvers with which Salinas was attempting to regain legitimacy for his administration, and Mumme notes that the endangered species decrees were "low-cost options with high public visibility" (Mumme 1992, 140, n. 8).

Perhaps Salinas's most visible decision regarding the environment was the dissolution of the Secretaría de Desarrollo Urbano y Ecología (SEDUE) and the creation, in its place, of the Secretaría de Desarrollo Social (SEDESOL, in May 1992. SEDESOL's two environmental branches (which are semi-autonomous institutions) are the Instituto Nacional de Ecología (INE, charged with creating environmental policies and norms) and the Procuraduría Federal de Protección al Ambiente (PFPA, the environmental attorney general, charged with enforcement of environmental law). Many Mexican environmental NGOs protested the change and felt that ecology, now without even a sub-secretariat, would be subordinated to social development, and particularly to Salinas's Programa Nacional de Solidaridad (PRONASOL), which is administered by SEDESOL.[7]

Several government officials called the creation of SEDESOL a "visionary" transformation, which, in joining ecology with the fight against poverty, confirms the Mexican government's commitment to sustainable development.[8] Critics felt the move was indicative of the government's treatment of environmental issues as an afterthought. An interesting development, however, was the appointment, late in Salinas's term, of several highly respected ecologists from the academic and nongovernmental community to high posts in SEDESOL—positions that often go to political appointees. The most important example was the appointment, in January 1994, of biologist Julia Carabias to head the INE. While environmental activists received the news enthusiastically, they also noted that many of Salinas's appointees would probably be out of office by late 1994, when his term ended. NGOs also contend with a constant changing of the guard at SEDESOL: for example, Mexico had three environmental attorneys general in less than two years.

The Mexico City government has also undertaken several highly visible measures to fight the capital's severe air pollution, the best known being Hoy No Circula (One Day Without a Car), a program that prohibits residents from using their cars one day a week. The program, originally proposed by environmental NGOs and begun in 1989 as a temporary measure, was made permanent soon afterward. It seems to have backfired in terms of intended results, however, as many who could afford it bought a second car to drive on their "off-day." The program's effectiveness has also been limited by corruption and by the government's failure to promote and improve public transportation more vigorously, thereby discouraging private vehicle use and gas consumption.[9]

During the Salinas administration, Mexico saw an increase in environmental technical norms and *reglamentos* (which are needed to implement laws), and Mexican environmental laws are considered quite strict. Enforcement is lacking, however, in part because of understaffing, underbudgeting,[10] and poor training of inspection officials. The Salinas administration also relied heavily on *convenios* signed between government and industry to redress violation of environmental norms. It is very difficult to verify whether fines are paid, however, and the policy relies greatly on voluntary action by both officials and manufacturers.[11]

An important aspect of the Salinas administration was its focus on Mexico's "modernization" and entrance into the industrialized world, and the centerpiece of this effort was the passage of NAFTA in 1993. As far as the Mexican public was concerned, NAFTA's negotiation process was kept behind closed doors. In the United States, several environmental NGOs were galvanized around the issue and played an important role in pressuring for the creation of the parallel Environmental Accord. In Mexico, environmental and other NGOs were kept in the dark about NAFTA's provisions and potential impact, and the treaty sailed through the legislature, despite public criticism and concern. Much of the information on NAFTA that reached Mexican NGOs came from their counterparts in Canada and the United States. The most active and important Mexican NGO network to form around the free trade issue was the Red Mexicana de Acción Frente al Libre Comercio (RMALC), but it too has been hampered by lack of access to information.[12]

While environmental NGOs lost considerable strength and visibility after 1988, in certain cases Mexico City organizations have joined with rural groups around specific issues, and these coalitions have been able to affect policy. Two notable examples are the suspension of the San Juan dam and the detour of a proposed highway in the Chimalapas rainforest, both in 1992. While these cases are quite complex, they are worth mentioning briefly as important examples of environmental mobilization that have changed the direction of policy.

In late 1990 the Consejo de Pueblos Nahuas del Alto Balsas (CPNAB) formed to protest the planned San Juan hydroelectric dam, one of a series of proposed dams on the Balsas River in Guerrero.[13] From 1990 to 1992 the CPNAB succeeded in bringing national and international attention to the dam project, which would have flooded almost twenty Nahuatl communities. It called in journalists and Mexican and international NGOs, and sent letters to local and foreign newspapers, as well as to the international lending institutions that were to finance the dam. The prestigious Group of 100 took out ads in major Mexican newspapers asking the government to suspend the project (Good 1992). In October 1992, the government suspended the dam,[14] and as Good has shown, "massive, highly publicized protest by Nahuatl Indians against the project was a crucial factor in the World Bank and Inter-American Development Bank decisions not to fund it" (Good 1992, 1).

A case with several similarities is that of the Chimalapas, a 600,000-hectare stretch of forest in southeastern Oaxaca (bordering on Chiapas), which is perhaps the area of greatest biodiversity in Mexico. In late 1991, the Comité Nacional para la Defensa de los Chimalapas (CNDCHIM), a national coalition of environmental NGOs, artists, intellectuals, researchers, and representatives of over forty local indigenous communities, formed to protest a proposed highway that was to run through El Ocote Reserve in Chimalapas, damaging an area of crucial biodiversity. The highway, supported by then-governor of Chiapas Patrocinio González Garrido and powerful economic interests in the area, would have shaved two hours off the drive from Tuxtla Gutierrez to Mexico City.

Headed by representatives of mostly *zoque* indigenous communities in Chimalapas, CNDCHIM used strategies that included demonstrations in Mexico City, use of the media to publicize the issue, and demands for meetings with government officials. CNDCHIM has also benefited from the experience and prestige of its members, some of whom are among the best-known environmentalists in Mexico. Several CNDCHIM members, through years of work with NGOs in the Chimalapas, had already formed extensive ties with indigenous communities there, and international organizations such as the Rockefeller Foundation and World Wide Fund for Nature have been instrumental in funding these NGOs' work.

In 1992, Salinas signed a decree changing the route of the proposed highway to prevent its passing through the Chimalapas. This outcome was due, in part, to timing: the government was concerned with its international image, and it was under scrutiny during both the Earth Summit in Rio de Janeiro and the NAFTA negotiations. It was also due in large part to the mobilizational efforts of the CNDCHIM, whose members even approached Salinas at the Earth Summit to press him on the issue. According to several NGO activists, Luis Donaldo Colosio, then head of SEDESOL, was also instrumental in opening a dialogue with NGOs about the proposed highway.

The government is presently exploring the possibility of establishing an ecological reserve in Chimalapas, to be run by local campesino communities. The creation of the *reserva* is one of the main goals of the Cndchim and local communities, but they have insisted it be postponed until the local agrarian conflict over land boundaries is resolved.[15] In both the San Juan dam and the Chimalapas cases, press coverage, timing, the government's image, international actors, and coalitions of local communities and Mexico City groups came together to sway policy.

Outlook and Future

Just as the preceding analysis is both positive and negative with regard to Mexican environmental NGOs and environmental policy, the outlook for the next sexenio seems mixed. On the negative side, Julia Carabias has astutely noted that the "conjunctural" quality of environmental groups (their concentration on localized or immediate environmental problems as opposed to a more global vision of the environment-development dilemma) has in part caused the Mexican government to react as it has: that is, responding to these problems one at a time, and according to the loudest demands.[16] Observers criticize the "bourgeois" character of many urban environmental NGOs and their lack of ties to rural counterparts. Within the NGO community itself, there is a definite schism between those who see themselves as "autonomous" from government, and those perceived as being "coopted," or in league with the government.

Cooptation, or the perception of it, is linked in part to the financial weakness of many NGOs (not just environmental) and their dependence on the government. This weakness in turn is partly due to the difficulty NGOs have in obtaining tax deductibility status from the government. Many NGO participants and lawyers believe this difficulty is one way the government "severely limit[s] the scope of [NGOs'] activities."[17] The cooptation of environmentalists—and their fear of it—seems to contribute to apathy and cynicism, and even to weaken the incentive to mobilize.

On the positive side, many environmental NGOs have progressed from their strategy of *denuncia* ten years ago, to concrete and pragmatic proposals today. There is evidence that some NGOs are attempting to join with local urban neighborhood associations—not necessarily *ecologista* in name—that have increasingly tied their environmental demands (clean water, green spaces, controls on construction) to demands for democracy, including access to information, participation in urban planning, and the right to elect their own leaders.[18]

Environmental NGOs are also increasing their ties to international counterparts—the Rio conference and NAFTA negotiations were especially important for strengthening these ties and improving Mexican NGOs' access to information and potential funding sources. Finally, there is an increasing professionalization and political sophistication among many environmental NGOs. While Mexico's laws do not lend themselves to class action or citizen suits, nor has political lobbying been an option for Mexican NGOs, some environmental activists are seeking legal and political redress in new ways. For example, in 1994 Greenpeace-Mexico prepared a proposal on the total ban of toxic waste importation into Mexico. The proposal generated surprising consensus across political parties in the Mexican legislature and was passed (with provisions) by the lower house on July 14. It awaited debate in the senate as of January 1995.

Mexico is facing a new sexenio, headed by a president who will likely continue Salinas's legacy of an increasingly streamlined state and heightened emphasis on technocratic solutions. The lack of an overall environmental plan in Mexico, and the government's neoliberal economic framework, with its emphasis on extensive agriculture, privatization of communal land, and urban commercial development, may well deepen Mexico's environmental problems. The role of environmental NGOs and their allies in the democratization process—demanding access to information, creating space for mobilization and policy debate, and pressing the government for accountability on the environment—will be an important part of what some see as a general mobilization of civil society in Mexico. Whether these groups will be able to advance the debate on sustainable development and the environmental problems caused by the present economic development model remains to be seen.

Notes

1. Many of the latter are linked to the Mexican business community and are generally more sympathetic to the government than are the former.

2. Sergio Aguayo, head of Alianza Cívica, an NGO network that formed in 1994 to help ensure clean elections that year, has noted that although Salinas reacted to NGOs in general with a certain "pragmatism" and flexibility, in fact his administration was hostile to NGOs (interview with the author, July 7, 1994).

3. These exceptions include the successful movement in the early 1980s of fishermen and environmentalists to prevent the construction of a nuclear experimental center on Lake Patzcuaro in Michoacán, and the mobilization in 1984-85 of Mexico City residents in the Ajusco area to protest the government's efforts to expel "irregular" settlers for "ecological" reasons. See Pezzoli, "Environmental Conflicts in the Urban Milieu."

4. The Green Party (PVEM) got its electoral register in 1991 and ran a candidate, Jorge González Torres, in the presidential elections of 1994. However, it is widely criticized as being a creation of the PRI to divide the opposition vote. Many Mexican environmental activists feel the PVEM has no real ecological platform and do not want to join it.

5. The plant opened for commercial use in 1990 but was actually in operation by 1988.

6. The Pacto was also split by the Lomas de Seminario incident in Mexico City, in which several members supported the government's expulsion of irregular settlers for allegedly ecological reasons, while other members condemned it.

7. PRONASOL, or Solidarity, is ostensibly meant to pump resources into needy communities and development projects but is widely criticized as an electoral vehicle of the PRI and a mechanism by which the party-state apparatus can target marginalized communities in areas where the PRI has lost favor.

8. Interviews with María Angélica Luna Parra, former directora general de concertación social, SEDESOL, February 22, 1994; Cristina Cortinas, directora de proyectos especiales, INE, January 5, 1994; and Arturo Alcocer Lujambio, subprocurador de participación social y quejas, PFPA, January 25, 1994.

9. The Mexico City government is presently studying the feasibility of suspending Hoy No Circula or waiving it for those who install catalytic converters in their cars.

10. While Mexico spent almost $80 million on the environment in 1992, a marked increase over 1988, newspapers reported that SEDESOL admitted in its 1991-92 report on the environment (released in late 1993) that problems such as air pollution, deforestation, and the handling of hazardous waste had not improved. See Angélica Enciso, "No se han resuelto problemas ecológicos, reconoce la Sedesol," *La jornada*, October 7, 1993, 25; Benjamin Powell, "INE Releases Environmental Report," *The News*, October 7, 1993, 1 & 38; and *México: Informe de la situación general en materia de equilibrio ecológico y protección al ambiente 1991-92* (Mexico City: SEDESOL, 1993), xii and passim.

11. Interview with Greg Block, Esq., February 1, 1994. See Laurelli, et al., "Incorporación de la dimensión ambiental en una administración sectorializada," 750-51. See also Mumme and Sánchez (1994, 11), and Block, "One Step Away from Environmental Citizen Suits in Mexico," 10350.

12. RMALC, made up of environmental NGOs, independent labor groups, fishermen's unions, and many other types of NGOs and social organizations, formed to protest the treaty's provisions and the negotiation process of NAFTA. It is now involved in monitoring NAFTA's effects, pressing for a renegotiation of the treaty's terms, and demanding more citizen participation on the trilateral commissions on trade, labor, and environment.

13. The following account is based on Good, " 'Making the Struggle, One Big One.' "

14. Salinas suspended the dam only until the end of his term; the CPNAB has continued to push for a definitive cancellation of the project. See "Exigen la cancelación de una obra hidroeléctrica," *La jornada*, October 27, 1993; and "Demandan cancelar el proyecto hidroel éctrico en Tetelcingo," *La jornada*, January 15, 1994, 23.

15. The complexity of the land problem cannot be covered here for reasons of space. According to Miguel Angel García, a key member of CNDCHIM and an anthropologist who has worked in the Chimalapas for over fifteen years, cattle ranchers and lumber merchants (with the Chiapas government's encouragement) have created a "false inter-

state conflict" by sending indigenous colonizers into the Chimalapas, fomenting their clash with indigenous groups already there. The cattlers and timber interests have thus been able to advance on the forest over several decades. They have not recognized the communal property rights of the *zoque* Indians, who purchased the land in 1687, and it is this boundary dispute that must now be resolved before the Reserva Ecológica Campesina is created (interviews with Miguel Angel García, Maderas del Pueblo del Sureste A.C., May 27, 1994, and Luis Miguel Robles Gil, Naturalia A.C., April 23, 1994).

16. Interview with Julia Carabias, January 4, 1994. The interview was conducted less than a month before Carabias was appointed to head the INE.

17. Interview with Betty Aridjis, Grupo de los 100, May 30, 1994.

18. In Mexico City, the mayor and *delegados* are appointed not elected. A major debate in Mexico City has formed around a proposed political reform that would allow for election of these officials.

Bibliography

Block, Greg (1993), "One Step Away from Environmental Citizen Suits in Mexico," *Environmental Law Reporter* 23, no. 6 (June): 10350.

Good, Catharine (1992), "'Making the Struggle, One Big One': Nahuatl Resistance to the San Juan Dam, Mexico." Paper presented to the Agrarian Studies Seminar, Yale University, October 30.

Laurelli, Elsa, et al. (1990), "Incorporación de la dimensión ambiental en una administración sectorializada" in Enrique Leff, ed., *Medio ambiente y desarrollo en México*, vol. 2 (Mexico City: UNAM, Centrao de Investigaciones Interdisciplinarias en Humanidades).

Mumme, Stephen (1992), "System Maintenance and Environmental Resorm in Mexico: Salinas' Preemptive Strategy," *Latin American Perspectives* 19, no. 1, issue 72 (Winter): 131.

Mumme, Stephen, Richard Bath, and Valerie Assetto (1988), "Political Development and Environmental Policy in Mexico," *Latin American Research Review* 23, no. 1: 20.

Mumme, Stephen, and Roberto Sánchez (1989), "Mexico's Environment Under Salinas: Institutionalizing Policy Reform." Paper presented at the XV International Congress of the Latin American Studies Association, Miami, December.

Nuccio, Richard, and Angelina Ornelas (1990), "Mexico's Environment and the United States" in Janet Welsh Brown, ed., *In the U.S. interest* (Boulder: Westview).

Pezzoli, Keith (1991), "Environmental Conflicts in the Urban Milieu: The Case of Mexico City" in D. Goodman and M. Redclift, eds., *Environment and Development in Latin America* (New York: Manchester University Press).

Quadri, Gabriel (1990), "Una breve crónica del ecologismo en México," *Ciencias*, especial 4 (Mexico City: UNAM, Centro de Ecologia): 58.

SEDESOL (1993), *México: Informe de la situación general en materia de equilibrio ecológico y protección al ambiente 1991–2* (Mexico City: SEDESOL).

24

DOUGLAS A. CHALMERS AND KERIANNE PIESTER

Nongovernmental Organizations and the Changing Structure of Mexican Politics

The growth of nongovernmental organizations highlights the changing structure of Mexican politics. Douglas Chalmers and Kerianne Piester trace their recent growth to government failure to respond adequately to emergencies, a desire for political reform, and the adoption of international norms that stress the private sector, which includes nongovernmental organizations. Some of the latter are grouped into networks that may help to provide coherent organization for civil society. Such networks increase the autonomy of organizations in their dealings with the state, obtaining resources and favorable regulations. Political parties do not dominate them, although Alianza Cívica, formed to favor a fair electoral process, was close to leftist opposition parties.

The multiplicity of issues and organizations points to increasing pluralism, in contrast to organization of the masses or a corporatist society. The nongovernmental organization networks are channels of communication but not of authority. The formation of nongovernmental organizations and their networks leads to internationalization of politics. Foreign foundations' and international interest groups' support of Mexican nongovernmental organizations necessarily influences Mexican politics, but this has not led to the objections that would arise from direct intervention by a foreign government.

One of the more subtle changes in Mexico in the last decade has been the expansion of independent associational life, sometimes referred to as the growth of civil society. If it continues to strengthen, we believe it will have a profound effect on the way Mexican politics is conducted. There are many significant forms of independent associations, including businesses, grassroots organizations, private universities, among others. We wish to describe some of the characteristics of political patterns emerging in the relationship between nongovernmental organizations (NGOs), the people, and the state—one important segment of this new level of associational life. Reversals and fundamental redirection are possible, and it is highly unlikely that these new styles of politics will ever completely eliminate other forms, but we believe there is a high probability that these characteristics will be part of Mexico's future.

In the last decade, there have been a rising number of NGOs. These are nonprofit, nonofficial organizations, whose members are generally educated and often professional. They often deliver some kind of service, for example, developmental assistance to the poor, or serve as an alternative policy "think tank." Our concern, though, is not with these activities in themselves, but with how NGOs and their networks fit into the political system and how they are, potentially, changing it.

This growth of associationalism is a common trend in many countries (Salamon 1993). It is probably better understood as the result of structural changes (which we will not try to discuss) than as particular governments' policies to promote associations, although government responses to crises generated by structural changes may be important in shaping their specific role. In Mexico, a key moment came in 1968 when popular reaction against violent government actions against protesters mobilized a number of movements. More recently, another moment came in the aftermath of the 1985 earthquake in Mexico City, when many citizens organized, either to take over relief from the slowly responding government, or to make demands on the government and influence the reconstruction.

Some characteristics of President Carlos Salinas de Gortari's term of office (1988–94) have also given a distinctively Mexican shape to this growth of civil society. As a result of the rise and subsequent frustration of opposition parties in 1988, and of widespread skepticism about the fairness of the elections that brought Salinas to power, many sought to organize politically, independent of the government. This impulse was strengthened when Salinas decided to downplay political reforms in favor of economic ones. The government's National Solidarity Program, a striking effort to deal with the problems of poverty and the economic dislocation through (at least nominally) demand-based development programs, was both a recognition of the growing number of popular organizations (by explicitly seeking to incorporate or preempt them) and a stimulus to the formation of new ones. Further, Mexico's turn outward, most obviously through negotiating NAFTA, has made international influences more legitimate in Mexico. International norms have been adopted, neoliberalism has pushed the "private sector," and internationally based "voluntary" and "nonprofit" organizations have become active. All of these promoted the growth of a "third sector."

In Mexico, which has had a strong state and a strongly statist culture, the growth of this sector gets less attention than it might elsewhere. Further, attention has focused on the so far incomplete process of democratization and the newly threatened state capacity to carry out economic reforms. In such a climate, it is easy to overlook the fact that there are incipient trends that would shift the structure of Mexican politics away from a long-established clientelistic and corporatist pattern. If the growth of associations continues, democratization and economic policy making will look quite different than they would if the state still dominated structurally and institutionally.

It is impossible at this stage to assess precisely the size and importance of this movement toward civil society and the growth of NGOs. NGOs are not a single movement or organization. They take multiple forms, are fragmented, change frequently, and there is no meaningful inventory that is useful for understanding their political role. But our strong impression is that growth of the number and significance of NGOs and other independent associations would be very difficult to reverse or hold back.

Therefore, although extrapolation is risky, we think it is worthwhile to point to the characteristics of this group of new organizations and the institutions, both formal and informal, that are emerging around them to suggest the possible directions of changes in Mexican politics. The question is, What new kinds of politics are being generated by these groups?

To begin exploring this question, a group of us carried out an investigation of four NGO networks in Mexico.[1] Networks may be considered a sort of super-NGO, in that they, too, are generally nonprofit, unofficial organizations, often staffed by professionals, that perform services. In this case, however, their principle bases are not directly in the grassroots but rather in a large number of other NGOs. They usually aim at serving to strengthen the impact of their constituent organizations, to provide them with a national presence giving them recognition in society, and to provide some protection for the autonomy of the NGOs, particularly from the state. NGO networks offer at least the potential of providing coherent organization for significant part of civil society. We wanted to know whether this potential was real. Our sample of four cases was too small to make conclusive results, but we are able to suggest some possible dimensions of change.

The first potential characteristic of the new structures of Mexican politics associated with the NGOs is that they are not creating a self-sufficient world *apart* from the state, but rather *enhancing the autonomy of societal organizations in order to deal with the state.* We are in an era in which one frequently encounters the rhetoric of "nongovernmental," "deregulation," "free enterprise," "limited role for the state," and "autonomous civil society." It is easy to imagine that the growth of NGOs might illustrate the creation of some sort of privatized world. In the case of nonprofit NGOs, however, quite the reverse is the case. The internationally based developmentalist NGOs have, for example, gone through periods of trying to stimulate self-sufficiency and complete autonomy—for example, among rural communities. But today the consensus seems to be that NGOs should promote the capacity of groups to extract resources and favorable regulation from the state. This is particularly so in the policy areas we looked at in our 1994 study: social policy and women's rights, environment and working conditions.[2] The sample of four NGO networks in our project appeared to have a common point of view on this question. They were all seeking to alter the relationship of people to the state, *not* break that relationship. This was obviously true of those who were interested in political practices, such as the network named the Convergence of Civil Organizations for Democracy (Convergencia), but also for those that focus on policy—for example, the Mexican Action Network on Free Trade (RMALC), which seeks to influence trade policy, and the Mutual Support Forum (FAM), which seeks to shape social policy.

Second, NGOs are building a politics that is not only independent of the dominant party, but in which *political parties do not dominate* the process. Mexico for some time has had a strong executive tightly linked to an "official" (i.e., ruling) party, the PRI. Concern for democratization has centered attention on the possibility of opposition parties successfully challenging the PRI. But NGOs and NGO networks are beginning to carve out an arena where political forces meet each other, and where both the official state party and the opposition parties are either marginally important, or take center stage only at some moment, such as election time, or in the legislature (Schmitter 1992).[3]

One example is the NGO network, Mutual Support Forum (FAM), which has created a structure to serve multiple local and church-affiliated groups at the community level, with the specific purpose of formulating and influencing social policy at the national level. While its origins are in the Catholic charitable and relief efforts, it has not affiliated with the Partido Accion Nacional (PAN), the party closest to the church, nor has it affiliated with the Partido de la Revolución Democratica (PRD), despite their shared commitment to the popular classes. The FAM has opted to maintain autonomous linkages, working with a variety of government institutions. Since it works with the government, a strict "we-they" attitude, not uncommon in some Mexican circles (probably most common among intellectuals), might argue that they were being coopted by the PRI establishment. But what seems more significant to us is that FAM appears to be establishing a space that is potentially autonomous from all parties, in which interests are developed, conflicts resolved, and policies promoted without direct involvement of political parties.

The issue is more complicated for NGOs concerned directly with political practices and democratic change. Alianza Cívica is a network of civic organizations, predominantly NGOs, which was formed to promote a fair electoral process for everyone. Since its formation, Alianca Cívica has struggled to be recognized as a nonpartisan organization and to remain one. On the one hand, the issue of fair elections in Mexico has meant, and continues to mean, challenging the PRI/government. It necessarily entails holding the PRI to standards it has accepted only reluctantly and partially—providing a level playing field for all participants and allowing transparent procedures that would risk a defeat for itself. Insistence on honest elections has long been defined as anti-PRI and has been a major banner of the opposition parties, the PAN and the PRD. Whatever its intentions, many thought the Alianza was "objectively" partisan, simply by working for honest elections. There was also no question but that the activists in the Alianza were generally more sympathetic to the PRD than to the PRI or the PAN. A widespread culture of "us versus them," in which people are categorized as either with the establishment or against it, an attitude characteristic of the opposition as well as the government, reinforces the assumption of partisanship. It conceptualizes the political process in terms of these broad groups, and not in terms of the specific patterns of organizations and institutions. But organizationally and institutionally, Alianza was clearly moving in the direction of staking out a nonpartisan institutional role. It is not clear at this writing whether, if it continues beyond the presidential elections, it will strengthen its nonpartisan quality or succumb to the assumptions of many that such a role does not exist on this issue.

Related to this separation from parties is a third aspect. The NGOs appear to be participating in the creation of *a kind of pluralism* and specifically undercutting any attempt to construct, or reconstruct, broad political blocs in society. This is important especially for the way popular sectors are represented in politics. Many, including Latin Americans, often look to the European model of mass movement mobilization. The social-democratic ideal was a single movement representing the entire lower class. In Latin America, this was often transformed into a state-sponsored populist-corporatist structure. In Mexico it was President Lázaro Cárdenas who built this mass bloc through the creation of corporatist organizations that were linked to the official party.

The rhetoric of the left opposition to the PRI has often echoed the ideal of a broad, united, and organized front representing "the people." "Vanguardism" was an extreme version of this view, and it may have been dealt a decisive blow with the collapse of the Soviet Union. But the idea of a broadly organized front is common to any view of politics as being divided along a simple division (class, religion, etc.), and which assumes that that struggle requires a kind of organized confrontation.

The NGO phenomenon, in harmony with the nonpartisan and specialized qualities of politics we have already described, constitutes a different sort of popular politics. Many of the NGOs, particularly those that have emerged out of grassroots organizing or national and international developmental projects, have a strong identification with "the people" or at least with causes that are meant to benefit the people.[4] Among them, the rhetoric of broad solidarity is still very common. The thrust of NGO organization and activity, however, is against such broad formations. An emphasis on dialogue and democratic procedures makes forming large bureaucratized organizations less likely. An argument can be made, in fact, that in contemporary Mexico, specialized and independent organizations are more rational. Building mass organizations, the argument would run, does not promise massive success. They are more likely to produce internal division, bureaucratization, and weakness.

In any case, the current thrust of NGO activity appears to work against organizational consolidation on the left and is much more pluralist, however much these groups still identify with the people in some general sense (Brachet-Marquez 1992).[5] Thus, the NGO networks have not led to the formation of peak organizations. Instead, the networks appear to be what the name infers, a channel of communication but not of authority, a link that expresses a generalized agreement on a general thrust of political activity, but not a commitment to a particular party or ideology.

A perhaps extreme example of this is the network called Ganando Espacios (Winning Space). It is a relatively small group of activists, loosely linked to a wide variety of women's organizations, which has taken as its goal increasing women's participation in elected and appointed offices. This specialized campaign has been carried out with minimal organization, even internally. But even an elaborate organization such as Convergencia does not operate as a peak organization and has no authority over its "constituent" organizations. It is a relatively stable organization, but its links with the NGOs are, as the name we have given it implies, in the form of networks, which leaves much room for divergence, bargaining, and, when necessary, going their separate ways.

A fourth direction toward which the NGOs might be pushing Mexican politics toward is the construction of a complex set of *organizations to provide specialized political services* to a range of what might be called "political clients." These specialized organizations do not so much have special *interests* as specialized *functions*. This is happening in many countries. Among the public, the interest groups, the parties, and the government, there has emerged a set of organizations that have professionalized public opinion polling, image construction, technically sophisticated policy making, and many other tasks. NGOs are contributing to this specialization of politics.

Some specialize in a policy area, becoming a space to mobilize opinion, trade information, and debate policy around a loosely stated goal. Convergencia began as a group to defend against the restrictive treatment of NGOs. The government had proposed to treat them in the same fashion as profit-making entities. The issue is still unresolved, and new legal definitions are in the works. Convergencia evolved, however, to focus on democratic change, being among the first to develop the capacity to observe elections. RMALC was formed as a coalition of labor, environmental, and other groups concerned with trade and opposed to NAFTA as it was shaped by the Salinas administration. Since NAFTA's passage, it has sought a new role, but still around the issues that emerged in that debate. FAM, though a relatively new network, has sought to formulate alternative social policies in the areas in which its members have some expertise, including social and rural development, housing, and care for children, the disabled, and the elderly.

Specialization also occurs with respect to functions. Alianza Cívica was an organization sponsored by Convergencia and other civic organizations specifically to observe the 1994 elections. This entailed a series of specialized capacities, including training a large number of observers, conducting a parallel vote count, conducting a broad campaign for civic education, and analyzing media coverage.

Specialization may take a wide variety of forms, and there was one case that even represented a function often thought to be quintessentially governmental, the management of crises. At the time of the Chiapas rebellion, a variety of NGOs came together in a network called CONPAZ in Chiapas, and then a national organization was created called ESPAZ, which sought to intervene to break the cycle of violence that threatened in that state. Dedicated to securing a peaceful solution to the crisis, they formed a human wall around the site of the negotiations, serving to insulate the process to some degree from possible disruptions from partisans of either side, but also from the various local political factions that were not formally at the table.

The general point is that the NGOs and networks we looked at are providing a range of specialized political services. Taken individually, they may have strong ties with one or another group and a sharply critical view of the government. Taken together, they constitute a kind of field in which specialized groups interact, bargain, trade services, and in many ways act more like a marketplace in which politics is, or may be, played than the imagined arenas of log rolling or mobilization we often think of.

A final characteristic of politics that NGOs represent is the *internationalization of politics*. NGOs and NGO networks have provided a way through which foreign-based groups—foundations, support and solidarity organizations, international policy networks, as well as international organizations and financial institutions—have been able to participate in Mexican politics, generally without generating a strong nationalist reaction. The opposite pole here might appear to be the ostensibly strict exclusion of any important political role of foreigners up to now, and certainly Mexicans have insisted as strongly as any country in the world on the inviolability of its political practices and institutions to foreign "intervention." In fact, of course, the presence of a very influential U.S. embassy and powerful multinational corporations are only two examples that have powerfully contradicted this rhetorical position.

Unlike the past, however, today the composition and the numbers of such intervening groups, and the degree to which they are becoming (at least informally) institutionalized within the system, are growing. There is no question that the NGOs, with their foreign funding, their involvement of international experts on policy, their involvement of foreign observers for the election and many other ways, facilitate the participation of an increasing number and complex set of foreign actors in Mexican politics. The lack of sustained outcry against the presence of these foreigners remains to be studied, but we suspect that it has something to do with the diversity of the foreigners involved (in place of the massive presence of the neighbor to the north), and with the fact that through the NGOs the foreigners' presence is in some sense institutionalized and tamed.

Election observation was a case in point. In many countries, observers are sent in by external organizations. In Mexico, although the government resisted for a long time accepting any foreign observers, they were finally admitted for the 1994 general elections. While a few came on their own, many obtained domestic sponsorship in order to have a much more systematic role. Many Mexican organizations did sponsor foreign observers (including the two authors). A significant segment of the foreign observers were trained and deployed by Alianza Cívica, for example. For many nationalists, the fact that the foreigners were not operating independently probably legitimized their role. The mutual benefits of foreign involvement are significant. From the point of view of the NGOs, outsiders bring funds and other resources that may be difficult to get internally without support from the state. FAM is a network that emerged out of the relief organizations channeling international relief funds from international church sources. FAM itself has become a channel, like many others, for involving international social policy expertise, as well as international project funding.

On the other hand, international donors and institutions are increasingly interested in NGO networks as a way to foster more cooperative relationships between NGOs and state agencies. In Mexico, the United Nations Development Program (UNDP), for example, has sponsored a project to improve communication and collaboration between NGOs, the government, and itself. This project, entitled International Cooperation for Social, Indigenous and Non-Governmental Organizations (more commonly referred to as the Ba Asolai project, which means "transparency"), is significant because it has involved representatives of thirteen NGO networks, together with representatives from three state agencies, in all levels of decision making concerning the project's objectives, funding distribution, and management. For various international institutions, networks are a way to promote more and better NGO-state partnerships.

Access to international media is among the most important resources provided by the international linkages for those NGOs directly involved with confrontations with the state. Convergencia, Alianza Cívica, and human rights organizations in Mexico systematically prepare for the mobilization of international opinion to support their projects. The mobilization of international opinion was even more direct with RMALC. It was founded with the active help of Canadian and U.S. environmental and labor groups, and the network continued to be very involved in mobilizing support from allies in those countries during the struggle over NAFTA (Heredia 1994). International support provided important leverage in dealing with the government, which in turn needed international support in the external, secondary arenas of Mexican politics, often located in Washington, D.C. The NGOs hardly had a monopoly on this track, and, in fact, the government itself began to lobby extensively in the United States, but the NGOs represent a strong push in the direction of making that international influence an enduring feature of Mexican politics.

The new administration in Mexico is confronting a severe economic crisis very early in its tenure, symbolized by the sudden devaluation of the peso before Zedillo's term was a month old. The consequences of this crisis, given the tensions within the PRI and the slowly growing strength of the opposition, could lead in a number of directions. These include a fundamental upheaval, or the weakening of the PRI to the point that it will begin to lose more elections—but also, extrapolating from past crises, it is always possible that the outcome will be merely a partially reformed political system.

We do not pretend to argue that the characteristics of Mexican politics we have spoken of will determine that outcome, and certainly not that the NGOs will be a dominant player in that drama. But we do argue that the trend toward a new pattern of politics in Mexico will have an effect whether Mexico is democratic or authoritarian, stable or unstable. A more plural, specialized, nonpartisan, and internationalized politics is likely to be an important part of its future. Democratic consolidation and political stability are both likely to require incorporating and institutionalizing this new form of politics.

Notes

1. This project was an investigation of NGO networks carried out during the summer of 1994 by the authors, with Judy Gearhart, Andrea Hetling, Adam Jagelski, and Caroline Tsilikounas. The full report of the project, entitled "Mexican NGO Networks and Popular Participation," is available from the Institute for Latin American and Iberian Studies, Columbia University. This was research sponsored by the North-South Center at the University of Miami.

2. See note 1.

3. The exploration of political structures that either bypass or reduce the role of political parties is not uncommon in other systems. See, for example, Phillippe Schmitter's observation concerning how a range of associations is likely to compete with parties to represent societal interests in arenas other than the electoral one, in "The Consolidation of Democracy and Representation of Social Groups," *American Behavioral Scientist* 35, no. 4/5 (March–June 1992): 422–49.

4. If one were to include the voluntary trade and lobbying organizations of the business community among the NGOs (whose usual definition would not exclude them), the picture would be different.

5. Note that we are using "pluralist" in a descriptive sense, as many competing and differentiated groups, rather than as a reference to a politically loaded paradigm of political development. For its use in the latter sense, see Viviane Brachet-Marquez, "Explaining Sociopolitical Change in Latin America: The Case of Mexico," *Latin American Research Review* 27, no. 3 (1992): 91–122.

Bibliography

Brachet-Marquez, Viviane (1992), "Explaining Sociopolitical Change in Latin America: The Case of Mexico," *Latin American Research Review*, 27, 3, 91–122.

Heredia, Carlos A. (1994), "NAFTA and Democratization in Mexico," *Journal of International Affairs* 48 (Summer): 13–38.

Salamon, Lester M. (1993), "The Global Associational Revolution: The Rise of the Third Sector on the World Scene," Institute for Policy Studies, Johns Hopkins University, Occasional Paper 15, April.

Schmitter, Phillippe (1992), "The Consolidation of Democracy and Representation of Social Groups," *American Behavioral Scientist* 35, no. 4/5 (March–June).

25

Joseph L. Klesner

The Evolving Party System: PRI, PAN, and PRD

Shifts in Mexican political structure reflect Mexico's economic modernization, which also altered the structure of Mexican society. Mexicans traveled to, worked and studied in, and read about the United States, and wanted its democracy for themselves. The electoral reforms of 1977 guaranteed seats in the Chamber of Deputies for representatives of PRI's opponents and made it easier to establish political parties.

The severe doubts that Carlos Salinas de Gortari would have been elected president without fraud led to demands for changes in Mexican political procedures. The governing party, PRI, was bypassed in appointing government executives. At the same time, government policies did not favor the peasant and labor groups that traditionally had supported the PRI. Instead, President Salinas tried to modernize the PRI by using primary elections within the party to select its candidates on some occasions and selectively recognizing the opposition's electoral victories. It began to replace corporatist structure with that of individuals and groups based on geography. Government spending was targeted to areas whose support PRI wished to regain, with considerable success.

Cuauhtémoc Cárdenas established the Partido de la Revolución Democrática (PRD) in the fall of 1988, hoping to unify left-wing opposition to the government. The PRD does not have an economic development strategy distinct from that of the PRI, although some of its members are loyal to doctrines of economic nationalism and import substitution. Despite internal divisions, the PRD has increased its strength, especially in the south. Greater gains recently have been won by the Partido Acción Nacional (PAN), which has represented legal and gradual reform, as well as opposition to state domination of the economy. The PAN won governorships in the north and has transformed itself from a middle-class party to a right-of-center party with a broader base. Mexico's political parties have become increasingly competitive, with strong regional divisions. Joseph L. Klesner believes that a broadly shared outlook between the PRI and the PAN will lead to respect for election results, but that sharp differences over policy between the PRI and the PRD may contribute to a continuation of intermittent political assassinations and rebellions in the south.

Before 1988, Mexico's Institutional Revolutionary Party (Partido Revolucionario Institucional, or PRI) had never lost a presidential, gubernatorial, or federal senatorial race it had contested since it was founded as the National Revolutionary Party (Partido Nacional Revolucionario, or PNR) in 1929. The PRI seldom won less than 98 percent of the federal deputy seats open each three years, even though the constitution's no-reelection clause meant that PRI candidates enjoyed no incumbency effect. Opposition party candidates infrequently contested and rarely won municipal elections. Political scientists felt comfortable in the 1960s and 1970s calling Mexico a hegemonic party system, distinguishing it from the single-party states of the former Soviet bloc because opposition parties could and did exist legally and politically, but also recognizing thereby that opposition parties posed no genuine challenge to the PRI.

PRI hegemony owed much to the party's revolutionary heritage as the party built by the victorious revolutionaries and as the party that brought land reform to the campesinos, labor rights to the working class, and economic development to Mexico as a whole. PRI hegemony was also due to its corporatist structure, which channeled the electoral and other political participation of Mexico's peasantry and unionized workers, and to a vast clientelistic network through which the ruling elite materially rewarded those ambitious politicians who sought social mobility through politics and those social groups the same politicians claimed to represent. The PRI's monopoly on the elected executive positions at the federal, state, and local levels gave PRI leaders access to the governmental resources that made clientelism easy, particularly in a state with an extensive bureaucracy and a tendency toward intervention in the economy. Opposition parties' failure to gain any executive positions made them unable to challenge the PRI electorally because they had nothing with which to reward their supporters.

Table 25.1 displays the extent of PRI domination of the electoral arena prior to 1988. Economic modernization did produce gradual erosion of the PRI's commanding position electorally, but the emphasis must be on the gradual character of that erosion. Opposition parties did markedly better in urban and industrial areas where the population had greater access to education and the mass media. In the vastness of rural Mexico, where the opposition feared to show itself, the PRI's vote totals sometimes reached numbers above the registered electorate. Whether such large numbers of campesinos voted enthusiastically for the PRI to reward it for giving them land or had their votes cast for them by rural bosses was unknown in individual districts because the urban press was no more willing to venture into such rural areas than were oppositionists. Endemic political corruption and electoral fraud ensured large vote tallies for the PRI, but even without them, the PRI would likely have been hegemonic because Mexican

Table 25.1

Federal Deputy Election Results, 1961–94 (in percent)

Year	PAN	PRI	PPS	PARM	PDM	PCM	PST PSUM PMS PRD	Other PFCRN
1961	7.6	90.3	1.0	0.5	—	—	—	—
1964	11.5	86.3	1.4	0.7	—	—	—	—
1967	12.5	83.8	2.2	1.4	—	—	—	—
1970	14.2	83.6	1.4	0.8	—	—	—	—
1973	16.5	77.4	3.8	2.0	—	—	—	—
1976	8.9	85.2	3.2	2.7	—	—	—	—
1979	11.4	74.2	2.7	1.9	2.2	5.3	2.2	—
1982	17.5	69.3	1.9	1.3	2.3	4.4	1.8	1.3
1985	16.3	68.2	2.1	1.7	2.9	3.4	2.6	2.9
1988	18.0	50.4	9.2	6.1	1.3	4.5	10.2	0.5
1991	17.7	61.4	1.8	2.1	1.1	8.3	4.3	3.1
1994	26.8	50.3	0.7	0.9	0.4	16.7	1.1	4.3

Source: Joseph L. Klesner, "The 1994 Mexican Elections: Manifestation of a Divided Society?" *Mexican Studies/Estudios Mexicanos,* 11, no. 1 (Winter 1995): 139.

Note: Annulled votes have been excluded.

PAN = Partido Acción Nacional, or National Action Party

PRI = Partido Revolucionario Institucional, or Institutional Revolutionary Party

PPS = Partido Popular Socialista, or Popular Socialist Party

PARM = Partido Auténtico de la Revolución Mexicana, or Authentic Party of the Mexican Revolution

PDM = Partido Demócrata Mexicano, or Mexican Democratic Party

PCM = Partido Comunista Mexicano, or Mexican Communist Party, which became the PSUM = Partido Socialista Unificado de México, or Unified Socialist Party of Mexico, which became PMS = Partido Mexicano Socialista, or Mexican Socialist Party, whose registration was converted to PRD = Partido de la Revolución Democrática, or Party of the Democratic Revolution

PST = Partido Socialista de los Trabajadores, or Socialist Workers' Party which became PFCRN = Partido del Frente Cardenista de Reconstrucción Nacional, or Party of the Cardenista Front for National Reconstruction.

public policy in the 1940s, 1950s, 1960s, and even into the 1970s produced rapid economic development for which the electorate rewarded the PRI, and because opposition parties presented no real alternatives to PRI governance or to the PRI development strategy.

Factors in the PRI's Decline

Table 25.1 also shows that the PRI no longer dominates the Mexican party system in the way it did only a decade ago. By mid-1995, the most successful party of opposition, the conservative National Action Party (Partido Acción Nacional, or PAN) held the governorships of four of Mexico's thirty-one states. In the past two presidential elections, the PRI has barely captured half of the valid votes. Two significant parties of opposition, the PAN and the leftist Democratic Revolutionary Party (Partido de la Revolución Democrática, or PRD), have emerged to challenge the PRI at all levels of government. Once of little interest to anyone other than the PRI politicians being elected to office, elections now receive intense attention from the press and are hard fought among the parties. What has changed Mexican electoral politics?

First, we must recognize that Mexico's economic modernization, a process at work since the 1940s, has altered the social structure upon which the PRI's hegemony was based. The Mexico of the 1980s was more urban, more educated, and more influenced by the outside world than the Mexico of the 1930s. Consequently, Mexicans of the 1980s were less subject to the control of the PRI's corporatist organizations, more informed about alternatives to the PRI, and more desirous of the democratic practices observed outside of Mexico, especially in the United States, than were Mexicans of the 1930s. A more complex social structure meant that public policy could not please all Mexicans all of the time. As economic development proceeded, opposition support grew. In more modern parts of the country, especially in cities, the opposition performed much better. But economic modernization does not explain the sudden fall in the PRI's electoral fortunes in 1988.

Second, seeking democratic legitimacy to supplement the support it received for producing economic success, the Mexican government encouraged the development of opposition parties through a long series of reforms that gradually opened the federal and state legislatures to representatives of the opposition. The most significant of these electoral reforms came in 1977 when the government of José López Portillo not only reserved one hundred of the four hundred seats in the Chamber of Deputies for opposition representatives but also relaxed the laws that had previously kept several opposition groups from becoming registered political parties. This permitted both the Mexican Communist Party (Partido Comunista Mexicano, or PCM) and groups that had formed out of the 1968 student movement to emerge and to compete for electoral support. The 1977 reforms reinvigorated the PAN, too, and the political debate in the 1980s became much richer than any time since the 1930s as a consequence.

The richness of the debate among the parties and the increasing electoral contestation in the 1980s owed their origins to more than just political reforms that permitted greater opposition activity, however. The economic crisis experienced by Mexico from 1982 onward undercut the legitimacy built up by the PRI as the result of decades of economic policy success and gave the opposition parties opportunities to attract the voters being lost by the PRI. López Portillo's populist last act, the nationalization of the banks in 1982, angered the private sector and much of the middle class, leading them into more vigorous electoral activity in support of the PAN. Miguel de la Madrid's administration (1982-88) chose to respond to the debt crisis with an austerity program that became a liberalization project that accelerated under Carlos Salinas (1988-94). The pain resulting from austerity and liberalization afflicted the peasants and workers particularly, the very sectors whose support played such a key role in PRI electoral victories. The sudden change in the development strategy also produced severe divisions within the PRI, leading by 1987 to Cuauhtémoc Cárdenas's defection from the party shaped by his father and his candidacy at the head of a union of parties and groups of the left.

Cárdenas's presidential candidacy, the first by a PRI maverick since 1952, ruptured the stability of the hegemonic party system. His success at drawing millions to his campaign rallies and then to vote for him indicated significant disaffection of the electorate with the ruling elite. To defeat Cárdenas, the PRI and the government had to take extraordinary measures, even by their own standards, to the extent that the electoral authorities' computer "crashed" on the night of the election, the vote tallies of nearly half of the polling places were never reported, and those ballots were subsequently destroyed. Even then, Carlos Salinas received only half of the votes. He entered office with the legitimacy of his presidency questioned by substantial portions of the Mexican population, the effective leader of a party whose capacity to carry elections had come under question, promising a program of accelerated economic liberalization likely to hurt the interests of the PRI's bedrock of support, peasants and workers.

How did Salinas respond to these challenges? How did economic restructuring affect the parties and the party system? What measures did he take to reinvigorate the PRI? How did the opposition parties respond to Salinas's very vigorous leadership? What have been the consequences for the electoral fortunes of the parties? We will first consider the major parties, and then the party system as a whole.

Reforming the PRI?

To understand the challenge of reforming the PRI, we must first grasp the real character of this "party" and its relationship to the Mexican state. Lorenzo Meyer, Mexico's foremost historian, has captured it well:

> The PRI ... was created to complement the institutional structure of the new regime, not to do battle with its political adversaries at the polls. It provides the forum for internal negotiations among the governing elite, for the distribution of political patronage awards, and for recruiting (fewer and fewer) and socializing new members. During electoral campaigns it acquaints the populace with its soon-to-be-elected officials, and it mobilizes specific sectors of society as needed for the preservation of the system. Between elections—excepting those occasions when government leadership needs limited mass mobilization—the official party practically disappears. Its activities are determined almost exclusively by the president and by the electoral calendar, not by grassroots interests or demands. (Meyer 1989)

In short, the PRI does not "rule" in the sense that we say the Conservative party rules in Britain. A self-reproducing civilian political elite rules in Mexico. It uses the PRI as an electoral organ to mobilize voters and thereby to win the elections so critical to creating a veneer of democratic legitimacy. Real political power is centered in the presidency, the key political institution in Mexico. Increasingly, recruitment to the executive departments controlled by the presidency has practically bypassed the party. However, electoral positions remain important as the patronage distributed by the party to sectoral groups whose votes the PRI counts on to produce electoral victories.

The economic strategies pursued by de la Madrid and Salinas created a gulf between the upper level of the political elite and the sectors of the party because the members of the labor and peasant sectors did not benefit from neoliberalism. In many ways the sectorial organization of the PRI created by Lázaro Cárdenas in the 1930s simply did not fit the Mexico of the 1980s and 1990s, a Mexico less rural, more educated, and more mobile than a half century ago. Increasingly, the sectors could only produce the votes needed for PRI victories through coercion or vote buying, or outright fraud. In this situation, elections did not legitimate the rule of the political elite but rather delegitimated that rule because they were so clearly fraudulent. Salinas was not the first president to see a need to reform the PRI to maintain it as the electoral tool of the political elite, but he saw an urgent need after the debacle of the 1988 elections. Salinas's strategy had two elements, one more successful, one less so.

First, Salinas sought to "modernize" the PRI. One aspect of modernization involved creating a more democratic image for the party, an image much tarnished by the massive fraud committed by the PRI in its contests with the PAN in northern states from 1985 onward and against Cárdenas's supporters in 1988. The more democratic PRI would use internal primaries to select its candidates for office, and it would recognize its losses when they occurred. Moreover, it would replace its sectoral organization and the bloc affiliation associated with the sectors with individual affiliation and geographical organization, similar to the organization of parties in the United States. These efforts failed for the most part. Internal primaries were used sparingly. They tended to exacerbate divisions already existing in state and local party organizations, and the president was unwilling to completely give up the opportunities for distributing patronage offered by the more traditional presidential designation of PRI nominees. Opposition victories in state and local elections were recognized, but selectively, and often despite local PRI unwillingness to admit its defeats. Salinas had to use presidential power to get PRI candidates to resign after they claimed victory in gubernatorial races marked by electoral fraud. And, threatened by the demonstrated strength of the left in 1988, Salinas permitted the PRI to use fraud and intimidation against the PRD even while encouraging the PRI to recognize PAN victories.

Another, more successful aspect of PRI modernization involved the introduction of more sophisticated campaigning tools: computers, polls, and better organization of the campaign. Under the leadership of Luis Donaldo Colosio (later assassinated during his own presidential campaign in 1994), a massive effort was unveiled in 1989 to create a network of get-out-the-vote promoters coordinated by the PRI's state organizations with connections down to the most intimate level of Mexican society. The plan targeted the 115 most important cities in the country. The plan also used a system of national surveys, which were designed to allow the PRI organization to tailor its candidacies and the campaigns of its nominees to meet the demands of the particular districts. While the PRI has always been able to mount a far larger and more richly funded campaign than its opposition, this was an unprecedented effort to reclaim the grassroots. Of course, such a massive effort could have been undertaken only with the support of government resources. But whether the PRI played fair in this effort or not, it produced results in 1991.

Second, recognizing the social costs to the Mexican people and the political risk to the PRI of economic restructuring, upon entering office Salinas immediately created the National Solidarity Program (Programa Nacional de la Solidaridad, or PRONASOL), a large and complex program aimed at ameliorating the burdens associated with economic restructuring in those areas in which poverty and costs associated with the economic crisis are the worst. Its major initiatives included building health care facilities in rural areas, extending telephone service to remote villages, and refurbishing schools. It is a form of welfare for the less fortunate, but one that emphasizes self-help through neighborhood committees, which are supposed to participate in the selection of projects and the supervision of their implementation. In the process, not only are poor people benefited materially, but they are organized for, among other things, voting for the ruling party. PRONASOL allowed the PRI to distribute from the pork barrel to those it felt it had to reclaim for the party, for the distribution of PRONASOL funds went disproportionately to areas where Cárdenas did well in 1988. Results in the 1991 elections suggest PRI success was at least partially explained by PRONASOL spending (Molinar Horcasitas and Weldon 1994).

The PRI remains the one truly national party in Mexico, but it is a party suffering many fissures as it tries to respond to pressures created by economic liberalization. Reformers such as Salinas and Colosio have tried to make the PRI a more modern political party, which should mean abandoning the more blatant practices of presidential imposition of candidates and electoral fraud. Salinas apparently found himself more convinced of the need to hurry forward with economic reform than to promote political reform, however. He stated: "When you are introducing such a strong economic reform, you must make sure that you build the political consensus around it. If you are at the same time introducing additional drastic political reform, you may end up with no reform at all. And we want to have reform, not a disintegrated country" (Salinas 1991). At times this has meant looking the other way when the PRI returns to its practices of old and therefore looking hypocritical about "modernization."

Creating a Party of the Left

Cárdenas's presidential campaign in 1988 had been postulated by a wide range of independent and collaborationist parties of the left under the umbrella of the National Democratic Front (Frente Democrático Nacional, or FDN), each of which maintained its separate legal identity while advancing Cárdenas as its presidential candidate. When Cárdenas proposed a united party of the left in the fall of 1988 to consolidate and channel the gains of 1988, three collaborationist parties (the Partido Auténtico de la Revolución Mexicana, or PARM; the Partido Popular Socialista, or PPS; and the Partido Frente Cardenista de Reconstrucción Nacional, or PFCRN) left the FDN. Eventually, the remnants of the FDN converted the registration of the Mexican Socialist Party (Partido Mexicano Socialista, or PMS) into the new PRD. But the PRD remains divided internally over ideological and strategic issues as well as personal differences among leaders. Therein lies one of its weaknesses.

Revolutionary nationalism motivates most members of the PRD, but most also recognize that economic nationalism and import-substituting industrialization will not bring Mexico out of economic crisis. The PRD has been unable to define a distinct development strategy, making it seem more a party of emotion than of reason on this critical issue. PRD militants hold very bad feelings toward the PRI as the fallout of the 1988 elections; the party has rejected compromise with the PRI and the government over electoral results and legislative proposals for electoral reform. This strategic intransigence may satisfy the PRD hardliners, but it probably gains the party few independent voters. As a party that came together out of other organizations of the left and from the defection of a substantial portion of the left wing of the PRI, the PRD remains faction ridden. PRD leaders continue to seek to reward those PRD members who have supported them over the decades at the expense of those who came from other organizations. Squabbles among leaders result, and the press reports them, contributing little to the party's public image. These internal weaknesses have made the consolidation of the PRD as the party of the left somewhat disappointing to those who saw bright opportunity in the 1988 Cárdenas campaign.

The PRD faces an equally difficult external challenge: the unwillingness of the PRI and the government to recognize its successes. Because of the strength of Cárdenas performance in 1988 and the PRD's ardent opposition to neoliberalism, the Salinas government felt more threatened by the PRD than by the PAN. Also, to members of the PRI, Cárdenas, Porfirio Muñoz Ledo, and other PRD leaders are, quite simply, traitors and hated for their betrayal of the PRI. While PAN triumphs in gubernatorial races were recognized by Salinas, when the PRD claimed victory, electoral authorities more often published results indicating PRI wins. In the states of Michoacán and México in 1989 and 1990, state and local elections produced intense conflicts between the PRD and the PRI, and the government sided with the PRI. The PRD may have exaggerated its performance, but it seems clear that the government permitted extensive fraud by the PRI.

In federal elections in both 1991 and 1994, the PRD finished third. Compared with the historical performance of the independent left, the PRD's 1994 finish indicates a significant advance. In the six years between 1988 and 1994, the PRD won over the bulk of the supporters of the collaborationist left; the PARM, the PPS, and the PFCRN all fell below 1.5 percent of the vote. For all intents and purposes, the PRD is now the electoral left in Mexico. Furthermore, the PRD has consolidated the second position electorally in many states in the south, especially Chiapas, Guerrero, Michoacán, Oaxaca, Tabasco, and Veracruz. In those states of the south where the effects of economic liberalization have been harsh for many campesinos, the PRD offers a voice of opposition.

The PAN: The Responsible Opposition?

The 1988 elections came as a disappointment to the PAN. Despite running a charismatic candidate for president (Manuel Clouthier), the PAN finished a distant third with no more than its usual share of the national vote, around 17-18 percent. Many analysts relegated the PAN to a permanent third position in light of the Cárdenas surge. However, since then the PAN has won four governorships. Its congressional delegation was instrumental in the passage of electoral reform legislation and laws altering the church-state relationship and the status of the ejido under Salinas. The PAN's acceptance of Ernesto Zedillo's presidential victory in August 1994 made the Cárdenas attempt to organize protest across the country ring hollow. Has the PAN become Mexico's loyal opposition?

Although the object of PRI-engineered electoral fraud in the north in 1985 and 1986, which led PAN leaders to organize massive demonstrations and hunger strikes in defense of the vote, the PAN must be recognized as the party of legal and gradual reform that it has been since its founding. The influx of middle-class and business militants into the party in the early 1980s may have made the PAN seem more stridently opposed to state intervention in the economy, but the PAN has always stood for constraints on state power. In short, ideologically and attitudinally, the PAN has changed less over the past fifteen years than many have suggested. Salinas's accession to power and the Cárdenas surge presented both the president and the PAN leadership with good reasons to seek accommodation in the 1990s: Salinas proposed to curtail state power and to initiate policy changes in directions favored by the PAN for decades, for which he needed the legislative help of the PAN; the PAN sought to avoid falling into obscurity as the result of the cardenista phenomenon and could accomplish that if Salinas recognized the PAN's victories when they occurred. This accommodation proved highly successful for each. The PAN won the gubernatorial races in Baja California and Chihuahua in 1989 and 1992 respectively, and saw Salinas force the resignation of PRI candidates for governor after blatantly fraudulent elections in Guanajuato and San Luis Potosí in 1991. Salinas appointed a PAN governor of Guanajuato. Salinas was able to point to PAN victories as evidence of political opening. The PAN achieved some electoral changes it sought through the electoral reform process while the PRD was left looking intransigent on this issue. Since Zedillo has taken office, the PAN has won the governorships of Jalisco and Guanajuato and nearly took the governorship of Yucatán.

Has this accommodation compromised the PAN's capacity to serve as a party of opposition? Former PAN leaders Jesús González Schmall, Pablo E. Madero, and Bernardo Bátiz argued that it did when they left the party, but the presidential campaign of Diego Fernández de Cevallos did not seem accommodationist in tone, particularly during the televised presidential debate. Why the Fernández campaign took a hiatus after the success of the debate has been the subject of much controversy, though, with some suggesting that Fernández may have been bought off. Overall, however, the PAN seems to be advancing electorally, and the experience of governing large states and municipalities will produce leaders capable of presenting themselves as realistic presidential candidates in the future, perhaps no one more so than the new governor of Guanajuato, Vicente Fox. Although it lacks the resources available to the PRI as the party of the state, the PAN runs far more professional campaigns than it could a decade ago. Still primarily a party of the middle class, the PAN could not win the gubernatorial races it has won without attracting working-class voters. Hence, the PAN has converted itself into a catchall party with a somewhat right-of-center ideology willing to work with the federal government legislatively but compete strongly with it when elections are held. This conversion is less the result of changes in ideology than changes in circumstance, principally the rise of the PRD.

The Shape of the Party System in the 1990s

The 1994 elections revealed two aspects of the evolving party system in Mexico. On the one hand, the 1994 election marks one more advance in the competitive character of the Mexican electoral system. Mexico's parties of opposition have shown greater capacity to contest elections than ever before. This contestation has spread to most parts of the country so that in few places does the PRI face no real challenge. Mexican voters now feel more free to cast ballots against the PRI; moreover, the electoral system contains more measures to insure that those votes are properly counted. It remains true that the playing field is not level, that the PRI has advantages associated with incumbency and with a mass media that overwhelmingly favors it, but Zedillo has shown a willingness thus far to play fair in state-level electoral contests. That bodes well for democratization in Mexico.

On the other hand, a deeper look indicates an increasing regionalization of partisanship in Mexico and suggests that Mexico is bifurcating. That electoral bifurcation reflects growing divisions between northern and western Mexico, a society increasingly integrated with the United States and likely to benefit from NAFTA, and southern Mexico, a society not prepared for that integration and not attracted to it. While Mexico may appear to have a three-party system, it may be more appropriate to call it two separate two-party systems. The PRI and the PAN face off in northern and western Mexico and in the Yucatán; the PRD and the PRI struggle in the south. Because both the PRI and the PAN favor integration and economic liberalization generally, they can cooperate legislatively even while they compete electorally.

The PRD and the PRI do not share economic policy perspectives. Their confrontations have thus been more violent, with the result that dozens of PRD activists have been killed in the last seven years. It is not coincidental that nonelectoral violence has flared in the south too, most notably, the rebellion in Chiapas. Because those in the south are less prepared for the consequences of economic liberalization and because Salinas seemed intent on pursuing it at almost any cost, the level of threat that each side poses to the other is high. In that circumstance, the electoral system may simply be unable to produce a democratic resolution (even if the real results are respected) sufficiently satisfactory to both sides that peace may reign.

Bibliography

Meyer, Lorenzo (1989), "Democratization of the PRI: Mission Impossible?" in Wayne A. Cornelius, Judith Gentleman, and Peter H. Smith, eds., *Mexico's Alternative Political Futures* (La Jolla: Center for U.S.-Mexican Studies, University of California at San Diego), 335.

Molinar Horcasitas, Juan, and Jeffrey A. Weldon (1994), "Electoral Determinants and Consequences of National Solidarity" in Wayne A. Cornelius, Ann L. Craig, and Jonathan Fox, eds., *Transforming State-Society Relations in Mexico* (La Jolla: Center for U.S.-Mexican Studies, University of California at San Diego), 123–41.

Salinas, Carlos (1991), "A New Hope for the Hemisphere?" Interview with Carlos Salinas, *New Perspectives Quarterly* 8, no. 1 (1991): 8.

26

JOSEPH L. KLESNER

Broadening toward Democracy?

Latin American constitutions are famous for expressing what a nation wants, or believes will serve as a means of giving legitimacy to its laws and practices. The Mexican constitution provides for democracy. Yet, despite formal elections, Mexico has long been dominated by the Institutional Revolutionary Party (PRI), whose interests were extensively intermingled with those of the state.

Joseph L. Klesner explores the features of the Mexican political system, and explains the events leading to its broadening toward democracy. The Mexican political system gives extensive powers to the presidency. The narrowness of President Salinas's election victory and the internal divisions within the PRI, however, required cooperation with another political party. On the other hand, the presidency probably maintained or increased its power with regard to that of localities. Although reforms had increased funds available to municipalities, the president retained considerable power by creating a new "solidarity" program (PRONASOL) to channel funds to areas important for elections. Further, local control is only beginning for the Federal District's 8.5 million people, who elect a city council but have a mayor appointed by the president.

Although provision is made for minority representation in the legislature, opposition parties have less access than the governing party to financial resources and to mass media. This limits their ability to win despite improved procedures resulting in cleaner elections.

An alternative path to democracy is being created by nongovernmental organizations, which address needs of localities, and national issues such as human rights and fair elections. Increased awareness of these issues, and international appreciation of them, led the government to negotiate with the Zapatista liberation army in Chiapas and urge it to convert itself to a political party, rather than take strong and consistent military measures against it. The government stress on electoral rather than military solutions, to be convincing, will require a broadening toward democracy, a process that Dr. Klesner believes will continue to progress, slowly.

How might we describe the Mexican political system? Emerging democracy? Authoritarian regime? Some kind of hybrid, unique to Mexico? For over three decades scholars have debated the character of the Mexican political regime. A central obstacle to characterizing the Mexican political system stems from the divorce between the formal, constitutional institutions of the political system and the practice of politics in the Mexican regime. In most democratic regimes, political institutions are designed to divide power among different agencies of government and to provide access to citizens seeking to participate in policy making. Furthermore, civil liberties are protected so that citizens can effectively participate politically. Political practice tends to conform to those ideals if the regime deserves the label democracy.

In clearly authoritarian regimes, a relative few have entry to the halls of power, civil liberties are frequently violated even if individual rights are recognized, and power is usually centralized, frequently leading to arbitrary rule.

Mexico's constitution laid out a presidential democracy with a federal structure, a separation of powers between executive and legislative branches of government, electoral selection of the principal executive and all legislative positions at all levels of government, and rights to free speech and free association for all citizens. These institutional arrangements have not, however, produced democratic practice, at least in the views of the majority of social scientists who analyze Mexican politics and of a vast number of Mexican citizens who have, particularly since 1968, demanded more democracy in their nation. Certainly not as harsh nor as arbitrary as the military regimes that governed the nations of the Southern Cone in the 1970s and early 1980s, the Mexican regime nevertheless remains highly centralized and relatively deaf to the criticism of political opponents, most of whom have no access to power, because the candidates of the Institutional Revolutionary Party (Partido Revolucionario Institucional, or PRI) nearly always win legislative and executive offices.

Mexico is neither entirely democratic nor authoritarian. In this chapter, I disaggregate these ideal types into some key features and explore movement by Mexico toward or away from democratic practice.

Presidentialism

Since the 1930s, presidentialism has defined the Mexican regime. Foreign observers have more frequently noticed the PRI's dominance of electoral politics, and certainly the PRI's electoral monopoly and presidentialism have been highly intertwined. However, a short acquaintance with Mexican politics will alert the observer to the centrality of the presidency and of the executive branch headed by the president. Presidents issue executive orders and sponsor all important legislative bills. Presidentially sponsored bills generally pass the Congress with few significant changes. Hence, in addition to being the chief executive, the president is the chief legislator. Moreover, the president controls monetary and other economic policy. In the past, with the Mexican state's large-scale owner-ship of industry, the president (through his power to appoint directors of parasta-tal firms) governed much of the economy, too.

For all the power a Mexican president has, his term lasts only six years and he cannot be reelected. Nor are other elected positions, including legislative seats, immediately reelectable. No one, in short, can develop independent institutional bases of power; heretofore, all political positions have required either the PRI's nomination or the president's appointment. The president is traditionally the effective head of the party, and his appointment power, in this system with such frequent turnover, makes almost everyone tremble before him, especially be-cause, as effective party leader, he has traditionally chosen his successor.

Carlos Salinas entered the presidency in 1988 promising political moderniza-tion. His election with barely 50 percent of the official vote may have meant that the era of the "virtual one-party system" has ended. That bare victory by the PRI also produced a Chamber of Deputies in which the PRI gained an unprecedent-edly small majority. After 1988, the president could not simply decree the changes he preferred on key issues. As a result, the Salinas government sought to negotiate with opposition parties for legislative support on key bills, such as those that altered the church-state relationship, changed rules about foreign in-vestment, and revised the status of the ejido, Mexico's traditional, communally held form of agriculture. Political reform measures, especially involving elec-toral issues, also required opposition legislative support. Salinas usually ap-proached the National Action Party (Partido Accion Nacional, or PAN) for that support and obtained it. The legislative cooperation between PRI and PAN indi-cates an increase in the importance of the congress in contemporary Mexican politics, a movement in a democratic direction.

In other realms, however, the presidency under Salinas grew stronger. Two areas stand out. First, Salinas more willingly removed state governors or forced their resignations than any recent president. In some cases these interventions came as the result of opposition protests of electoral fraud, for instance in the 1991 gubernatorial contests in Guanajuato and San Luis Potosí. In each case, faced with large demonstrations of opposition supporters who claimed that the local PRI stole the gubernatorial race, Salinas stepped into state politics and forced the resignations of the PRI governors-elect, replacing one with a PAN member, the other with a PRI member, neither of whom had been candidates in those contested elections. By compelling the PRI candidates to withdraw, Salinas recognized the demand for democracy made vocal by citizens in Guanajuato and San Luis Potosí. However, by imposing alternatives to the PRI candidates, Sali-nas strengthened the role of the presidency. This strong presidency may be needed to eliminate local and regional roadblocks in the path of democratization in provincial Mexico, or in the cases of union bosses such as the oil workers' Joaquin Hernandez Galicia ("La Quina") or the teachers' Carlos Jonguitud, both ousted by Salinas early in his term.[1]

Second, the most publicized initiative of the Salinas presidency, the National Solidarity Program (Programa Nacional de Solidaridad, or PRONASOL), likewise enhanced presidential power. This program promised to contribute to alleviation of poverty by providing federal grants to local groups who organized themselves to address problems of poverty in their localities and who put forward proposals that included local contributions of their own time and money. PRONASOL grew out of ideas developed by Salinas in his doctoral dissertation at Harvard.

PRONASOL founders intended to bypass the corporatist organizations of the PRI and thereby marginalize the caciques who traditionally siphoned off the federal funds distributed to states and localities. To this extent, PRONASOL showed democratizing characteristics. Much discretion in the distribution of PRONASOL funds remained in the hands of the president's staff, and hence presidential authority was enlarged. Furthermore, Salinas often invented new Solidarity programs on the fly, and in doing so improved his own personal reputation as a man of action and the public perception of the presidency as the locus of change in Mexican politics.

Salinas thus bequeathed to Ernesto Zedillo a much enhanced presidential power in a polity already dominated by the president. However, scandals associated with the outgoing administration, including the assassinations of PRI presidential candidate Luis Donaldo Colosio and PRI Secretary-General José Francisco Ruiz Massieu and the growth of a drug-trafficking mafia protected by political elites, reveal the dangers of excessive power centered in the office of the presidency.

In the early days of Zedillo's administration, the presidency has suffered significant damage. Two aspects of this should be mentioned, and Salinas himself plays important roles in each. First, many suspect that the Salinas family profited handsomely by the privatization of Mexican parastatal firms owing to access to inside information and to outright favoritism in the sales of such firms. In addition, Salinas's brother Raul Salinas and other top officials in his administration are suspected of shielding the development of a drug mafia and have been indicted in the assassination of Ruiz Massieu. A somewhat unrelated accusation against Salinas concerns his refusal to devalue the overvalued peso, both because of its ramifications for national politics in a presidential election year and because he did not wish to have his international reputation damaged at a time when he contended for the presidency of the new World Trade Organization. Of course, the devaluation Mexico was forced to make after Salinas left office in December 1994 has produced a profound economic crisis. These revelations have greatly damaged the reputation of the former president and of the presidency in general. Second, Salinas has publicly criticized Zedillo's management of the devaluation in such a way as to weaken Zedillo's authority, suggesting Zedillo mismanaged what should have been a far less traumatic devaluation.

Decentralization?

The power of the presidency has permitted an extreme centralization of power in Mexico, a country formally federal in structure. The Mexican central government generates a higher percentage of revenue and has a higher percentage of government expenditures than any other Latin American state except Chile, a formally centralist regime (Bailey 1994, 104–5). However, under Miguel de la Madrid, Salinas's predecessor, the Congress reformed the constitution to permit greater financial autonomy to the municipal governments so that they can both use disbursed federal monies with fewer constraints imposed from above and generate more revenues from their own sources.

To the extent that completion of this municipal reform agenda rested on presidential initiatives, little progress was made under Salinas. Indeed, as suggested above, PRONASOL permitted greater central government interference in local government affairs, because PRONASOL officials had the power to grant or withhold PRONASOL funds to municipalities. However, opposition governments came to power in some municipalities during the de la Madrid and Salinas administrations, and some of those opposition municipal governments were able to break the extreme control of local affairs by federal officials, primarily by developing their own sources of revenue and thereby creating some effective autonomy for themselves. Interestingly, one study of opposition governments concludes that while most PRI municipal governments did not take the initiative offered to them by the municipal reforms of de la Madrid to raise their own sources of revenue, those PRI mayors who followed the PAN municipal governments to power in Chihuahua and Ciudad Juarez made good use of that autonomy and in fact even improved those bases of revenue (Rodriguez 1995, 153–72). My conclusion, however, is that decentralization remains a project waiting to be achieved.

Related to the extreme centralization of power in the capital is the absence of effective self-rule for the Federal District's 8.5 million population. The president appoints Mexico City's mayor, while other mayors across Mexico are elected. Opposition parties and activists from Mexico City have long demanded the democratization of the Federal District's government. Mexico City now has an elected assembly, which is the equivalent of a city council, but its powers are limited because the mayor remains a presidential appointment and a member of the president's cabinet. Recently, though, the president of the PRI has called for the direct election of the Mexico City mayor. In mid-June 1995, it seemed likely that these elections would be held in 1997.

Electoral Reform and the Issue of Representation

Two key issues dominate this discussion. First, does the Mexican political system permit effective representation of diverse currents of opinion in its executive and legislative offices? Second, does the electoral process have integrity, and is the playing field level for the contending parties? The answer to both those questions remains no, but the situation has moved in more democratic directions over the past two decades as the result of a series of political reforms.

There are two major obstacles to representativeness: the PRI's domination of the electoral process and the insignificance of legislative organs in the policy-making process. To address the former, Mexican presidents since the early 1960s have advanced political reforms designed to reserve seats for opposition parties in the federal Chamber of Deputies. The most significant such reform came in 1977: it relaxed rules that had previously restricted the registration of opposition parties and reserved one-quarter of the seats (one hundred of four hundred) in the Chamber of Deputies for opposition parties selected on the basis of proportional representation. Opposition parties were stimulated by this reform. However, since the barriers to entry for new parties were set quite low, the opposition parties of the left remained divided and small.

In 1986, the de la Madrid government doubled the number of deputies chosen by proportional representation to two hundred (increasing the Chamber of Deputies to five hundred seats at the same time), but the PRI became eligible for some of those seats, so that if it lost significant numbers of the three hundred single-member district seats, it would still receive seats in proportion to its national vote share. This was crucial to the PRI in 1988 when it lost many more of the three hundred single-member district seats than it ever had.

The lesson of the PRI's bare victory in 1988 was not lost on the Salinas government. In 1990, in the first electoral reform of his term, the Salinas administration added a governability clause to the constitution whereby the largest party (presumably the PRI), if it received more than 35 percent of the popular vote, would receive at least 51 percent of the seats in the Chamber of Deputies, thereby avoiding the possibility of a divided government. Many members of the PAN, whose congressional votes were necessary to pass this constitutional reform, supported it because of the governmental stability it promised.

The undemocratic character of this governability clause received strong criticism from many elements of Mexican society, especially the left. To assuage these critics, in September 1993 an agreement between the PRI and the PAN led to the elimination of the governability clause and its replacement with a new constitutional provision whereby the maximum number of seats that a single party could hold in the Chamber was set at 63 percent, or 315 seats. Hence, no single party can reform the constitution on its own, lacking the two-thirds majority necessary for that purpose. Additionally, the 1993 political reform opened the Senate to minority-party representation. Previously, the Senate was composed of two members from each of the thirty-one states and the Federal District, chosen in winner-take-all elections. Henceforth, the Senate will have four members from each state, with the party gaining the most votes in a state being awarded three of the state's seats and the fourth going to the second-place party.

These reforms (and the creation of an Assembly of Representatives for the Federal District) make Mexico's legislative organs more representative than they were twenty years ago. Yet, as the Salinas government's effort to place a governability clause in the constitution indicates, the governing elite has sought to permit minority representation only if it has no consequence for the executive's capacity to govern as it will. This points to the other side of the representativeness issue: The PRI controls nearly all executive positions at the federal, state, and local levels. Minority parties have a voice in the legislatures of Mexico, but no effective vote because PRI majorities continue to dominate those legislatures, which therefore do not threaten the prerogatives of PRI presidents, governors, or mayors.

Winning mayoral, gubernatorial, and presidential elections has proven exceedingly difficult for the opposition, however, especially when the electoral playing field tilts in the PRI's favor. Two problems for the opposition are the degree of independence of the electoral authorities who ascertain the results and the cleanness of the elections and the disproportion in financial resources and access to the mass media available to the parties. In the former, real progress toward democracy took place during the Salinas administration, but the latter remains problematic.

In the past, the government and the PRI have had an effective majority on the Federal Electoral Commission and its successor, the Federal Electoral Institute (Instituto Federal Electoral, or IFE). Even the 1990 electoral reform legislation left the Federal Electoral Institute controlled by a majority of members associated with the PRI. In this situation, other aspects of the electoral process remained suspect: the accuracy of the electoral register (where many opposition supporters found their names absent when they appeared to vote), the capacity of the PRI to stuff the ballot box, the fairness of the vote count itself. The Federal Electoral Institute or one of its subsidiary bodies at state and local levels ultimately rules on each of these issues. Throughout the Salinas term, the opposition kept pressing the government to enact reforms that would create a truly independent electoral authority and contribute to a fairer and cleaner electoral process. As a result, the Congress enacted reforms as late as June 1994 for the August 1994 elections. Progress toward democracy came in the following areas: a completely new voter registration list was created, and each voter received a new voter registration card with his or her picture on it that was supposedly tamper proof; both domestic and international observers were granted greater access to the electoral process; the autonomy of the IFE was increased, the vote counting procedure was made simpler, and voting results were to be issued for even the precinct level; and stiffer penalties were created for those caught in acts of electoral fraud. Without doubt the electoral process is cleaner and more subject to observation than a decade ago when the PRI stole many elections in northern Mexico. At the same time, in southern Mexico, especially in rural localities where the opposition has no presence and the national media do not enter, where the leftist Party of the Democratic Revolution (Partido de la Revolucion Democratica, or PRD) forms the PRI's major opposition, these measures do not in themselves ensure clean elections.

Nationally, the inequitable access to financial resources and to mass media attention continues to hinder the opposition. Party finances, especially of the PRI, have been anything but transparent. Almost everyone believes that the PRI obtains a large portion of its revenues from government sources, although the lack of transparency makes that hard to prove. A particularly glaring example of PRI use of government resources for its campaign financing seems to have come to light in Tabasco, where the PRD gubernatorial candidate, Andres Manuel López Obrador, alleges that the PRI stole the election from him, in part by using massive funds from state coffers. López Obrador and PRD leader Porfirio Muñoz Ledo have presented boxes of PRI campaign receipts to the press that were allegedly paid for by the Tabasco government. López Obrador has made PRI fraud in Tabasco a national issue by leading a march, the Exodus for Dignity in Tabasco, from Villahermosa to Mexico City.

Furthermore, in an infamous dinner in February 1993, Salinas asked thirty of Mexico's most successful businessmen to contribute US$25 million each to a trust fund for the PRI. The disproportion in resources available to the parties is obvious. In an effort to level the playing field, the opposition parties pressed for campaign spending limits. The principle of campaign spending limits became law with the September 1993 reforms, with the General Council of the Federal Electoral Institute responsible for setting the actual limits in particular races. A problem persists here, however, because the spending limits have been set at very high levels: US$42 million for the 1994 presidential election, some eight times higher than what the PAN said it planned to spend (The Council of Freely Elected Heads of Government 1994, 26). Media bias in favor of the PRI, especially on radio and television, where the PRI and its candidates receive three or more times as much attention as the nearest rivals, has likewise impaired the opposition. Very little has been accomplished in this realm, where the major television and radio stations are privately owned and charge high advertising rates that clearly give the PRI advantage.

Some Additional Comments on the Mass Media

The broadcast media's prejudice in favor of the PRI at election time parallels its overall uncritical attitude toward the Mexican state and toward closeness in U.S.-Mexican relations. The major private television network, Televisa, which owns major radio stations as well, developed with close ties to former president Miguel Aleman Valdes. The state owns the other major television stations. The uncritical attitude of television news toward the government inhibits the kind of public debate about major public issues essential to democracy, especially because the majority of Mexicans rely on television and radio for their news.

In contrast, the print media has become much more critical of the political system and of specific public policies in the past twenty years. Mexico City and the cities of the north are especially well served by newspapers that have shown a willingness to criticize the government and in which opposition politicians and intellectuals can add their perspectives to the debate about public policy. Newspapers such as *Unomasuno* and *La Jornada* and magazines such as *Proceso* and *Nexos* have given a voice to the left and permitted investigative journalists to publish articles that reveal government corruption and describe the way some critical public decisions have been made. The degree of independence of these alternative press outlets will only grow as the liberalization of the economy diminishes the importance of advertising by the state and parastatal firms (advertising sometimes is withheld from overly critical periodicals), and as sources of newsprint other than the state-owned former monopolist Productora e Importadora de Papil, S.A. (Sociedad Anónima) (PIPSA) become available.

Nonelectoral Associations: Alternative Path to Democracy?

Mexico, like several other Latin American countries, has experienced a surge in the organizing of popular organizations or social movements, especially in the aftermath of the 1968 student movement. These organizations vary widely in their size, the issues they address, and the extent to which they try to maintain a distance from the government. In the 1980s, popular movements, most of which had sprung up at the grassroots, in poor urban neighborhoods as well as among peasant communities, began to make connections among themselves, thus forming networks of popular movements, sharing ideas and seeking collective responses to the government. Many of those who have studied such popular movements argue that they hold more promise for a democratization of Mexican life than the political parties and that the flowering of popular organizations witnessed in the past two decades indicates that many Mexicans increasingly wish to create a more participatory society.

Popular organizations typically begin with very local objectives that are closely related to the material needs of their members, such as clean water or other city services, the regularization of land titles, or the government's response to the 1985 Mexican earthquake. Veterans of the 1968 student movement organized many such organizations, but others have sprung up as the result of local leaders' initiatives. Often popular movements have an explicit commitment to internal democracy. Moreover, in both membership and leadership, popular movements tend to redress the gender imbalance otherwise evident in Mexican public life.

These local organizations have slowly established links with each other and thereby created more broadly oriented social movements. Movements have tended to focus on either socioeconomic or political issues but seldom both. In the 1970s and 1980s, popular movements more heavily emphasized socioeconomic issues. Moreover, they have sought to avoid being captured by the PRI's corporatist structures. Until the 1988 presidential candidacy of PRI dissident Cuauhtémoc Cárdenas, most of these organizations were explicitly abstentionist in electoral politics, seeing electoral politics as an arena of corruption and a distraction from more important local concerns that would never be affected by electoral politics anyway. In 1988, though, after six years of economic austerity under Miguel de la Madrid, a time marked by unusually low responsiveness of the Mexican state to the needs of the poor, some popular organizations and many popular organization members supported the Cárdenas candidacy since he promised to reject the neoliberal development model and return Mexico to a concern about social justice.

Most of those who call the Mexican regime authoritarian nevertheless recognize that the Mexican ruling elite has shown an unusually high capacity for creating programs intended to coopt most expressions of independent mobilization. Facing a legitimacy crisis following his highly contested and fraud-ridden victory in 1988, Salinas initiated the National Solidarity Program described above. PRONASOL was designed to help redress the adjustment burdens associated with the economic liberalization program that had contributed to the mushrooming of popular organizations. PRONASOL funds typically went to projects intended to improve the physical (sewage and potable water systems, street paving, electrification) or social (health, education, food distribution) infrastructure of poor urban neighborhoods or rural villages, precisely the areas where popular movements had sprung up.

PRONASOL funding required recipients to form local Solidarity committees. Consequently, it promised to either incorporate existing popular organizations, marginalize those that did not choose to become involved with PRONASOL, or head off the creation of independent popular organizations where they had not yet formed. Further, all of this has taken place outside of the PRI's traditional corporatist structure, which allowed Salinas to bypass those elements of the ruling elite, labor and peasant sector leaders, whom he considered most reticent to change Mexico's development model and least likely to concede at least some autonomy to these new associational forms that have emerged in Mexico's cities, towns, and villages. Equally important to Salinas, PRONASOL helped to distance many popular organizations and their leaders from Cárdenas's coalition and the newly created PRD. Although the PRD has made an explicit effort to recruit popular organization leaders as electoral candidates, this effort has faced two constraints. First, tensions invariably arise between long-standing party activists whose rewards are postponed when popular organization leaders are given PRD nominations. Second, lacking control of state governments and with few municipal governments in PRD hands, the party cannot effectively meet the material needs of popular organizations that cannot forget the bread-and-butter issues that initially motivated their members.

While PRONASOL thus allowed the government to recapture the initiative in its long-standing effort to incorporate expressions of independent political mobilization before they become partisan opponents, it should also be recognized that PRONASOL has permitted more autonomy and encouraged more local organization and participation than previous such efforts and than the corporatist sectors of the PRI ever permitted.

In addition to the growth of popular movements concerned primarily with the socioeconomic needs of localities, Mexico has witnessed the emergence of movements more focused on political regime issues. These include human rights organizations and associations dedicated to promotion of fairer elections and a more democratic regime. These organizations have broader membership and a more national scope than the popular movements described above. Middle-class professionals constitute a far larger share of the membership than in urban popular movements.

Human rights associations began to form in the late 1970s and early 1980s and proliferated in number. A relatively freer print media, which was willing to report instances of political corruption, police abuse, and political violence; support from international human rights organizations; and a record of assassinations of Mexican journalists all helped to motivate this movement. The Catholic church and church-based groups have contributed to the development of human rights associations. The Salinas government responded to the growth of attention to human rights by creating a National Human Rights Commission staffed by highly respected people committed to human rights, who were permitted to investigate reported instances of human rights abuses. We should note in passing that it should not be surprising that the technocrats associated with the Salinas government have been willing to abide the creation of human rights associations. Largely from upper-middle-class Mexico City backgrounds and educated in the United States and Europe, these technocrats find political violence distasteful, even when it is primarily practiced by their fellow PRI associates, the old-style politicians of the provinces and of the PRI's labor and peasant sectors, who, it should be remembered, are the chief adversaries of the technocrats within the party.

During the 1994 election campaign, civic associations came into prominence because of their role (largely self-appointed) in watching over the electoral process. The best known of these is the Civic Alliance, a self-described nonpartisan network of organizations dedicated to protecting the right of Mexicans to have a free and fair electoral process. While the nonpartisan nature of the Civic Alliance might be questioned because many of its most prominent members sympathized with or belonged to the PRD,[2] certainly the development of such associations dedicated to promoting more democratic practices in Mexican politics contributes to a less authoritarian political system. In addition, the open sympathy of many such organizations and human rights groups toward the rebels in Chiapas has served to constrain government abuses in putting down that rebellion and kept the pressure on the government to find a political solution to the armed resistance there.

Toward Democracy?

This brief survey has suggested that over the past two decades or more, and particularly in the past six years, there has been a liberalization of the Mexican regime, although there sometimes are reversions to past practices. Thus, the Chiapas uprising reveals the cross-cutting pressures on the Mexican elite and its difficult path to democracy. Many of the social reforms of the Mexican Revolution never reached Chiapas, an economically backward state where political violence and caciquismo reached notorious levels. Economic liberalization in the 1980s and 1990s meant that economic elites in Chiapas—for example, ranchers and timber cutters—could benefit greatly by foreign trade, but most Chiapas residents found themselves increasingly marginalized economically, unable to survive on the small plots of land to which they had access and forced to search further and further afield for agricultural jobs that paid little. The Mexico City elite was content to allow regional strongmen to govern as they always had, so long as the economic liberalization project was unhindered.

Human rights promoters, including Bishop Samuel Ruiz, however, encouraged the organizing of human rights and other popular organizations among the long-exploited indigenous communities of Chiapas. Hence, despite their political oppression, the people of Chiapas had a high capacity for the expression of their democratic orientation and their real economic and political needs. When the Zapatista National Liberation Army rose up against the government on January 1, 1994, it effectively articulated its differences with the Salinas government and its development project (choosing the day the North American Free Trade Agreement became effective to indicate its objection to economic liberalization) and found sympathy with its cause both in Chiapas and around the nation. Indeed, many other popular organizations took up the cause of the Zapatistas in public demonstrations. The national and international press willingly published the communiques of Subcommander Marcos, to the embarrassment of the government.

The Salinas government quickly recognized that in the age of satellite and other international electronic communication, it would not do to simply crush the Zapatistas militarily. That would look too much like the act of a scared authoritarian regime, even though it was by no means clear that anything approaching a majority of Mexicans agreed with the Zapatistas' goals or their methods. The Salinas government designated a negotiator to find a solution. The negotiation continues to this day in mid-1995. Negotiating with rebels damaged the reputation of the presidency and made the 1994 elections much more difficult for the PRI than had been expected. Moreover, it threatened to create the dangerous precedent that rebellions of sufficient scale would be met by compromises, thereby encouraging revolution as a path of resistance to PRI rule. Crushing the rebellion would have satisfied the president's neoliberal allies, but likely would have greatly damaged the regime's reputation on human rights, even more than the rebellion had already done.

Yet, the electoral opposition could not effectively exploit the Chiapas situation for its advantage. The conservative PAN did not sympathize with the rebels. It rejected both their methods and their ideology. The PAN probably benefited by the damage to the PRI's reputation because the PRD, the other potential recipient of anti-PRI votes, made little or no headway. The PRD clearly sympathized with the Zapatista cause. Advocating violent revolution is difficult for an electorally oriented opposition to do in Mexico, however, because its registry could be threatened by it. The Zapatistas were not won over by the PRD, either, because the electoral path did not seem particularly promising. Indeed, when they met, Subcommander Marcos strongly criticized the PRD presidential candidate, Cuauhtémoc Cárdenas. Meanwhile, the local PRI arranged to steal the Chiapas governor's race when it was held in August 1994, and local landowners and ranchers organized militias to use against the Zapatistas.

Carlos Salinas once said that for Mexico economic reform of the neoliberal variety had to come first and political reform could follow. He may have envisaged the working out of a version of modernization theory: economic reforms would promote economic prosperity; that economic prosperity would contribute to the growth of a middle class much invested in the economic model; that middle class would have the responsibility and the inclination to practice a moderate form of democratic politics. Such a process takes much time, and in the meantime political stability must be preserved. As Keynes said and many Mexicans seem to have recognized, in the long run we are all dead. The demands for democratization, such as expressed violently in Chiapas, by popular organizations in their daily struggles to win concessions from the still-pervasive state, and by masses of citizens appalled when electoral fraud denies the opposition parties victories they have won, indicate that Mexican society is impatient for greater freedom and more responsible participation in the institutions of the Mexican political system.

The regime's many strategies for forestalling such democratization have put the achievement of a more democratic Mexico off for many years. In his public speeches, Ernesto Zedillo has suggested that the time for such democratization has arrived. He has called for a separation of the PRI and the government and for greater transparency in all aspects of Mexican political life. Each of the past four Mexican presidents have begun their terms with promises of political reform or political modernization, however, and Mexico still lives under several nondemocratic practices and institutions, as this chapter has argued. Mexico may be broadening toward democracy, but that broadening has been most gradual and promises to continue to progress slowly.

Notes

1. See Cornelius, "Mexico's Delayed Democratization," 53–71.
2. See M. Delal Baer, "Observing the Mexican Election Observers," *Wall Street Journal*, June 3, 1994, A11.

Bibliography

Bailey, John (1994), "Centralism and Political Change in Mexico: The Case of National Solidarity" in Wayne A. Cornelius, Ann L. Craig, and Jonathan Fox, eds., *Transforming State-Society Relations in Mexico: The National Solidarity Strategy* (La Jolla: Center for U.S.-Mexican Studies, University of California at San Diego).

The Council of Freely Elected Heads of Government (1994), *Elections in Mexico*, 3rd report, August 1 (Atlanta: The Carter Center of Emory University).

Cornelius, Wayne A. (1994), "Mexico's Delayed Democratization," *Foreign Policy*, no. 95 (summer): 53–71.

Rodriguez, Victoria E. (1995), "Municipal Autonomy and the Politics of Intergovernmental Finance: Is It Different for the Opposition?" in Rodriguez and Peter M. Ward, eds., *Opposition Government in Mexico* (Albuquerque: University of New Mexico Press).

27

MARIÁ ALICIA PUENTE LUTTEROTH

Opening to the Church

The broadening toward democracy includes both new political parties and the recognition of nongovernmental organizations, which provided additional means of access to the government. Historically, the most important nongovernmental organization in Mexico is the Catholic church.

Mariá Alicia Puente Lutteroth points out that the Constitution of 1917 denied recognition of the legal personality of the church. In 1992, the constitution was amended to permit it at a time when religious diversity was increasing. Catholics formed "base communities" for greater coparticipation in liturgical and social activities, whose methods differed from those of the traditional church hierarchy.

She believes that recognition of religious associations increased knowledge about them and accentuated the government's control over their income, goods, and activities. A major question, however, is which group in the church is chosen to represent it. Puente Lutteroth suggests that the group selected was expected to support the government and restrict activities by its opponents. Traditional groups benefited from the appointment of Apostolic Nuncio Gerónimo Prigione, who has limited the activities of radical groups in the church, whose best-known leader is the Bishop of San Cristobal de las Casas, Don Samuel Ruiz, who has denounced injustice and violations of human rights and is a mediator between rebels in Chiapas and the government.

Ten years ago, the legal personality of the church was not recognized by the Mexican government. Today, relations with the Vatican have been reestablished. This change is part of a long, historic process. The anticlerical laws, from the middle of the nineteenth century, were directed to eliminate the economic, political and cultural power of the Catholic authorities. These laws always were considered to be a triumph, first of the liberal regimes and later of the revolutionaries. The liberals established the separation of church and state,

---

Translated by Laura Randall.

emancipating the latter from its dependence on the church during some decades of the nineteenth century. The revolutionaries accentuated the restrictions of the Reform Laws. The Constitution of 1917 made explicit a refusal to recognize the juridical personality of the church. It was a political conviction that these laws were untouchable. For this reason, the rapid approval of the constitutional modifications promoted in 1992 during the presidential regime of Carlos Salinas de Gortari was surprising.

The Social and Political Background

This surprising change in the law relates not only to the deficiently denominated church-state relations, but also to fundamental practices of the believers of whichever religion, given that they all are citizens that as a whole participate in the construction of their society (Guzmán 1992; Alonso et al. 1992). The background for understanding the context of changes in church-state relations is the great impoverishment of the majority of the population, who suffer from the effects of a great inequality and distance between a few who daily increase their wealth and the great majority that find that what increases is their inability to satisfy basic and elementary needs for survival.

It is in this context, accentuated by the indiscriminate aggression against autochthonous peoples, that one explains the armed rising of January 1, 1994, in Chiapas, which was made known by the Declaration of the Lacandon Forest, whose demands of land, home, health, education, food, work, independence, liberty, democracy, justice, and peace are a priority over the length and breadth of our territory.

Religious diversity is an increasingly evident fact in our traditionally Catholic country. Twenty years ago the census registered some 96.87 percent adherents of Catholicism and 1.81 percent of Protestantism. The census of 1990, however, for a population of 71 million over five years of age, registered 89.66 percent Catholics, 4.88 percent Protestants or evangelicals, 0.08 percent Jews, 1.44 percent of other religions, and 3.24 percent of Mexicans who identify themselves as pertaining to no religion. Here it is necessary to distinguish between those who consider themselves "baptized in a religion" and those who actively participate in their church, in whose case, according to personal appraisals of evangelicals and Jews, the percentage is notably reduced to less than half.

It is important to accept that this presence of other religious groups has served to erode but not to eliminate the cultural force of the dominant Catholicism, which includes groups with different tendencies.

These diverse pastoral plans can be qualitatively classified in two extremes: first, that of the majority of the bishops and priests whose relation to their faithful tends to a verticality in which men and women, consequently, only tend to carry out—as much in liturgical acts as in decisions about their life—that which the ecclesiastical functionaries say by means of doctrinal formulas and in which the indicators of fulfilling their obligations as Catholics are their attendance at mass and their provision of sacraments for their families.

The other pastoral option begun in some dioceses but widely known and the object of strong controversies is that of the few bishops and increasing number of priests who recognize that the faithful are capable of coparticipation in liturgical and social activities. It is a communitarian response in which bishops, priests, and lay people produce a spiritual nourishment. They form groups calling themselves *communidades de base*, catechistic groups, etc., abandoning being "the object of decisions of others and of being subjects of their own history" to live their faith not separated from but in relation to the social conditions of their life (Ruiz 1993). This pastorate is characterized by a tendency to horizontality in the relations between religious authorities and believers.

It is important to underline that in the last decade there has been increasing public participation by Christians and other believers in citizens' groups that as civil associations fight for the respect of basic rights, for facilitating the supply of basic needs in poverty zones, because of the increased awareness and civic-political organization, and because the immunity and impunity of public officials is disappearing with regard to acts that affect basic human rights. This is an indication of the weakening of the PRI, which therefore found it necessary to forge, reconstruct, or reform relations with potential allies—the Catholic episcopate and the hierarchies of other churches, the Partido Accion Nacional and other real or simulated opposition parties, businessmen, etc. In order to do so, it was necessary to amend the Constitution of 1917, which increased the anticlerical character of the laws. These were put into effect with the Regulating Law of 1926 that indicated the sanctions for every violation of the constitution in religious matters. Conflicts between civil and religious authorities with massive participation by the believing public were common during the following decades (Meyer 1974; Bailey 1974; Puente 1992).

Some verbal accords between the bishops and the president ended the armed phase of this movement. Relations remained tense until 1938, when, because of the oil expropriation, the bishops changed from an antigovernment position to that of total approval because of the boycott the oil nationalization had generated.

From 1940, *private* relations were established between President Avila Camacho and the archbishop of Mexico, D. Luis Ma. Martinez. Thus began the "modus vivendi" that has been prolonged for five decades, until 1992, in which for political reasons constitutional modifications were introduced.

Political weakness and cultural force in this respect, it is important to take into account the peculiar Mexican experience that speaks of a church subordinate to a state, whether this be a monarchy, republic, or revolutionary government. Initially, the pope made the kings of Spain "patrons" of the church and enabled them to intervene in the naming of bishops, extension of bishoprics, distribution of tithes, etc. This refers to the legal concept called *patronato* that lasted during three centuries of colonial dependence. During the independence period, in the nineteenth and twentieth centuries, new concepts opposed to the patronato appeared: the Reform Laws and the Constitution of 1917, with its Regulating Law of 1926 that, however, culminated in a control, a supremacy of the political power over the ecclesiastical. In colonial times there was a church that was recognized but subordinate; in the new independence period there was a church that was separated but controlled by means of the refusal to recognize its legal personality. The modification of the laws in 1992 by the recognition of the churches only accentuates the control over its income, goods, and activities. Nonetheless, the churches in Mexico cannot be described as a unity, and even less as monolithic. Referring to the Catholic church, there are diverse attitudes and concepts among believers.

The majority are believers that base their participation in their church in political, liturgical, or devotional acts and relate to them by obedience to priests and bishops. Other believers are involved in confessional groups or others but attempt to stem the social advances signaled by the Vatican Council II and the Latin American Conferences of Bishops in Medellin, Puebla, and Santo Domingo. Another significant group of Christians with a clear relationship to the popular processes has converged with other political actors in the battle for a social transformation.

Two relevant actors in the struggle within the church are Samuel Ruiz Garcia, Bishop of San Cristobal de las Casas, and Gerónimo Prigione, current apostolic nuncio. The actions of the Bishop of San Cristobal de las Casas are based on a recognition of the other members of his diocese: religious congregations, priests, the faithful, catechists of autochthonous peoples, who animate the construction of a church with an Indian face whose pastoral responses are not limited to giving speeches to those who need bread, health, and housing. This type of priesthood, which raises the consciousness of the rights and capacities of the people, constitutes a danger for the centers of power and for the interests of diverse groups. Similarly, the rising of the EZLN has been a cry to the conscience of the nation. Don Samuel was a mediator for the EZLN and the government, as well as a clear asset in the battle for peace with justice and dignity for the Indian peoples.

The constitutional modifications with respect to the church and the establishment of relations with the Vatican formally gave the government an opportunity of control, of subordination, and of braking of selected bishops and pastoral projects in Mexico by means of its ally the apostolic delegate—now nuncio—who already during the last decade has taken measures in this sense. Coadjutant bishops were named, who operated as a brake on the pastoral actions of the few bishops pledged to the people. Seminaries' curriculum was reorganized; ecclesiastic organization was restructured—the resignations of bishops because of their age were either immediately accepted or held at discretion. Bishops and priests were named so that 60 percent of the current diocesan structure depends on the good will of M. Prigione.

From the time that Don Samuel brought John Paul II his pastoral letter, *En esta hora de gracia*, during the latter's second visit to Mexico, denouncing injustice and daily violations of human rights, the Bishop of San Cristobal increasingly became an annoyance for the regime. Therefore the threats, the attempts to dismiss him, the unproved accusations of theological, pastoral, and doctrinal errors, adding to the defamations. Aggressions of all kinds increased with the declaration of the intention to arrest the leaders of the EZLN and to prove that the bishop had directly aided the Zapatistas.

In the face of these accusations, hundreds of people from various villages formed a twenty-four-hour guard around the cathedral, in order to impede the passage of the military. There has been continuous and increasing national and international aid by people and groups to the work of Don Samuel and that of Comisión Nacional de Intermediación (CONAI) for the immediate cessation of the armed conflict. They helped to establish conditions of respect for and give aid to the people in greatest need.

Legal Modifications, Popular Exigencies, and Ecclesiatical Demands

Although in practice coercions and restrictions are indicated for education by the church (Article 3 of the constitution), for its ability to acquire property (Article 27), for the religious manifestations of the people (Article 24), and for the political manifestations of the clergy (Article 130), these restrictive laws have always been a sword of Damocles. It is necessary to recognize that a continual violation of these laws existed.

As we have seen, social and political conditions in Mexico have generated a growing public presence of ecclesiastical actors and a certain need for the government to form new alliances in order to increase its strength. The opposition parties circulated their initiatives and thoughts about modifying the constitution. One of them, the PAN, affirmed that it was necessary to assure all citizens the full exercise of their natural rights and therefore "cancel for all time the dichotomy of the Mexican"—that there should not continue to be one, a Mexican believer, and the other, a Mexican citizen. An active participant from "the left" affirmed that "it is not possible to defend the Constitution and at the same time the violation of the Constitution" (*Relaciones* 1990).

On December 1, 1988, as part of his address on assuming the presidency of Mexico, Carlos Salinas de Gortari announced the necessity of "modernizing church-state relations." In June 1988, the Mexican bishopric, in continuity with other ecclesiastic authorizations previously emitted, formalized the aspiration of the bishops from half a century before and requested President Salinas to amend the articles that restricted the church and the rights of its parishioners.

The church officials and Catholics were able to agree on the revision of the constitution, even though not everyone agreed on the degree to which it was needed, and even less, to which it was prioritary. The great differences were about why, for whom, and how to do it.

In his third State of the Nation address, Salinas announced that he would send Congress a series of initiatives that would reform the constitution. This fact condensed a series of encounters and dialogues between representatives of the government and some bishops, initiated by the then apostolic delegate Gerónimo Prigione.

This was a striking announcement if one takes into account that barely two years before the strength of liberal convictions was manifested and permission was denied for "the insertion of the clergy in political matters." In the face of the church-political polemic that occurred because of the declarations of the bishops in the face of the 1985 and 1986 electoral frauds, Miguel de la Madrid, in a meeting of governors of all the states of the republic, stated "that those who believe it is the moment to destroy the Revolution or betray the nation should lose all hope" (Manifesto 1986).

Thus, during the next presidency, Salinas's initiative of reformulating the constitution is viewed as taking place because the government needed to repair its political weakness. He looked for the approval of possible allies, among them the ecclesiastical hierarchy, religious institutions, especially the Catholic one, that is important in spite of everything, having a great cultural weight. It was a way of returning to a de facto patronato. For this reason some analysts asked whether one was observing a modernization or, better said, a historic regression (Guzmán García 1991).

Even when there were negative reactions by those who considered anticlerical postures as a historic advance that could not be placed in doubt, a great number of citizens indicated that it was time to revise the constitution and bring it up to date.

The secretario de gobernacion initially suggested that three principles would be untouchable: the separation of the church and state, religious freedom, and lay education. Only two of these were maintained, since lay education was applied only to public schools.

An accelerated approval in the Chamber of Deputies permitted the publication of the decree that modified the articles whose application in 1926 led to the christero movement (*Diario* 1992). Six months later, in June 1992, the Law of Religious Associations and Public Worship was ready, which made the constitutional amendments effective. Both proceedings took place without a broad debate in which the majority of the population participated. Thus, in the Catholic church, the CIRM—the Conference of Religious Institutions and the Mexican Social Secretariat—made public their preoccupation that this new rule would tie these modifications to a privatizing and neoliberal mentality, which would limit the social mission of the church.

Relations with the Vatican: A Different Initiative

A series of events illustrate the process of the opening to the church. In February 1964 the dean of the College of Cardinals of the Vatican, in a private visit to

Mexico, spoke of the necessity of normalizing relations with the Vatican. Ten years later, in February 1974, President Luis Echeverría surprised the nation with a visit to Pope Paul VI in the Vatican and with the naming of a chargé d'affaires. Article 130 of the Constitution of 1917 did not recognize any legal personality of the churches, and recognized even less the pope as head of a state that was not recognized. Among the diverse reactions of those who saw in this an augury of a coming subjection to the Vatican, the president of the PRI and other official spokesmen affirmed that this fact did not bring any possibility of changing the policy of the revolutionary regimes.

In 1979, Pope John Paul II initiated his pontificate with a visit to Mexico that abundantly demonstrated the cultural force of Catholicism and, therefore, its apparent great political strength. The second visit of John Paul II occurred in the regime of Salinas de Gortari, which from its beginning indicated its intention to modify the traditional anticlerical positions. Among some unexpected acts we could point out: the presence of six church officials in the inauguration of the new president (1988); the request of officials of the secretary of treasury to the presidents of the Latin American Episcopal conferences, of Canada and the United States, in Monterrey in May 1989, to obtain their approval of the renegotiation of the Mexican debt; the interchange of personal representatives of John Paul II and Salinas de Gortari in 1990; and the reception by the president of Mexico of the pope in the Mexico City airport (May 1991). (It was announced, in 1990–91, that the papal representative would be a Mexican bishop who was expert in canon and constitutional law. However, the apostolic delegate was selected, which generated fears that the dependence of the Mexican bishopric would be accentuated.)

The rapid change of direction in church-political relations occurred in 1992. Constitutional modifications and especially the establishment of relations with the Vatican increased the power of the apostolic delegate, who formally obtained the rank of nuncio, of ambassador. Yet the Catholic church in Mexico is split into groups of bishops who echo the nuncio in his political alliances with the regime, and groups who maintain or increase their distance from him in their fight for an autonomy that allows them to carry out their ecclesiastic mission to the least favored sectors of the country. In this division within the church, one of the bishops who was seen as an obstacle to the political needs of the central power was Monsignor Samuel Ruiz, Bishop of San Cristobal de las Casas. It is thus that during the month of October 1993, it was announced that he would be asked to respond to accusations of doctrinal, pastoral and theological errors.

This fact immediately united groups of priests, religious and lay persons all over Mexico in collective action requesting a direct dialogue with the nuncio in which these errors would be demonstrated, but in the contrary case, demanding that the political authorities apply Article 33 of the constitution—expulsion of foreigners for intervening in domestic political affairs in Mexico—to Monsignor Gerónimo Prigione.

In relation to this conflict, a political-cultural fact of major significance was the approval of more than 15,000 Indians of Chiapas, that from diverse autochthonous villages came to San Cristobal. The mountains, woods, and roads from the diocese were covered with clothing, posters, songs, and prayers with all kinds of tzotzil, tzeltal, chole, tojolobal expressions by those walking miles to congregate in San Cristobal and by their presence in the cathedral now called La Paz, indicating their support of Tatie Samuel against the decisions of the apostolic nuncio.

In Synthesis:

1. During the last half century Mexico lived a legal fiction: Catholic schools were not allowed, but there were thousands; public demonstration of belief could not be made without permission of the government, but in all the villages religious festivals were celebrated; there could not be relations and agreements between church and state, but secret or discrete conversations existed.

2. During the last decade, the exacerbation of conditions of social injustice, of impunity, and of electoral fraud led some bishops to make public declarations and to make clear decisions in favor of the people, which hardened the official anticlerical positions during the presidency of Miguel de la Madrid.

3. We have witnessed the form and mechanisms that exclude a broad cultural debate, as well as a rapid approval of the amendments to the law during the presidency of greatest political weakness of the regime which searched for allies and offered concessions to strengthen its image.

4. In the case of the Catholic church authorities, one can distinguish two different attitudes toward the same demand for modification of the restrictive laws: that of the delegate, now nuncio, marked by an approach to and collaboration with the government that expressed itself as mutual recognition and exchange of favors. And the position of those like the Bishop of San Cristobal de las Casas, whose relation to the regime is based on an autonomy that allows an approach that gives rise to popular processes that increase the value of the cultural rights of the majority of the Mexican people.

5. By the current results, it is possible to affirm that the regime did not duly empower the diverse ecclesiastic groups. It considered that offering a major political weight to the delegate and transforming it into a nuncio would strengthen an alliance with the state, whose repercussions could constitute a brake on pastoral projects that tend toward an ecclesiastical and social democratization. Episcopal fragmentation is in sight between, on the one hand, the groups of religious actors who maintain their approval of the regime of the nuncio, and, on the other, the bishops, priests, and faithful who bet on an unpostponable alternative to current conditions.

The recognition of legal personality has been expensive. Who has benefited from the "opening"? The government through the secretaria of gobernacion now has valuable information that it lacked before about religious associations with a series of data that permits it to put into effect the "discretionality" that the Law of Cults and Religious Associations authorizes.

Bibliography

Alonso, Jorge, Alberto Aziz, and Jaime Tamayo, eds. (1992), *Nueva Imágen*, U. de G. and CIESAS (México).

Bailey, David (1974), *The Cristero Rebellion* (Texas).

Diario Oficial de la Federación, January 28, 1992 (Mexico).

Guzmán, Luis (1992), "El nuevo estado mexicano y los cristianos. ¿Estado neocolonial: con y sobre qué creyentes?" in *El Nuevo Estado Mexicano*, vol. 3.

Guzmán García, Luis (1991), "Iglesia-Estado ¿modernización o regresión histórica?" in *Las Relaciones Iglesia Estado en México* (CAM, CEE, CENCOS, CRT) (México).

"Manifesto Presidencial de Tijuana" (1986), in *Novedades y El Día*, February 16, 1986, p. 1 (Mexico).

Meyer, Jean (1974), *La cristiada*, 3 vols. Siglo XXI (México).

Puente, Ma. Alicia (1990), *Relaciones Iglesia Estado, Cambios Necesarios. Tesis del Partido Accion Nacional*. EPESSA (Mexico).

————. (1992), *Movimiento cristero: afirmación y fisura de identidades* CIESAS (México), Ph.D. thesis.

Ruiz, Don Samuel (1993), Carta Pastoral *En esta hora de Gracia*, Ediciones Dabar (México).

28

MIGUEL ALBERTO BARTOLOMÉ

Indians and Afro-Mexicans
at the End of the Century

Recognition of nongovernmental organizations is a way of increasing com-munication with, and influencing the conditions of, disparate groups in Mexico. Not all groups, however, are recognized by the government or subject to policies directed to them. This is partly a result of culture and ideology. There is no scientific basis for determining "race," so that poli-cies directed to "racial" groups do not exist. On the other hand, cultural identification—for example, as "Indians"—is an important determinant of how people are treated.

Miguel Bartolomé states that persons who racially are Indian can present themselves, culturally, as part white. However, those identified as Indian have incomes 36 percent of that of other Mexicans; 48 percent of pay differentials between Indians and other Mexicans cannot be explained by education, skills, or other measured characteristics.

Afro-Mexicans live in Veracruz and part of the coasts of Guerrero and Oa-xaca. A number of African cultural characteristics persist. The government has no specific policy for the Afro-Mexican population.

In contrast, government policies have a striking impact on Indian communi-ties and are beginning to be explicitly directed to them. For example, Bartolomé believes that the reform of Article 27 of the constitution, which permits the sale of ejidal and communal lands, could be considered an attack on Indian territo-ries—if land is thought of as belonging to "Indians" as part of their "national territory," rather than to individuals. Although an amendment of Article 4 of the Constitution said that in agrarian proceedings, Indian practices and legal tradi-tions would be taken into account, the law putting that provision into effect has not yet been promulgated.

The 1991–94 plan for development of Indian peoples was part of the National

Translated by Laura Randall.

Solidarity Program. It intended to increase Indian participation in all decisions that would affect them, while programs were designed to aid them. These policies did not sufficiently alleviate rural Indian misery, which led to the rebellion in Chiapas. The failure to ameliorate the exploitation of Indians leads Bartolomé to believe that Indian autonomy within Mexico could be an alternative to government goals.

It is not easy to make a rapid panoramic sketch of the situation that ethnic groups in Mexico have undergone during the last decade. The complexity of the situation includes not only the changing economic, ideological, and national political scenario, but also problems of the definition and self-definition of ethnically differentiated populations. This constitutes not just a formal academic dilemma but a crucial aspect of the understanding of the political processes in which ethnic identity is involved.

In the first place, it must be emphasized that in Mexico race is neither a relevant nor a sufficient indicator to denote membership in a specific ethnic group. The process of *mestizaje* (achieving the status of part-white part-Indian) has been not only biological but also cultural. Thus, persons who racially are Indian have been able to present themselves culturally as mestizos. This act supposes the acceptance of an alternate style of life as much as the negation of one's own. The reverse process rarely occurs, that is, that racially "white" individuals claim an Indian identity. However, these same persons often consider Indians as their ancestors, founders of the "Mexican nation," which now pertains to them as inheritors. The Indian thus exhibits a great historic influence, even though modern-day Indians are generally stigmatized, being considered an anachronism that should disappear to give way to a modernity understood as westernization. And if race is not a relevant indicator, then "style of living" often cannot be used to determine the presence of cultural boundaries. In fact, many peasant communities that do not speak their native languages anymore do preserve economic, social, and cultural practices that are not very different from those that are being placed within Indian villages. To assume an Indian identity represents then an act of existential affirmation that implies overcoming the denigrating stereotypes assigned to being Indian.

Usually these observations are lacking within the political literature on this topic. Paraphrasing the Brazilian Florestán Fernández, one can propose that we Latin Americans have "the prejudice of not having prejudices." Racist ideology, however, which concerns both Indians and Afro-Mexicans, continues to imprint a colonial hue on interethnic relations. For this reason it is very difficult to know the exact number of the national Indian population, given that estimates depend on how many the censuses assume are such. The only indicator currently used is comprehension of a native language, but many bilinguals could deny it. The foregoing explains the great variation of the estimates of the size of the Indian population according to the different criteria taken into account. To better understand the complex contemporary situation we must remember the historical process that gave birth to the contradictory present, in which the initial populations of the region appear as ethnic minorities.

History, especially that of this century, reflects a process of de-Indianizing Mexico. It has been estimated that Mexico was peopled by about 25 million people in pre-Hispanic times. After the European invasion, around 1650, there were 130,000 mestizos, 120,000 whites, and 1,270,000 surviving Indians.[1] In the twentieth century, the 1921 census stated that of 14,344,780 Mexicans, 4,179,000 identified themselves as Indians, but they used an imprecise racial definition (Valdéz and Menéndez 1987). After 1930, only a linguistic indicator was used, registering 2,251,086 native speakers in that year and 6,282,347 (over five years old) in 1990. Once again using other cultural features, some of which are a bit dubious,[2] the Instituto Nacional Indigenista (Embriz 1993) estimates that the total number of Indians rose to 8,701,688 people at the beginning of 1990, that is to say, about 10 percent of the population; other estimates range from 9 to 14 percent. The Indian population is increasingly literate but has illiteracy rates that are probably almost double those of other Mexicans. Their income was roughly 36 percent of that of other Mexicans, and Indians were nine times more likely to suffer severe deprivation, probably because those with comparable skills, education, and other characteristics working in Indian areas are paid significantly less than those working in other parts of Mexico. Forty-eight percent of pay differentials between Indians and other Mexicans cannot be explained by typically measured characteristics. Moreover, poverty forces Indian children to leave school earlier than others; their work provides a larger share of family income.

Indians are divided into fifty-six ethnic groups that refer as much to linguistic as to cultural or political/organizational affiliation. There are approximately 2,000 Indian communities, whose recognized lands are some 16 million hectares (1 hectare = 2.47 acres), which represents 8 percent of Mexican territory.

In spite of having a diminishing percent of population, in absolute terms Indians have undergone an extraordinary demographic recuperation in recent decades. This is a result of the notable contribution of preventive medicine in rural areas, especially vaccination campaigns and eradication of endemic diseases such as malaria. Traditionally a native family would have as many children as possible, because only very few would survive infant illness. Preventive medicine has multiplied the rate of survival, but the practice of having as many children as possible tends to be maintained. For example, the total Indian population of the state of Oaxaca has grown from about 520,000 people in 1930 to more than 1,300,000 in 1990. In the case of the Mayas in Yucatán, life expectancy, which was only 23.35 years in 1930, has risen to more than 60 now. Thus, the peninsular Mayan population has tripled in the last forty years, now showing more than a million people.

The transformation of the Indian majority into a minority is not the result of immigration of massive contingents of European migrants. De-Indianization thus should be understood not as a biological process, but as a political and ideological one, in which the native population was progressively required or induced to renounce its linguistic and cultural heritage. In this way, as emphasized by Guillermo Bonfil (1987, 42) many people who are socially considered as "mestizos" are actually de-Indianized Indians. From Independence on, national goals excluded Indians, because the Independence leaders were criollos and mestizos. But it was after the Revolution of 1910 that the repression of cultural plurality intensified, despite the rhetorical exegesis of the Indian past. It was assumed that cultural homogenization was a necessary condition for the configuration of a modern nation. Educational policies therefore were oriented toward requiring Spanish and abolishing native cultures, which were believed to cause Indian poverty (Heat 1972). Even the Mexican Constitution of 1917, because of its egalitarian emphasis, neither alluded to nor registered the existence of ethnic groups; the Indianist profession, which in fact recognized Indian presence, had to be realized by means of decrees, given that there was no precise legal definition (Nahmad 1988, 303–5).

The population with black ancestors, until recently forgotten, merits separate paragraphs. We still owe much to the studies of Gonzalo Aguirre Beltrán (1946, 1958, 1982). The first black slaves entered in the early Colonial period as servants of the Spanish invaders. In the following decades, Veracruz was the port of entry for slaves from Guinea and Cape Verde, destined for the mines, plantations, and domestic service, because the native population had undergone a terrible demographic decline, despite being relatively protected by colonial ordinances that claimed to impede Indian slavery. By 1570 there already were more than 20,000 blacks in New Spain, 10 percent of whom fled and were known as *cimarrones*.[3] In the years that Mexico became independent, toward 1810, there were only an estimated 10,000 Africans, but almost 625,000 mulattoes, who constituted 10 percent of the total population. That is to say, they were a defined and demographically significant presence. However, this important component of society has, up to now, been diluted and has not achieved a clear social visibility.

Currently, the population of African descent is especially visible in various zones in the state of Veracruz and in part of the coasts of the states of Guerrero and Oaxaca, in the region known as Costa Chica. But in almost all the rest of the nation, one can find regions and communities whose inhabitants show Afro-Mexican racial characteristics. An investigation designed to do so would appreciate the existence of a multitude of characteristics and cultural practices in which it is possible to trace an African origin. Nonetheless, in many cases African affiliation has disappeared from the group memory, skin color being attributed to God's will. Thus there is, for example, a Veracruz community where racial origin reappears only at Carnaval in the dance of the "disguised Afro-Mexicans," by which the community briefly reencounters its history (Cruz, Martínez, and Santiago 1990). Perhaps we could propose that only the Costa Chica has developed a social characterization or reconfiguration that can be described in ethnic terms. In this area, the descendants of cotton plantation slaves married to descendants of cimarrones represent tens of thousands of people who have constructed a vast organizational fabric that connects numerous communities of both groups. Here Afro-Mexican ethnicity is based not on possession of a language and an alternate culture, but on its unique organization, in the endogamous tendency, and in the persistence of ancient interactive boundaries with the surrounding population. This does not exclude the presence of some African cultural characteristics, such as round houses, masks, and dances. But local "black identity" encounters greater support in belonging to a social group articulated in itself, than in the racial phenotype. It must be stressed that the government has no specific policy for the Afro-Mexican population.

Returning to the Indian question, it should be pointed out that during the presidency of Carlos Salinas de Gortari (1989–94), legislative reforms were enacted that had and have a high level of potential impact on Indian peoples. Perhaps the most debated was the reform of Article 27 of the constitution, which established that ejidal and communal lands could not be sold or subjected to corporate exploitation, and gave rural communities a priority right to land. The Salinas government said both that there was no more land to distribute and that Article 27 had to be modified in order to attract investment in agriculture. The new Article 27 implied that these lands could be sold and rented by ejiditarios as well as bought by mercantile societies. This reformulation, expressed concretely in 1992, provoked an intense polemic; it was accused of favoring the development of new forms of latifundismo, thus annulling the achievements of the agrarian reform and facilitating the concentration of income. From another perspective it could be considered as an attack on Indian territories, given that it immediately made possible the sale, no longer of productive personal property but of part of an ethnic territory. If a mestizo peasant sells his ejido lands, I believe that he would be exercising an individual right, but if an Indian sells it, he is compromising the collective territorial right of his people, even though sale of ejido lands to outsiders must be approved by a majority of the ejido's general assembly. This interpretation underscores the difference in legal concept between land as something that can be sold, and land as part of an inalienable national territory. We must point out, however, that the right of Indian people to their own territory still is not recognized by national laws, although it is increasingly demanded.

Undoubtedly, the most important legislation in relation to Indian peoples during the sexenio was represented by the reform of Article 4 of the national constitution. On December 7, 1990, a paragraph was added to this article that said:

The Mexican nation has a pluricultural composition originally sustained by Indian peoples. The law will protect and promote the development of their languages, cultures, uses, customs, resources and specific forms of social organization and will guarantee to their members effective access to the jurisdiction of the state. In the agrarian judgments and proceedings that pertain to them, their practices and juridical customs will be taken into account in the terms which the law establishes.

But in spite of the juridical innovation represented by this constitutional reform, the law regulating Article 4 has not yet been promulgated because of the conflicts generated among the various interest groups. We should point out that until a few years ago Mexico defined itself as a mestizo nation, a concept that claimed to synthesize the composition of the population, but which in reality excluded all those ethnically differentiated from the reference group. For this reason, the constitutional reform had a strong political and ideological impact on many of the social sectors who saw their "national vision" altered. The future implementation would open legal doors to the political configuration of a pluriethnic state that already exists in fact.

The Instituto Nacional Indigenista (INI) is the institution officially charged with designing and executing government policies with respect to Indian peoples. In 1989, President Carlos Salinas installed the Comisión Nacional de Justicia in the Instituto Nacional Indigenista. The Comisión Nacional de Justicia designed the Programa Nacional de Desarrollo de los Pueblos Indigenas 1991–1994, placing it within the Programa Nacional de Solidaridad, which represents the social aspect of the reigning neoliberal agenda. This commission took off from an analysis in which indicators of the regional concentration of poverty were specified, which always coincided with the areas of greatest density of Indian population. The sanitary and nutritional conditions of ethnic regions are the most precarious in the nation, reaching indices of 53 percent for infant malnutrition in Oaxaca, the state with the largest number of Indians.

In order to transform this situation, the commission elaborated a plan that proposed to respect Indian cultures by means of increasing Indian participation in all decisions that would affect them. Specific programs were proposed to aid Indian languages, education, culture, health, and economies (INI 1990). In general, the effective achievements of these proposals were extremely modest, because they only acted as palliatives of a situation of marginalization and structural domination. Today in Mexico being Indian is a synonym for being poor.

The clearest and most dramatic expression of the failure of the government Indian policy and the negative impact of measures such as the reform of Article 27 is the massive outburst of Indian insurrection that detonated January 1, 1994, in Chiapas. For decades researchers and social analysts from different national and foreign institutions have documented the continuance of a neocolonial interethnic system in Chiapas, whose economy registers archaic forms of exploiting Indians by the mestizo population, locally called "ladinos." In spite of this, there was not a defined political will, either by President Salinas or his predecessors, to change a centuries-old situation of social injustice. The discontent, fermented during generations and expressed in various rebellions that occurred in past centuries, exploded through the Ejercito Zapatista de Liberación Nacional. Despite the presence of non-Indian leaders in its ranks, and the probable existence of political interests from outside the region, it cannot be doubted that the rebels counted on a defined Indian social base. No group of activists could have achieved the armed mobilization of thousands of native men and women if profound reasons did not feed the discontent and nourish the rebellion. It is very difficult at this time (December 1994) to speculate about the political and military process generated by the guerrillas. The configuration of future scenarios is still uncertain. However, the EZLN has projected the ethnic question in Mexico to its true political dimension, moving it from the restrictive label of assistance and development practices. Proposals about the future of Mexico can no longer ignore the presence of ethnic groups and their long-standing, just demands for economic, political, and cultural autonomy—autonomy that does not indicate separation from the state but recognizes that the goals of ethnic groups, although parallel, could be (an) alternative to government goals.

Notes

1. Toward the end of the eighteenth century, the Indian population showed signs of demographic recuperation, registering 5,200,000 persons of this identification, in contrast to 2,270,000 members of the so-called other castes, which included criollos, mestizos, negroes, and mulattoes (Wolf 1967, 206). At the beginning of the War of Independence, in the last century, 60 percent of the population was characterized as Indian, contrasted to only 17 percent as mestizos (Noriega in Aguirre Beltrán 1946, 223). For this period, 85 percent of the districts in the valley of Mexico were populated by Indians; Mexico City was 24 percent Indian (Carrasco 1991, 3).
2. Some of the criteria utilized by the INI are hard to quantify, given that among them appear relation to nature, forms of organization of work, imparting justice, values, and forms of thought. Others are more precise, such as including 1,129,625 potential speakers of Indian languages less than five years old and taking into account the self-identification manifested.
3. For 1646, there were 35,000 Africans and around 120,000 mulattoes. In 1742, there were a little more than 20,000 Africans, but those classified as mulattoes grew to about 270,000 persons.

Bibliography

Aguirre Beltran, Gonzalo (1946), *La población negra de México* (Mexico City: Fondo de Cultura Económica).
———. (1958), *Cuijla: esbozo etnográfico de un pueblo negro* (Mexico City: Fondo de Cultura Económica).
———. (1982), "El negro, la esclavitud y su proyección en la formación social mexicana" in *Africa en América* (México: Centro de Estudios Económicos y Sociales, CEESTM).

Bonfil Batalla, Guillermo (1987), *México Profundo. Una civilización negada.* SEP-CIESAS, Colección Foro 2000 (Mexico).

Carrasco, Pedro (1991), "La transformación de la cultura indígena durante la colonia" in *Los Pueblos de Indios y las Comunidades* (Mexico City: El Colegio de México).

Cruz, S., A. Martínez, and A. Santiago (1990), "Los negros disfrazados" in *México Indígena*, no. 10 (Mexico City).

Embriz, Arnulfo, ed. (1993), *Indicadores socio-económicos de los pueblos indígenas de México, 1990* (Mexico: Instituto Nacional Indigenista).

Heat, Shirley Brice (1972), *La política del lenguaje en México: de la colonia a la nación* (México City: Instituto Nacional Indigenista, No. 18).

Instituto Nacional Indigenista (1990), *Programa Nacional de Desarrollo de los Pueblos Indígenas, 1991–1994* (Mexico City: Instituto Nacional Indigenista).

Nahmad, Salomón (1988), "Indigenismo oficial y luchas indígenas en México" in R. Stavenhagen, ed., *Derechos Indígenas y Derechos Humanos en América Latina* (México City: El Colegio de México-IIDH).

Valdés, Luaz, and Menéndez, Ma. Teresa (1987), *Dinámica de la población de habla indígena (1900–1980)* (México: Colección Cinetífica No. 62, INAH).

Wolf, Eric (1967), *Pueblos y Culturas de Mesoamérica* (México: Ediciones ERA).

29

ANNA. M. FERNANDEZ PONCELA

The Political Participation of Women in Mexico Today

Discrimination against women in Mexico is part of the culture. For example, the Mexican constitution did not deny women political rights; it ignored them. Mexican women's right to vote was recognized in 1953. They were guaranteed legal equality in 1974. However, a 1993 recommendation to political parties about nominating women to electoral office was withdrawn.

Women do not lack a voice. They provide most of the members of social movements and popular organizations. In contrast, they are largely absent from formal politics. They tend to vote for the PRI, reflecting their lower income and greater rural residence and older age than that of men, who tend to vote for the opposition.

Women first entered the Chamber of Deputies in 1952, the Senate in 1964, and the Cabinet in 1981. Their participation in the legislature fell during the Salinas administration but rose at the beginning of President Zedillo's term of office. Anna Fernández notes that women in high office are not usually involved in combating discrimination against women. Greater participation in politics therefore would provide only part of the changes necessary to improve their lot.

It is not a surprise to say that in no country nowadays do women in the realm of formal politics have access, status, or any sort of influence equal to that of men (United Nations 1992; Nelson and Chowdhury 1994).

The relation between women and formal politics—the institutional political system—has always been complex and difficult. Everything from women's recent acquisition of the vote in the 1930s and 1940s to the persistence of traditional values and the domestic role of women—apparently disassociated from the public sphere—has acted as a barrier to women's political participation. Moreover, women have continued to be ignored by

---

Translated by Laura Randall.

contemporary political theory (Jaquette 1976; Chaney 1983; Vargas 1985; Kirkwood 1990; Jones 1992).

History of a Long-Standing Exclusion in Mexico

If we carry out a historical comparison, we see that there have been advances: from the appearance of more positive legislation concerning women, to the slow but steady increase in the number of women in positions within political parties, in the Chamber of Deputies and the Senate, and in the executive branch of the federal government.

The Mexican Constitution did not deny women their political rights; however, this is due to the fact that they were not taken into account (Ojeda de Siller 1976; García Orozco 1989).

The first calls for women's suffrage date from the end of the last century. The demand for suffrage was important in the revolutionary period and increased during the 1930s (INFONAVIT 1975; ICAP 1984; Farías 1988; Tuñón 1992), but women's right to vote was not recognized until 1953, when Article 34 of the constitution was amended (Secretaría de Gobernación 1983). Moreover, it was not until 1974 that women were guaranteed legal equality, by the reform of Article 4 (IFE 1994a). Even as late as 1993, the Federal Code of Electoral Institutions and Proceedings (COFIPE) withdrew a "recommendation" to political parties about the nomination of women to electoral offices (IFE 1994b).

Not only have women historically been excluded from politics, but their themes, interests, and needs have also been ignored and postponed, despite the fact that women have participated in well-recognized ways in historic events in Mexico, from the colonial to the revolutionary period. They were important in workers' movements at the beginning of the century, have been soldiers and generals, members of liberal clubs, activists in women's movements, salaried workers and teachers, participants in peasant, worker, and feminist organizations, as well as in political parties.

Disinterest and Absenteeism

On the other hand, compared to men, women hardly seemed to demonstrate an interest in institutionalized politics. This is in striking contrast to politics understood as the resolution of daily problems through social movements and popular organizations, where in the Mexican case the figures for participation of men and women are inverted, and 80 percent of the members are women.

According to information from research in the 1970s and 1990s, as well as the information from surveys of the August 21, 1994, election, women have little interest in politics. Not only that, women don't talk much about politics, election campaign meetings matter less to them than to men, and they have a higher rate

Table 29.1

Presence of Women in the Chamber of Deputies and the Senate, 1952–55–1994–97

	Chamber of Deputies			Senate		
		Women			Women	
Legislature	Total number	Number	%	Total number	Number	%
1952–55 (XLII)	161	1	0.6	64	0	0
1964–67 (XLVI)	210	13	6.2	64	2	3.1
1982–85 (LII)	400	46	11.5	64	6	9.4
1988–91 (LIV)	500	60	12.0	64	10	15.6
1991–94 (LV)	500	42	8.4	64	3	4.7
1994–97 (LVI)	495	70	14.1	127	15	11.8

Source: Table elaborated on the basis of "Participación social y política de las mujeres en México: un estado de la cuestión," in Anna M. Fernandez Poncela, ed., *Participación política: las mujeres en México al final del milenio* (Mexico City: PIEM-COLMEX, 1995).

of abstention and a smaller belief that elections are clean and the vote respected (Blongh 1972; Acosta et al. 1991; Excelsior 1994).

At the time they voted, moreover, their vote seemed to be "conservative." For example, according to surveys about the August election, more women voted for the PRI (Partido Revolucionario Institucional), which is the official party—50 percent of the women in contrast to 42 percent of men—while more men voted for the opposition parties, PAN (Partido Acción Nacional) and PRD (Partido de la Revolution Democratica). The conservative choice of women in voting is not homogeneous and depends on several factors. The grouping of these factors is similar to that of their male counterparts: less income and education, more rural residence, and greater age (Nexos 1994; Voz and Voto 1994).

Curiously, when they were in power, the more "progressive" tendencies and governments denied the right to vote to women, and, ironically, women voted conservatively, while other political options apparently paid more attention to the details of their current needs. Mexican political culture and the worldwide complex relation between women and formal politics are the keys to understanding this reality (Fernandez Poncela 1994).

Four Decades of Participation

Women entered formal politics by exercising their right to vote, which created an important landmark despite restrictions on voting itself by historic fraud and irregularities in Mexican elections.

However, their inclusion in some positions in the Mexican political system is

Table 29.2

Percentage of Women in the Principal Organs of the Political Parties, 1960–94

	CEN (National Executive Committee)				CPN (National Political Council)	CE (State Commit- tees)	MP (Total Political Militance)
	1960	1980	1990	1994	1994	1994	1994
PAN	—	6.3	17.9	11	5	3	44
PRI	4.2	10.8	12.5	13	12	9	—
PRD	—	—	20	23.8	21	8	—

Source: Same as Table 29.1.
Note: In 1992, 20 percent of the CEN of the PRI were women; in 1993, 16 percent were women.

a recent phenomenon and is not comparable to their percentage in the electoral register, where they account for 51.6 percent of the population over eighteen years old. With regard to their presence in the Congress, participation in the Chamber of Deputies dates from the 1950s (1952) and the next decade (1964) as senators. From 1964, the total number and share of women have constantly increased, although slowly and gradually (Table 29.1).

In the 1960s the first women affiliated with political parties appeared, women who also held jobs in major federal bodies. This occurred first in PRI, next in PAN, and most recently in PRD (Table 29.2). With regard to the executive branch and government administration, the first woman was appointed as sub-chief of staff for the Department of Public Education in 1958; the first chief clerk of the secretary of foreign relations in 1970; and the first secretary for tourism in 1981. It was in these first years of the 1980s that some women reached high positions (Farías 1988; Leal 1992).

Only three women have served as heads of (cabinet-level) departments: Tourism in 1982, Fishing in 1989; and the General Accounting Office in 1989. They have been governors of only three states: Colima in 1979, Tlaxcala in 1987, and Yucatán in 1991. In the judiciary, the first woman was named magistrate of the Federal District's Supreme Court in 1929 (Fernandez Poncela 1995).

Women's Presence in the Salinas Administration (1988–94)

As Mexico has been transformed during the past decades, from 1930 to 1995, through migration, urbanization, industrialization, and economic growth, women have been brought into different "social spaces," although they still suffer from discrimination. However, the changes directly related to women—the control of fertility; the increasing presence of women at all educational levels; the growth in participation in the labor market, with diversification in their occupations and in the composition of women's work—have not led women to representative or decision-making positions at policy-making levels.

In some cities, 35 percent of women were economically active (García and De Oliveira 1994), 40 percent of enrollment at universities was female (Morales 1993), and about 15 percent of households were headed by females (Acosta 1991); yet the average participation of women in the organizational structure of PRI, PAN, and PRD in 1994 was 14.3 percent (Table 29.2); participation in congressional seats was 7.9 percent before the 1994 elections, while in the current legislature (1994–97) there was a notable increase (Table 29.1.).

In the executive branch, some 79 women had jobs in 1993, 6.7 percent of the 1,162 jobs in this category (Presidencia de la República 1993). In the judicial branch, women held 39 of 291 positions (13 percent) (Presidencia de la República 1993).

As a matter of interest, in the last legislature there was a decline in women's membership in the Chamber of Deputies and in the Senate, falling from 12.0 to 8.4 percent in the former and from 15.6 to 4.7 percent in the latter. (Table 29.1). There was, moreover, a decline in women's participation in the national organizations of political parties, except for PRD, where their presence appears to have increased (Table 29.2).

Parallel to this reduced political participation is women's weak qualitative participation, that is, the positions they hold, the tasks they carry out, and the decision-making power they really have. Women who have entered the world of formal politics in Mexico have been placed in technical and administrative jobs, which usually are related to social and welfare tasks. These jobs and arenas are considered reserved, or "appropriate for," women, and the women in them are of a certain socioeconomic and cultural level and mainly belong to the party in power (Fernandez Poncela 1995).

On the other hand, these professional political women have no reason to involve themselves in the issue of discrimination against women. In general, they lack that kind of consciousness and do not collaborate to include such themes in the nation's political agenda (ICAP 1984).

Final Considerations: Balance and Perspectives

We conclude that women's participation in high positions in the Mexican political system is quantitatively reduced and qualitatively weak. There have been advances and losses, but the predominant note is that formal political participation is out of step and does not interact with other levels of society, such as education and work. On these levels there have been transformations with respect to the introduction and participation of women, and changes in fertility that have directly influenced women's lives.

The most recent government was that of Carlos Salinas de Gortari. In spite of his campaign speeches and those he made as president in favor of women, women's participation in high-level positions not only did not increase but declined (Salinas 1987a, 1987b, 1987c; Lamas 1988; PAN 1989a, 1989b; CIM 1991a, 1991b; PRI 1993; CMC 1994). This happened despite the efforts of women in political parties, and in feminist movements, for the organization of women's candidacy for office and specific campaigns (Robles and Cepeda 1991; Mercado and Tapia 1991; Lovera and Casas 1992).

At the present time, a women is president of PRI—Maria de los Angeles Moreno—and three women are in the cabinet of the new president, Ernesto Zedillo—Julia Carabias, Silvia Hernández, and Norma Samaniego—all of whom were named to their positions at the end of 1994.

The late incorporation of women in the formal political system, the low level of interest in politics, the reduced access to jobs in political parties and in government, and a conservative electoral behavior are some of the most notable features of women's participation in politics. The political world continues to be a masculine space. The extension of political rights to women has not changed its androcentric conception and structure.

Obviously there are interpretations and explanations of these difficulties, obstacles, and limitations to women's political participation. These cover the configuration of the institutional political system, Mexico's political culture, the economic and social problems of society as a whole, and the psychological problems of women themselves (Fernandez Poncela 1994).

There are suggested affirmative strategies to overcome this low participation. These range from quotas for positions within political parties and for positions determined by election for feminist women or those who defend women's rights, to the presence of women's themes and interests in Mexico's political agenda, to changes in law, education, and the media (Fernandez Poncela 1994). The most difficult change and perhaps also the most important is the transformation of mentalities, the change in the cultural model that perpetuates subordination.[1]

We live in the historic moment of a transition crisis, and it is precisely in times of war, crisis, and revolution that women have participated most actively in society. However, the crisis of values and concepts has brought us a certain conservatism and intolerant attitudes, which are extremely opposed to the supposed interests of women and of feminism.

One of the many challenges to the Mexican political system today regards women's access and participation in the institutional political life. It is necessary to think of strategies and seek solutions. Women must enter politics talking,

---

[1]As an informant remarked to me during field work in the city of León (Nicaragua) in 1991, "It is easier to win a battle—and I have been in the war—than to change people's mentality," that is, the local version of Einstein's famous comment, "It is easier to smash an atom than a prejudice."

negotiating, participating. Remaining outside of politics is equal to giving up the fight by a posture of sterile aesthetic purity. Entering politics can run the risk of being absorbed and co-opted by the very practices and forms that one has criticized. Looking for a middle ground, participating but without losing the capacity for criticism, is perhaps the most reasonable option. Looking for equilibrium between "reformist demands" and "utopian ideals"—understood as "that which doesn't exist but is possible"—and politics—as "the art of the possible."

References

Acosta, Ma. Teresa, Javier Uribe, Concepción López, and Angélica Millán (1991), "Participación electoral femenina: De la representación social de la política al voto" Iztapalapa, no. 23, Mexico City.

CIM (Consejo para la Integración de la Mujer) (1991a), "Qué es el Consejo para la Integración de la Mujer?" Mexico City.

———. "Evaluación y perspectivas del Movimiento Femenil de PRI." Mexico City.

CMC (Congreso de Mujeres por el Cambio) (1994), "Documentos básicos 1994. Declaración de Principios. Programa de acción. Estatutos." Mexico City.

Chaney, Elsa M. (1989), Supermadre. La mujer dentro de la política en América Latina. (Mexico City: FCE).

De Oliveira, Orlandina, and Brígida García (1990), "Trabajo, fecundidad y condición femenina en México," Estudios Demográficos y Urbanos, no. 15, (Mexico City).

Este País (1994), "Resumen de una encuesta sobre preferencias electorales en México," Esta País, no. 44 (November).

Excelsior (1994), "Resultados de la encuestra," August 12, Mexico City.

Farías Mackey, Ma. Emilia (1988), "La participación de la mujer en la política" in Varios Autores México 75 años de Revolución. Desarrollo Social II. (Mexico City: FCE-IN-EHRM).

Fernandez Poncela, Anna M. (1994), "Cultura política y participación femenina. Algunas reflexiones sobre la diferente intervención política según los sexos" Ponencia presentada al Sexto Encuentro Nacional de Investigadores en Estudios Electorales, Mexico City.

———. (1995), "Participación social y política de las mujeres en México: un estado de la cuestión" ed. Anna M. Fernandez Poncela Participación política: las mujeres en México al final del milenio. (México: PIEM-COLMEX [en prensa]).

García, Brígida, and Orlandina De Oliveira (1994), Trabajo femenino y vida familiar en México. (Mexico City: COLMEX).

García Orozco, Antonio (1989), "Ley electoral de 1857" in Legislación Electoral Mexicana 1812–1988 (Mexico City: Aedo).

ICAP (Instituto de Capacitación Política) (1984), Participación política de la mujer en México. Siglo XX. (Comp. de la ANFER, Agrupación Nacional Femenil Revolucionaria) (Mexico City: ICAP-PRI).

IFE (Instituto Federal Electoral) (1994a), (Mexico City: IFE).

———. (1994b), Código Federal de Instituciones y Procedimientos Electorales. México: IFE.

INFONAVIT (Instituto del Fondo Nacional para la Vivienda de los Trabajadores) (1975), "1916 Primer Congreso Feminista de México," Mexico City.

Jaquette, Jane (1976), "Female political participation in Latin America" in June Nash, and Helen Safa, eds., Sex and Class in Latin America (New York: Prager Publishers).

Jones, Kathleen B. (1992), "Hacia una revisión de la política" *Política y Cultura*, no. 1 Mecico City: UAM-Xochimilco).

Kirkwood, Julieta (1990), *Ser política en Chile. Los nudos de la sabiduría feminista* (Santiago: Cuarto Propio).

Lamas, Marta (1988) "Las mujeres y el poder político" *Doble Jornada* March 7, (Mexico City).

Leal Duck, Luisa María (1992), "Condiciones de la mujer en México," *Quorum*, 1, no. 7 (October) (Mexico City).

Mercado, Particia, and Elena Tapia (1991), "La participación en las elecciones de agosto de 1991" *Doble Jornada*, no. 56 (September 2) (Mexico City).

Morales Hernández, Liliana (1993), "Mujer que sabe latín: la mujer en la educación superior en México," *El Cotidiano*, no. 53 (March-April) (Mexico City).

Nelson, Barbara J., and Najma Chowdhury (1994), *Women and Politics Worldwide* (New Haven and London: Yale University Press).

Ojeda de Siller, Renée (1976), "Los derechos de la mujer mexicana," *Pensamiento Politic*, 21, no. 81 (Mexico City).

PAN (Partido Acción Nacional) (1989a), "Reglamento de la Secretaría de Promoción Política de la Mujer" (Mexico City).

———. (1989b), "Foro Nacional. La mujer . . . origen y destino" (Mexico City).

Presidencia de la República (1993), *Diccionario Biográfico del Gobierno* (Mexico City).

PRI (Partido Revolucionario Institucional) (1993), "Documentos Básicos. México 1993" (Mexico City).

Robles, Rosario, and Ana Lilia Cepeda (1991), "Las mujeres ye las elecciones de 1991," *El Cotidiano*, no. 44 (November) (Mexico City).

Salinas de Gortari, Carlos (1987a), "La integracián de la mujer: un desaflo de modernidad," *Discurso*, December 19 (Mérida, Yucatán, Mexico City).

———. (1987b), "Las mujeres, suma de voluntades para México," *Discurso* (November 20) (Uruapan, Michoacán, México).

———. (1987c), "La mujer, elemento indispensable para el cambio," *Discurso* (December 15) (Mexico City).

Secretaría de Gobernacián (1983), *Constitucián Politica de los Estados Unidos Mexicanos* (Mexico City).

———. (1983), "Código Federal de Instituciones y Procedimientos Electorales" (Mexico City).

Tuñon, Enriqueta (1992), *Mujeres que se organizan. El Frente Unico Pro Derechos de la Mujer. 1935–1938* (Mexico City: UNAM-Porrúa).

United Nations (1992). *Woman in Politics and Decision-Making in the Late Twentieth Century.* Dordrecht, (The Netherlands: Martinus Nijhoff Publishers).

Vargas Valente, Virginia (1985), "Las mujeres en movimiento. O de cómo somos políticas las mujeres" Documento mimeografiado, Lima.

Voz y Voto (1994), "Razones del voto," *Voz y Voto*, no. 21 (November) (Mexico City).

30

MERCEDES BLANCO

Women's Employment and Careers in Mexico

*Mercedes Blanco analyzes women's employment and careers in Mexico. She indi-
cates that a major change in the lives of women is their increased participation in
the paid urban labor force. Censuses and surveys of employment, with somewhat
different coverage, provide an overview of women's employment. The share of
women over twelve years old who were economically active increased from 16
percent of Mexican women in 1970 to 31 percent in 1991. This reflects the fact that a
larger share of married women with children are in the labor force, although
childless women continue to have a higher labor force participation rate.*

*Some 70 percent of economically active women are in the services sector, and
20 percent work in industry, especially in* maquilas *(industries that have received
U.S. tariff preferences) in the northern border area. In Mexico, salaried jobs
grew during the 1970s, but from the 1980s on, the economic crisis led to an
increase in self-employment, especially among women. Over three-fifths of Mexican women who work in commerce or in the rural sector are self-employed.*

*According to the census, women are most often employed in education and
health. The census does not include unsalaried work. Employment surveys that
include it show commerce as the most frequent occupation.*

*The salaried occupation most often held by women is administrative and
office work, replacing domestic service as the most frequent occupation. Moreover, women increasingly hold professional and technical jobs. Nonetheless, they
hold less skilled, less well paid jobs than men. There is no government policy to
broadly remedy this inequality, although during the eighties it began some training programs for rural and poor urban women. This effort continued in the
Women in Solidarity program during the Salinas administration, which trained*

Translated by Laura Randall.
I am grateful for the helpful comments of Edith Pacheco and Susan Parker in the
elaboration of this article.

women and created production projects they carried out, mainly in rural areas. Nonetheless, the economic crisis and poor position of women in the labor force make it hard to say that their increased participation in it increases their status or level of living.

Introduction

The objective of this article is to offer an overview of the principal transformations that occurred in the participation of Mexican women in the urban labor force during the 1980s and the first years of the 1990s. To this end, reference will be made to the levels and tendencies of this participation, to some of its sociodemographic determinants, as well as to the sectorial and occupational distribution of the labor force, concluding with some comments on public policies and employment in Mexico.

The principal sources of information at the national level on the labor market are the population censuses and employment surveys. Both present advantages and limitations that have been analyzed by various authors (García 1988 and 1994; Oliveira 1989; Rendón and Salas 1987).

Briefly, one can say that if the censuses indeed offer useful information on labor force participation and the economy, gathering the information in them always has brought problems derived from a group of factors. Among them is the elaboration of the questionnaire, which, among other things, implies the necessary limitation of the number and extent of questions, making it impossible to explore labor market topics more profoundly. It is for this reason that the employment surveys, especially those designed to measure diverse variables of the employment picture, capture information on situations that go unnoticed by the censuses, as, for example, the measurement of women's employment in part-time, precarious, or unremunerated work.

In Mexico, the first survey of employment appeared in 1975. It was called the "Continuing Survey of Occupation" (Encuesta Continua Sobre Ocupación—ECSO). In 1983, it underwent substantial modifications and received the name "National Survey of Urban Employment" (Encuesta Nacional de Empleo Urbano—ENEU), which it has kept until now. These two surveys are directed especially to metropolitan areas in the entire nation. They began in 1975 with only three cities (Mexico, Guadalajara, and Monterrey) and increased their coverage: in 1993 they included thirty-seven cities. Finally, starting at the end of the eighties (1988), a national survey was carried out, the National Employment Survey (Encuesta Nacional de Empleo—ENE), which provides information about cities larger and smaller than 100,000 inhabitants.[1]

The Economic Participation of Women

Through both the censuses and the employment surveys, one can obtain an overview of the economic participation of women and men at different moments of time. Beginning in the decade of the seventies, the economic presence of women began to increase slowly. During the eighties it grew more rapidly. Thus, in 1970, according to the census of population, 16 percent of Mexican women twelve years and older said that they were economically active.[2] In 1979, according to ECSO, it was 21 percent, and by 1991 it had reached 31 percent, according to the ENE.[3]

This growing incorporation of women in the labor market is due to a complex series of factors, among which must be considered both the previously mentioned tendency of the slow incorporation of women into the productive sphere and the effect of the economic crisis that began in 1982 (García, Pacheco, and Blanco 1994). It is also necessary to take into account the socioeconomic and sociodemographic determinants that explain a part of this group incorporation of women into the labor market.

Some Sociodemographic Determinants

The sociodemographic characteristics of women who carry out some activity outside of the home has undergone some changes, above all during the past few years. Traditionally it was young (from twenty to twenty-four years), unmarried, and childless women who had the highest rate of participation in the labor market. However, beginning in the nineties, the age group with the highest participation became the thirty-five- to thirty-nine-year group.

Data from various sources indicate that, for example, in 1979, according to ECSO, the highest rate of women's participation (33.4 percent) was given in the 20–24 age group. For 1991, according to ENE, it increased to 40.4 percent, being surpassed by two percentage points by the 35–39 age group (42.5 percent) and following that of the 30–34 age group (40.7 percent) (García 1994, 67).

These figures indicate, among other things, that now women in conjugal unions and with children are joining or remaining in the labor market, as distinguished from their earlier behavior in which they generally left the labor force at the time of marriage or, above all, when they had children. In other words, single women in the past have had higher levels of participation than married women. However, the incorporation of the latter in the labor market has acquired a more accelerated pace than in earlier epochs.[4]

Similarly, the presence of children has had an inhibiting effect on women's work outside of the home, so that women without children participate more than those with children. Note, however, the increased presence in the labor market of women between thirty-five and thirty-nine years, an age by which most women have completed their fertility, demonstrating that children have had a less inhibiting impact on the probability of women working than in the past (García, Pacheco, and Blanco 1994).

This situation could be attributed, in part, to the deteriorating level of well-being brought about by the crisis of the 1980s and the consequent incorporation of women and children into the labor market as a way to counteract falling real income levels (Oliveira 1989). It is also necessary to take into account the effect of economic policies that have favored the creation of certain labor enclaves, such as the increases of maquiladora enterprises in the north of the country.

Sectorial Distribution of Women in the Labor Force

Our starting point is that the tertiary sector, which includes services and commerce, has absorbed the largest share of women's employment in the eighties and the first years of the nineties. Approximately 70 percent of the population of economically active women is found in this group of activity.[5] Another 20 percent of economically active women is found in industry, above all in a sector where their presence is very important, that of the maquiladora firms located in the northern border of the nation. Note, however, that the percentage of women occupied in the industrial sector fell by about 1.5 percentage points in the first half of the 1990s (García 1994, 37).

Given the heterogeneity of the Mexican labor market, enormous differences can exist within sectors as regards position in occupation (salaried work, commission, self-employed, unpaid work, employer, etc.). We now turn to a brief discussion of salaried and nonsalaried work. In reviewing the evolution of salaried and nonsalaried work in its various forms in Mexico in the last decades, García (1988) observes that generally speaking there was a process of salarization until 1980. That is to say, until the end of the seventies as much in the industrial sector as in that of services (including commerce) there was an increase in salaried work. Her work refutes the hypothesis that industry could no longer generate employment by the 1970s and therefore encouraged the expansion of the informal sector.

However, toward the end of the seventies and already fully in the eighties this situation underwent various changes in the opposite direction, which became even more pronounced during the nineties. In the eighties and nineties, Mexico has been characterized by successive economic and political crises, and has seen the greater appearance of nonsalaried workers (self-employed, unpaid employment) and unemployed workers.

In this process it is women, in relation to men, who have most rapidly increased their classification as nonsalaried workers. This situation can be appreciated by looking at the relative distribution in the occupational structure. Whereas in 1979, 28 percent of women who worked were unsalaried, by 1991 they had increased to 36.2 percent. In contrast, the data for the masculine population was 35.4 percent and 36.8 percent, respectively (García 1994, 45).

These figures include three broad sectors: agriculture, industry, and services/commerce. Among these, in the case of women, it is in the tertiary sector, and within this especially in commerce, that there is the larger proportion of unsalaried workers—62 percent in 1991. Note that in rural areas, 65 percent of the workers can be classified as unsalaried labor (García 1994, 45 and 47).

It is clear that the changes in the markets and labor force have been centered in the expansion of manual and nonsalaried labor.

Occupational Distribution of Women in the Labor Force

A second approximation to the heterogeneity of economic sectors, especially of the tertiary, and to the transformations that women's participation in the labor market have undergone is possible by an analysis of the occupations performed by women. It should be noted that different studies represent distinctive levels of disaggregation and make comparisons difficult. The problem, as described above, is that sources such as the censuses of population and the surveys of employment present results that do not coincide because they refer to different occupational groups.

Thus, for example, the tertiary or services sector is that in which the majority of women performing work outside the home belong. But at the subgroup level of activity, the census of 1990 indicates that it is community and social services, above all those of education and health, that give greatest employment to women (21.33 percent). This is partly because the census highlights the formal and salaried labor market, because it was the labor market activity best recorded (Jusidman and Eternod 1994). In contrast, the ENE of 1991 indicates that 24.7 percent of economically active women were in commerce, which includes various kinds of nonsalaried activities, which is precisely what the census does not capture well.

Considering the salaried employment of women, the 1990 census reports that 21.22 percent of the economically active women are in administrative and office employment, representing the largest occupational group. The second largest category of principal occupation for women is domestic services, at 11.31 percent. It should be noted that occupation in domestic services has been decreasing over time[6] (García and Oliveira 1994; Pedrero 1990).

In conclusion, the employment surveys as well as other sources of information about work confirm the tendency of growth of numbers of women who work in the informal occupations. However, this is not to ignore other occupations that, although proportionally a minority, have presented rapid growth rates, such as professional and technical workers, who, according to the census of 1990, have the highest growth rate (7.26 percent) of all the other occupational groups,[7] even though this refers to the universe of salaried workers in the formal sector.

Finally, owing to the limitation of space, it is not possible to develop more fully the theme of conditions of employment that prevail in different occupational groups, in which one would have to refer to variables such as the amount of income, the number of hours worked, and fringe benefits.

In respect to the first, in addition to the generalized loss of salaried workers' purchasing power during the eighties and nineties, women obtain lower income than men (Pacheco 1994). One school of interpretation argues that this situation is due to the fact that women work fewer hours than men, and that, for this reason, it is logical that they receive smaller incomes. This either could be because many women have to work at part-time jobs because of their domestic responsibilities or because they cannot find jobs with better conditions of work. However, it is also true that in the same occupations and working the same number of hours, women receive lower salaries, although they have higher levels of education on average than men (Parker 1995). Exacerbating the situation is the segregation of occupations by sex, as women are less likely to be found in high-paying occupations such as managerial occupations. Here a reference can be made to the nonexistence of public policies.

Public Policy and the Employment of Women

The decade of the eighties represented for Mexico not only a period of economic crisis but also one of important transformations in diverse fields. As indicated above, the participation of women in the labor market, its levels, determinants, and kinds of employment underwent changes that have increased in the first years of the nineties and that in the light of the new crisis in 1994 appear to be becoming even more acute.

During the regime of President Salinas de Gortari (1988–94) there were moments in which some macroeconomic indicators appeared to signal the improvement of the national economy in spite of the fact that living conditions for broad groups of the population did not improve. However, at the end of his six-year term it was evident that the result of the policies continued to be the generalized deterioration of standards of living, the loss of purchasing power of salaries, and increased unemployment and self-employment, phenomena that have worsened with the beginning of the administration headed by President Zedillo.

In the first months of 1995, there have been debates in diverse forums about the magnitude and characteristics of employment in Mexico, above all, the unemployment that has been generated by the most recent economic crisis. There is no consensus among the diverse actors (among others, government agencies, employers groups, labor unions, and scholars) regarding these points. However, they agree that there clearly exists a disequilibrium between supply and demand of labor and on the need to increase the growth of employment. It is for this reason that speaking about public policies directed to the diverse problems of labor must first refer to the development model or to the means and policies of economic adjustment and restructuring that Mexico has undergone during the most recent presidencies.

In regard to women, government efforts directed especially to the development of programs of employment for specific groups have been very limited. During the eighties, as part of a broader social policy, some government organisms began training programs basically for rural women and those in poor urban areas. During the regime of Salinas de Gortari, the creation in 1989 of the so-called Programa Nacional de Solidaridad (PRONASOL), directed to attend to the most unfortunate sectors of the population, stands out. PRONASOL is composed of various subprograms, one of these being Women in Solidarity (Mujeres en Solidaridad); this includes both training and creation of productive projects carried out by women, for the most part in the rural sector (Pedrero, Rendón and Barrón 1995).

Both PRONASOL as a whole and the subprogram dedicated to women have received many criticisms, which range from planning errors and ignorance of national reality to its utilization for electoral ends. Despite this, its contributions have also been acknowledged and, above all, the experience that it generated suggests it should be utilized in future plans and programs. If indeed during the first months of the regime of President Zedillo PRONASOL has not officially disappeared, its existence and permanence for the moment are uncertain, given that not only has it been questioned but also its inability to attack the basic problem of national poverty has been recognized, given that this requires structural changes in the economy as well.

In the light of the recent economic crisis, which has been evident since the end of 1994, the overview of employment in Mexico, both for women and for men, does not present encouraging perspectives, but only the reverse. It is for this reason that the population will have to continue to undertake strategies that generate income as well as reduce consumption. That is to say, families will have to continue to send their women and children to the labor market. In view of the structural situation and the low qualifications of these workers, they are likely to find space only in the informal sector, with its characteristics and limitations. In this way, although the economic participation of women continues to increase and its provision is essential for family survival, if this employment continues to be precarious and badly paid, it is difficult to consider how this will permit the elevation of the standard of living.[8]

Notes

1. The ENEU is elaborated and applied by the Instituto Nacional de Estadística, Geografía e Informática (INEGI), and the ENE also is carried out by INEGI but in collaboration with the Secretaría del Trabajo and Previsión Social (STPS).
2. The economically active population (PEA) includes employed workers (salaried and nonsalaried) as well as unemployed workers searching for work in the reference period (in some cases, the previous week).
3. A consensus exists among scholars of employment in Mexico that the 1980 and 1990 censuses have important gaps in their coverage of economic activity in general and of women in particular, for which reason the surveys are a better source for a description of women's work.
4. The specific rate of women's activity by civil status at the national level, according to the ENE of 1991 was 37.5 percent for single women, almost the same as those not united in formal marital unions (37.3 percent), and 25.5 percent for married women (García 1994, 71).

5. For 1979, 49.9 of the women's economically active population was in services and 21.7 percent in commerce. For 1991 the proportions changed a little: 46.1 percent in services and 23.6 percent in commerce (García 1994, 37).

6. García and Oliveira (1994) have used sources such as the Encuesta Nacional Demográfica for 1982 and the Encuesta Nacional de Fecundidad y Salud of 1987 to student tendencies and determinants of women's work in México. Based on employment data from these sources, the authors point out that between 1982 and 1987 the percentage of women who worked as domestic servants fell from 11.4 percent to 7.5 percent of women between twenty and forty-nine years old.

7. The growth rate of the total economically active population, according to the census of 1990, was 2.94 percent, and that of women was 4 percent (Jusidman and Eternod 1994, 36).

8. There are various studies that indicate that the traditional relation between unsalaried labor and lower earnings than that of salaried labor is changing. For example, self-employed workers could receive income equal to and even greater than that of salaried workers in similar jobs, so that self-employment sometimes is a better alternative than the search for a job in the formal sector of the economy.

Bibliography

García, Brígida (1988), *Desarrollo Económico y Absorción de Fuerza de Trabajo en México* (Mexico City: El Colegio de México).

———. (1994), *Determinantes de la Oferta de Mano de Obra en México.* Cuadernos de Trabajo No. 6 (MexicoCity: Secretaría del Trabajo y Previsión Social).

García, B., and O. de Oliveira (1994), *Trabajo Femenino y Vida Familiar en México.* (Mexico City: El Colegio de México).

García, B., E. Pacheco, and M. Blanco (1994), *El Trabajo Extradoméstico de las Mujeres Mexicanas. Documento preparado para el Comité Nacional Coordinador para la IV Conferencia Mundial de la Mujer, 1995* (Mexico City: En Prensa).

Jusidman, C., and M. Eternod (1994), *La Participación de la Población en la Actividad Económica en México* (Mexico City: INEGI/ISS-UNAM).

Oliveira, O. de (1989), "Empleo femenino en México en tiempos de recesión económica: tendencias recientes" in Cooper, et al., eds., *Fuerza de Trabajo Femenina Urbana en México.* vol. 1 (Mexico City: UNAM/Porrúa).

Pacheco, Edith (1994), *Heterogeneidad Laboral en la Ciudad de México a Fines de los Ochenta* Doctoral thesis, (CEDDU / El Colegio de México).

Parker, Susan (1995), "Niveles salariales de hombres y mujeres: diferencias por ocupación en las areas urbanas de México: 1986–1992." Paper presented at the 5th Annual Meeting of the Mexican Society of Demography, Mexico City, June 5.

Pedrero, Mercedes (1990), "Evolución de la Participación Económica Femenina en los Ochenta," *Revista Mexicana de Sociología,* ISS-UNAM (January–March).

Pedrero, M.; T. Rendón; and A. Barrón (1995), *Desigualdad en el Acceso a Oportunidades de Empleo y Segregación Ocupacional por Género. Situación Actual en México y Propuestas. Documento elaborado para el Fondo de Desarrollo de las Naciones Unidas para la Mujer para la IV Conferencia Mundial de la Mujer, 1995.*

Rendón, T., and C. Salas (1987), "Evolución del Empleo en México: 1895–1980," *Estudios Demográficos y Urbanos* 2, no. 2 (May–August).

31

ALICIA ELENA PÉREZ DUARTE Y N.

Legal Reform in Mexico and Its Effects on Women, 1984–94

The changing condition of women in Mexico reflects modifications both of culture and of the law. Alicia Elena Pérez Duarte y N. points out that expanded access to education has benefited women more than any other factor. The Mexican Constitution provides the legal basis for this by consecrating the right to education, which is to teach the ideal of avoiding privileges based on sex. It recognizes women's right to informed motherhood and protection of their health; to employment without discrimination and equal pay for equal work; and maternity leave. Mexico ratified the international Convention on the Elimination of All Forms of Discrimination Against Women in 1981, which obligates it to establish policies that will eliminate discrimination against them.

Some of the most important laws impacting women are those covering marriage and divorce. Mexican law tends to maintain men's power in marital relations. Although in some federal entities each spouse must contribute to family expenses in proportion to his or her income, in other states, men must pay for the home and children, while a wife must follow her husband and take care of the children. State laws vary as to whether a wife may work outside the home automatically or only with her husband's permission.

From 1975 to 1983, if a divorce was contested, the guilty party paid for support. If the divorce was voluntary, a man did not have to support his wife after the union was dissolved. As of 1983, a husband must support a divorced wife for as long as the marriage lasted if she does not remarry. Similar terms apply to support by his wife of a husband unable to work.

The National Development Plan of 1989–94 proposes the full integration of women in national development. However, the outlook for the future is that solution of the political and economic crisis in general will take precedence over the improvement of the conditions faced by women in particular.

Translated by Laura Randall.

Structures and Institutions

It is hard to evaluate the effects that the reforms of the Mexican legal system have on the condition of Mexican women because in reality we have many significant differences of class, generations, ethnicity, ideology, region, education, etc., so that we find a heterogeneous and unequal panorama of conditions and opportunities among different groups of women. That is to say, the analysis and evaluation of the condition of Mexican women should begin with the recognition of two characteristics of our nation's social structure: heterogeneity and inequality.[1]

Focusing our analysis on the aspect of production and labor, it can be affirmed that in the last decades the nation's structures have undergone changes as one of the reflections of the economic crisis that we have undergone for many years, which has forced the integration of women into the paid labor force. However, this has not significantly modified the traditional division of labor between men and women within the nuclear family. Women continue to have the role of mother-wife and housewife, and the man that of the breadwinning head of family. Thus we can ask if social structures effectively have been modified, or if these changes have only been superficial. It is also important to think about the causes of these changes.

In this context, it is possible to affirm that the access to education places women in more favorable conditions than those of their mothers and grandmothers and that this has repercussions, much more than any public policy, on the change in our social, political, and economic condition.

If we shift the focus of analysis toward work in national politics, we find that the massive access of women to paid labor has not had a proportional impact on our role in this area. Until recently, this sector has been dominated by men. Our participation has come about much more slowly, with advances but also with significant regressions.[2]

The Current Legal System

Together with these structural changes, the Mexican legal system has undergone reforms. Those which increase legal equality between men and women are emphasized. In this context, it is necessary to clarify that the recognition of women's rights has not been a gracious concession of our patriarchal society. It has been the result of a long struggle, of the constant effort of many. For this reason, one cannot say that it is the result of government actions or government planning directed toward this end. However, it is undeniable that the reforms of the Mexican legal system in the last two decades have made certain inequalities disappear and have narrowed the gap between them, although not sufficiently.

The Mexican legal system is based on the federal constitution and includes, moreover, international treaties and conventions subscribed to by Mexico, as well as federal and state laws. Currently, Article 4 of the constitution indicates, in addition to equality between men and women, two basic principles that correspond to the demands for recognition of rights that women have demanded throughout history: a right to free, responsible, and informed motherhood, and the right to protection of health.

Article 3 of the constitution consecrates the right to education. There is no specific mention of equality between men and women. However, it indicates that education should sustain the "ideals of fraternity and equality of rights of all men, avoiding privileges based on race, religion, group, sex, or individuals."

For its part, Article 123 of the same basic document contains, from 1917 on, workers' rights, among those that of women to be hired without discrimination and to receive a salary equal to that of men for equal work. It includes the basic rules governing absence for maternity and nursing, which are categorized as rules for protection of childhood and as a recognition of the social function of motherhood.[3]

In regard to political rights, it is only from the reform of Article 30 in 1953 that Mexican women finally achieved the recognition of their unrestricted citizenship.

In the international sphere, the parameters for evaluating legal standards of women's rights was established by the Convention on the Elimination of All Forms of Discrimination against Women, ratified by Mexico in May 1981, by which it obligated itself to establish a policy directed toward the elimination of discrimination against women; to modify sociocultural standards of conduct, practices, customs, and prejudices based on the idea of the inferiority of either of the sexes; to guarantee that family education include an adequate understanding of motherhood as a social function and the recognition of the joint responsibility of men and women for the education and development of their sons and daughters.[4]

Rules and secondary laws are derived from the constitutional provisions referred to above. Such laws include the Federal Labor Law, which protects equality of salaries, conditions of work, the right to training, social security, and absences for motherhood and nursing; the General Population Law, which tangentially refers to reproductive rights; the Agrarian Reform Law, which creates Industrial Agricultural Units for women (UAIM); and the General Health Law, which details the standards governing the right to health, including reproductive rights.[5] Likewise, the civil and penal[6] codes of each of the thirty-one states and the Federal District should be taken into account.

Both Mexican domestic legal structure and its international legal obligations proclaim a strong discourse of equality between men and women. The Convention requires Mexico to go beyond simple declarations and brings attention to uses and customs that perpetuate the condition of subordination, which means, among other things, revising sex education schemes that favor inequality of opportunity and changing the entire domestic legal standard so that laws do not project, ad infinitum, patriarchal structures of Mexican society that consider women almost quasi incompetent and requiring tutelage and protection equal to that required by minors.

In summary, there have been important advances in the fight for women's rights and in the achievement of equality of law and opportunity between men and women. The criticisms that have been made about the reforms signify that the structures that maintain inequality are weakening, that we can hope, quantitatively and qualitatively, for improvements in the near future.[7]

Marriage and Divorce in Mexico

Family structures are a magnificent thermometer that measures for us, with sufficient precision, the legal condition of women in a society.[8] Mexican legislation in this area has been very advanced, given that in 1917 the Law of Family Relations made the first declaration of legal equality between men and women.[9]

However, even today, man's marital power is maintained in some of the Civil Codes of our republic, especially by means of the strict distribution of family obligations between men and women, which favor the economic dependence of women on men and, by this means, submit them to his authority.

In this context, in Mexico, only civil marriage is recognized, that is to say that performed by the authorities legally entitled to carry it out. Within civil marriage, there are two forms of ownership of the couple's goods: that of marital ownership and that of separation of goods. The former creates a community of goods between the man and the woman in such a way that both are owners of half of all of the goods acquired during the marriage and while the marital regime lasts. The community of goods could be liquidated during the life of the conjugal union or after its dissolution. Under the separation of goods regime, both partners keep their ownership of their personal property.[10]

Independent of patriarchal authority in marriage, there are different requirements in relation to the economic contribution that each of the spouses should make to support the marital household. On the one hand, some federal entities establish that both of the spouses should decide, of common agreement, about establishing their household and that both should contribute resources, in proportion to their income, for the maintenance of the home and their sons and daughters.[11] In other states, it is pointed out that women have the obligation of following their husband to wherever he would establish the couple's home, and that the husband is required to maintain the home and the children, while the wife is to care for and attend to the needs of the children.[12]

Between these two extremes, there are some variables, however, coinciding with them, on the one hand, civil codes that do not restrict women from carrying out remunerated work outside of the home and those that expressly state that the wife will be allowed to work outside the home only when her husband permits it and always given that such work would not prejudice the obligations that she has for the home and children.

In regard to divorce, Mexico follows the structure of the Napoleonic Code with required and voluntary divorce. In almost all of Mexico, there are sixteen causes of divorce, all of which refer to undesirable conduct on the part of one of the spouses, so that the dissolution of the marriage is converted into a punishment for the guilty partner.[13]

There is also voluntary divorce, and that which has been called de facto divorce, which is to say, a separation for more than two years without taking into account the reason that led to the separation.[14] This latter cause of divorce was added in 1983. It was thought that it would promote an avalanche of divorces, but that didn't happen. The procedural obstacles for divorce continued to exist in all of Mexico because it is considered that marriage is an institution whose continuation is of public concern and that divorce only can be decreed if the cause for which it is invoked is fully proved.

In the same divorce proceeding, the judge should take the necessary measures to cover the needs of the children of the marriage: food, custody,[15] and, when this is the case, the loss of the father's rights.[16] The judge has the broadest powers to do this, being required, at all times, to attend to the higher interest of the children. In relation to food, it is pointed out that after the divorce both parents continue to be obliged to maintain their sons and daughters and a stipend sufficient to cover their needs should be established. Between the spouses, starting in 1975 and up to 1983, only the guilty party was condemned to pay the monies for support, and when the other partner had insufficient resources to attend to his or her own support. In voluntary divorces—in honor of the legal equality between men and women—the provision that obliged the man to support his wife once the union was dissolved was eliminated.

From 1983,[17] the existence of a real disequilibrium within the nuclear family was recognized. For the first time, a principle of placing a monetary value on work in the home (contained in Article 288 of the Civil Code of the Federal District) establishes that "in the case of divorce by mutual consent, the wife has the right to receive support for food for the same period of time as the marriage, a right which she will enjoy if she has insufficient income and while she does not contract new marriages."

The same right will be had by the husband who is unable to work and lacks sufficient income, while he does not contract a new marriage or concubinage. The difference between the two is that the man must demonstrate his incapacity to work, while in the case of the woman support is a recognition of the years she dedicated to attending to the home, thus losing her competitiveness in the labor market.

Of course, an important element in the dissolution of a marriage is the distribution of goods that were acquired during it. In the Mexican system, although this aspect is highly conflictive because of the emotions that surround the legal process, in reality, the only possibility that exists is dividing property in half if the marriage was carried out under the form of marital society, or leaving to each partner his or her own property, if they were married under the regime of separation of goods.[18]

Public Policies in the Government of Salinas de Gortari

The National Development Plan of 1989–94 contains a section that refers to the participation of women in development programs and actions during the last presidency. The reference standard was defined in the following manner:

> Despite the greater participation of women in the various areas of national life, important differences and inequalities remain in regard to the number and quality of opportunities that are offered to women in education, work and political and social organizations. This situation is incompatible with our democratic aspirations and we must transform it. To this end, the government will aid and promote the full integration of women in national development and its benefits, responding to the legitimate demand of opening more spaces to their participation at all levels.[19]

This declaration specifies that change and modernization include not only material concepts, but also a transformation of attitudes and behavior that favor a culture of equality. In this same document, specific mention of women is made in regard to public health and population policies. In the first group, exact reference is made to maternal and child health, and in the second the reduction of the rate of population growth by means of actions that would motivate a reduction in fecundity.

In this context it is pointed out that the following should be encouraged:

> ... structural transformations that are related to changes in reproductive behavior of couples, noting the evidence that increasing equality between the sexes in educational and productive labor, together with increasing the level of living, has a clear demographic impact. In our regime of liberty, family planning is a decision that belongs exclusively to the couple; it is the task of government and society to promote responsible motherhood and fatherhood and to create conditions for the free and beneficial development of the family.[20]

Finally, it should be pointed out that this National Plan indicates the importance of encouraging the active participation of women in the fight against extreme poverty and in favor of the improvement of the living conditions of the population. For this we anticipate the promotion and recognition of the work we have already undertaken and the strengthening of our capacity of integrating ourselves into productive activities, for our own benefit, as well as that of our families and communities.[21]

Included in this task is PRONASOL (Programa Nacional de Solidaridad), in which women were a group receiving priority and whose basic document recognizes the outstanding role women have played, as much in domestic work—and the responsibility that this signifies in the physical development of our sons and daughters—as in the processes of production and commercialization, especially in agriculture (PRONASOL 1990, 103).

Outlook for the Future

Although toward the end of 1993 there was a favorable outlook for the consolidation of concrete actions with a view to improving the condition of Mexican women in all aspects, to capitalize gains more rapidly than in the last two decades, the events which shook the country during 1994, uniting us in an unprecedented political and economic crisis, darkened the outlook because priority was given to the solution of more urgent problems.

For Zedillo's government, achieving definitive peace in Chiapas is more urgent than creating a body whose task is the design of public policy for women and the follow-up of international promises in this area. Slowing the decline in value of our money and the collapse of an economic policy that appeared viable are two problems to be resolved before thinking about providing greater numbers of women access to management posts in local and federal government. Fighting delinquency, which grows daily in urban areas, is more important than combating subtle discriminations against women, for example, in access to work.

Of course, I believe that if solving these problems is a basic task in this moment of our history, the Mexican government should not lose sight of the fact that improvement of the living conditions of women not only indicates improvement of living conditions of 51 percent of the population, but also that this has a multiplying factor that, by itself, would help to resolve other kinds of problems, including those given priority.

It is not possible at this time to present the aspects of Zedillo's political program that are related to women, because the National Development Plan for his term of office has not yet been presented, but the outlook is not very promising if we keep in mind that during his political campaign there were very few concrete references to reforms leading to equality of opportunity between men and women, and if we consider that in the recent reform of the federal judiciary, the first of his administration and the most drastic in Mexican history, only one woman was named to the Supreme Court as minister,[22] so that the percentage of women decreased as a result of the December reform from about 20 percent to less than 10 percent.

However, there are also positive signs. In the midst of the most severe crisis since the triumph of the Mexican Revolution and a search for alternatives that would permit it to maintain its power, the official party named, for the first time in its history, a woman as its national president. In the Cabinet, there are—also for the first time in history—three women as secretaries of state. There also is a woman in one of the most important subsecretaries of the minister of the interior. How much will this be reflected in the improvement of social, political, and economic conditions of Mexican women? We don't know. The presence of women in decision-making positions does not necessarily indicate benefits for other women.

In the academic sector, the efforts of university programs and institutions are united, which was not seen before.[23] In civil society there are instances of coordination of nongovernmental organizations with wide membership,[24] all of which allows us to think with some hope of the near future, because this work, in the past, has been a determining factor of the changes that have been achieved.

Notes

1. *The Technical Group on the Participation of Women in Public Life and Access to Decision Making of the National Coordinating Committee for the IV World Conference on Women* (Hierro, Graciela, Lorenia Parada, and Gloria Careaga, April 1994) indicates, for example: "In the last decades, an important group of urban women who have obtained a high level of education have been able to separate sexuality from reproduction, in spite of the force of religion and of the traditional models of socialization. That is to say, these women have faced a series of conflicts to arrive at their views of imposed motherhood and reject the excess burden of children and of domestic work that is implied by their maintenance and care," a situation that does not prevail among women of the upper class or of the lower middle class, or among women who have less than average education, or among rural women or those in other ethnic groups.

2. The same document listed in note 1 underscores the inclusion of women in national political life is given as an extension of their role of mother, because they are given tasks considered to be "feminine." It also points out the differences in policy making between men and women, which impede our access to formal areas with recognition of our potential as interlocutors in this task.

3. These rights include a maternity leave of forty days, which can be divided among days before and after childbirth, although it is preferred that all be taken after. Full salary is paid during this leave. Similarly, working mothers have the right to nurse their baby during two half-hour periods during the day. Their income is not reduced because of this.

4. We must point out that these promises have not been fully carried out because women still endure discrimination in various aspects of daily life.

5. In this regard, it is specifically pointed out that family planning, as well as the health of mothers and children, is a priority activity of the so-called Health Sector, so that during the Salinas regime plans and programs were constructed to attend to the largest possible number of people who requested such services. However, it has to be pointed out that certain programs were severely criticized, especially those related to family planning, because they paid more attention to figures about birth control than to giving informed attention to women of reproductive age.

6. In the category of penal law, we must ask: How much does free sexual and bodily development of the woman matter? To answer this question a comparative analysis was made between two crimes: simple rape, and cattle rustling or the stealing of one or more head of cattle. In the majority of the states of the republic, the penal code provides greater punishment for cattle rustling.

7. There is still much to do; the legislature has not filled in gaps in legislation that continue to permit discrimination against women.

8. For this reason feminist literature exhibits a justifiable interest in the themes of the family, of women's participation in it, of the conditions governing daily relations between men and women in it, etc. These themes are related to that of family law.

9. However, it is necessary to point out that for many years, despite the fact that this declaration clearly delimited the sex-determined roles and responsibilities—the woman at home, the man providing support—these definitions were slowly modified. When the Civil Code of 1928 was promulgated, it conserved the declaration of juridical equality between the man and the woman with a rationale that was clearer and broader than those previously given. However, within the family structures, the figure of marital power was conserved for many more years until 1954, when this concept was eliminated, even though other forms were maintained, which indirectly led to the same subjection of the woman to her husband. In 1975, an attempt was made to eliminate all distinctions that favored the figure of male-head-of-family or male-provider and an effort was begun to eliminate language that could damage women by the use of generic masculine terms.

10. These two regimes governing goods of married couples exist, with slight variations, in all the states of Mexico.

11. This case includes the Federal District and the state of Guerrero, for example.

12. This is the case in the states of Quintana Roo and Durango, for example.

13. Thus, for example, causes of divorce include: adultery; that a woman give birth to a child conceived before the marriage that would judicially be declared illegitimate; the husband's proposal of prostituting his wife; immoral acts carried out by the husband or wife with the aim of corrupting the children, as well as tolerating their corruption; suffering from chronic and incurable sexually transmitted disease; incurable impotence that occurs after marriage; incurable mental derangement; unjustified abandonment of the home for more than six months; great cruelty, threat, or injury by one spouse to the other; unjustified refusal of a spouse to contribute to the expenses of the home and the maintenance of the children; and habits such as gambling, drunkenness, or drug addiction, among others.

14. This is the most recent reform of divorce law in the Federal District; it is not being considered in any other federal entity. It could be invoked by either of the spouses, with the difference from earlier provisions that it could only be used by the innocent party.

15. At the present time, either parent could obtain custody of the children. Custody is to be decided after hearing both partners; the judge will decide which would be better in each case, although the express disposition exists that, except in cases of grave risk, those under seven years will stay with the mother.

16. Previously there were specific dispositions to condemn the guilty party to the loss of rights within the family (*patria potestad*) automatically. However, the criterion is now prevalent that conflicts between parents should have the least possible effect on their children. Thus, these rights are lost only if the conduct leading to divorce also includes one of the causes for loss of family rights.

17. The reform originated in the Federal District and gradually was incorporated in other federal entities.

18. For more information on these regimes, see Martinez Arrieta, *El régimen patrimonial del matrimonio en México.*

19. Page 50.

20. Page 108.

21. Page 129.

22. Although appointments suggested by the president have to be approved by the

Senate, on this occasion a list was drawn up of eighteen candidates for eleven positions, and the list included only three women.

23. The three most important academic centers of the country—UNAM (Programa Universitario de Estudios de Género), UAM (Programa de la Mujer), and Colegio de México (Programa Interdisciplinario de Estudios de la Mujer)—provide instances of academic groups dedicated to the analysis of women. We also have national organizations such as the Mexican Organization of University Women.

24. And even in the working groups brought together by the government, such as the National Coordinating Commission for the IV World Conference on Women, whose convoking, for the first time in history, was not based on women in government, but brought together academic women and those who carried out work in community groups.

Bibliography

Martínez Arrieta, Sergio (1984), *El régimen patrimonial del matrimonio en México* (Mexico City: Porrúa).

PRONASOL (1990), *El combate a la pobreza* (Mexico City: PRONASOL).

32

ANA LANGER AND RAFAEL LOZANO

The Health of Women in Mexico: Current Panorama and Future Prospects

Health care in Mexico improved during the 1980s, despite the economic crisis. Life expectancy increased by four years. Intensive vaccination and measures against cholera and diarrhea reduced infant mortality, while the general fertility rate fell. Health problems shifted from those of the young to those of the old. Yet there are vast differences in health within Mexico, the poorest, rural states suffering severe problems. Mexico's inadequate spending on health especially damages women, "the poorest of the poor," who increasingly are heads of households and earn less than minimum wages.

Ana Langer and Rafael Lozang indicate that women, however, are not discriminated against in health care. Girls are fed as well as boys and use health services more often. Recent attention has focused on women's health related to reproduction. Maternal mortality rates declined but were triple the national average in the south and one-fifth of it in the north. Complying with its international commitments, Mexico established maternal mortality committees and a program for maternal and child health, in order to improve the coverage and quality of family planning and health services.

Six times as many men as women in Mexico have AIDS. AIDS was first found in a Mexican woman in 1985. Because it was transmitted by contaminated blood, in 1986 and 1987 the government prohibited the buying and selling of blood and required AIDS testing in blood banks. This contributed to the result that in 1994, 68 percent of AIDS infections were sexually transmitted, yet there is little AIDS among commercial sex workers as a result of efforts that have led them to negotiate the use of condoms with their clients.

Cervical cancer, which is a "secondary" illness associated with sexually transmitted disease, is the leading cause of death among women aged thirty to forty-four. It is increasing among those over fifty and is most prevalent among women from low socioeconomic backgrounds. The high death rate results from the low coverage and poor quality of detection programs; the lack of a system for notifying women of the results of tests and referring them to a specialized health care facility; and the lack of trained personnel and hospitals. Increased political will and government action could help to improve women's health in Mexico.

Introduction

In response to the grave crisis that occurred in the eighties, Mexico began a process of structural reform aimed at stabilizing the economy, improving the distribution of income, and reducing public expenditures. At present, the area of health reflects the effects of the crisis and of efforts made subsequently to overcome it. The result is a situation characterized by general improvement in health conditions, a change in patterns of sickness and death, and a marked imbalance among regions, states, and social groups in the distribution of morbidity and the resources available for health care.

Traditional indicators demonstrate the improvement. Life expectancy has been lengthened by more than four years as of 1980, reaching seventy-three for women and sixty-nine for men at present (Consejo Nacional de Población 1992). Since the beginning of this century infant mortality has had a downward curve, with a less pronounced drop between 1968 and 1982, as of which time it regained the pace of its downward trend. Were this tendency to continue, a rate of 25 per 1,000 live births is estimated for the year 1998 (Dirección General de Estadística . . . 1983–93).[1] The general fertility rate dropped from 7 children per woman in 1970 to 3.4 in 1990. Changes taking place in the birth and death rates have led to significant shifts in the population pyramid.

Within this context, a process is taking place that has been referred to as epidemiologic transition (Frenk et al. 1991). As a consequence of new lifestyles, urbanization, and changes in the demographic structure deriving from the decline of both fertility and mortality (in other words, the relative "aging" of the population), an epidemiologic pattern has been observed involving a decline of infections and nutritional deficiencies as the cause of sickness and death, and a rise in chronic ailments—cancer, cardiovascular disorders, diabetes—and lesions. This process is typical of the transition from a health profile characteristic of an underdeveloped country to that of an industrialized one. Nevertheless, in the case of Mexico national averages conceal profound differences among regions and social groups in the country ("epidemiologic polarization"). Suffice it to say that infant mortality in the five poorest states is twice that of the five richest ones; the weight of infectious diseases, malnutrition, and reproductive problems is 2.2 times as great per inhabitant in rural areas as it is in urban zones (Frenk et al. 1994), and maternal mortality is eight times as great among illiterate women as among those who finished high school (Langer et al. 1993).

Such imbalances are also evident in the distribution of resources for health care within an overall framework of an increase in expenditures in this area in recent years. As a result of structural change, public spending on health currently surpasses the levels reached prior to the economic crisis of the eighties measured in terms of the proportion of the gross domestic product (GDP): In 1992, federal government expenditures reached 2.76 percent, and private expenditures, a similar figure (thus, the total expenditure on health was around 5.3 percent) (Frenk et al. 1994). Gauged as a proportion of the government's budget, in 1990 spending on health reached its highest level in the past twenty years (12 percent) (Valdés Olmedo 1991). These proportions represent an expenditure per person per year ranging from 185 to 220 U.S. dollars (Frenk et al. 1994). Despite such increases, we are still far from complying with international recommendations and are at a disadvantage when this level of expenditure is compared with that of other countries in the region classified, like Mexico, as middle-income. To this must be added inequity in the distribution of these resources: the poorer a state is, the lower the public expenditure on health, and the poorer a particular family is, the greater the proportion of its income spent on health care (Frenk et al. 1994).

In the eighties, it became apparent that the recession was having a particularly serious effect on women. At that time, an expression was coined, i.e., "women, the poorest of the poor" (De los Ríos 1993). Besides conditions involving economic poverty, women also had to deal with those resulting from an inferior position in society.

The status of women is the product of a confluence of general living conditions, of the different values ascribed to females and males, and of discriminatory treatment by gender. Formal education is an appropriate sphere in which to study discrimination against women, as can be seen in data from Asia and Africa (UNFPA 1992). In Mexico, however, when comparing the average level of schooling between men and women we find that the differences that existed a few decades ago have now disappeared among our youth (Instituto Nacional de Estadística, Geografía e Informática 1990).

Employment is another realm in women's lives in which discrimination can be plainly seen. In Mexico, women have come to play an increasing role in the labor market. Whereas they represented 13 percent of the economically active population in 1950 and 25 percent in 1981, they accounted for approximately 34 percent in the country's major cities in 1988 (García et al. 1989). Women's labor patterns reflect gender inequalities: they are concentrated in the service sector, their income is generally lower than that of their male counterparts, and they mostly hold temporary jobs or do not work on a steady basis. This is determined, to a great extent, by their reproductive functions and by their responsibilities in the home (Barquet 1994).

Among the living conditions causing problems for women we should mention a phenomenon that is increasingly frequent: women as the head of the household (Acosta Díaz 1993). In Mexico, 14.1 percent of all households are headed by women, of which 86 percent are located in cities (Secretaría de Salud 1987). Moreover, 63.9 percent of female household heads who work earn minimum wage or less (in the case of men, this figure is 46.3 percent), and 27.5 percent have not had formal schooling (as opposed to 16.4 percent for men) (Acosta Díaz 1993).

What can be said about girls and women in the area of health? Discrimination in this area is often expressed in terms of nutrition, as can be seen in studies conducted in different parts of the world (Jain and Bongaarts 1981; Waldron 1987). In Mexico, however, nutrition among male and female children is similar, and there is no evidence that would indicate discrimination against females (Secretaría de Salud 1988).

The use of health services can be considered another indicator of discrimination (Das Gupta 1987). In Mexico, we looked for associations between consultations by sex and morbidity by analyzing the data on prevalence and the use of health services among the population aged 0–4 related to falls, diarrhea, and acute respiratory infections (Secretaría de Salud 1987). Contrary to what could be expected, the findings indicate a systematic unfavorable pattern for males: higher morbidity in boys, accompanied by a lower rate in the use of services (Lozano et al. 1993).

Lastly, we examined the situation of girls in terms of infant and preschool mortality. An excess mortality among female children should be viewed as a warning sign of discrimination (World Health Organization 1989). In our country, trends in infant mortality (under 1 year old) and preschool mortality (1–4 years of age) by gender between 1930 and 1990 fail to reveal disadvantages for females (Gómez de León and Partida 1992).

Insofar as reproductive health care is concerned, we will mention some indicators illustrating the differences between women from different social groups. Of the 2.8 million births recorded for 1993, 68 percent were attended by medical personnel, with enormous variations by state: professional coverage reached 96 percent in Mexico City and was less than 40 percent in the poorest states (Secretaría de Salud 1992). A similar pattern of geographic distribution can be observed in contraceptive use (Consejo Nacional de Población 1994). In conclusion, available data point to a difficult situation for women in Mexico, stemming not so much from gender discrimination as from the poverty and inequality still prevalent throughout the country.

In recent years, health care for women has become a priority objective in government discourse. At the same time, interest on an international scale (Starrs 1987; Ashford 1995) has helped create an awareness and encourage the channeling of funds toward research and action. Thus, an analysis of the status of women's health is particularly relevant at the present time. The field is vast; a thorough inquiry into it is beyond the scope of this article. We have therefore chosen to focus our analysis on three pertinent problems: maternal mortality, as an example of a reproductive health problem; AIDS, an epidemic that has had an increasing effect on women; and cervical cancer, which is one of the most frequent problems for perimenopausal women.

Maternal Mortality

In our country, maternal mortality (MM) has declined significantly in recent years: from a rate of 53 per 10,000 live births (LB) in 1940, to 4.5 in 1993.[2] Nevertheless, this drop has not been uniform or constant: as of 1985, there was a relative standstill as compared to the trend in previous years. Taking into account the fact that vital statistics are underestimated by anywhere from 37 to 50 percent (Reyes Frausto 1944; Hernández et al. 1994), it is possible to estimate a national rate of approximately 9 maternal deaths per 10,000 LB, with a high degree of regional variation: in Oaxaca, the figure would be 26.8—that is, above the levels to be found in Central American countries—and in Nuevo León it is 1.8, which is a fourteenth of the rate for Oaxaca and lower than the rates for Cuba and Costa Rica, the countries with the best health indicators in Latin America.

Maternal mortality also shows significant differentials according to individual sociodemographic characteristics. Thus, the risk of dying from causes related to reproduction varies greatly according to schooling. Of the total number of maternal deaths that occurred between 1986 and 1991, 26 percent were women who had not attended school, 33 percent were women who had not completed elementary school, 24 percent had only completed elementary school, and 16 percent had completed junior high school or more (Langer et al. 1993).

If we use as a basis for analysis *zones with different levels of development* in the country, we find that taking into account maternal mortality, Mexico can be divided into three major regions: the north, where MM is low; the central region, where MM is average; and the south, where it is high. When comparing maternal mortality in these regions over the past fifteen years, we find that the ratio between the states with high and low MM was 2.4 from 1980 to 1984 (the worst years of the crisis during that decade), and that it dropped to 2.13 in the following five-year period (Reyes Frausto 1944). Similar patterns are found when we analyze MM according to community size and marginalization.

Social Response

The activities undertaken in Mexico to reduce maternal mortality are within the framework of international agreements, with two milestones: the International Safe Motherhood Conference, held in Nairobi, Kenya, in 1987 (Starrs 1987), and the World Summit for Children, convened in 1990 by the United Nations (Organización de las Naciones Unidas 1990). In the latter, a commitment was made to reduce MM by 50 percent by the year 2000 with regard to the rate for 1990 (Organización de las Naciones Unidas 1990). In general, there is an overall consensus regarding basic strategies: to influence the status of women in society, and to improve the coverage and quality of family planning services and health care during pregnancy and delivery.

In keeping with these commitments, Mexico has put into practice a series of measures. "Maternal mortality committees" have been set up in all the country's health institutions,[3] and a National Program for Maternal and Child Health has been drawn up. This program includes activities for increasing obstetric coverage, training primary health care personnel and traditional birth attendants, promoting health in the community, fostering cooperation among public, private, and nongovernmental organizations, and improving information systems and statistics. Different activities have been implemented with varying degrees of intensity, and studies have not been conducted to evaluate their impact.

Parallel to these government efforts, a National Safe Motherhood Conference was held in our country in 1993. Legislators, public and private institutions, researchers, women's groups, journalists, and representatives of the states, international organizations, and donors attended. At the close of the conference, the Mexican Declaration for Safe Motherhood (Comité Organizador . . . 1993) was announced, and a commission was set up, which continues to meet on a regular basis for the purpose of promoting compliance with the commitments made.

This group has played an important role; among its activities are conducting regional conferences and, subsequently, creating local committees; publishing a dossier on the subject for journalists; including a question about whether the woman was pregnant in death certificates for women of reproductive age; incorporating the detection of complications during pregnancy as another component of the campaigns called National Health Weeks, and carrying out research projects.

Conclusions and Recommendations

Maternal mortality has practically disappeared as a public health problem in developed countries or in social groups with access to suitable living conditions and health services. In view of the existence of technical and scientific tools by which it is possible to avoid over 90 percent of maternal deaths, the persistence of this problem is inexcusable.

The data commented on in this chapter illustrate that MM is still a priority public health problem in Mexico, due both to its overall levels and to the striking differences found among social groups. Moreover, if we were to exemplify social inequality with regard to death by using a single indicator, maternal mortality is one of the most revealing ones.

Nevertheless, there are some elements that enable us to have a certain degree of optimism: the attention that is being given to MM; the improvements in information systems and statistics; the existence of data and methodologies allowing for an increasingly objective assessment of the situation and the formulation of concrete proposals that can be evaluated; and growing cooperation among international, national, governmental, and nongovernmental organizations. However, since official statistics are not very reliable, it is not possible to ascertain precisely the degree to which we are coming close to the goals set for the year 2000.

The challenges to be met are huge: in the first place, to achieve changes in the social position of women and in their living conditions is a long-term objective that can be attained only within the framework of Mexico's social development. In recent years, substantial progress has not been made in this sense. In the second place, it is essential to widen the coverage of family planning and maternal services; such efforts should be directed, above all, toward those regions in greatest need and to underprivileged social groups. Analyses of the current situation indicate that in order to reduce levels of MM by as much as 50 percent in the next five years it would be necessary to maintain present coverage and the intensity of programs in the more favored states in the north and central regions of the country, increase medical care during delivery by 50 percent, and increase the proportion of users of family planning methods by 10 percent in the rest of the country. Efforts must be consistent, sustained, multisectorial, and well grounded if they are to have an impact.

Acquired Immune Deficiency Syndrome (AIDS)

It is now beyond question that AIDS is a serious health problem for women, particularly in developing countries. According to the World Health Organization (WHO), in the world there are approximately four million cases of AIDS and over sixteen million adults infected with the HIV (human immunodeficiency virus), of which 40 percent are women (Gómez 1993).[4]

In Mexico, the first case of AIDS in women was recorded in 1985. That year, the male:female ratio for this disease was 14:1. In 1987, the rise in cases among women, the majority of which were the result of transmission by contaminated blood, caused a drop in the ratio, which reached 12:1. In the following four years, this tendency continued, leading to a ratio of 5:1; subsequently the ratio was reversed slightly and leveled off at 6:1.

The breakdown of the means of transmission has changed considerably throughout the history of the epidemic. In 1986, all cases of AIDS among women were attributable to blood transfusions, whereas currently this figure has gone down to 32 percent (*Boletín Mensual* 1995). In contrast, infections acquired by sexual transmission went from 0 to 68 percent of the accumulated prevalence up to 1994 (Del Río 1995). In effect, sexual intercourse with a heterosexual partner now represents the major risk factor for women.

The AIDS epidemic among women in Mexico poses two significant differences vis-à-vis what is occurring in other countries. In the first place, the prevalence of infection among commercial sex workers (CSW) is very low, as can be seen in seroepidemiologic studies and sentinel surveys conducted among these groups. This situation can be explained by the still low prevalence of the infection among the heterosexual population; the practically nonexistent addiction to drugs administered intravenously among CSWs; and the effect of the intensive work that has been done for several years now with CSWs to empower them to negotiate the use of condoms with their clients.

The second differential characteristic of the epidemic in Mexico is the noticeable decline in the rate of transmission by blood, which has yet to be observed in other underdeveloped countries. In fact, said decline is "concealing" the rise in the number of cases due to sexual transmission, since when both epidemics are combined, one on the rise and the other declining, one gets the impression that they are stabilizing.

Social Response

Recognition of AIDS as a priority problem for women has been long in coming throughout the world, and Mexico has been no exception. As the epidemic has increased among women, the tremendous personal, familial, economic, and social impact these cases have and will continue to have in the future has begun to be acknowledged.

Among the first measures introduced in the fight against AIDS was one we have already mentioned, i.e., the control of infection via blood transmission. The prohibition of the buying and selling of blood and the compulsory nature of AIDS testing in blood banks were decreed in 1986 and 1987; the results are now apparent.

Since 1989, the Mexican National Council for the Fight Against AIDS (Consejo Nacional de Lucha contra el SIDA, or CONASIDA) has placed particular emphasis on women in its mass media campaigns, with increasingly explicit messages, despite the more or less active opposition of the church and certain organized citizens' groups. These efforts notwithstanding, the potential impact of the campaign will probably be limited due to the inevitable nonspecific nature of any campaign aimed at the general public, and because of the very nature of the message, which questions religious and moral principles upheld by wide sectors of Mexican society. It is important to admit, though, that the impact is still hard to evaluate due to the period of latency that elapses between the campaign implementation and the potential effects.

Another important action has been the inclusion of cervical cancer as an "associated disease" in the definition of a "case of AIDS" in the Mexican Official Norms (*Norma Oficial Mexicana* 1995). That can make a significant contribution toward improving record keeping of cases and toward making available to the women who need them drugs and medicines that are only authorized for AIDS cases and not for apparently asymptomatic infected individuals.

Insofar as activities directed toward specific groups are concerned, especially worth mentioning are those conducted by CONASIDA with prostitutes. From

1989 to 1993, a research project was carried out for the purpose of ascertaining factors related to the risk of infection: sexual behavior, sociocultural aspects, risk practices, ability to negotiate, etc. On the basis of the findings, educational actions were designed, supplemented by pamphlets and posters made with the help of CSWs (Uribe 1995). This effort, which is still underway, may have contributed to the low prevalence of HIV among this high-risk population in Mexico.

For the women who come to CONASIDA's Information Centers, special groups were set up whose composition and dynamics differ from those of groups created for men; participating in the women's groups are mothers, abandoned women, rape victims, and others who suspect that their husband is being unfaithful and who cannot protect themselves (Uribe 1995).

Conclusions and Recommendations

The Mexican anti-AIDS program is without a doubt among the best in Latin America. Nevertheless, the characteristics of the epidemic and the difficulties involving prevention that are faced by women throughout the world make it imperative to step up efforts. The tasks that should be undertaken can be summed up as follows:

Improving care for women. Activities involving HIV/AIDS detection, diagnosis, and care should be included in services related to family planning, sexually transmitted diseases, and prenatal and maternal-child care. These efforts are in keeping with the international recommendation for establishing comprehensive reproductive health care services in which, regardless of the reason for the consultation, women receive adequate counseling, information, and attention for all their needs.

It is equally important to strengthen programs for detecting cervical cancer, a disease associated with HIV infection. Similarly, it is necessary to promote the organization of support groups for HIV-positive women and to ensure that all infected pregnant women have access to AZT (azidothymidine) treatments.

Last, in centers where medical care is provided, there should be an interdisciplinary team that, aside from medical problems, also sees to the grave psychological, economic, and legal problems faced by infected women.

Perfecting epidemiologic monitoring systems. This action is essential for conducting proper follow-up on the evolution of the epidemic, for making basal diagnoses allowing for the design of interventions, and, later, for assessing their impact. Special efforts should be made to improve systems for detection, notification, and record keeping in rural areas. Similarly, it is important to ensure that the definitions and criteria used in Mexico are kept up to date with regard to those followed internationally.

Promoting health education. Educational programs aimed at adolescents and young women should be reinforced and extended in schools, community centers, workplaces, and through the mass media, etc. These informational and educational activities should be complemented by indications of places where it is possible to receive counseling, and with easy and economical access to condoms. All women should know the channels by which the disease is transmitted. They should be aware of the risk of contracting the disease when engaging in heterosexual intercourse and should be able to implement preventive measures.

Enhancing the social condition of women. Changes in this area are the most difficult to achieve, since this implies overcoming values and behavior patterns firmly rooted in society, as well as instituting a social development policy placing special emphasis on women. A position of equality for women in society and within couples, as well as greater power for negotiation and decision making, are indispensable if we are to effectively control the AIDS epidemic in Mexico.

Along with general social measures, it is necessary to strengthen programs for defending women's human rights; to help them solve the economic and social problems they face when they are infected and, above all, when they are the sole support of the family unit; and to set up programs aimed at the most vulnerable women: refugees, CSWs, women suffering from extreme poverty, Indian women, etc. Last, it is essential to foster the support of families and communities for women with HIV/AIDS, their children, parents and older relatives, and other dependents.

The epidemic, the circumstances causing it, and the context are so complex, there are still so many gaps in our knowledge of it, and such diversified actions are needed that only with coordinated and sustained efforts on the part of the government, national and international foundations, research institutions, non-governmental organizations, and feminist groups, to mention only a few, will it be possible to achieve favorable results.

Cervical Cancer

As a result of the epidemiologic transition occurring in Mexico, the weight of chronic diseases has been increasing steadily. Neoplasias are the primary cause of death for women, and, among these, cervical cancer ranks first (*Mortalidad . . .*). In fact, this cancer is the leading cause of death among women aged 30–44. In 1991, mortality due to cervical cancer was slightly higher than the rate recorded for 1985: 49.3 vs. 47.2 per 100,000 inhabitants. Among women aged 50 or older, mortality due to this type of cancer presented a significant upward tendency (Lazcano and Lozano 1994). In terms of morbidity, 5 percent of the cases are in an advanced, invasive stage when detected (*Morbilidad . . .* 1993), a high rate for a neoplasia that can be diagnosed in its very early stages.

Cervical cancer is more frequent among women from low socioeconomic backgrounds. The unequal distribution of and access to services and programs offering testing for early detection (Pap smears) and treatment partially account for this. Also contributing to a high prevalence in certain groups are risk factors for this neoplasia such as sexual behavior patterns characterized by early commencement of sexual activity and many partners, as well as genital infection with the human papilloma virus (HPV) and genital herpes (Lazcano et al. 1993; Lazcano et al. 1994).

It is important to emphasize certain distinctive traits of this neoplasia. In the first place, its evolution is very slow, lasting for years, from the initial lesions to dissemination. On the other hand, technologies are available allowing for early detection as well as treatment, which, when applied to initial lesions, is highly effective. Last, cervical cancer is strongly associated with the above-mentioned genital viral infections (human papilloma virus and genital herpes) (Lazcano et al. 1993; Lazcano et al. 1994) that can be prevented or at least detected and treated opportunely. That is why the fact that cervical cancer continues to be the first cause of death among women in Mexico, and that a downward trend has yet to be observed, is unacceptable.

Social Response

As of 1974, gynecological cancers were acknowledged in Mexico as a priority health problem, and a national program was established to combat them. The general guidelines and strategies of this program were updated and modified between 1988 and 1994 (*Norma Oficial Mexicana* 1995). Among the major activities comprising the current program are mass media campaigns; revision and updating of the official norms, in which stress is placed on the importance of early detection; and an increased coverage and a general improvement of the National Cancer Registry. Despite these advances, the country's epidemiologic situation has not exhibited positive changes. Several factors help explain this lack of impact:

Low Coverage of Detection Programs

During the seventies, a program for the early detection of cervical cancer was launched in Mexico (López Carrillo et al. 1994). From the beginning, the Papanicolaou test was the basic tool of this program. Currently, some 17.5 million women are potential targets. Unfortunately, the program covers only 20 percent of women with a right to social security health services and 15 percent of the population without a right to said services (Escandón et al. 1992).

This deficiency in coverage is due not only to an inadequate supply of services, but also to a demand pattern that varies significantly according to the social group. In effect, the benefits of such testing are concentrated among the women who put a priority on their health and make use of preventive services, who are aware of the seriousness of the problem and acknowledge the fact that early detection of cancer is essential, who are familiarized with their own bodies and agree to undergo gynecological examinations, and who have access to a health facility with the capability of conducting this type of testing.

Poor Quality of Detection Programs

Whereas theoretically, the Papanicolaou test detects 80 percent of all cases, due to the actual conditions of the program in Mexico it is possible to diagnose only 20 percent of the affected women who take the test (Escandón et al. 1992). This is due to poor quality in sampling, observation, and interpretation of results, as well as the time that elapses between sample taking and interpretation (Lazcano et al. 1994).

Lack of Tracking and Referral Systems

A considerable proportion of women who take the Papanicolaou test do not return to find out the results, and there is no way of notifying them. Added to this is the lack of a referral system between primary health care centers and specialized institutions, with the exception of women belonging to the social security health care system.

Insufficient Capacity for Treatment

Last, Mexico suffers from a lack of infrastructure and technical capacity for providing these services to all the women who require them. Hospital infrastructure and the number of trained personnel are not sufficient and would be even less so were the demand to grow as a result of efficient detection campaigns.

Conclusions and Recommendations

Despite the fact that cervical cancer has been acknowledged as a priority problem, the measures implemented have not been sufficient to achieve true impact. In order to attain substantive results, it will be necessary to:

• Allocate resources for equipping laboratories, training staff for mass detection programs, and increasing the capacity of treatment services.

• Institute comprehensive programs and assess their feasibility and cost effectiveness.

• Improve the system for notification and registration statistics so as to understand the magnitude of the problem and be in a position to assess the impact of programs and activities.

• Conduct research in order to ascertain the reasons women fail to demand services; design mass campaigns for reversing this trend; and evaluate their impact.

• Contribute to the enhancement of the status of women in society in such a way that women assign a higher priority to their health, are familiar with the risks they face, and are able to negotiate in the areas of sexuality and the search for proper attention to their needs.

Final Considerations

An analysis of the effects that periods of crisis or economic and social adjustments have on health meets with at least three types of difficulties:

1. The type, quality, and timeliness of the information available, which includes, on the one hand, data from cross-sectional surveys, which is very useful but discontinuous and therefore does not allow for longitudinal analysis; on the other, the continuous data from vital statistics, which is seriously under-registered and limited to the extreme of the range of health problems, i.e., death.

2. The lack of specific projects, methodologies, and experience needed to evaluate the impact of macrosocial conditions on health. In effect, the great body of literature dealing with the crisis and/or structural changes and their impact on health has been devoted to examining budgetary allocations and restrictions. Much more research is needed regarding the substantive effects economic conditions have on health (Langer et al. 1991).

3. The very dynamics of the processes being studied—their complexity, multicausality, and chronology (especially the time elapsing between changes in the milieu and their effect on health)—make it impossible to draw definitive conclusions. In general, it is only possible to pose hypotheses to be verified through specific studies.

To conclude, we should point out that in order to improve women's health, there are no "magic bullets," unlike what occurs, for example, in the case of child health. Fortunately, we can achieve substantial improvements in health during childhood through the implementation of vaccination programs or campaigns against infections, as can be seen in the dramatic decline in infant mortality witnessed in recent years in Mexico. But unfortunately, actions geared toward women have no counterparts in this sense. The complexity of women's health problems and of the underlying causes requires long-term multisectorial activities for which a necessary but insufficient condition are a political will and government action.

Notes

1. The decline in infant mortality was especially significant between 1991 and 1992: 23 percent after correction for under-registration. It is assumed that the drop was a result of intense vaccination campaigns, as well as measures taken to fight cholera and diarrhea.

2. Maternal deaths are those occurring during pregnancy, labor, or puerperium as a consequence of a health problem associated with reproduction or aggravated by it. Maternal mortality (MM) is measured by the following formula: maternal deaths/women of childbearing age, when the denominator is available, x 100,000. When the denominator is not available, maternal mortality is measured as follows: maternal deaths/live births x 10,000.

3. These committees are comprised of physicians and nurses working at each health institution. Their task is to review the cases of women who die, in order to pinpoint errors and responsibilities, and to gain detailed knowledge regarding the process that led to their death.

4. The greater vulnerability of women to the infection is due to various factors:
(a) *Biological factors*. The amount of the virus found in semen is greater than that in vaginal fluids; the vaginal and rectal mucous membranes are more vulnerable to infection than the epithelium of the penis; and in these areas the virus remains viable for longer and the contact surface is larger.

(b) *Epidemiologic factors*. Due to complications arising during pregnancy and delivery, women need blood transfusions more frequently than men; thus, they are more susceptible to becoming infected by this means.

(c) *Social factors*. It is common for women to get involved sexually with older men who are more experienced and therefore more likely to be infected. In addition, there are significant differences between the genders in their patterns of sexual behavior, in their power for decision making related to sexual practices, and in their status within the family and the community, all of which determine greater vulnerability on the part of women (Del Rio et al. 1995). In practice, women still do not have barrier methods that would afford them protection from infection without requiring the consent of their partner. In fact, women depend solely on the willingness of men to use condoms.

Bibliography

Acosta Díaz, F. (1993), "Mujeres jefes de hogar y bienestar familiar en México." ICRW and the Population Council (mimeographed).

Ashford, L.S. (1995), "New Perspectives on Population: Lessons from Cairo," *Population Bulletin* 50, no. 1 (March) (Washington, D.C.: Population Reference Bureau).

Barquet, M. (1994), "Condicionantes de género sobre la pobreza de las mujeres" in *GIMTRAP. Las mujeres en la pobreza* (Mexico City: El Colegio de México), 73–89.

Boletín Mensual de SIDA/ETS (1995), Año 9 (1).

Comité Organizador e la Conferencia para una Maternidad Sin Riesgos (1993), *Declaración de México para una Maternidad Sin Riesgos* (Cocoyoc, Morelos, México).

Consejo Nacional de Población (1992), *Esperanza de vida al nacimiento, 1980–2000* (Mexico City: CONAPO).

————. (1994), *Situación de la planificación familiar en México. Indicadores de anticoncepción* (Mexico City: CONAPO), 15.

Del Río, A.L. Liguori, and C. Magis (1995), "Epidemiología del SIDA y las mujeres," *Letra S* (suplemento del periódico *El Nacional*) no. 5: 3.

Das Gupta, M. (1987), "Selective Discrimination against Female Children in Rural Punjab, India," *Population and Development Review* 13: 77–100.

De los Ríos, R. (1993), "Género, salud y desarrollo: un enfoque en construcción" in Gómez, E., ed., *Género, Mujer y Salud en las Américas* Scientific Publication no. 541, (Washington, D.C.: Pan American Health Organization) 3–18.

Dirección General de Estadística, Informática y Evaluación, SSA (1983–93).

Escandón, C., M.G. Benítez, J. Navarrete, et al.. (1992), "Epidemiología del cáncer cérvico-uterino en el Instituto Mexicano del Seguro Social," *Salud Pública de México* 34: 607–14.

Frenk, J., J.L. Bobadilla, C. Stern, T. Frejka, and R. Lozano (1991), "Elements for a Theory of the Health Transition," *Health Transition Review* 1, no. 1: 21–38.

Frenk, J., R. Lozano, and M.A. González-Block (1994), *Economia y Salud. Propuestas para el avance del sistema de salud en México. Informe Final.* (Mexico City: Fundación Mexicana para la Salud).

García, B., O. de Oliveira; and B. Christenson (1989), "Los múltiples condicionantes del trabajo femenino en México," *Estudios Sociológicos* 20.

Gómez, E., ed. (1993), *Gender, Women and Health in the Americas* Scientific Publication No. 541 (Washington, D.C.: Pan American Health Organization).

Gómez de León, J., and V. Partida (1992), "Niveles y tendencias de la mortalidad en los primeros años de vida, 1930–1990." Documento de Trabajo del Centro de Estudios de Población y Salud, DT 1–1992.

Hernández B., J. Chirinas, M. Romero, and A. Langer (1994), "Estimating Maternal Mortality in Rural Areas of Mexico: The Application of an Indirect Demographic Method," *International Journal of Gynecology and Obstetrics* 46, no. 3: 285–89.

Instituto Nacional de Estadística, Geografía e Informática (INEGI) (1990), *XI Censo Nacional de Población y Vivienda* (Mexico City).

Jain, A., and J. Bongaarts (1981), "Breastfeeding: Patterns, Correlates and Fertility Effects," *Studies in Family Planning* 12: 79–99.

Langer, A., R. Lozano, and J.L. Bobadilla (1991), "Effects of Mexico's Crisis on the Health of Women and Children" in M. González de la Rocha and A. Escobar Latapí, eds., *Social Responses to Mexico's Economic Crisis of the 1980s* (San Diego: University of California), 195–219.

Langer, A., R. Lozano, and B. Hernández (1993), "Mortalidad materna. Niveles, tendencias y diferenciales," *Demos* 6: 10–11.

Lazcano, E., and R. Lozano (1994), "Tendencia de la mortalidad por cáncer cérvicouterino en México." Instituto Nacional de Salud Pública, mimeographed.

Lazcano Ponce, E., P. Alonso de Ruiz, L. López Carrillo, M.E. Vázquez Manríquez, and M. Hernández Avila (1994), "Quality Control Study on Negative Gynecological Cytology in Mexico," *Diagn Cytopathol* 10: 10–14.

Lazcano Ponce, E., L. López Carrillo, P. Alonso de Ruiz, I. Romieu, and M. Hernández Avila (1994), *Etiología y factores predisponentes del cáncer cérvicouterino en la Cd. de México. Un estudio de casos y controles* (Instituto Nacional de Salud Pública, Informe Técnico-Académico).

Lazcano Ponce, E.; R. Rojas Martínez, M. López Acuña, L. López Carrillo, and M. Hernández Avila (1993), "Factores de riesgo reproductivo y cáncer cérvicouterino en México," *Salud Pública de México* 35: 65–73.

López Carrillo, L., S. Vandale, C. Fernández-Ortega, and S. Parra-Cabrera (1994), "Cáncer cérvico-uterino y mamario en la mujer mexicana" in A. Langer and K. Tolbert, *La salud reproductiva de la mujer en México: Una agenda para la investigación y la acción* (Mexico City: Population Council).

Lozano, R., C. Infante, L. Schlaepfer, and J. Frenk (1993), *Desigualdad, pobreza y salud en México* (Mexico City: Consejo Consultivo del Programa de Solidaridad).

Morbilidad por neoplasias malignas en el Distrito Federal, 1982–1989 (1993), (Mexico City: Secretaría de Salud).

Mortalidad por Tumores, 1922–1990. Perfiles Estadísticas. (Mexico City: Secretaría de Salud).

Norma Oficial Mexicana NOM–010–SSA2–1993, para la prevención y control de la infección por Virus de la Inmunodeficiencia Humana (1995). Diario Oficial. Tomo CDXCVI (12, 17).

Norma Oficial Mexicana NOM–014–SSA2–1994, para la prevención, tratamiento y control del cáncer del cuello del útero y del la mama en la atención primaria (1995). Diario Oficial, January 16. II Sección, Secretaría de Salud.

Organización de las Naciones Unidas (1990), *Declaración mundial sobre la supervivencia, la protección y el desarrollo del niño* (New York: United Nations).

Reyes Frausto, S. (1944), *Mortalidad Materna en México* (Mexico City: Instituto Mexicano del Seguro Social).

Secretaría de Salud (1987), *Encuesta Nacional de Fecundidad y Salud* (Mexico City: Secretaría de Salud).

———. (1988), *Encuesta Nacional de Nutrición* (Mexico City: Secretaría de Salud).

————. (1992), *Estadísticas Vitales 1992* (Mexico City: Secretaría de Salud).

Starrs, A. (1987), *Preventing the Tragedy of Maternal Deaths: A Report on the International Safe Motherhood Conference, Nairobi, February 1987* (Washington, D.C.: World Bank).

UNFPA (1992), *The State of the World Population 1992* (New York: United Nations Population Fund).

Uribe, P. (1995), "En la prevención, aprovechar las armas de la mujer," *Letra S* (Suplemento del periódico *El Nacional*), no. 5: 8.

Valdés Olmedo, C. (1991), *Bonanza, crisis,..¿Recuperación?* (Mexico City: Fundación Mexicana para la Salud).

Waldron, I. (1987), "Patterns and Causes of Excess Female Mortality Among Young Children in Developing Countries," *World Health Statistics Quarterly* 40: 194–210.

World Health Organization (1989), *The Health of Youth. Facts for Action.* Technical Discussions A42 (Geneva: World Health Organization).

Part V

Regional Structures

33

WILLIAM SIEMBIEDA AND RAMON RODRÍGUEZ M.

One Country, Many Faces: The Regions of Mexico

William Siembieda and Ramon Rodríguez M. outline the characteristics of Mexico's regions. Population density varies from 14/km² in the north to 275/km² in the east central region, which includes the Federal District. The south has agricultural activity, many speakers of indigenous languages, and great poverty. The richer northeast leads in industrial employment, while Mexico City and the surrounding area dominate secondary and tertiary activities. The ratio of economically active to dependents has increased, especially in the north.

Almost one-fifth of the population changed where they lived between 1985 and 1990, as Mexicans moved to areas with employment opportunities. The authors describe the leading cities in each region. Migration to the east central region slowed, because of policies established during President Miguel de la Madrid's administration. Constitutional reforms in 1983 gave cities greater control over their fiscal and infrastructure development. President Salinas increased spending in the poorest areas. Decentralization, in part reflecting a shortage of federal resources, is continuing under President Zedillo. Siembieda and Rodríguez argue that neoliberal policies do not provide a mechanism for regional equity, and that the state, not the market, must take an active role in achieving it.

Introduction

Mexico is a mosaic of diverse landscapes, cultural groups, and economic areas. It is also a big country of ninety million people living on some 1,970,000 square kilometers, of which nearly 10,000 kilometers is coastline along the Pacific, the Gulf of California, the Gulf of Mexico, and the Caribbean.[1] Sometimes it seems as though there are many countries within the whole. Yet, within this diverse land there exists a strong nationalism and a desire on the part of each regional group to maintain its rich culture and heritage. There is also a pronounced inequality of wealth distribution among the regions, in large part due to the concentration of capital and political power of the Mexico City region, plus a modernizing northern and a lagging southern region. All of this is occurring during the emergence of a multiparty political system in a country that is more urban than rural.

The purpose of this chapter is to discuss the various regions of Mexico and examine some of the policies of the last two administrations related to regional development. In the sections below, the regions are defined and some socioeconomic differences are presented. This is followed by a brief synopsis of the major cities and their roles within each region. Finally, there is a brief examination of some major legislation and policy actions that have influenced regional development in Mexico.

Regional Divisions

Geographer Angel Bassols Batalla (1979) defined eight large regions that account for Mexico's political-administrative divisions, the diverse levels of production and distribution, consumption and wealth, and its demographic patterns.[2] The regions (as shown in Figure 33.1) are used herein. They represent, as well as any other grouping, the diversity that exists in the country. The regions and their major cities are:

1. *Northwest.* Composed of the states of Baja California, Baja California Sur, Nayarit, Sinaloa, and Sonora; the major cities in this region include Tijuana, Mexicali, Hermosillo, Culiacán, Mazatlán, Ciudad Obregón, and Tepic.

2. *North.* Composed of the states of Coahuila, Chihuahua, Durango, San Luis Potosi and Zacatecas; the major cities in this region include Ciudad Juárez, Torreón, Chihuahua, San Luis Potosi, Saltillo, and Durango.

3. *Northeast.* Composed of the states of Nuevo León and Tamaulipas; the major cities in this region include Monterrey, Tampico, Nuevo Laredo, Matamoros, Ciudad Victoria, and Reynosa.

4. *West central.* Composed of the states of Aguascalientes, Colima, Guanajuato, Jalisco, and Michoacán; the major cities within this region include Guadalajara, Morelia, Aguascalientes, León, Guanajuato, Irapuato, Salamanca, and Celaya.

5. *East central.* Composed of the states of Hidalgo, Mexico, Morelos, Puebla, Querétaro, Tlaxcala, and the Federal District (D.F.), the federal capital of government, which is without status as a separate state; other important cities in this region include Toluca, Cuernavaca, Pachuca, Tlaxcala, Puebla, and Querétaro.

6. *East.* Composed of the states of Tabasco and Veracruz; the major cities in this region include Veracruz, Orizaba-Córdoba, Jalapa, and Villahermosa. Also in this region is the industrial corridor of Coatzacoalcos-Minatitlán.

7. *South.* Composed of the states of Chiapas, Guerrero, and Oaxaca; the major cities in this region include Acapulco, Oaxaca, and Tuxtla Gutiérrez.

Figure 33.1 **States Grouped into Major Regions**

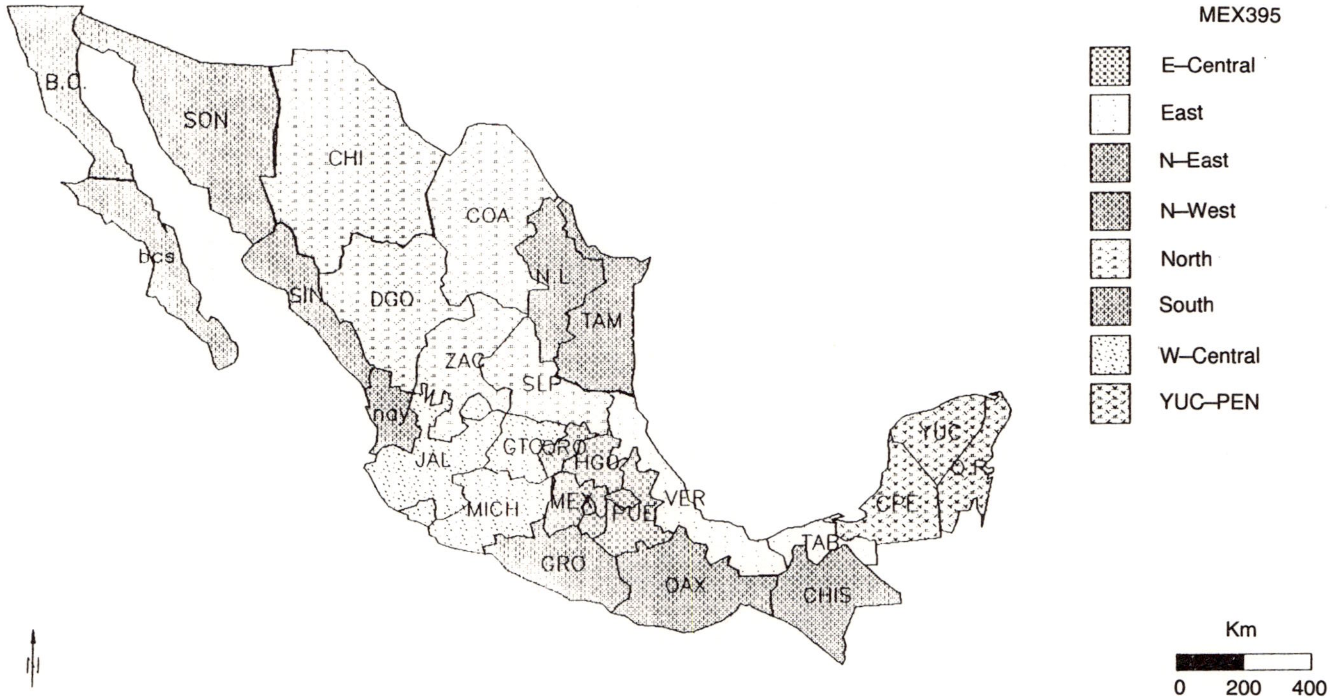

B.C.
SON
CHI
COA
bcs
N L
SIN
DGO
TAM
ZAC
SLP
nay
JAL
GTO
QRO
HGO
MICH
MEX
PUE
VER
GRO
OAX
TAB
CHIS
YUC
Q.R.
CPE
MEX395
E–Central
East
N–East
N–West
North
South
W–Central
YUC–PEN
Km
0
200
400

Table 33.1

Population, Area, and Density, 1990

Regions	Pop. (000's)	% Pop.	% Area	Den.[a]
Northwest	6,831	8.40	21.3	16.48
North	9,043	11.12	33.3	13.78
Northeast	5,348	6.58	7.3	37.04
West central	13,982	17.21	9.3	76.97
East central	27,074	33.32	5.0	274.89
East	7,730	9.51	4.9	79.3
South	8,851	10.89	11.8	37.98
Peninsula of Yucatán	2,391	2.97	7.1	16.89
Total	81,250	100.00	100.0	41.3

Source: General Census of Population and Housing, 1990. INEGI.
[a]Population/km^2.

8. *Peninsula of Yucatán.* Composed of the states of Campeche, Quintana Roo and Yucatán; the major cities in this region include Mérida, Cancún, Ciudad del Carmen, Campeche, and Chetumal.

Socioeconomic Characteristics

The average population density of the county is 41.3 persons per square kilometer (see Table 33.1). This average is deceptive, however, because the highest density, 274.89 persons per square kilometer, is found in the east central region, reflecting the influence of the Mexico City and the Federal District (D.F.). The lowest density, 13.78/km^2, occurs in the north region, where farming, cattle, and open spaces dominate. When the regions are grouped together, two facts are quite evident: the majority of the population lives on the smallest land area in the central part of the county (50 percent population on 14.3 percent of the land), and density is lower in the north.

The strong cultural diversity of the country is demonstrated by the fact that in Mexico more than five million people speak more than twenty-five different indigenous dialects (see Table 33.2). The south is the most diverse region, with more than two million indigenous speakers. Indigenous languages tend to be spoken less in the northern regions and are almost absent from the northeast region.

The labor force and jobs both grew between 1970 and 1990, with the labor force growing faster than employment (see Tables 33.3 and 33.4). Employment, as counted by the federal government, is reported by three large sectoral groups: primary (agriculture, fishing, and related activities), secondary (mining, manufacturing, energy, and construction), and tertiary (trades and services). These

Table 33.2

Native Language Spoken, 1990

Region	Native Speakers (000's)	%
Northwest	124.4	1.80
North	289.0	3.20
Northeast	13.4	0.25
West central	141.5	1.01
East central	1,308.4	4.83
East	628.4	8.13
South	2,032.6	22.96
Peninsula of Yucatán	745.0	31.16
Total	5,282.7	6.50

Source: General Census of Population and Housing, 1990. INEGI.

Table 33.3

Available Labor Force 12 Years + 1970–90 (000's)

Region	Pop. 1970	Labor Force 1970	%	Pop. 1990	Labor Force 1990	%
Northwest	2,386.0	1,034.7	43.4	4,771.9	2,173.1	45.5
North	3,557.8	1,482.6	41.7	6,223.7	2,610.9	41.9
Northeast	1,963.6	866.6	44.1	3,866.9	1,746.8	45.2
West central	5,127.7	2,164.5	42.2	9,381.8	3,924.7	41.8
East central	9,704.9	4,537.6	46.7	19,057.7	8,390.4	44.0
East	2,809.6	1,205.0	42.9	5,274.6	2,198.4	41.7
South	3,156.2	1,313.9	41.6	5,708.7	2,287.0	40.1
Yucatán	701.6	304.5	43.4	1,628.7	731.9	44.9
Total	29,407.4	12,909.4	43.9	55,914.0	24,063.2	43.0

Source: General Census of Population and Housing, 1970 and 1990. INEGI.

categories can be viewed in sectorial and regional terms. In 1990, the tertiary sector played the strongest role in employment. In some sense, Mexico can be said to be following the global trend toward an expanding service economy. Regional variation tells a different story. Secondary sector activities are strongest in the north and central parts of the country and lagging in the south. The northeast, containing the large industrial city of Monterrey, leads all regions with 36 percent employment in the secondary sector and has very little agricultural activity. The highest agricultural activities (as a percent of all employment) occur in the south and east regions. The east central region containing D.F. and surrounding states dominates the country in terms of secondary and tertiary

Table 33.4

Employment by Activity Sectors, 1990

Region	Employed Pop. (000's)	Primary %[a]	Secondary %[b]	Tertiary %[c]	Other %[d]
Northwest	2,124.9	25	23	48	4
North	2,530.4	23	31	42	4
Northeast	1,694.1	10	36	50	4
West central	3,821.7	22	31	44	3
East central	8,157.3	13	31	53	3
East	2,135.5	39	21	37	3
South	2,220.5	50	15	32	3
Yucatán	720.5	27	21	48	4
Total	23,404.9	23	28	46	3

Source: General Census of Population and Housing, 1990. INEGI.

[a]Primary sector: Agriculture, cattle raising, forestry, hunting, and fishing.

[b]Secondary sector: Mining, extraction of oil and gas, manufacturing and industry, electrical energy generation, and construction.

[c]Tertiary sector: Trade and services.

[d]Other: Unspecified or reported activities.

activities, reinforcing the historical forces that brought economic wealth and power to the country's center.

Income distribution in Mexico is uneven by both region and social class. Most of the population earns one to two minimum salaries (between $5 and $10 a day U.S.). Table 33.5 shows us the monthly revenue received by region. The south has the largest percentage of people who do not receive income at all, while at the same time the highest percentage of those who receive more than five minimum salaries are situated in the northwest, closely followed by northeast, north, west central, and east central regions in the country.

Mexico has a rapidly expanding population, growing from some 48 million in 1970 to over 81 million in 1990, and is projected to reach 100 million by the year 2000 (Lemus 1994, 27). The rate of annual population expansion between 1970 and 1990 was 2.6 percent, lower than the 1950–70 rate of 3.2 percent annually. However, the average household size of five persons does not vary much by region. This reflects the sociocultural tendency for larger families, although the urban area has about half the family size of rural areas. Mexico's long-term, United Nations-supported program of birth control has achieved lower birth rates and family size in the urban areas compared to the countryside by almost a two to one ratio. The results of this effort are shown in the population cohort distribution between 1970 and 1990. In 1970, 46 percent of the population was under 14 years of age. This fell to 38 percent in 1990. Also the 15–64-year-old cohort in 1970 was 50 percent of the total population, and in 1990 it increased to 57

Table 33.5

Monthly Revenue Received by Employed Population, 1990

Region	Population employed	Does not receive income %	Less than 1 min. salary %	1 to 2 min. salaries %	+2 and –3 min. salaries (%)	3–5 min. salaries (%)	+5 min. salaries (%)	(%)ᵃ
Northwest	2,124.5	3	10	37	21	14	10	5
North	2,530	8	17	38	15	10	8	4
Northeast	1,694.1	3	16	41	17	11	9	3
West central	3,821.1	7	15	35	17	11	8	7
East central	8,157.4	5	19	40	15	10	8	3
East	2,135.6	10	26	34	13	8	5	4
South	2,220.2	20	31	25	10	5	4	5
Yucatán	720.5	7	27	33	14	9	6	4
Total	23,403.5	7	19	37	15	10	8	4

Source: General Census of Population and Housing, 1990. INEGI.
ᵃUnspecified.

percent. The percentage of people 65 years and older was 4 percent of the population in both periods (see Table 33.6). In regional terms, the northeast and the northwest approached 60 percent of the total population between 15 and 64 in 1990. This translates into high demands for housing and urban services and forms the basis for much of the urban crisis experienced by states along the border (*la frontera*).

Migration within the country is on the rise. The 1990 census reported that more than 17.4 percent of the population has moved to their place of residence since 1985. Intraregional movement was highest in the northeast, northwest, peninsula of Yucatán, and the east central regions, respectively (see Table 33.7). The industrial expansion along the U.S.-Mexico border and the continued integration of border economies with the United States explains the "pull" effect of the northern region, jobs drawing workers. The Yucatán has been an important tourist area, with an expanding service-sector employment base, while the east central remains the country's economic heartland. The poorer regions have experienced the most population loss, the results of the "push-pull" factor operating within the country.

Regions and Their Economic Activities

The center of the country's financial, industrial, and political power is located in the east central region, containing more than twenty million people. This concentration is the basis of the economic and social inequalities that exist in other

Table 33.6

Population by Age Groups, 1970-90

Region	Tot. Pop. 1970 (000's)	0–14 years (%)	15–64 years (%)	65 and more years (%)	Tot. Pop. 1990 (000's)	0–14 years (%)	15–64 years (%)	65 and more years (%)	(%)
Northwest	3,908	47	49	4	6,831	37	58	4	1
North	5,900	48	48	4	9,043	38	57	4	1
Northeast	3,151	45	51	4	5,348	34	61	4	1
West central	8,470	47	48	5	13,981	40	54	5	1
East central	15,931	45	51	4	27,073	37	59	4	0
East	4,584	46	50	4	7,730	39	56	4	1
South	5,181	47	49	4	8,850	43	52	4	1
Yucatán	1,098	43	52	5	2,391	38	56	4	2
Total	48,223	46	50	4	81,247	38	57	4	1

Source: General Census of Population and Housing, 1990. INEGI.
a Unspecified

Table 33.7

Internal Migration, 1990 (according to birthplace)

Region	Residents	% Immigrants	% Migrants	% Balance Net
Northwest	6,687.6	22.9	11.7	11.2
North	8,916.0	11.9	22.7	−10.7
Northeast	5,263.0	23.3	10.1	13.2
West central	13,750.0	11.1	17.6	−6.5
East central	26,820.2	26.2	20.2	5.9
East	7,672.1	9.5	13.5	−4.0
South	8,740.8	4.6	16.5	−12.0
Yucatán	2,347.3	19.7	12.4	7.3
Total	80,197.0	17.4	17.4	0.0

Source: General Census of Population and Housing, 1990. INEGI.
Note: These figures do not include indigenous tribes or migrants who leave the country.

regions. In this region is found the Federal District, containing the central functions of all federal bureaucracy and Mexico City, as well as many of the country's
largest universities, leading services, commercial enterprises, and of course the
central bank. Deconcentration is occurring within this region with people migrating to the cities of Toluca, Cuernavaca, and Querétaro, and industrial activities
moving to the cities of Puebla, Pachuca, and Tlaxcala. Migration in this region
began to slow down during the last decade, due in part to the urban development
policies established during the presidency of Miguel de la Madrid (1982–88).

The west central region is dominated by the city of Guadalajara, the nation's
second largest metropolitan area (4,000,000 people) and the capital of Jalisco
state. Guadalajara's economy is based in agricultural processing, commerce,
and a growing electronics manufacturing sector. The second most important
city in the region is Morelia, the state capital of Michoacán. It has experienced
rapid growth since the 1980s due in part to being a functioning far-off "suburb
of D.F.," and to the fact that many people moved there after the D.F. earthquake
of 1985. Morelia, a UNESCO Cultural Heritage City, has grown to more than
500,000 people in its metropolitan area. Lázaro Cárdenas, the port city on the
coast of Michoacán, was constructed during the presidency of Luis Echeverría
(1970–76) to serve as a "growth pole" for exportation of oil products and goods
to the markets of Asia. Lázaro Cárdenas never fulfilled its objectives, however,
as the true economic flows for Mexico were in a North-South direction (United
States and Latin America), not toward the west (to growing Asian markets).
The cities in the state of Guanajuato, including Léon, Irapuato, Salamanca,
Celaya, and Guanajuato, have become important centers of industry, agriculture, and services.[3]

The northeast region is dominated by the city of Monterrey, the country's third largest metropolitan area (2,600,00 people in 1990). Monterrey is the center of heavy industry such as chemicals, steel, beer, electric parts, and glass. It is also home to the Tecnológico de Monterrey, which is one of the best technical universities—and the largest private university—in the country. The industrial and economic power of Monterrey influences all the surrounding parts of the region. Tampico is the major seaport of the region, located on the Gulf of Mexico. It has facilities to handle large cargo container ships and the exportation of petroleum, and it functions as an important center for the seafood industry. In the last ten years, the expansion of maquiladora industries (assembly plants serving foreign parts manufacturers) has tied the region more closely to development along the U.S.-Mexico border.

The north region bases its riches in agriculture (fresh produce), cattle, forestry, and minerals and also its proximity to the U.S. market. The maquiladora sector has profoundly impacted this region and has joined in international commerce.

The northwest region has a varied economic base, and much of its economic activity is tied to relations with the United States. The maquiladora sector has had a most profound impact on the region, especially the Tijuana metropolitan area. Tourism and fishing also play an important role in the region. The cities of Tijuana, Ciudad Juárez, and Mexicali are the most important points of international commerce in the region. The city of Mazatlán plays an important tourist role in the region, along with serving as a center for cattle, agriculture, and mining.

The south region is the poorest in the country and has the highest numbers of people speaking indigenous languages. The city of Acapulco is an important tourism center, serving as a weekend second home center for many of D.F.'s middle and upper class. The newly completed toll highway (*autopista*) has reduced driving time from D.F. to Acapulco to three hours, a short drive to escape the stress of urban life. The cities of Oaxaca and Tuxtla Gutiérrez are noted for their tourism (crafts, ancient ruins, and indigenous art) and are centers of state government. In the state of Chiapas, the federal government has made important investments in the hydroelectric sector. Also located in Chiapas is the zone of the Isthmus of Tehuantepec. Because it has a relatively small neck of land connecting the Pacific and Gulf of Mexico via the cities of Salina Cruz and Coatzacoalcos, this zone has been earmarked to play the transshipment function between the two bodies of water.

The east region's cities are important corridors of industry. These include Córdoba and Orizaba, where cement, textile, and beer industries can be found. Coatzacoalcos-Minatitlán is an important center of oil refineries. Villahermosa has experienced important growth in the last thirty years and is considered to be an important center for petroleum and cattle.

The peninsula of Yucatán has experienced notable growth in the last fifteen years. The region's largest city, Mérida, has traditionally been the center of commerce, the cement industry, and beer. It is also known as the gateway to the Mayan ruins, which contain artifacts of the region's important cultural heritage. Historically, Mérida has been influenced by European tourists, and its ambiance reflects this relationship. New deposits of petroleum have been discovered along the coast near Campeche (the state capital). This oil discovery has made the port city of del Carmen an important new economic expansion center. Campeche and Chetumal are the capitals of their states and have important roles as seats of government. Through federal initiatives begun during the presidency of Luis Echeverría, the city of Cancún has become one of Mexico's most important tourist destinations and is the most visited tourist destination area for foreigners in Mexico.[4]

Policy Initiatives for Regional Development

A set of national policies influencing regional development began with the presidency of López Portillo (1976–82) when the National Human Settlements Law was adopted (Ley General de Asentamientos Humanos, 1978). This act established a framework for the regulation of future growth of cities and regions and signaled the first attempt to shift the management control over some urban functions from the federal to lower levels of government.

During the presidency of Miguel de la Madrid, the framework of the law was used as a tool to strengthen the state and municipal governments, which were suffering under the burdens of the nation's international debt crisis and the 1985 peso devaluation. In 1983 de la Madrid established constitutional reforms allowing municipal governments more direct power and control over fiscal and infrastructure development. Also in the de la Madrid era, Mexico began to move toward neoliberal macroeconomic policies, which were required under the external debt renegotiation with the International Monetary Fund (IMF).

Although the major amendments to the Human Settlements law were undertaken in 1983 and 1994, the impact of the law as a tool for governmental reform did not change the political ties that linked them to the federal budget. In 1989 President Salinas de Gortari created the National Program of Solidaridad— PRONASOL (a national antipoverty, jobs, and infrastructure program). One element of PRONASOL was a continuation of the basic ideas of the Human Settlements law, but through a different form of regional and municipal development. A second Salinas effort was the National System of Collection and Distribution of Taxes. The current president, Ernesto Zedillo, continues the decentralization theme by pointing out the importance of transferring to the states and municipalities the authority, resources, and decision-making power necessary to produce local self-sufficiency and increase local citizen participation. Zedillo's actions reflect the limitations of federal assistance available under present economic conditions.

Movement toward Regional Improvement

Roberto Ortega Lomelín (1994) identifies a series of forces that shape the federal budget in the areas of fighting poverty and regional inequality. From 1989 to 1992 these efforts include an increase of 17.1 billion pesos, for works undertaken for solidarity and regional development. The scope of these expenditures can be viewed in terms of percentage increases to the entire federal budget. In 1989 only 1.9 percent of the budget went to solidarity and regional development, but by 1992 nearly 4 percent went to the same budget categories.[5] Additional support was provided by various federal agencies that developed fourteen development programs for specific underdeveloped regions. Forty-nine percent of all these programs operate in the states of Chiapas, Oaxaca, Yucatán, Mexico, Michoacán, and Guerrero.

In 1992, 4.4 percent of the income collected from the federal government went to local governments (at the municipal level), as compared to 1.5 percent in 1980. In the area of federal tax distribution, Ortega Lomelín (1994), after analyzing operations between 1989 and 1992, came to the following conclusion. The majority of states benefited from the new system of the federal government paying them a large share of revenues on the first day of each month and the remainder later on in the month. This system assisted the poor states of the country a great deal by stabilizing their income flows.

Summary Observations

Due to historical and political circumstances, for many regions uneven development is a continuous condition. However, the policies of the previous two administrations have at least one common denominator, an attempt to integrate the regions into the national economy. During the Salinas presidency the federal government used policies aimed at both reducing the external debt and targeting poverty and inequality. Parallel with these grand external and domestic policy actions there has been reform in the federal system of revenue collection and distribution, which has helped the finances of municipal government. These efforts alone are not enough to combat the regional disequilibrium and the excessive centralism that has taken wealth from the regions. Without an effort to increase the minimum wage, stimulate the production of domestic product for internal consumption, and stimulate small-scale business activity, the country cannot move forward at any meaningful level (Barkin 1990). The next generations of federal administration must recognize that neoliberal policies do not provide a mechanism for regional equity. The state, not the market, must play an active and consistent role in resolving past abuses and providing the leadership needed for true development.

Time is now the most important variable for Mexico, for time is needed to put its economy in order and to create the policies appropriate to its new economic circumstance, as well as to strengthen the regions of this multifaceted country.

Notes

1. Mexico is a mountainous country. Nearly 71 percent of its territory is located more than 300 meters above sea level, and 28 percent of the land has a slope greater than 25 degrees. There is a great variation in climate, soil type, and vegetation, including tropical, subtropical, and arid ecologies with an average annual rainfall of 717 mm.
   2. Bassols Batalla's definitions are still used as major administration divisions. The PRI urban platform book *Retos y Propuestas* used similar regional groupings.
   3. Léon for shoes, Guanajuato also for tourism.
   4. The Secretary of Tourism created FONATUR as a development agency for actually building tourism projects. FONATUR built Cancún and various other resort areas in the country.
   5. In 1992, 60 percent of the expenditures were directed at activities that permitted the immediate betterment of the quality of life of the population, 21 percent for new employment opportunities for areas of economic difficulty, and 19 percent for the construction of infrastructure in very poor regions of the country.

Bibliography

Barkin, David (1990), *Distorted Development: Mexico in the World Economy* (Boulder: Westview).
Bassols Batalla, Angel (1979), *México—formacion de regiones economicas* (Mexico City: UNAM).
Lemus, Mariano G., ed. (1994), *Retos y propuestas* (Mexico City: Fundación Mexicana Cambio XXI, Luis Donaldo Colosio).
Ortega, Lomelín Roberto (1994), *Federalismo municipio* (Mexico City: F.C.E.).

34

BORIS GRAIZBORD AND CRESCENCIO RUIZ

Recent Changes in the Economic and Social Structure of Mexico's Regions

Boris Graizbord and Crescenio Ruiz detail the changing structure of Mexico's regions. Mexico has had both spatially oriented and "nonspatial" policies since 1978, which led at first to the increasing urbanization of Mexico and more recently to the decentralization of its manufacturing sector. The economic reforms of the eighties and early nineties had impacts that differed among regions and cities. Thus, general policies may have had a stronger impact on the location of economic activity at this time than policies specifically directed to this end.

During the eighties, the economic units in the central region fell from 41 percent to 36.5 percent of the national total. The share of manufacturing increased in the center north, western, and south pacific regions. Manufacturing was not able to substantially increase employment, so that trade and services increased their importance for the labor market. Large cities saw the growth of low-skilled services and skilled consumer services, such as teaching and social assistance. The center and northeast had large increases in labor productivity, as well as higher than average salaries, although in all sectors and regions average salaries decreased. Productivity increased in manufacturing and trade but decreased in services, especially construction.

Mexico's rapid urbanization began in the fifties and continued more slowly during the next two decades. In the eighties, the growth of large cities decreased in comparison to the national total; smaller cities grew in importance. The increased number of poor people and increasingly unequal distribution of income had regional impacts: the poorest states had decreasing shares of national income.

Introduction

Since the late seventies, Mexico has made remarkable efforts to direct urbanization and industrialization processes. These efforts began with a National Urban

Development Plan (1978–82); subsequently, two national urban development programs appeared (1984–88, 1990–94) and were followed by other spatial-oriented strategies such as the National Industrial Development Plan (1979). Nonetheless, "nonspatial" policies have deeply affected decision making, and the spatial behavior of economic agents and factors of production.[1]

"Workers to work" or labor migration, rather than "work to workers,"[2] is the pattern that most neatly reflects Mexico's urbanization process during its initial stages. However, considered as an ongoing demographic, economic, and social transformation within the national geographical space, this process has led to an increase in the number and size of cities. Quantitatively, this meant a larger volume and share of the national population living in urban locations[3] and a higher ratio between urban population increase and overall population growth. From the qualitative standpoint, both the sociodemographic profile and the political behavior of Mexican society have undergone important changes.

At present there is no doubt that urbanization is inevitable, and directly related to the country's economic and social development, urban population growth, and number and size of cities; however, certain countries have experienced recent changes in both their regional economic and social structure and their urbanization patterns, giving way to a reconsideration of this relationship. Indeed, recent innovations in the fields of communication and information technology have shown the way toward the globalization and liberalization of national economies, enabling the fragmentation of production processes and their moving away from traditional input sources (energy, labor force, natural resources, or raw materials) and from consumption and product markets. Thus, where scale economies were once accountable for the geographic concentration of the population and economic activities (Mera 1973), decreasing scale economies (Piore and Sabel 1984) now explain the decentralization of economic activity, mainly in the manufacturing sector.

In this essay we discuss briefly the relationship between economic policies and trade liberalization, and how both have influenced regional development and the well-being of the different economic sectors and social classes, these last considered here as income groups within the capital-labor dichotomy. Apart from this introduction, this chapter includes five sections. The first summarizes the main elements of Mexico's economic development strategy during the eighties; the second describes sectoral changes that affected the country's regional structure; the third summarizes the evolution of demographic and economic variables along the last twenty years; the fourth gives an account of the effects that these processes have had on the employment and income levels of Mexicans, and the last section concludes with a brief summary of the main ideas permeating the chapter.

Mexico's Development Strategy during the Eighties

As known, in 1982 Mexico's economy confronted a deep crisis, and early in 1986 certain signs of recovery began to appear. It was during the latter year that a trade strategy was implemented to accelerate the integration of the Mexican economy to the world system.

The 1980–90 decade can be analytically divided into two periods. As a matter of fact, during the first five years of the eighties economic crisis became evident: subsequent devaluations; an annual inflation rate of over 100 percent; a current account deficit of 2,685 million dollars in 1982; a public sector deficit equivalent to 17 percent of the GDP; and an external debt of approximately 85 billion dollars. Apparently, the crisis was not merely circumstantial but had deep structural roots, as experts in this field indicated (see, among others, Bravo Aguilera 1993 and several articles in Bazdresch et al. 1993).

The debt problem marked an important point of inflection in Mexican development. When during the late sixties Mexico displayed high economic growth rates and vast oil reserves, it received a large share of the financial credits aimed at developing countries. However, as of 1982 external indebtedness became the main constraint to the country's growth. Subsequent monetary devaluations turned the debt interests into a heavy encumbrance that combined with restricted access to external funding during the years that followed. In 1980 the national debt represented 27.6 percent of the GDP, and in 1986 it reached 79.5 percent. In 1987 the total debt amounted to 102.4 billion dollars (Wong González and Salido 1991, 13).

When the crisis reached its peak, the Mexican economy was dependent on oil exports, as these represented 75 percent of the total value of exports. A gradual reduction of international demand and the collapse of oil prices offered a glimpse of the serious problems in store for Mexico's economy. Eventually, the government recognized the problems posed by this heavy dependence, and alongside pressures from international financing agencies (International Monetary Fund and the World Bank) arguments in favor of a greater export diversification began to emerge. Thus, during the second half of the eighties, the government expressed its decision to improve its balance of payments and recover its credit capacity, and it encouraged non-oil exports within the framework of greater economic liberalization. This resulted in a higher proportion of intermediate and durable consumer goods in the export account.[4]

The encouragement of exports called for the implementation of new policies and measures, among which the following can be mentioned: fiscal incentives; export rights; tax reduction in imports required by exporters; administrative simplification for exports; etc. These measures were institutionalized through different normative instruments such as the 1986 Foreign Trade Act (Ley de Comercio Exterior); the 1984–88 National Program for Industrial Encouragement and Foreign Trade (Programa Nacional de Fomento Industrial y Comercio Exterior); the 1985 Program of Overall Encouragement to Exports (Programa de Fomento Integral a las Exportaciones); and, recently, the National Program of Industrial Modernization and Foreign Trade (Programa Nacional de Modernización Industrial y del Comercio Exterior, PRONAMICE) (see Bravo Aguilera 1993, 321–

34). Furthermore, additional measures such as economic reforms were implemented to increase investment from abroad in productive areas previously prohibited to foreign capital. Once the economy began to show signs of stability, particularly after 1985, an increase of capital investments from other countries was registered. Simultaneously, in order to strengthen its finances, the government implemented a policy for the privatization of public enterprises. This took place gradually after 1986, and in February 1990 the privatization or, where applicable, the sale of 891 entities had been achieved, to conclude with a total of 691 cases (Córdoba Montoya 1993, 434).

Summarizing, the above measures indicated a final transition from the old model of import substitution or "inward growth" toward a new pattern of outward or export liberalization, and the consequent decentralization, in accordance with the demands of the new international division of labor and globalization. At the same time, the new economic policy programs and the recent 1994 enactment of the North American Free Trade Agreement (NAFTA) are evidence of the high priority presently conferred to the production of export goods and the integration of multilateral commercial blocks. The territorial impacts (negative or positive) that may derive from these changes are not yet clear for the country as a whole, but they are already felt within certain regions and cities, as we will try to demonstrate in the following sections.

1980–88 Regional Restructuring

This section is based on the 1980 and 1988 economic censuses data. It attempts to depict changes registered in the regional participation of manufacturing activities, construction, trade, and services, as reflected in the number of economic units (EU), occupied personnel (OP), total payments in salaries and wages of occupied personnel (SW), and value added (VA), and to evaluate these in relation to the average size of economic units, average income per worker, and productivity of the labor force or value added per capita in each of these sectors by regional aggregates.[5]

Number of Economic Units (EU)

As shown in Table 34.1, there is an increase in the number of manufacturing, construction, trade, and service establishments at the national level, although in varying proportions for each sector, as their participation in the total is lower in the case of the first three sectors, and only higher for the service sector, which increased from 28 percent of the total in 1980 to 31.5 percent in 1988.

During these years, the weight of regions and their sectors with respect to the national total greatly changed. The most remarkable changes are in detriment of the central region, which from concentrating almost 41 percent of the country's economic units decreased to only 36.5 percent. In this region, all sectors lost

Table 34.1

Percent Distribution of Selected Economic Variables for Economic Sectors by Region, 1980–88

| | Economic Units (EU)[a] | | | |
| | 1980 | | 1988 | |
Regions/Sectors	Regional	Sectorial	Regional	Sectorial
National	100.00	100.00	100.00	100.00
Manufacturing	100.00	12.95	100.00	10.59
Construction	100.00	0.49	100.00	0.40
Trade	100.00	58.43	100.00	57.55
Services	100.00	28.13	100.00	31.46
I. Northwest	6.35	100.00	6.67	100.00
Manufacturing	5.17	10.54	5.16	8.19
Construction	8.44	0.65	10.15	0.62
Trade	5.59	51.42	6.22	53.68
Services	8.44	37.39	7.96	37.52
II. North	6.00	100.00	6.40	100.00
Manufacturing	5.14	11.10	6.40	10.58
Construction	5.46	0.44	9.19	0.58
Trade	5.91	57.59	6.11	54.94
Services	6.58	30.87	6.90	33.90
III. Northeast	6.53	100.00	7.11	100.00
Manufacturing	6.18	12.26	6.61	9.85
Construction	10.40	0.78	10.47	0.60
Trade	6.06	54.21	6.80	55.07
Services	7.61	32.76	7.79	34.49
IV. Center-North	9.76	100.00	10.43	100.00
Manufacturing	10.43	13.84	11.40	11.58
Construction	5.86	0.29	13.66	0.53
Trade	10.43	62.41	10.54	58.20
Services	8.14	23.45	9.84	29.70
V. West	12.86	100.00	12.98	100.00
Manufacturing	13.41	13.50	14.08	11.48
Construction	9.37	0.35	8.48	0.26
Trade	12.92	58.72	12.91	57.26
Services	12.53	27.42	12.78	30.99
VI. Center	40.89	100.00	36.49	100.00
Manufacturing	43.57	13.80	36.78	10.67
Construction	51.47	0.61	30.46	0.34
Trade	41.08	58.71	37.19	58.65
Services	39.08	26.88	35.19	30.34
VII. Gulf	7.46	100.00	7.94	100.00
Manufacturing	5.96	10.35	7.03	9.37
Construction	4.20	0.27	6.90	0.35
Trade	7.54	59.06	7.76	56.30
Services	8.03	30.31	8.57	33.97
VIII. South Pacific	7.27	100.00	8.56	100.00
Manufacturing	6.90	12.29	9.00	11.12
Construction	1.90	0.13	5.09	0.24
Trade	7.74	62.28	9.01	60.56
Services	6.54	25.30	7.64	28.07

(continued)

Table 34.1 (continued)

	Economic Units (EU)[a]			
	1980		1988	
Regions/Sectors	Regional	Sectorial	Regional	Sectorial
IX. Yucatán Peninsula	2.88	100.00	3.43	100.00
Manufacturing	3.24	14.59	3.55	10.95
Construction	2.91	0.49	5.60	0.66
Trade	2.73	55.30	3.45	57.94
Services	3.03	29.62	3.32	30.45

	Employment (Occupied personnel)			
	1980		1988	
Regions/Sectors	Regional	Sectorial	Regional	Sectorial
National	100.00	100.00	100.00	100.00
Manufacturing	100.00	41.70	100.00	38.43
Construction	100.00	8.69	100.00	4.98
Trade	100.00	28.81	100.00	31.57
Services	100.00	20.80	100.00	25.02
I. Northwest	6.74	100.00	8.03	100.00
Manufacturing	5.11	31.63	6.69	32.00
Construction	5.98	7.71	6.79	4.21
Trade	8.35	35.70	8.93	35.09
Services	8.08	24.95	9.21	28.69
II. North	6.52	100.00	9.41	100.00
Manufacturing	7.00	44.73	12.33	50.36
Construction	3.69	4.91	7.43	3.94
Trade	6.93	30.60	7.61	25.54
Services	6.20	19.75	7.58	20.16
III. Northeast	9.62	100.00	10.03	100.00
Manufacturing	11.16	48.41	11.56	44.29
Construction	11.38	10.29	10.93	5.43
Trade	7.74	23.20	8.81	27.73
Services	8.37	18.11	9.04	22.55
IV. Center-North	7.22	100.00	9.21	100.00
Manufacturing	7.42	42.83	9.89	41.28
Construction	3.04	3.66	9.79	5.30
Trade	8.72	34.79	9.35	32.07
Services	6.50	18.72	7.86	21.35
V. West	10.29	100.00	10.78	100.00
Manufacturing	9.22	37.36	9.37	33.39
Construction	6.02	5.08	7.23	3.34
Trade	12.37	34.62	12.38	36.25
Services	11.35	22.94	11.65	27.02
VI. Center	47.96	100.00	38.97	100.00
Manufacturing	52.97	46.05	41.20	40.62
Construction	56.00	10.15	45.02	5.76
Trade	40.35	24.24	35.95	29.13
Services	45.09	19.56	38.16	24.49
VII. Gulf	5.37	100.00	6.02	100.00
Manufacturing	3.69	28.65	4.96	31.64
Construction	7.15	11.58	4.46	3.69
Trade	6.94	37.23	7.14	37.42
Services	5.83	22.55	6.56	27.24

(continued)

Table 34.1 (continued)

Employment (Occupied personnel)
1980 · 1988

Regions/Sectors	Regional	Sectorial	Regional	Sectorial
VIII. South Pacific	4.07	100.00	4.58	100.00
Manufacturing	1.73	17.69	2.36	19.80
Construction	5.30	11.31	3.38	3.68
Trade	5.96	42.16	6.41	44.17
Services	5.64	28.83	5.92	32.35
IX. Yucatán Peninsula	2.21	100.00	2.96	100.00
Manufacturing	1.70	32.15	1.64	21.25
Construction	1.44	5.67	4.97	8.36
Trade	2.65	34.52	3.42	36.45
Services	2.94	27.66	4.02	33.94

Total salaries and wages (SW)[b]
1980 · 1988

Regions/Sectors	Regional	Sectorial	Regional	Sectorial
National	100.00	100.00	100.00	100.00
Manufacturing	100.00	57.08	100.00	58.73
Construction	100.00	8.33	100.00	3.97
Trade	100.00	18.94	100.00	19.76
Services	100.00	15.65	100.00	17.54
I. Northwest	5.80	100.00	7.23	100.00
Manufacturing	4.03	39.65	5.47	44.41
Construction	6.37	9.14	6.54	3.59
Trade	9.66	31.54	10.88	29.75
Services	7.30	19.67	9.17	22.26
II. North	5.99	100.00	9.51	100.00
Manufacturing	6.19	58.97	11.34	70.06
Construction	4.01	5.57	5.48	2.29
Trade	7.24	22.90	7.29	15.15
Services	4.81	12.57	6.78	12.50
III. Northeast	11.80	100.00	11.99	100.00
Manufacturing	13.27	64.17	12.62	61.84
Construction	10.93	7.71	12.00	3.97
Trade	9.06	14.54	10.79	17.79
Services	10.24	13.58	11.20	16.40
IV. Center-North	4.79	100.00	7.45	100.00
Manufacturing	5.41	64.53	8.47	66.80
Construction	2.99	5.20	5.87	3.12
Trade	4.74	18.76	6.79	18.03
Services	3.52	11.51	5.11	12.05
V. West	7.89	100.00	8.33	100.00
Manufacturing	7.64	55.23	7.83	55.22
Construction	5.97	6.30	5.41	2.58
Trade	9.65	23.15	10.00	23.17
Services	7.72	15.32	8.78	18.49
VI. Center	55.65	100.00	45.69	100.00
Manufacturing	57.95	59.43	45.75	58.81
Construction	49.30	7.38	55.33	4.80
Trade	49.98	17.01	42.54	18.40
Services	57.50	16.17	46.86	17.99

(continued)

Table 34.1 (continued)

Regions/Sectors

VII. Gulf	4.44	100.00	5.50	100.00
Manufacturing	3.66	47.03	6.18	66.10
Construction	10.55	19.80	3.66	2.64
Trade	5.26	22.46	5.41	19.46
Services	3.04	10.71	3.70	11.81
VIII. South Pacific	2.33	100.00	2.35	100.00
Manufacturing	0.85	20.80	1.47	36.69
Construction	8.57	30.70	2.10	3.54
Trade	2.78	22.62	3.34	28.06
Services	3.85	25.88	4.25	31.71
IX. Yucatán Peninsula	1.30	100.00	1.97	100.00
Manufacturing	1.00	43.81	0.87	26.04
Construction	1.31	8.39	3.61	7.28
Trade	1.62	23.46	2.95	29.67
Services	2.03	24.34	4.15	37.01

	Value Added (VA)[c]			
	1980		1988	
Regions/Sectors	Regional	Sectorial	Regional	Sectorial
National	100.00	100.00	100.00	100.00
Manufacturing	100.00	51.94	100.00	57.24
Construction	100.00	10.07	100.00	2.49
Trade	100.00	21.14	100.00	27.35
Services	100.00	16.85	100.00	12.93
I. Northwest	6.25	100.00	6.68	100.00
Manufacturing	3.60	29.26	4.14	35.49
Construction	10.28	16.58	7.03	2.62
Trade	10.29	34.83	10.90	44.59
Services	6.91	18.63	8.94	17.30
II. North	5.65	100.00	9.01	100.00
Manufacturing	5.60	51.50	10.67	67.77
Construction	9.18	16.38	6.67	1.84
Trade	5.31	19.87	7.27	22.06
Services	4.11	12.25	5.80	8.33
III. Northeast	10.48	100.00	11.21	100.00
Manufacturing	12.43	61.58	12.56	64.13
Construction	7.08	6.80	13.81	3.06
Trade	8.97	18.10	8.79	21.45
Services	8.41	13.52	9.84	11.35
IV. Center-North	4.64	100.00	8.19	100.00
Manufacturing	5.41	60.57	9.60	67.08
Construction	1.61	3.50	6.04	1.83
Trade	5.45	24.80	6.86	22.91
Services	3.07	11.13	5.18	8.18

(continued)

Table 34.1 (continued)

Regions/Sectors	Regional	Value Added (VA)[c]		Sectorial
		Sectorial	Regional	
V. West	8.31	100.00	8.64	100.00
Manufacturing	8.41	52.61	7.39	48.91
Construction	5.95	7.22	4.98	1.43
Trade	10.18	25.90	11.30	35.75
Services	7.04	14.27	9.29	13.90
VI. Center	54.73	100.00	46.28	100.00
Manufacturing	59.02	56.01	47.12	58.27
Construction	36.66	6.75	53.62	2.88
Trade	48.92	18.90	43.04	25.43
Services	59.62	18.35	48.00	13.41
VII. Gulf	4.96	100.00	5.05	100.00
Manufacturing	3.67	38.41	5.36	60.77
Construction	12.74	25.86	3.21	1.58
Trade	5.43	23.15	5.03	27.25
Services	3.70	12.57	4.06	10.39
VIII. South Pacific	3.16	100.00	3.11	100.00
Manufacturing	0.89	14.68	2.30	42.28
Construction	14.62	46.66	2.01	1.61
Trade	3.22	21.57	3.96	34.83
Services	3.20	17.09	5.12	21.28
IX. Yucatán Peninsula	1.83	100.00	1.83	100.00
Manufacturing	0.97	27.45	0.87	27.27
Construction	1.88	10.36	2.62	3.56
Trade	2.23	25.82	2.85	42.56
Services	3.94	36.38	3.77	26.61

Source: INEGI (1988 and 1993), XI and XIII Censos Economicos for Manufacturing and Construction 1981 and 1989; VIII and X Censos Economicos for Trade and Services, 1981 and 1989, Mexico.

Note: According to the Programa Nacional de Desarrollo Urbano 1990–94, SEDUE, Mexico, 1990, the individual states corresponding to the nine regions are: 1) Northwest: Baja, CA, Baja, CA sur, Sonora y Sinaloa; 2) North: Chihuahua, Durango y Coa huila; 3) Northeast: Nuevo Leon y Tamaulipas; 4) Center-North: Zacatecas, Aguascalientas, San Luis Potosi, Guanajuato y Queretaro; 5) West: Nayarit, Jalisco, Colima y Michoacan; 6) Center: Districto Federal, Mexico, Morelos, Tlaxcala, Hidalgo y Puebla; 7) Gulf: Veracruz y Tabasco; 8) South Pacific: Guerrero, Oaxaca y Chiapas; 9) Yucatán Peninsula: Yucatan, Campeche y Quintana Roo.

[a]Equivalent to number of establishments.

[b]Pesos of 1980.

[c]Pesos of 1980.

their share in reference to their national total, particularly the manufacturing sector, which decreased from 43.6 percent in 1980 to only 36.8 percent in 1988. This represents an absolute loss of about 4,000 manufacturing outlets, from 55,000 to 51,000, which in itself constitutes an unprecedented fact in the country's history. Other sectors (trade and services) registered an absolute increase in the number of economic units; this enabled them to preserve and, in the case of services, to increase their weight within the region.

The relative loss (not necessarily in absolute numbers) of the manufacturing sector in each region, and the relative gain in the case of services is a widespread phenomenon. Simultaneously, all (except the central region) enlarged in absolute terms their number of manufacturing economic units, increasing, consequently, their share in this sector at the national level. Moreover, the manufacturing sector acquired a greater sectoral share within regions than at the national level, thus allowing an industrial manufacturing specialization in the case of the center-north, western, and Pacific regions, whereas the Yucatán peninsula and the central region, as already mentioned, receded in this sense.

Occupied Personnel

Census data show a loss in the capacity of the manufacturing sector to generate employment to the extent that occupied personnel in certain subsectors (paper, basic metallic and nonmetallic minerals) increased scarcely 5 percent during the eight-year period. Several factors explain this: the contraction of the internal market as a response to the crisis; technological innovation; conspicuous presence of foreign goods; etc. (Rendón and Salas 1992, 20). On the other hand, there is a clear tendency of trade and service activities to increase their importance for the country's labor market, thus contributing to a marked *tertiarization* of the economy. The increase of unpaid personnel, particularly in retail trade and consumer services, must be emphasized. This meant greater employment generation capacity of the tertiary sector, not just because it attracted new medium- and large-scale investments from the industrial sector in search of more profitable markets within wholesale trade and producer services, but rather due to the proliferation of small-scale, own-account or unpaid occupations that show an increasing precariousness of tertiary employment (Aguilar 1993).

The sectoral structure of the labor force within the different regions experienced significant transformations during the period under analysis. We shall first consider the manufacturing sector. Within five regions of Mexico (northeast, center-north, west, center, and Yucatán) the percentage of occupied population in this sector decreased given the increasing importance of tertiary activities. However, only in the central region this five-point percent decrease implied a loss of occupied population in absolute numbers (around 31,000 employment positions). On the other hand, the regions that most contributed to employment generation in this sector were, above all, the north and center-north, and then the northwest and northeast, which as a whole contributed more than 80 percent of the net increase of employment in this sector. The same happened in the construction industry, that from concentrating 56 percent (246,000 out of the 440,000 workers employed countrywise in 1980) decreased to 45 percent (154,000 out of the total 342,000 in 1988).

It can be said that it was basically the central region, which includes Mexico City Metropolitan Area (MCMA), that faced greater difficulties for employment generation in the manufacturing industry, and thus new and more dynamic industrial firms looked for advantageous location in other regions, mainly in northern Mexico.

Second, trade activity showed net employment increases in all regions. However, in two of these (north and center-north) the percent participation of this sector decreased during the period of reference. The higher increases occurred in three regions: center, west, and north. However, it is worth pointing out first that the regions where these increases occurred are not the same as those that registered the most important manufacturing increases, except for the center-north, which had the second most important manufacturing gain, and second, that the solid increase in the trade sector is related to the existence of large national urban concentrations (Mexico City, Puebla, Guadalajara, and Monterrey), which are located precisely within those regions that show that sector's largest increases. During the last decade, the economy of the large Mexican cities was in fact characterized by a huge growth of retail trade, particularly own-account activities (itinerant vendors, for example). Unpaid jobs in this sector represented 50 percent or more of the net increase registered in the west, center, center-north, Gulf of Mexico, and south pacific regions (Aguilar 1993). It was in those regions that the contraction of paid activities obliged the population to turn to own-account trade activities as an alternative for safeguarding or increasing their income.

Finally, it must be highlighted that employment in the service sector displayed net positive and percentage increases in all regions during the eighties. The central region stands out with the largest increases in all kinds of services, although consumer services have a large share in this increase, indicating a thriving of low-qualification activities (for example, trading with food, garments, or personal services); producer services also increased, which seems to indicate that some manufacturing industries either have not lost dynamism or have undergone internal restructuring and demand these support services. Additionally, community services (teaching, social assistance, etc.) increased their importance, especially as a result of the demand generated by large urban concentrations. These positive changes reflect interestingly complex productive restructuring processes within this region. The western region shows the second largest increase among all sectors, and particularly in consumer and community services, but not so in producer services. This is most surely due to the scarce growth of the manufacturing sector. Also important are increases registered in the northern regions (northwest, northeast, north, and center-north), where consumer services have the highest participation; the same can be said of all the remaining regions. In the case of producer services, employment growth relates to the increase in manufacturing activities, mainly in the in-bond (maquiladora) industry (Aguilar and Graizbord 1995).

Value Added

Real growth (in 1980 pesos) of the total value added during the period was only 30 percent, attributed paradoxically to the manufacturing sector by two-thirds, and the rest corresponding to the trade sector. On the other hand, the service sector, while preserving its absolute volume, decreased from 16.8 percent to only 13 percent of the total, whereas the other two sectors showed an increase in their relative participation from 52 percent to 57.3 percent the manufacturing sector, and from 21 percent to 27.4 percent the trade sector. By regions, the north and center-north considerably increased their importance in regard to their VA, and, once again, the central region receded in its contribution to the total value added from 54.7 percent at the beginning of the period to only 46.3 percent at the end of it.

Analytical Relationships among Variables

Sectorial and regional economic restructuring, which began during the eighties, was produced by both the crisis and the so-called globalization that affected national economy. The following description of analytical relationships among the variables described above hopefully enables an evaluation of their effects.

In all regions, and nationally, the average size of manufacturing units (OP/EU) increased during the period under consideration. This is not so for the construction sector, in which the size of economic units decreased in all regions (except the Yucatán peninsula, reflecting massive hotel building in Cancún). Contrarily, the trade and service sectors register, in all regions, a slight increase in the average size of their economic units. This is important in general for consumer services and, in certain regions, for production services, as in the case of the northeastern, northern, and Yucatán peninsula regions. It is noteworthy that the average size of economic units in the northern (northwest, north, and northeast) and central regions in both years exceeds that of the country as a whole, with important relative growths for the north and northwest, and a decrease in the northeast and center between the first and last years (Table 34.2).

In the case of labor productivity (VA/OP), which in Mexico decreased from 226.1 in 1980 to 217.9 in 1988 (in 1980 pesos), higher values are observed for both years only at the central region (14 percent in 1980 and 19 percent in 1988) and the northeast (9 percent in 1980 and 12 percent in 1988). The same happens with the average income per worker (SW/OP). Only in these two regions work-

Table 34.2

Selected Analytical Relations by Region and Economic Sector, 1980–88

Regions/Sectors	Size (OP/EU) 1980	Size (OP/EU) 1988	Productivity (VA/OP)[a] 1980	Productivity (VA/OP)[a] 1988	Avg Salary (SW/OP)[a] 1980	Avg Salary (SW/OP)[a] 1988
National	5.20	5.24	226.11	217.87	89.81	64.57
Manufacturing	16.73	19.02	281.65	324.50	122.93	98.68
Construction	92.75	64.51	262.04	108.71	86.06	51.39
Trade	2.56	2.87	165.91	188.71	59.04	40.41
Services	3.84	4.17	183.15	112.62	67.59	45.28
I. Northwest	5.51	6.31	209.66	181.24	77.38	58.11
Manufacturing	16.53	24.65	198.55	200.99	96.98	80.62
Construction	65.71	43.12	450.68	112.58	91.73	49.49
Trade	3.83	4.12	204.53	230.32	68.34	49.26
Services	3.68	4.82	156.58	109.27	61.01	45.07
II. North	5.65	7.70	195.73	208.57	62.51	65.22
Manufacturing	22.76	36.67	225.36	280.66	108.77	90.73
Construction	62.60	52.16	652.38	97.53	93.50	37.86
Trade	3.00	3.58	127.09	180.18	61.73	38.70
Services	3.61	4.58	121.37	86.12	52.51	40.45
III. Northeast	7.65	7.40	246.49	243.40	110.25	77.15
Manufacturing	30.21	33.28	313.58	352.43	146.16	107.15
Construction	101.54	67.29	162.96	137.42	82.62	56.46
Trade	3.27	3.72	192.31	188.29	69.11	49.49
Services	4.23	4.84	184.00	122.50	82.66	56.10
IV. Center-North	3.84	4.63	145.32	193.76	59.53	52.21
Manufacturing	11.90	16.50	205.48	314.85	89.68	84.48
Construction	48.06	46.24	139.14	67.04	84.68	30.79
Trade	2.14	2.55	103.59	138.40	32.10	29.35
Services	3.07	3.33	86.43	74.22	36.59	29.46
V. West	4.16	4.35	182.46	174.68	68.87	49.90
Manufacturing	11.51	12.66	256.96	255.91	101.82	82.54
Construction	59.62	55.00	258.96	74.85	85.30	38.49
Trade	2.45	2.76	136.53	172.28	46.06	32.64
Services	3.48	3.79	113.51	89.87	45.98	34.15
VI. Center	6.09	5.60	258.05	258.71	104.21	75.70
Manufacturing	20.34	21.30	313.83	371.11	134.49	109.58
Construction	100.93	95.34	171.51	129.46	75.76	63.16
Trade	2.52	2.78	201.16	225.88	73.14	47.82
Services	4.43	4.52	242.15	141.69	86.18	55.61
VII. Gulf	3.74	3.98	208.85	182.55	74.19	58.93
Manufacturing	10.37	13.42	280.03	350.57	121.80	123.08
Construction	158.10	41.76	466.62	78.28	126.90	42.10
Trade	2.36	2.64	129.88	132.96	44.77	30.64
Services	2.79	3.19	116.47	69.63	35.22	25.54

(continued)

Table 34.2 (continued)

Regions/Sectors	Size (OP/EU)		Productivity (VA/OP)[a]		Avg Salary (SW/OP)[a]	
	1980	1988	1980	1988	1980	1988
VIII. South Pacific	2.91	2.80	175.43	148.06	51.35	33.12
Manufacturing	4.19	4.99	145.53	316.12	60.36	61.37
Construction	258.72	42.84	723.70	64.82	139.36	31.91
Trade	1.97	2.04	89.76	116.76	27.55	21.04
Services	3.32	3.23	103.96	97.37	46.09	32.46
IX. Yucatán Peninsula	3.99	4.52	186.86	134.99	53.01	42.93
Manufacturing	8.79	8.78	159.51	173.26	72.23	52.60
Construction	45.90	57.25	341.58	57.44	78.48	37.40
Trade	2.49	2.84	139.77	157.63	36.03	34.95
Services	3.72	5.04	245.75	105.82	46.56	46.81

Source: INEGI (1988 and 1993), XI and XIII Censos Economicos for Manufacturing and Construction 1981 and 1989; VIII and X Censos Economicos for Trade and Services, 1981 and 1989, Mexico.
[a]Thousands of 1980 pesos per capita.
OP Occupied Personnel
EU Economic Units
VA Value Added
SW Total Salaries and Wages

ers obtained higher salaries in comparison to the national average. It is worth mentioning that for the last year, the northern region shows an average value somewhat higher than the national, although only 1 percent, whereas the central region's is 17 percent higher and the northeastern's is 19 percent.

In this respect, it would seem that those workers who remained in the central region during the crisis, or those who arrived in it or at the north and northeastern regions were able to lessen the effect of the general collapse of the average salary, which decreased nationally, as observed in Table 34.2, from 89.8 (in 1980,000 pesos) at the beginning of the decade, to 64.6 by the end. Both years register important regional variations in the four sectors. However, in all sectors and regions the average salary per worker (SW/OP) systematically decreased between 1980 and 1988. Not one single sector or region shows an actual gain, despite the fact that in some of them the total payroll did increase in real terms, as in the case of subsector 35 (chemicals) nationally, and subsector 38 (metal-mechanics) in almost all regions, but never proportionally to the increase of the corresponding VA. This may be suggesting a relatively higher "exploitation" of the labor force or, in functional terms, a more "efficient" use of labor. From this perspective, and taking into consideration that in the trade sector (both wholesale and retail) the total volume of salaries and wages (SW) increased in absolute terms (in 1980 pesos), it is also possible to think that the cost of labor in this activity increased, giving employees in these occupations a chance to recover buying power in relative terms. This is not valid for this sector in all regions, since in some of them the increase of occupied personnel was either higher than the increase in the payroll, or proportional, enabling the preservation of an average salary-income per worker equivalent to that of the first year.

It can be concluded that while the decrease of the average income of labor was a widespread fact during the period, workers increased their average productivity (VA/OP) in the manufacturing industry and trade at the national level, and in all regions of Mexico, whereas in services, and most extraordinarily in the construction industry, their productivity invariably decreased between 1980 and 1988. Thus, whereas for the first sector the capital-labor relationship was positive, for the second it was negative for both factors, as the number of occupations did not grow either in the service sector or in construction, and in this last one total value added alarmingly collapsed.

Urban Evolution and Industrial Growth

The centripetal and concentrating phase—which caused Mexico City's rapid demographic and economic growth—extends from 1950 through 1970. Some analysts divide the postwar period into two periods. The first (1950–80) referred to a "stabilizing development" or "Mexican miracle," and the second (1980–90) known as the "lost decade," began to appear following the first worldwide oil crisis in the seventies. Here we consider a period of rapid demographic growth (from 1950 through 1970), a second period (1970–80) during which population growth rates slow down,[6] and a third period (1980–90) during which the country openly enters urban transition (Zelinsky 1971). Urban transition took the form of economic and demographic decentralization in favor of middle-size secondary cities (100,000 to one million inhabitants) whose population and manufacturing employment experienced higher growth rates than the primary city's.

Mexico's contemporary urbanization and economic development began during the second half of the twentieth century. Agricultural employment and production experienced an abrupt decline during the fifties, and this resulted in high levels of rural-urban migration. Few cities received investment in urban services, which only some state capitals offered—although incipiently. It was Mexico City, however, that received the largest share of rural migration and benefited from large investments of economic and social capital (physical and social infrastructure), which the government recognized as efficient during the country's industrial take-off. Thus, concentrated urban growth enabled rapid economic growth through import substitution. The country's urban population grew from 14.4 million in 1960 to 24 million in 1970 and 38 million in 1980; this is more than 40 percent of the total population in 1960, almost 50 percent in 1970, and more than 55 percent in 1980. At the same time, cities with 50,000 inhabitants and more in size increased their number from forty-six in 1960 to sixty in 1970 and seventy-six in 1980. By the middle seventies (Ledent 1982; Graizbord 1984b) the urbanization rate started to slow down from an annual 1.85 percent average during 1960–70 to only 1.3 percent between 1970 and 1980, whereas in 1950–60 it had reached its historical 3.8 percent maximum (Garza and Rivera 1994, Table 1.3).[7]

During the 1950–60 decade Mexico City was only beginning to expand physically and functionally, already showing its metropolitan character. By 1980 the number of metropolitan areas in the country would reach twenty-six (Negrete and Salazar 1986), and Mexico City, which in the thirties became a millionaire city, would shelter in 1960 more than 5.4 million inhabitants, and 9.1 million in 1970. By this time, the urban area of the capital had already overgrown the limits of the old city and occupied the territory of eleven municipalities of the state of Mexico, which surrounds the Federal District in the east, west, and north. The population of Mexico City's Metropolitan Area, of more than 13 million inhabitants in 1980, would represent between 20 and 22 percent[8] of the country's total population, and combined with other areas (Guadalajara, Monterrey, and Puebla) would concentrate more than one-half (51.3 percent) of the total urban population. During the eighties, the process reached a point of inflection, and the concentration trend began to revert openly, that is in absolute and relative terms. Indeed, urban primacy, which characterized the national urban system (NUS), reduced itself as the Mexico City population, which in the seventies and eighties was equivalent to that of the twenty-three cities that followed it in size, in 1990 was only equivalent to the total of the following fourteen cities. Moreover, its population decreased to 18 percent of the national total, and as far as the four great metropolises are concerned, their added population, which accounted for 51.3 percent in 1980, decreased to 45.1 percent in 1990. Additionally, the urbanization rate for the whole urban system was only 0.8 percent during this last year despite the fact that their population represented more than 60 percent of the urban total (locations with 15,000 or more inhabitants).

As with the population, economic growth also focused primarily on Mexico City's Metropolitan Area up to the seventies, and on the metropolitan areas of Monterrey, Guadalajara, and Puebla secondly until the eighties. Sectorially, the MCMA represented 46 percent of the industrial GDP in 1960, and in 1980 it reached 48 percent. This latter year, these four metropolises contributed 68 percent to the country's industrial GDP (Garza and Rivera 1994, 248). During the 1980–90 decade the demographic growth in these large cities decreased in comparison to the national total, and their industrial economic importance also began to decrease: the MCMA declined from 46 percent to 32 percent, and Monterrey's MA reduced its participation from 10.3 percent to 6.7 percent, whereas Guadalajara's MA slightly increased from 5.2 percent to 6.3 percent and Puebla remained with 3.7 percent.

The above changes pose certain difficulties in establishing possible "causal associations" between positive demographic and economic growths, or between the economic crisis and population and employment decentralization. On the one hand, the 1982 oil crisis seemed to trigger an increasing contribution of secondary or middle-size cities—mainly those in the range of 250,000 to 500,000 inhabitants—to Mexico's industrial and total GDP; on the other hand, the redistribution of urban population and rapid population growth in secondary cities (excluding the other three large metropolises, which during the decade of the seventies had shown higher rates than the MCMA itself) coincides with the relative loss of importance of the central region in favor of the country's peripheral regions. With respect to the time dimension, the previous considerations lead to questioning whether the changes in the pace and direction of urbanization and economic development are merely circumstantial—dependent on six-year government periods, for example—or structural and derived from relatively independent processes, as seems to be the case of demographic growth in Mexico and other countries, regardless of their development level and political systems.

From our standpoint, population distribution in the Mexican territory followed, in the long-term, a pattern independent from economic circumstances, even though both factors have mutual effects. In any case, the relationship between them does not immediately or automatically follow in time. This becomes quite clear when we see that state efforts to retain labor force in its place of birth or where it hardly finds the means to survive remain only in writing. This is particularly evident, even despite monetary or fiscal policies, when due to production costs or average income differentials, or economic, political, or social change expectations, both employers and workers (capital and labor) decide to find better locations and the first change their suppliers and clients while the latter change their dwelling and working places. This does not mean, of course, that state actions, most of the time delayed, do not strengthen or modify location-related decision making in a reciprocal relationship: greater public regional expenditure induces local decision making in favor of these privileged areas or sites, and unusual economic and demographic growth in a certain region or place demands public response (investment) concerning physical and social infrastructure, and so on. . . .[9] This could occur automatically and immediately only if full information was readily available without cost and without frictions, and would not be possible where the factors of production's main characteristic is a huge spatial and sectoral differentiation and heterogeneity.

Effects of economic policy (nonspatial in nature) can be best observed in the urban sector of the economy. As a matter of fact, in 1990 the main 127 Mexican cities, according to the value of their GDP,[10] produced 73 percent of the national GDP and more or less eight out of ten pesos of the total gross product of manufacturing, trade, and services (see Table 34.3). In 1970 Mexico's major 118 cities[11] contributed 64.6 percent of the GDP, 71 percent to the GDP of the manufacturing sector, and more or less 75 percent to that of the trade and service sectors (see Tables 34.3 and 34.4). Thus, while the cities remarkably increased their weight for the national and sectoral GDP (from 64.6 to 72.9 percent), the MCMA only did so slightly (from 28.6 to 30.6 percent of the total), despite having lost importance within the manufacturing sector (from 37.5 to 33.7 per-

Table 34.3

Gross Domestic Product by Sector and Selected Groups of Cities, 1990
(in millions of 1980 pesos)

	Total	%	Manufacturing	%	Trade	%	Services	%
National GDP	5,255,777 (100.0)	100.00	967,063 (100.0)	18.40	1,334,967 (100.0)	25.4	1,466,361 (100.0)	27.9
127 Cities GDP	3,831,461 (72.9)	100.00	769,782 (79.6)	20.01	1,075,983 (80.6)	20.01	1,205,348 (82.2)	31.5
4 Metropolitan areas	2,196,918 (41.8)	100.00	476,762 (49.3)	21.80	624,764 (46.8)	28.5	793,301 (54.1)	36.2
Mexico City metropolitan area	1,608,268 (30.6)	100.00	325,900 (33.7)	20.30	456,559 (34.2)	28.4	633,468 (43.2)	39.4
Monterrey, Guadalajara, and Puebla Metropolitan areas	583,391 (11.1)	100.00	150,862 (15.6)	25.90	168,206 (12.6)	28.8	159,833 (10.9)	27.3

Source: Table II.2 in Garza and Rivera (1994) and Banco de México (1991).

Table 34.4

Gross Domestic Product by Sector and Selected Groups of Cities, 1970
(in millions of 1980 pesos)

	Total	%	Manufacturing	%	Trade	%	Services	%
National GDP	2,168,056 (100.0)	100.00	487,813 (100.0)	22.5	682,937 (100.0)	31.5	429,275 (100.0)	19.8
118 Cities GDP	1,400,564 (64.6)	100.00	345,939 (70.8)	24.7	508,106 (74.4)	36.2	324,961 (75.7)	23.3
4 Metropolitan areas	834,701 (38.5)	100.00	251,245 (51.3)	30.1	293,663 (43.0)	35.2	191,886 (44.7)	23.1
Mexico City Metropolitan area	620,064 (28.6)	100.00	183,539 (37.5)	29.6	219,223 (32.1)	35.3	145,953 (34.0)	23.6
Monterrey, Guadalajara, and Puebla Metropolitan areas	197,293 (9.1)	100.00	62,345 (13.8)	31.6	74,440 (10.9)	34.7	45,932 (10.7)	21.5

Source: Table II.1 in Garza and Rivera (1994) and Banco de México (1991).

cent). This gain of two percentage points was due to the minor increase in trade (32.1 to 34.2 percent) and its relative advantage (in both quality and location) in all kinds of services, which increased their sectorial importance from 34 to 43.2 percent.

Summarizing, figures show a decentralization of the manufacturing sector from the MCMA toward other cities and metropolitan areas in the NUS, and a concentration of services (29.6 to 20.3 percent and 23.6 to 39.4 percent, respectively). Additionally, there was a loss of importance of manufactured products in the generation of the national GDP (22.5 to 18.4 between 1970 and 1990) and in the corresponding products of total cities (24.7 to 20.1 percent), as well as in the total of the four major metropolitan areas (30.1 to 21.8 percent) (see Table 34.4).

Therefore, tertiary activities dramatically increased their importance at the national, urban, and metropolitan levels. Thus, what during the sixties and part of the seventies was a population transference from the countryside to the cities, and of labor force from agricultural activities to secondary ones, in the eighties became a transference of labor force from the secondary to the tertiary sector, and of population and employment in manufacturing activities in the metropolises to most of the middle-size cities of the NUS. This deeply affected the urban quality of life, employment, and the structure of the labor force, as well as the interregional share of income and production. Undoubtedly, a new geography of production and consumption emerged, equivalent, to some extent, to the axis shift or change of geographical weights in the United States from east to west and south, during the decade of the sixties, whereas in Mexico this rather represented an urban hierarchical filtering. At the same time, if we consider the social costs of restructuring, the differences pointed out since the sixties by Paul Lamartine Yates (1962) between central and northern states and those of the south, have been exacerbated during the last six-year period. In this sense, alongside the actual increase between 1970 and 1990 of the national product (2.4 times),[12] workers' income and wages have alarmingly collapsed; in consequence, poverty, measured in terms of the number and percent of individuals and families considered poor and extremely poor, increased during the last years, which was not the case during the previous decades. In the following section we will analyze this "reverse side of the coin."

The Reverse Side of the Coin

At the closing of President Salinas's government, Mexico was a country that proclaimed the advantages of market forces and privatization over state participation and regulation. During Salinas's sexenio the economy grew outward, and, consequently, protectionism gave way to competitiveness and efficiency.

At the same time, and as the reverse side of the coin, the living standards of the majorities dramatically deteriorated; the numbers of poor and extremely poor individuals were noticeably enlarged; the income of workers and families collapsed to a low similar to that of "fourth world countries"; "open" and "disguised" unemployment (in informal or marginal activities with very low remuneration, extremely long or very reduced working shifts, etc.) alarmingly intensified. As a matter of fact, a reduced capability for employment generation,[13] public control of wages and salaries and the influx of workers entering the labor market for the first time reduced the share of occupied personnel remunerations in the GDP from 37 percent, which had prevailed during the seventies and eighties to only 26.4 percent at the end of the six-year presidential term that concluded in 1994. In 1994, the minimum-wage buying power fell to 40 percent of what it was in 1982, and wages in the manufacturing sector were reduced to only 85 percent of those of the earlier years.

The number of poor people increased from 31 to 41 million between 1981 and 1988, and the number of people in extreme poverty, 13.7 million in the early eighties, increased to 17.3 million by the end of the decade; of these, seven out of ten live in rural areas.[14] On the other hand, family income distribution suffered a regression as households in the last four deciles with the lowest incomes reduced their share of the total family income from 14.4 percent in 1984 to 12.7 percent in 1992, whereas the two deciles with highest incomes increased theirs from 49.5 to 54.2 percent of the total; consequently, those deciles corresponding to middle strata, from the third to the sixth, also reduced their share from 36 to 33 percent.[15]

Emphasis must be given to the fact that from 1984 through 1989 the highest decile was the only one that gained percentage points in the distribution of the national income, and it did so extraordinarily. Indeed, in only five years it concentrated 5.2 additional percentage points of the national income, as it increased from 32.8 to 37.9 percent. All other deciles lost points, although from 1989 to 1992 both the first and second deciles increased their respective shares: from 37.93 to 38.16 percent and from 15.62 to 16.02 percent respectively. Thus in 1992 only 20 percent of the population concentrated more than 54 percent of the total national income.

The above is closely related to unemployment. In 1993 only 3.5 percent were unemployed in the thirty-seven cities included in the Mexican Urban Employment Survey (ENEU) taken by INEGI. However, if we consider as unemployed those whose income is less than one minimum salary (8.5 percent of the economically active population), unemployment results in a total of 12.4 percent. Additionally, it is generally accepted that "disguised" unemployment in Mexico might be affecting close to 30 percent of the economically active population.

Not all problems lie on the reverse side of the coin. Firm profits strengthened regressive concentration as they absorbed 59.3 percent of the national income available in 1992 (against somewhat less than 53 percent in 1981). Additionally, the national production apparatus, according to the analysts of CANACINTRA is "tied" to imports. As a matter of fact, in certain manufacturing industries the rate of integration is not over 5–10 percent of total inputs (20 percent on average), and therefore "not only in the production of export goods, but also in those oriented to the domestic market . . . a real import substitution would be hardly attainable,"[16] if that were the purpose, in view of the new and unsteady dollar exchange rate. Apparently, for Mexican entrepreneurs it is easier to overcome product market deficiencies, shortages, and lack of quality of local goods and services by importing the majority of their inputs, with the consequent imbalance in the foreign trade balance.[17]

It is important to emphasize that the economic policy of the past two sexenios (de la Madrid and Salinas) encouraged exporting manufactured goods (see note 4). This is in itself relevant, especially if we take into consideration that manufacturing activities, as already seen, have gradually acquired greater importance in the economic base of secondary cities. Nonetheless, sectorally and regionally, Mexican exports of manufactured goods are concentrated and vulnerable,[18] as 76.3 percent of the total is exported by only three industrial classes—machinery and equipment; chemicals; and food, beverages; and tobacco—73 percent of exports are concentrated in twenty-five products commercialized by only 2 percent of the national firms, and three-fourths is traded with the United States—which in fact explains the advantage offered by location in the states of northern Mexico. Indeed, firms located there, mainly in-bond (maquiladora) industries, are solely accountable for the increase of industrial employment during the last ten to twelve years.

Poverty is also unevenly distributed in space. The poorest states register a decremental participation in national wealth. Two southeastern states (Chiapas and Oaxaca), a central one (Hidalgo), and Yucatán in the peninsula have traditionally been the poorest: 40 percent and 28 percent of the occupied population of the first two obtain incomes below the official minimum wage, and in the case of the last two, this figure is over 30 percent. On the other hand, the geographical polarization of wealth and money is remarkable: the Federal District, Jalisco, Nuevo León, Veracruz, and Tamaulipas concentrate 77 percent of bank savings and credit and 95 percent of the total investment banking. In those states where the three largest metropolitan areas of Mexico are located (Mexico City, Guadalajara, and Monterrey), commercial banks acquired in 1994 almost eight out of every ten pesos of their available resources. Perhaps one should not worry too much, as money has greater relative mobility than individuals. Consequently, one would expect decentralization to benefit from investment opportunities, once these are detected. Undocumented workers that try their luck in the U.S. economy, California in particular, on the other hand, show there is no reason to remain in their place of origin. Their tolerance levels have been outgrown, not only due to the enormous income differentials between Mexican and United States workers, but also because of the inability of the economy to generate employment and meet the monetary and nonmonetary expectations[19] of the poorer but, as far as one can foresee, less docile Mexican labor force.

Conclusions

To say that the explicitly territorial actions of the state have not directly or substantially influenced the geographical distribution of the population and urban growth does not necessarily mean we are neglecting public policies. On the contrary, it expresses our concern over the conceptual bases and instruments used to direct, control, or modify the spatial and economic behavior of all social agents.

This chapter highlighted/described some of the changes experienced by Mexico in regard to its regional structure and urbanization process, particularly during the late eighties and early nineties. The questions we tried to answer are related to the role played in those changes by the economic policies of President Salinas's government and that of his predecessor, during which the neoliberal model was first sketched. Thus, to approach the questions What kind of changes? Which policies? How do the latter relate to the former? Difficult as they might be and despite possible multiple answers to them, we opted to reduce them to their urban and regional dimensions. We must emphasize our doubts about the effectiveness of public policies in meeting spatial goals and objectives, such as a balanced spatial distribution of the population. Similarly, we hardly believe that one sole cause, in this case the state or the crisis, determines decision-making and spatial behavior,[20] whether it concentrates or deconcentrates economic activities and production factors (capital-labor).

Certain authors consider that the state is omnipotent and ubiquitous, and that its actions and policies determine the way in which all other economic agents— social groups in general—arrive at their decisions. Others consider that those decisions correspond to multiple variables, and that the state and its policies constitute only additional aspects to be taken into consideration. Similarly, the state is not homogeneous; sectorially and at multiple levels its operation is fragmented, and its results are often contradictory. Consequently, they propose that economic, social, demographic, geographical, and political phenomena—without disregarding the importance of the last—are relatively autonomous.

In any case, the changes described above are enough evidence, in our opinion, to accept that Mexico is now in a regional economic development process that is already affecting the country's traditional center-periphery structure and will contribute to consolidate a most complex regional and urban system.[21] The regional economic structure of Mexico was modified, as in the case of post-industrial capitalist countries, due to a transference of capital and labor; not from agriculture toward the secondary sector, as in 1950 and 1970, but from the manufacturing sector to tertiary activities. This last sector became most important nationally and regionally. Nevertheless, during the eighties Mexico's economy also experienced a process of reindustrialization whereby the manufacturing sector, although it lost employment positions and number of economic units, increased in "size" and productivity. In this process, the central region, historically the axis of the country's urban and industrial development despite having relatively lost industrial importance and leadership, preserved, in general terms, the largest economic units, greatest productivity, and better paid jobs, although the northern regions came closer to it, and a few sectors in other regions also registered positive changes during the period under analysis.

During the last fifteen years the country suffered, with the 1982 crisis, the restructuring and readjustment of its urban-based activities (manufacturing, construction, trade, and services) at the same time that the labor factor relapsed in all or almost all sectors. Despite policies, and as far as national, regional, and sectoral income is concerned, changes have been important but did not occur or favor everyone simultaneously and at the same place, and they jointly display the two sides of the same coin, undoubtedly marking the conformation of a new geography of economic and social development in Mexico.

Notes

1. See evaluations made by Garza (1983); Garza and Puente (1989); Graizbord (1984a, 1985, and 1990); and Ruiz (1993); among others.
2. Richardson (1969) described in those terms both extremes of regional development policies for the British case.
3. Those with 2,500 inhabitants according to population censuses up to 1970, and between fifteen and twenty thousand inhabitants according to different criteria accepted by international agencies and analysts with a view to comparing among countries and/or economic systems.
4. An indication of this would be the varying composition of exports, which well into the eighties were mainly based on the extraction sector (particularly oil). This sector concentrated more than two-thirds of the 1980 total, 40 percent in 1986, and by the late eighties (1989) it had decreased to one-third, making way for manufacturing industry products, which increased from 23 percent in 1980 to almost 60 percent of total exports by the end of that period. See NAFINSA (1990).
5. The country has been divided into nine regions, which are usually used by academics, the ministries of Programming and Budget and of Social Development, and INEGI for state programming and analytical purposes.
6. The demographic transition experienced in Mexico since the fifties (Mier y Terán and Rabell 1993) affected the fertility and mortality rates and is related, among other factors, to the extension of public urban services and the social policy implemented by the country's revolutionary governments.
7. This urbanization rate compares percentages of the urban population (in locations with 15,000 inhabitants or more) at the end and the beginning of the period under consideration and represents the annual mean increase of urban population.
8. The official 13.9 million figure for MCMA according to the 1980 population census is higher than other estimations that report scarcely 13 million; this is equivalent to 22 or 20 percent of the country's population, respectively.
9. Direct state investment or activity has drastically decreased in Mexico, and the privatization of certain sectors (oil, communications, electric power) considered strategic and untouchable is now under discussion.
10. Estimations for each city were made indirectly (see Garza and Rivera 1994), based on employment as a factor to weight the sectoral value of the state to which each city belongs.
11. The difference of nine cities between 1970 and 1990 does not significantly change proportions and does not affect conclusions.
12. During those twenty years, the urban population increased 2.07 times (from 23.8 to 49.4 millions) and the economically active population grew 1.8 times, from 12.9 to 23.4 millions.

13. Independent sources, published in the press, and the Cámara Nacional de la Industria de Transformación (CANACINTRA) foresee that, with an economic growth of 3.5 percent in 1995 (probably to be zero or negative), it will not be possible to create the one million jobs required to cover accumulated lags.

14. According to INEGI and ECLA's data, 9.9 million individuals out of 84 million Mexicans in 1992 were living in conditions of extreme poverty, quoted in Gollás (1994).

15. See Table 11 in Gollás (1994) and "La deuda social heredada por el nuevo gobierno . . . " *El Financiero*, January 26, 1995, p. 28.

16. "Amarrado a importaciones el sistema productivo nacional: CANACINTRA" *El Financiero*, January 26, 1995, p. 22.

17. In 1993, foreign trade in Mexico concluded with a deficit with respect to North America (–4,500 million dollars) and ALADI countries (–500 million dollars), whereas with respect to the European Community it had a favorable balance (4 billion dollars). Data taken from Table 12 in Gollás (1994).

18. The deep integration of foreign inputs in manufacturing was reflected in a very rapid increase of imports (of capital and intermediate goods) during the nineties, to the extent that, since 1989, the foreign trade balance began to have a deficit that amounted to 17 billion dollars in 1994 (Gollás 1994, 51).

19. The Chiapas upheaval of January 1994 might be seen as an example of this combination of economic and political frustrations.

20. All of them, if rational, can be considered economic, including the number of children, age at marriage, beginning of any activity, change of residence and work, etc.

21. Until the eighties the approaches and interpretations of Mexico's regional development insisted on the imbalances and concentration that occur in the framework of a center-periphery model (Mendoza Berrueto 1969; Appendini, Murayama, and Domínguez 1972; Unikel 1975; Unikel et al. 1976; among others). The city systems approach has recently begun to be accepted (Graizbord and Garrocho 1987).

Bibliography

Aguilar, A.G. (1993), "Dinámica Metropolitana y Terciarización del Empleo, 1970–1990." Paper presented at the Seminario Nacional de Alternativas para la Economía Nacional, Instituto de Investigaciones Económicas, UNAM, November, México.

Aguilar, A.G., and B. Graizbord (1995), "La reestructuración regional en México: Cambio de la actividad económica urbana 1980–1988," *Comercio Exterior* 45, no. 2: 140–51.

Appendini, K., D. Murayama, and R. Domínguez (1972), "Desarrollo desigual en México (1900–1960)," *Demografía y Economía* 6, no. 1: 1–40.

Banco de México (1991), *Informe Anual 1991*, Mexico City.

Bazdresch, Carlos, et al., eds. (1993), *México, Auge, Crisis y Ajuste*, Lecturas No. 73, Vol. 3, Fondo de Cultura Económica, Mexico.

Boltvinik, J. (1994), "La magnitud de la pobreza. Prioridades de asignación del gasto público social," *Demos* 7: 29–31.

Bravo Aguilera, L. (1993), "La apertura comercial 1983–1988. Contribución al cambio estructural de la economía mexicana" in C. Bazdresch, et al., eds., *México, Auge, Crisis y Ajuste*, vol. 3, (Mexico City Fondo de Cultura Económica).

Córdoba Montoya, J. (1993), "La reforma económica de México" in C. Bazdresch et al., eds., *México, Auge, Crisis y Ajuste*, vol. 3, (Mexico City: Fondo de Cultura Económica).

Garza, G. (1983), "Desarrollo económico, urbanización y políticas urbano-regionales en México (1900–1982)," *Demografía y Economía* 17, no. 2 (54): 159–80.

Garza, G., and Puente, S. (1989), "Racionalidad e irracionalidad de la política urbana en

México: el Plan Nacional de Desarrollo Urbano, 1978" in Garza, Gustavo, ed., *Una década de planeación urbano-regional en México, 1978–1988*, (Mexico City: El Colegio de México).

Garza, G., and Rivera (1993), "Desarrollo económico y distribución de la población urbana en México, 1960–1990," *Revista Mexicana de Sociología*, no. 1:177–212.

————. (1995), *Dinámica macroeconómica de las ciudades en México*, (Mexico City: Instituto nacional de Estadistica Geografica e Informatica, Mexico).

Gollás, M. (1994), "México 1994. Una economía sin inflación, sin igualdad y sin crecimiento," Documento de Trabajo, CEE, El Colegio de México, Mexico City.

Lamartine Yates, Paul (1962), *Desigualdades Regionales en México* (Mexico City: Banco de México).

Graizbord, B. (1984a), "Desarrollo regional, ciudades intermedias y descentralización en México. Observaciones críticas al Plan Nacional de Desarrollo Urbano (1978–1982)," *Demografía y Economía*, 18, no. 1: 27–47.

————. (1984b), "Perspectivas de una descentralización del crecimiento urbano en el sistema de ciudades de México," *Revista Interamericana de Planificación* 18 (71): 36–58.

————. (1985), "Un escenario del crecimiento metropolitano para la ciudad de México," *Diálogos* 21, no. 11 (131): 9–14.

————. (1990), "Programa Nacional de Desarrollo Urbano, 1990–1994: Aspectos cualitativos y cuantitativos para una evaluación *ex-ante*," *Estudios Demográficos y Urbanos* 5, no. 3 (15): 755–63.

Graizbord, B., and C. Garrocho (1987), *Sistemas de ciudades. Fundamentos teóricos y operativos*, Serie Cuadernos de Trabajo, (Mexico City: El Colegio Mexiquense).

Ledent, J. (1982), "Rural-urban Migration, Urbanization and Economic Development," *Economic Development and Cultural Change* 30: 507–38.

Mendoza Berrueto, E. (1969), "Implicaciones regionales del desarrollo económico de México," *Demografía y Economía* 3, no. 1: 25–63.

Mera, K. (1973), "On the Urban Agglomeration and Economic Efficiency," *Economic Development and Cultural Change* 21: 309–24.

Mier y Terán, Martha, and Rabell, Cecilia (1993), "Inicio de la transición de la fecundidad en México. Descendencias de mujeres nacidas en la primera mitad del Siglo XX," *Revista Mexicana de Sociología*, no. 1: 41–81.

NAFINSA (1990), *La Economía Mexicana en Cifras 1990* Mexico City.

Negrete, M.E., and Salazar, H. (1986), "Zonas metropolitanas en México, 1980," *Estudios Demográficos y Urbanos* 1, no. 1: 97–124.

Piore, M., and C. Sabel (1984), *The Second Industrial Divide: Possibilities for Prosperity* (New York: Basic Books).

Rendón, T., and C. Salas (1992), "El mercado de trabajo no agrícola en México. Tendencias y cambios recientes" in *Ajuste estructural, mercados laborales y TLC*, (Mexico City: El Colegio de México, Fundación Friedrich Ebert, El Colegio de la Frontera Norte).

Richardson, H. (1969), *Elements of Regional Economics* (New York: Penguin).

Ruíz, C. (1993), "El desarrollo del México urbano: cambio de protagonistas," *Comercio Exterior* 43, no. 8: 708–16.

Unikel, L. (1975), "Políticas de desarrollo regional en México," *Demografía y Economía* 11, no. 2: 143–81.

————. et al. (1976), *El Desarrollo Urbano de México*, El Colegio de México, Mexico City.

Wong González, P., and P.L. Salido (1991), "Libre comercio, integración internacional e impacto territorial en México," *Estudios Sociales, Revista de Investigación del Noroeste* 2 no. 4: 7–44.

Zelinsky, W. (1971), "The Hypothesis of the Mobility Transition," *Geography Review* 61: 219–49.

35

JAVIER BERISTAIN

Mexico City: Toward Its Sustainable Development

Mexico is an urban nation, and Mexico City is its most important city. Javier Beristain points out that its basic needs for drinking water and sewage, electricity, and housing are being met, despite the highly unequal income distribution. Mexico City's municipal policies included increased public transport; reduced air and water pollution; housing construction and legalization of squatters' settlements; greater economic and political autonomy of the Federal District; and reconstruction of historic sites.

Mexico City policies are similar to those at the national level. The government hopes to strengthen its tax administration, reduce subsidies such as that of transport; privatize public services; improve administration; and improve the environment. Beristain believes that Mexico City is on the road to becoming a global business center linking all of the Americas.

Mexico City's Recent Economic Development

Local city governments face extraordinary dilemmas every day: economic growth or environmental protection, public participation or a centralization of the decision-making process, promotion of free speech or authoritarianism, the protection of individual rights or the pursuit of the public interest. Mexico City—with its complex history, enormous size, and changing economics—is not the exception. From 1950 to 1970 its population grew at an annual average rate of 5 percent. Although by 1990 the rate had decreased to 1 percent, the population of the Federal District is now about 8.5 million, which, added to the population of the nearby municipalities, makes a population of 17 million in the Metropolitan Area of Mexico City.

But demographics are a source of opportunities, not only of problems. Mexico City provides a $100 billion market. Its labor force is, relatively, the best educated, the most mature, and the most politically participating of the nation. It is not by chance that the political elections in the city are among the tightest in the country—in 1988 the opposition parties obtained 72 percent of the votes, although in 1994 the proportion was reduced to 57 percent.

The resources needed to satisfy the basic needs of the population are considerable, yet in the Federal District these are being met: 98 percent of the households have drinking water and sewage, 99 percent have electricity, and 75 percent have more than three rooms. Two-thirds of total housing is owned by its dwellers. In Mexico City, income per capita is three times the national average, though its distribution is still far from being equitable: 10 percent of the total population receives 40 percent of total incomes. Furthermore, in 1990, as many as 60 percent of family heads received less than two minimum wages about US$8 in November 1994; Mexico City's daily minimum wage was 18 pesos per day, equal to $2.70 at the beginning of May 1995. It was estimated that four minimum wages were needed to purchase a basic weekly basket of goods. Industrial employment is 20 percent of the city total, ten points lower than what it was in 1970. This trend has been reinforced by the economic development program of the country, oriented to the global markets, and by increasing constraints to polluting activities. Today, seven out of ten jobs are in the service sector, and one in every four is in the public sector. Economic activity in the city is turning, inevitably, toward the service sector. The challenge is to prevent the loss of productivity that follows the decay of industrialization.

During recent years, the city has implemented several policies and programs to improve the living conditions of the inhabitants:

1. It has increased and reorganized the supply of transport services. In the last three years, twenty-three miles of additional subways have been added. Strict environmental standards apply in the transport sector.

2. Pollution levels due to the presence of lead, sulfur, carbon monoxide, and nitrogen dioxide were extremely high; now they do not violate international standards. PEMEX has greatly reduced lead in gasoline, and unleaded now has about 40 percent of the gasoline market. Sulfur emissions have been reduced because the major electric utility, CFE, is using natural gas, and also because the sulfur content of diesel has been lowered. Carbon monoxide has been reduced by vehicle inspections and the introduction of catalytic converters since 1991. Nitrous oxide is not adequately controlled: the ozone problem persists.

3. Programs for the efficient use of water have been implemented. Private operation of water treatment plants is encouraged and a public organism oversees all related water activities—previously scattered throughout Mexico City's government. The city has promoted private participation in metering and billing water consumption.

4. Public action has been directed toward social equity. One hundred thousand lots that originally were squatter settlements have been legalized; the government has constructed twenty-eight thousand living quarters, increased the

water distribution system, improved potable water distribution, and disposed of increasing volumes of residual water and solid waste.

5. New policies that help create one hundred thousand jobs every year are being implemented. Private investment is encouraged to turn Mexico City into a major financial, commercial, tourist, and export center. In the Hispanic world, only Spain's GDP is significantly higher than that of Mexico City's Metropolitan Area.

6. Public finances are now healthy, and are to be maintained by increasing revenues and controlling current expenditures, without sacrificing public investment. The city has moved from a financial deficit of 16 percent of the budget in 1988—covered by federal grants—to a situation close to equilibrium in recent years. However, during the late 1980s, federal financing overall had covered over half of the Federal District's expenses. The reduced role of the federal government in financing the Federal District and the recently introduced direct election of its mayor suggest greater political and financial self-reliance of Mexico City in the immediate future.

7. The Historical Center and other such symbols of the city have been regenerated so that the general public and visitors can enjoy them once again. Today, there are more than five hundred restoration works in the downtown area. Simultaneously, work on the rehabilitation of old neighborhoods, parks, and public spaces is under way; other works include the provision of metropolitan ecological parks and the rehabilitation of Mexico City's Zoo and the National Auditorium.

Toward Sustainable Development

A necessary condition for economic development is the creation of better and new employment opportunities, in sectors where social and private productivity levels are highest, in clean industries and services. Economic growth has to be compatible with the preservation of our environment, and with the conservation of natural resources: our water, air, and soil. If not, the survival of the Mexican capital is at stake.

Income distribution has to improve. Presently, it is extremely concentrated. Without better income distribution, economic growth is short lived. Every economic program has to balance efficiency with equity and justice in the distribution of its benefits. The road to a better distribution passes through investment in human capital and requires economic stability. Thus a sustainable, long-run economic program can be pursued instead of a policy of "laissez-faire." The agenda includes:

1. The strengthening of public finances, with better tax administration. This is necessary to compensate for the relative decrease in the percentage that Mexico City receives from federal revenues, as well as the reduction of subsidies that the city used to get from the federal government.

2. The revision of policies that subsidize private consumption of public services. Transportation is a case in point. The Federal District operates three transport systems: buses, trolley buses, and underground trains. Fares account for only a third of the operation costs of these services, per passenger. Given that the Federal District has to build the infrastructure for these systems, as well as cover their operating deficits, the public transport system absorbed more than 20 percent of the total expenditure budget for 1994.

3. New incentives to attract private investment to the supply of public services. The contracting of private firms, granting of operating permits, and privatization of public enterprises will continue in Mexico City as a means of using private savings and market guides to supply public services. Examples abound: water treatment plants, maintenance of the distribution network, metering and billing consumption, among others. Furthermore, the city has contacted entrepreneurs interested in the collection of toxic and industrial waste, in recycling and disposal of solid waste, and in private generation of electricity.

4. Changes in the regulatory practices of government agencies to eliminate red tape, increase legal certainty for investors, and reduce the transaction costs of economic activity.

5. Zoning policy improvements. Specially, the city is eliminating over-regulation in the commercial sector, where the informal sector has grown at incredible rates and creates considerable social costs.

6. Adequate management of externalities, with rules and regulations, and economic instruments that internalize social costs, when possible. Schemes to account for the social costs of pollution from mobile sources, in the price of fuel, parking lot fees, taxes on the use of cars, among others, have been applied. Furthermore, residual discharges in the drainage system are being taxed. For refuse disposal, a differential tariff system has been approved by Congress, to encourage recycling and private transportation to sanitary landfills.

7. Investment in infrastructure: both "hardware," such as roads, drainage systems, waste disposal, hospitals, schools, and telecommunications systems; as well as "software," like new forms of urban services provision, state-of-the-art technologies, and joint programs with universities and technology development centers.

8. Attacks on poverty and inequality, with programs that include legalization of squatters' property rights, continued investment in drainage, water, and electricity systems, access to the health infrastructure, and access to employment and education.

Toward its sustainable development, Mexico City is designing environmental policies that have achieved:

- the improvement of the quality of fuels, which beginning in 1991 required unleaded gasoline;
  - the permanent closing down of the fuel refinery at Azcapotzalco;
  - the continuous—but slow—modernization of industrial processes;

- the promotion of new enterprises with up-to-date technology;
- the promotion of environmental research, without which any policy is bound to be cost ineffective.

There are four areas of direct government responsibility and involvement that have required specific measures:

1. In public transportation, two new Metro system lines that add thirty-eight kilometers and provide transportation to one million passengers. In addition we introduced:

- the changes of engines of the Ruta–100 bus system, reducing their diesel emissions;
- the introduction of catalytic converters in all new vehicles in the 1991 model year;
- a biannual verification of the emission of vehicles, which must pass inspection in order to be allowed to continue to circulate.

2. The government of the city has also invested in the reforestation of the Metropolitan Area of Mexico City with millions of trees planted and the Sierras de Santa Catalina and Guadalupe reforestation and environmental protection programs. This primarily will help control air pollution, and in some areas will help control water runoff and therefore contribute to stabilizing the water table.

3. In solid waste management we have achieved:

- the permanent closure of "open air" disposal sites;
- the design of a toxic waste disposal program.

4. In water management we have also made progress through:

- the ecological rescue of the floating gardens of Xochimilco, one of our most precious zones;
- the operation of secondary treatment plants.

The results so far in the area can be summarized as follows: Mexico City has reduced emissions of sulfur, nitrogen oxides, carbon monoxide, and lead to comply with international standards. Although ozone levels have decreased, further reduction through fuel improvements, control of industrial and vehicle emissions, and better research in the field are needed.

To be sure, Mexico City has still many public policy challenges to confront. Nevertheless, a carefully planned and market-oriented economic policy with society's participation can rise to the challenges posed by Mexico's new development model. While the country is entering this new stage of economic life, Mexico City is on the road to becoming a global business center linking all of the Americas.

Index

Mexican Institute of Water Technology, 232

Mexican Method for Ordering Forests, 220, 221

Mexican National Council for the Fight Against AIDS (CONASIDA), 340–41

Mexican National Fertility and Health Survey, 201

Mexican Petroleum Institute (IMP), 125, 181

Mexican Socialist Party (PMS), 270

Mexico City, 210, 244, 354, 359, 375, 379, 380, 391–95

  air pollution in, 207, 208, 214, 215–16, 392

  air quality in, 211–12

  earthquake in, 243

  economic development of, 391–93

  employment survey, 316

  environmental policy, 246

  investment in, 393, 394

  mobile source control in, 212–14

  sustainable development of, 393–95

México state, 220, 352, 362

Meyer, Lorenzo, 267

Michoacán, 271, 352, 362

Middle class, 5, 158

Migration, 145–56, 160

  and agrarian policy, 150–51

  bilateral accord for, 146

  and currency devaluation, 153–55

  illegal, 149

  and income distribution, 156, 157

  internal, 351, 357, 359

  labor, 366

  return, 148

  surge in, 152–53

  types of, 149

Minimum wage, 385, 392

Ministry of Labor, 141

Ministry of Public Education (SEP), 171

Modernization, 5–6, 7, 10–12, 127, 266

  and labor relations, 138

Modernization *(continued)*

  politics of, 59–61

Monetary policy, 29, 32, 35

Monterrey, 210, 225, 316, 352, 355, 360, 375, 380

Monterrey Technological Institute (ITESM), 173, 360

Morelia, 352, 359

Morelos, 352

Mortality rates. *See* Death rates

Motherhood, 325

Mumme, Stephen, 245

Muñoz Ledo, Porfiro, 270, 282

Mutual Support Forum (FAM), 256, 258, 260

N

NAFTA. *See* North American Free Trade Agreement

Nahuatl Indians, 247

National Agreement to Improve Quality and Productivity (ANEPC), 138

National Autonomous University of Mexico (UNAM), 170, 172–73, 174, 181

National Council for Science and Technology (CONACYT), 177, 178, 180–81

National debt. *See* Debt, national

National Employment Survey, 316

National Evaluation Commission (CONAEVA), 176

National Human Rights Commission, 285

National Human Settlements Law (1978), 361

National Irrigation Commission, 229–30

Nationalism, 7–8, 270

  revolutionary, 56

National Land Clearing Program, 220

National Plan for Family Planning, 198, 200

National Polytechnic Institute (IPN), 170, 172–73, 174

National Poverty Abatement Plan, 157

About the Editor

Laura Randall is a professor and graduate adviser in the Department of Economics of Hunter College of the City University of New York. She is the editor of *Reforming Mexico's Agrarian Reform*; and the author of T*he Political Economy of Brazilian Oi*l; *The Political Economy of Mexican Oil*; *The Political Economy of Venezuelan Oil*; *An Economic History of Argentina in the Twentieth Century*; *A Comparative Economic History of Latin America*; and other books and articles.